Practice Wisdom

Practice Futures

VOLUME 3

Series Editor

Joy Higgs (*Education, Practice and Employability Network, Australia*)

Advisory Editorial Board

Steven Cork (*Australian National University, Australia*)
Geoffrey Crisp (*University of Canberra, Australia*)
Debbie Horsfall (*Western Sydney University, Australia*)
Will Letts (*Charles Sturt University, Australia*)

Scope

The way people act and work – and are enhanced or replaced by technology – in employment and practice settings in the future, will inevitably evolve incrementally or radically. This series considers *probable, possible* and *preferable* practice futures and employability, along with accompanying educational influences and support. Wisdom is a key dimension of our discussions of practice and education. The books in this series examine directions that are currently underway, future visioned and at the edge of imagination in transforming practices. The authors reflect on how these transformations are being or could be influenced by many factors including changes in society, nations and global connections, in the physical environment, workplaces (physical and virtual) and in the socio-economic-political contexts of the world and its nations. The authors in this series bring a rich range of practical and academic knowledge and experience to examine these issues. Through the conversations in these books readers can enter into these debates from multiple perspectives – work, organisations, education, professional practice, employability, society, globalisation, humanity, spirituality and the environment.

The titles published in this series are listed at *brill.com/pfp*

Practice Wisdom

Values and Interpretations

Edited by

Joy Higgs

BRILL
SENSE

LEIDEN | BOSTON

All chapters in this book have undergone peer review.

The Library of Congress Cataloging-in-Publication Data is available online at http://catalog.loc.gov

ISSN 2665-9263
ISBN 978-90-04-41047-3 (paperback)
ISBN 978-90-04-41048-0 (hardback)
ISBN 978-90-04-41049-7 (e-book)

Copyright 2019 by Koninklijke Brill NV, Leiden, The Netherlands, except where stated otherwise.
Koninklijke Brill NV incorporates the imprints Brill, Brill Hes & De Graaf, Brill Nijhoff, Brill Rodopi, Brill Sense, Hotei Publishing, mentis Verlag, Verlag Ferdinand Schöningh and Wilhelm Fink Verlag.
All rights reserved. No part of this publication may be reproduced, translated, stored in a retrieval system, or transmitted in any form or by any means, electronic, mechanical, photocopying, recording or otherwise, without prior written permission from the publisher.
Authorization to photocopy items for internal or personal use is granted by Koninklijke Brill NV provided that the appropriate fees are paid directly to The Copyright Clearance Center, 222 Rosewood Drive, Suite 910, Danvers, MA 01923, USA. Fees are subject to change.

This book is printed on acid-free paper and produced in a sustainable manner.

CONTENTS

Preface vii

Acknowledgement ix

Part 1: Understanding Practice Wisdom

1. Appreciating Practice Wisdom 3
   Joy Higgs

2. Wisdom, (Moral) Virtue and Knowledge 15
   David Carr

3. Social Practice Wisdom 29
   Bernard McKenna

4. Mindfulness and Practical Wisdom 39
   Diane Tasker and Joy Higgs

5. Practice Wisdom and Professional Artistry: Entering a Place of Human Flourishing 47
   Angie Titchen

6. A Place for Phrónêsis in Professional Practice: A Reflection of Turbulent Times 57
   Allan Pitman and Elizabeth Anne Kinsella

7. Resilience, Self-management and Agency: Living Practice Wisdom Well 69
   Rachael Field

Part 2: Practice Wisdom and Society

8. Contested Practice: Being "Wise" in an Age of Uncertainty 81
   Nita L. Cherry

9. Practice Wisdom and the Sociological Imagination 95
   Jan Fook

10. A Lived Experience of Aboriginal Knowledges and Perspectives: How Cultural Wisdom Saved My Life 107
    Sandy O'Sullivan

11. Practical Wisdom and Ethical Action 113
    Karolina Rozmarynowska

12. Developing Wise Organisations 127
    Bernard McKenna

CONTENTS

13. Learning Practice Wisdom from Elders: Wisdom Moments and How to Recognise Them   141
    Barbara Hill, Aunty Beryl Yungha-Dhu Philip-Carmichael and Ruth Bacchus

14. Bringing Spirituality and Wisdom into Practice   155
    John Wattis, Melanie Rogers, Gulnar Ali and Stephen Curran

Part 3: Practice Wisdom in Practice

15. Practice Wisdom Development   171
    Joy Higgs

16. Master Mariners and Practice Wisdom   185
    Bradley Roberts and Joy Higgs

17. Learning Embodied Practice Wisdom: The Young Sapling Learning from the Old Tree   201
    Angie Titchen and Niamh Kinsella

18. Practice Wisdom of Expert Inquirers   211
    Phillip Dybicz

19. Skill Acquisition and Clinical Judgement in Nursing Practice: Towards Expertise and Practical Wisdom   225
    Patricia Benner

20. Health and Human Service Professionals and Practice Wisdom: Developing Rich Learning Environments   241
    Lester J. Thompson

21. The Place of Wisdom in Clinical Practice: Taking a Vygotskyian Approach   255
    Rodd Rothwell

22. Wisdom and Ethico-Legal Practice: Ways of Seeing and Ways of Being   265
    Deborah Bowman

23. Valuing Critical Reflection and Narratives in Professional Practice Wisdom   277
    Laura Béres

24. Embodied Wisdom in the Creative Arts Therapies: Learning from Contemporary Art   289
    Joy Paton and Sheridan Linnell

25. Wise Practice for Teaching: Messages for Future Generations of Teachers   299
    Janice Orrell

Notes on Contributors   311

PREFACE

The authors in this book are strong supporters of practice wisdom. We see this as valuable and aspirational rather than obvious and essential; something that is achieved by some, but not all practitioners. In the face of different foundations for good practice (like evidence-based practice, practice judgements, decision making strategies and research or protocol guidelines), practice wisdom provides something extra that outstanding practitioners offer. These are wise practitioners or sometimes emerging practitioners who show growing wisdom in aspects of their practice.

Our authors explore what practice wisdom means to them and their academic and practice communities. And, we consider the value of practice wisdom in the context of practice today alongside other practice dimensions (such as judgement, professional knowledge and practice ethics) and practice foundations (such as evidence-based practice, practice codes of conduct, standards and accountability requirements). Value here means both what value wisdom in practice is seen to have and how it is valued and recognised. These determinations are made in relation to practice effectiveness and outcomes as well as its approaches and perceptions. Further, the perspectives (e.g. by clients, practitioners, peers) and practice standards against which good practice is judged make considerable difference to the way that practice is valued and judged, as does the viewpoint of who is making this decision. What a client wants and expects, for instance, can differ considerably from what an expert in the field considers is best practice. Also, we acknowledge that clients, not just professionals, are contributors of wisdom. Clients may well know most about their situation and bring rich wisdom of this life experience to the discussion table.

Practice wisdom interpretations and models have been the subject of much research, scholarship, debate and critique over different eras. These views and classifications range from Aristotle to ethical practices, from social practice wisdom to sociological imagination and new interpretations. Practice wisdom is interpreted by the authors in multiple contexts across professional development, mindful practice, dealing with moral issues, embodied practice, practice ecologies, critical reflection, ethico-legal situations, dealing with modern wicked problems in the age of certainty and dealing with cultural and ethical matters.

We invite our readers to reflect on the place of practice wisdom in pursuing good practice outcomes amidst the turmoil and pressure of professional practice today and consider whether the imperatives of evidence-based practice and triple-bottom-line accountability leave enough space for wise practice or if wisdom is seen by modern practice worlds as unnecessary, antiquated, unrealistic and redundant.

In this book *Practice Wisdom: Values and Interpretations* we bring diverse views and interpretations to what wisdom in professional practice means academically, practically and inspirationally. We consider core dimensions of wisdom in practice like ethics, mindfulness, moral virtue and metacognition, and we tackle the challenges that practice wisdom seekers encounter including the demand for resilience, finding credibility in practice wisdom and linking wisdom into evidence for sound, human-centred professional decision making.

Joy Higgs

ACKNOWLEDGEMENT

The editor wishes to acknowledge the excellent support received by Kim Woodland in book management and copy editing.

PART 1
UNDERSTANDING PRACTICE WISDOM

Guarding precious eggs,
Your bird-ness and your fury
Captured in black ink

Yet my grasp is tentative
Transfixed 'tween your wing and tail

Bradley Roberts
Sumi Bird: Ink on rice paper. 2012, Helsinki

JOY HIGGS

1. APPRECIATING PRACTICE WISDOM

This chapter opens the discussion in this book by exploring the merger of practice and wisdom into three inter-related constructs: wise practice, practice wisdom and practising wisely. The deliberate reversal of the nouns and adjectives in the first two of these terms expresses the respective value placed on both practice and wisdom; further, it denotes an appreciation of practice that is wise beyond both technical expertise and the objective and efficient performance of accountable practice, and it is an appreciation of wisdom that is grounded and realised in practice. The third term draws into the discussion the rich and broad arena of the verb, of *practising* wisely as doing, knowing, being and becoming (Higgs, 1999) as a phenomenon of appreciation, interpretation and enactment of wisdom in comparison to the nouns *practice and wisdom, being about these two*. The focus of this chapter is on practice wisdom, meaning broadly wisdom associated with practice (particularly professional practice) which encompasses but extends beyond Aristotle's practical/ethical wisdom or *phrónêsis* (discussed further in subsequent chapters).

WISDOM

Wisdom is construed in many different ways. In the following definitions we see ideas of wisdom ranging from generic wisdom to practice wisdom, and wise practice being inseparable from practical wisdom. In an extensive reflection on various interpretations of wisdom across chapters in a book on wisdom Birren and Fisher (1990, pp. 325-326) concluded:

> Wisdom brings together experience, cognitive abilities and affect, in order to make good decisions at an individual and societal level. These conceptualizations of wisdom can be placed on a continuum, with wisdom as solely a cognitive ability at one end (Baltes and Smith) and some higher integration of cognition with affect (Kramer) or other subjective forms of knowing (Labouvie-Vief) at the other. Cognitive abilities, action and affect each appear to be a necessary but not sufficient component of wisdom for most authors in this volume.

> Wisdom results from the application of successful intelligence and creativity toward the common good through a balancing of intrapersonal, interpersonal, and extrapersonal interests over the short and long terms. Wisdom is not just a way of thinking about things; it's a way of doing things. If people wish to be wise, they have to act wisely not just think wisely (Sternberg, 2003, p. 188).

Practice wisdom requires the building and critical use of multiple practice knowledges. Aristotle spoke of three forms of knowledge: *epistêmê* (which is today characterised as *epistêmic* or scientific, invariable, context-independent knowledge, *tékhnê* (which is characterised as technical knowledge) and *phrónêsis* (which is characterised *as* pragmatic, variable, context-dependent and oriented toward action). Knowledge for professional practice requires all three of these. Taylor (2010) provides the following perspective which reflects a blending of these three knowledges:

> In my opinion, medical wisdom is the capacity to understand and practice medicine in a common-sense manner that is scientifically based, sensitive to patient needs, ethically grounded and professionally satisfying. (p. 6)

In this way, practice knowledge incorporates learned propositional knowledge about practice, and is enriched through experience-based knowledge gained through professional practice. These two knowledges (propositional and experience-based-knowledge) merge and are continually refined through critical reflection, critical self-appraisal (metacognition) and reflexivity (including professional development).

There is a rich variety of sources of experiential and lived knowledge including knowledge of the lived experience of practitioners, colleagues and clients; openness to these multiple constructed realities provides a space of diverse and complex understanding of dialectics through ontological appreciation. Knowledge is also manifest in the visible and invisible, explicit and tacit, robust and ephemeral dimensions of practice.

> Immeasurables are those typically deep aspects of practice that are impossible or difficult to measure and, at times, to articulate. They are often deliberately or inherently hidden and undisclosed, they are often marginalized, they are essentially invisible, unobserved or unspoken, they can be complex and hard to articulate and they are difficult to name. (Higgs, 2014, p. 257)

The sum of a practitioner's professional knowledge and capacity to use this knowledge in practice is progressively transformed and enhanced, becoming qualitatively different. This increasingly complex phenomenon becomes practice wisdom when it is practised and actuated wisely. This is illustrated in the use of professional judgement, particularly in situations of great complexity and uncertainty where rules and prescribed findings from research are inadequate to deal with wicked problems and lack the essential wisdom of particularity and situatedness.

Practice wisdom is finely illustrated in advanced forms of decision making such as in medical decision making which has been portrayed as extending from the novice to expert forms of professional decision making. The novice's learned process of hypothetico-deductive reasoning is enhanced through practice experience with practice scripts and emerges into the expert reasoning of pattern recognition (see Boshuizen & Schmidt, 2019). Practice wisdom occurs in spaces beyond the notion of expertise and learned reasoning. Such practice wisdom holds no less responsibility for the quality of practice for the client, but rests on an inherently richer, deeper and more humanly complex realisation of lived reality, creative understanding and human interests.

PRACTICE

Practice is the context for, origin of and purpose for practice knowledge and wisdom. The phenomenon of practice is a social construct in that to understand it we need to give meaning to it: this is a social rather than individual process of meaning making and attribution. A (collective) practice comprises ritual, social interactions, language, discourse, thinking and decision making, technical skills, identity, knowledge and practice wisdom, framed and contested by interests, practice philosophy, regulations, practice cultures, ethical standards, codes of conduct and societal expectations. For instance, if we talk about another construct, "the *practice* of justice", we could examine its dimensions and enactment through the living words of language and the documented words of the discourse of justice in general, or the various models through which it is realised or enacted in different places. If we talk about "the *practice* of medicine" we could define it broadly in comparison to the practices of other established professions such as law and theology, considering the differences and similarities in the way these practice communities "walk", "talk" and "think" their practices. Dunne (2011) contends:

> by a practice, I mean a more or less coherent and complex set of activities that has evolved co-operatively and cumulatively over time, and that exists most significantly in the community of those who are its practitioners – so long as they are committed to sustaining and developing its internal goods and its proper standards of excellence. (p. 13)

Practice is "situated and temporally located in local settings, life-worlds and systems, as well as international discourses, and it is grounded and released in metaphor, interpretation and narrative" (Higgs, 2012a, p. 3). Being social and situated, practices are not just shaped by the experience, intentions, dispositions, habitus and actions of individuals (Kemmis & Grootenboer, 2008). They are also shaped and prefigured intersubjectively by *arrangements* that exist in, or are brought to, particular sites of practice.

A practice extends beyond what the individual enacting a practice brings to a site as a person (e.g. beliefs, physical attributes and abilities); it also encompasses arrangements found in or brought to the site, arrangements with which the individual interacts and without which the practice could not be realised. Like the person enacting the practice, practices are always embodied (Green & Hopwood, 2015); these arrangements thus form a crucial part of the ontological ground that makes a practice possible.

Practice and Practices

Practice (a noun, concept, phenomenon) (Higgs, 2011, 2012b) can be understood as:

- a *domain,* a particular field of study, a discipline, a knowledge base (about the phenomenon of practice). Within the field of study of practice there are a variety of traditions or schools of thought.[1] In this domain context interest lies in the nature of the phenomenon represented in the field and how it is/can be interpreted,

conceptualised and planned. The field deals with the big picture of *why* and *what* the phenomenon is about, and this understanding is needed for evaluation of *how well* and *against which* frame of reference the phenomenon is realised/enacted;
- **the** practice *of a particular community of practice, profession or occupation*. This is practice that is field-owned, field-appraised (and encompasses "recognised good practices in the field") and practices that are field-regulated (as in being held to and monitored by sets of practice standards or codes of conduct);
- **the** practice *of an individual*; here a practitioner's practice is derived from the practice of his or her practice field, but is also made unique through the practitioner's personal frame of reference and agency;
- **a** practice (or a set of practices) within the above interpretations refers to *one of a group of* strategies or approaches in that field. In this context the interest lies in the realisation of the phenomenon and *how (where, with whom, when)* it is/can be implemented. For instance, professional decision making is a practice within the broader scope of professional practice.

The term *practices* refers to customary activities associated with a profession, occupation or discipline, and to the chosen ways individual practitioners implement their practice/profession. Examples of practices are ethical conduct, professional decision making, client–practitioner communication, consultation and referral, and interdisciplinary team work. Practices prefigure individual actions (Schatzki, 2001).

The construct *practice* can be seen to transcend other core domain level terms. For example, pedagogy as a domain is the practice of teaching, pertaining to the ways educators frame and enact their teaching and curricular practices and their teaching relationships, to enrich their students' learning experiences. Such pedagogy is informed by the teachers' interests, personal frames of reference, practice knowledge, theoretical frameworks, reflexive inquiries and capabilities, in consideration of contextual parameters, educational theory and research. Within the domain of pedagogy reside a variety of shared pedagogical practices and various ways different teachers practise their pedagogies.

In action, *practice* can be collective (e.g. a profession's practice) and individual (i.e. an individual practitioner's practice). The practice of a community of practice comprises ritual, social interactions, language, discourse, thinking and decision making, technical skills, identity, knowledge and practice wisdom, that are framed and contested by interests, practice philosophy, regulations, practice cultures, ethical standards, codes of conduct and societal expectations. An individual's practice model and enacted practice are framed and construed by the views of the practice community as well as the practitioner's interests, preferences, experiences, perspectives, meaning making, presuppositions and practice philosophy.

Importantly, in today's age of rapidly changing work demands and environments, there is considerable interest in practitioners' capacity for work and practice and their employability. This exceeds the scope and the ability of workers beyond the technical aspects (knowledge and skills) of performing the professional role to include generic abilities to act as capable and informed individuals, social citizens and professionals. McIlveen (2018) contends that "employability is not knowledge and skills per se; it is the propensity (of individuals) to understand their personal value and act toward their acquisition for deployment in a specific context" (p. 2).

Both within and across fields of practice, practices can be thought of in terms of *ecologies of practice* (Kemmis et al., 2012) in which practices co-exist, are interconnected, and adapt and evolve in relation to other practices across regional and chronological variations (Mahon et al., 2017). This practice interpretation builds on Capra's (2005) principles of ecology, sustainability, community and basic facts of life: networks, diversity, cycles, flows, nested systems, interdependence, development and dynamic balance. Using this ecological lens, Kemmis et al. (2012) view practices as relating "to one another as living entities in living systems" (p. 48).

Practice Characteristics

The nature of practice not only demonstrates its inherent complexity, it also sets wicked challenges for practice wisdom. That is, the practice of an occupation, profession or discipline is a multidimensional and dynamic phenomenon that is:

– socioculturally, historically and politically constructed – it is a product of its time, place, peoples and evolving interests
– shaped by the narrative, discourse and evolution of the discipline/occupation
– temporally located in eras, generational contexts and prevailing professional, policy and political drivers
– situational – what practices are useful, optimal and most relevant *depends* on the circumstances, geography, systems and persons involved
– ethical (ideally) – since practice is bound up in issues of moral purpose. This can range from contractual obligations to clients and practice communities to professional services with inherent duty of care to clients
– responsible – as enacted by both the practice community (collectively) and practitioners (personally)
– consequential – practice in occupational contexts has purposes and consequences if those purposes are not met or if actions taken have negative outcomes
– embodied – manifested, owned, enacted and realised.[2] Further, Green and Hopwood (2015) emphasise the notion of corporeality, contending that explicit attention to the body "informs and extends our current understandings and conceptualisations of (professional) practice" (p. 4)
– agential – pertaining to the will and capacity of the practitioner to choose and implement actions and influence
– owned and interpreted by practice to respect both the norms and standards of the practice community and the personal values and interests of the practitioner
– governed (regulated, led, managed, monitored) by its practice community(ies)
– current (up-to-date) in the present and future-oriented in its evolution

- person-centred – people (their interests, characteristics and needs) are the focus and purpose of practice, without the practice creators, receivers and collaborators practice has no meaning or purpose
- realised through and embedded in partnerships and collaboration with practice stakeholders including clients, colleagues, employers, practice community leaders and society
- dynamic, adaptable, flexible and creative – both proactively and in response to changes in circumstances and practice settings
- encompassing of praxis which refers to "acting for the good", "right conduct" (adopting a neo-Aristotelian view) and as "socially responsible action" (using a post-Marxian view) in the professions. Praxis is inherently reflexive. Praxis is informed by historically generated practice traditions that give substance to praxis, so that praxis is evaluated against historical and evolving standards and expectations that shape and frame the collective practice of professions as well as the conduct of individual practitioners.

Practice Theory

To understand practice wisdom it is useful to explore practice theory which examines all kinds of activity, contextually, through the lens of practice. According to Nicolini (2012) the value of practice theory lies in taking a practice-based view of social and human phenomena which allows us to take "radical departure from the traditional ways of understanding social and organizational matters" (p. 6).

Green (2009) identifies two distinct philosophical meta-traditions in practice theory work: *neo-Aristotelianism* and *post-Cartesianism*. The first stems from the philosophies of Aristotle and the Greeks and is linked to the work of 20th century scholars including Alisdair MacIntyre, Hans-Georg Gadamer and Joseph Dunne. Green (ibid) considers that "[t]he hallmark of this work is the notion of *integrity*— that is, that authentic practices contain within themselves their own integrity" (p. 5), and being true to itself. The second meta-tradition, the post-Cartesian, supports the critique of Cartesianism in Western culture and philosophy. Green argues that "perhaps the key organising issue here is what has been called the problem of *subjectivity* ... (recognising) that subjectivity is constituted in and through the practices (and discourses) of available cultures and traditions" (p. 5).

Practice Theory Themes

Rouse (2007) identifies six key practice themes explored by practice theorists. These themes, argues Rouse, provide "some unity to the various projects in sociology, anthropology, social theory and the philosophy of social sciences" (ibid, p. 528) that comprise practice theory contributions.
- *reconciling social structure of culture with individual agency*
Practice theories tend to support the value of both individual actions and agency along with culture and society. While society provides the framework (both

constraining and facilitating), the individual is influenced by and can influence the system (see also *habitus* above).

– *practices, rules and norms*
Critical to the philosophical background to practice theory are Wittgenstein's work on rule following and Heidegger's account of understanding and interpretation. "The notions that society or culture is the realm of activities and institutions governed or constituted by rules, of meaningful performances rather than merely physical or biological processes, or of actions according to norms rather than (or as well as) causally determined events are ubiquitous" (Rouse, 2007, p. 502).

– *bodily skills and disciplines*
Human bodies and bodily performance play a central role in practice. Bodily agency, expressiveness, intentionality and affective responses are shaped by social normalisation but human beings have freedom to act in ways that realise these system-led normative constraints.

– *language and tacit knowledge*
Practices have crucial tacit dimensions yet they can be described in linguistically expressed terms. Language and discourse can be considered as practices.

– *social sciences and social life*
Many practice theorists have focused on theorising the relationship between social inquiry and social life.

– *practices and the autonomy of the social*
An ongoing point of debate is location of practice study in disciplines, some contending that practices itself is the proper domain of the social sciences.

PRACTICE WISDOM

What is the wisdom of practice? It is not to have attained a state of superabundance or skills and abilities that in no way can be improved upon. Paradoxically, to think that you have attained wisdom, means that you are not wise. Rather, wisdom is a disposition to go on developing and learning in a world of contingency and happenstance. (Hager & Halliday, 2009, p. 232)

Practical wisdom is more than the possession of general knowledge just because it is the ability to actuate this knowledge with relevance, appropriateness, or sensitivity to context. In every fresh actuation there is an element of creative insight through which it makes itself equal to the demands of the new situation. (Dunne, 2011, p. 18)

Practice wisdom is 'an embodied state of being, comprising self-knowledge, action capacity, deep understanding of practice and an appreciation of others, that imbues and guides insightful and quality practice'. (Higgs, 2016, p. 65)

FROM PRACTICE TO PRACTICE WISDOM: DOING, KNOWING, BEING AND BECOMING

In this section I pick up the notion of practice introduced above as encompassing doing, knowing, being and becoming (Higgs, 1999) and draw it into the space of practice wisdom through exploration of these four terms when the wisdom and practice tensions are explored (see Figure 1.1). Being, Doing, Knowing and Becoming in practice broadly become refined in practice wisdom into *Dasein*, *Agentia*, *Sapience* and *Eudaimonia* (see Figure 1.2).

Figure 1.1. From Practice (Doing, Knowing, Being and Becoming) into Practice Wisdom.

Agentia

Agentia (Latin), or agency, encompasses a range of ideas including choice, capability, dispositions, self-critique and choice of action and practices. Professional practitioners need to pursue agency on their own behalf in the implementation of their roles and responsibilities and they often act as agents and advocate for their clients. Their behaviour is informed both by their own self-directed practice decision making and through the culture of their profession.

Sapience

Knowing extends far beyond having knowledge. Professionals need to be able to derive knowledge from, and use knowledge in, practice. And, beyond knowledge as noun, is the verb knowing. Knowing includes appreciating (with inbuilt critique, valuing and using knowing to generate ideas and judgements), mindfulness (with heightened awareness and attitudes of attentiveness to other and other ideas), self-awareness (self as presence and agent in situations), and being a knowing being with abilities of discernment, metacognition and self-awareness. Such a being is *sapient* (Old French, Latin),[3] meaning having good sense, intelligence, wisdom and the capacity to perceive. Professionals need to develop not just their practice epistemology and have this inform their practice knowledge, critical appreciation and development, they also need to develop epistemological fluency.

APPRECIATING PRACTICE WISDOM

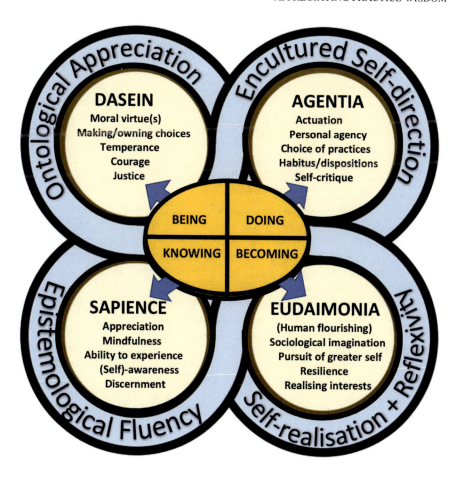

Figure 1.2. Practice Wisdom: Agentia, Sapience, Dasein and Eudaimonia.

The idea of fluency, typically applied to language, the spoken word and interactive communication, is particularly useful when thinking about knowledge and professional decision making. First, it refers to having a command of the language, and experienced practitioners need to have this ability. Jargon/technical language of the practice community provides the means and tools for communicating with colleagues using the rich knowledge and shared understanding embedded in the discipline-specific language of the profession (see Higgs, 2019).

Professionals are not simply third-party receivers of the knowledge and wisdom of others. Instead they are critical consumers of the knowledge of their own and other relevant fields plus the vast knowledge (as well as the lesser entity, information) that pervades the Internet and industry/professional work spaces. With these tools they are capable of using knowledge in action, to make judgements, to guide and promote human interaction, to make sense of experiences and to inform behaviour, particularly wise and moral practice such as ethical conduct, benevolence, practice decision making and the promotion of social justice. Further, they are knowledge generators, being responsible for creating and critiquing practice-based knowledge from their own practice and contributing this to their field and the wider professional knowledge base.

Dasein

Being in professional practice demands the pursuit of moral virtues as part of professionalism and expects the use of ontological appreciation of practice worlds and worldviews to foster understanding, recognition and appreciation of the multiple worldviews of the many participants in professional practice and recognition of the many interests (see Habermas, 1972) that different people, cultures and contexts contribute to the given situation. Practitioners are not just expected to act in line with sound practices of their professions and follow norms and codes of ethical conduct, they are also required to make and enact their own judgements, decisions and practice models and sustain as well as evolve these in the face of uncertain and complex situations, taking responsibility for their choices. Professional practice requires being a person of courage, temperance, virtue and justice. I have chosen the label of *Dasein* for this space: *Dasein* (German: da "there"; sein "being") or presence. Heidegger used the expression *Dasein* to refer to the experience of being that is peculiar to human beings.[4]

Eudaimonia

Neither as self/person or professional/practitioner worthy of the label, does a professional graduate act as a static or non-evolving being. Instead, just as their world of practice and knowledge is growing and changing around them, so too are they developing. People describe this development in many ways. From the general term becoming, there are many other options to be considered.

Eudaimonia (Greek) is typically translated as human flourishing and living well. In Aristotle's works, *eudaimonia* was used as the term for the highest human good. In practical philosophy the aim is to consider what *eudaimonia* is and how it can be achieved. In pursuit of human flourishing the individual benefits from an understanding of the human world, a sociological imagination, resilience and creativity. Embedded in human flourishing are the ideas of *arête* (virtue and excellence) and *phrónêsis*.

> [In modern times] we tend to think of 'wisdom' as the opposite of 'practical.' Wisdom is about abstract, ethereal matters like 'the way' or 'the good' or 'the truth' or 'the path.' And we tend to think that wisdom is something for sages,

gurus, rabbis, and scholars ... Aristotle's teacher, Plato shared this view that wisdom was theoretical and abstract, and the gift of only a few. But Aristotle disagreed. He thought that our fundamental social practices constantly demanded choices – like when to be loyal ... and that making the right choices demanded wisdom. ... The wisdom to answer such questions and to act rightly was distinctly practical, not theoretical. It depended on our ability to *perceive* the situation, to have the appropriate *feelings* or desires about it, to *deliberate* about what was appropriate in these circumstances and to *act*. (Schwartz & Sharpe, 2010, p. 5)

CONCLUSION

Understanding and employing practice wisdom is a journey of appreciation and realisation. The use of this interpretation of practice wisdom is a useful means of exploring how the complexities of practice wisdom and the many possibilities of wisdom can be brought together to create realisations of this absorbing phenomenon.

NOTES

[1] See, for instance, various perspectives on practice theory in Higgs (2019).
[2] A related idea is "lived body", which refers to the way that we use our body in any given context, for example, the influence emotions or gender have on our body in actions and interactions (Karin, Nyström, & Dahlberg, 2008).
[3] https://www.etymonline.com/word/sapience#etymonline_v_37645
[4] https://plato.stanford.edu/entries/heidegger/#Bib

REFERENCES

Birren, J. E., & Fisher L. M. (1990). The elements of wisdom: Overview and integration. In R. J. Sternberg (Ed.), *Wisdom: Its nature, origins and development* (pp. 317-332). Cambridge, England: Cambridge University Press.

Boshuizen, H. P. A., & Schmidt, H. G. (2019). The development of clinical reasoning expertise. In J. Higgs, G. Jensen, S. Loftus, & N. Christensen (Eds.), *Clinical reasoning in the health professions* (4th ed., pp. 57-65). Edinburgh: Elsevier.

Capra, F. (2005). Speaking nature's language: Principles of sustainability. In M. K. Stone & Z. Barlow (Eds.), *Ecological literacy: Educating our children for a sustainable world* (pp. 18-20). San Francisco, CA: Sierra Book Club Books.

Dunne, J. (2011). Professional wisdom in practice. In L. Biondi, D. Carr, C. Clark, & C. Clegg (Eds.), *Towards professional wisdom: Practice deliberations in the people professions* (pp. 14-26). Farnham, England: Ashgate.

Green, B. (Ed.). (2009). *Understanding and researching professional practice*. Rotterdam, The Netherlands: Sense.

Green, B., & Hopwood, N. (2015). The body in professional practice, learning and education: A question of corporeality. In B. Green & N. Hopwood (Eds.), *The body in professional practice, learning and education* (pp. 15-33). Dordrecht, The Netherlands: Springer.

Habermas, J. (1972). *Knowledge and human interest* (J. J. Shapiro, Trans.). London, England: Heinemann.

Hagar, P., & Halliday, J. (2009). *Recovering informal learning: Wisdom, judgement and community*. Dordrecht, The Netherlands: Springer.

Heidegger, J. (1962). *Being and time* (J. Macquarrie & E. Robinson, Trans.). Oxford, England: Basil Blackwell. (Original work published 1927)

Higgs, J. (1999, September). Doing, knowing, being and becoming in professional practice. *Master of Teaching Post Internship Conference*, The University of Sydney, Australia.

Higgs, J. (2011). *Practice-based education: Enhancing practice and pedagogy* (Final Report for ALTC Teaching Fellowship). Sydney, Australia: Australian Learning and Teaching Council.

Higgs, J. (2014). Assessing the immeasurables of practice. *Asia-Pacific Journal of Cooperative Education, Special Issue, 15*(3), 253-267.

Higgs, J. (2012a). Practice-based education: The practice-education-context-quality nexus. In J. Higgs, R. Barnett, S. Billett, M. Hutchings, & F. Trede (Eds.), *Practice-based education: Perspectives and strategies* (pp. 3-12). Rotterdam, The Netherlands: Sense.

Higgs, J. (2012b). Practice-based education pedagogy: Situated, capability-development, relationship practice(s). In J. Higgs, R. Barnett, S. Billett, M. Hutchings, & F. Trede (Eds.), *Practice-based education: Perspectives and strategies* (pp. 71-80). Rotterdam, The Netherlands: Sense.

Higgs, J. (2016). Practice wisdom and wise practice: Dancing between the core and the margins of practice discourse and lived practice. In J. Higgs & F. Trede (Eds.), *Professional practice discourse marginalia* (pp. 65-72). Rotterdam, The Netherlands: Sense.

Higgs, J. (2019). Exploring practice in context. In J. Higgs, S. Cork, & D. Horsfall (Eds.), *Challenging future practice possibilities* (pp. 3-16). Rotterdam, The Netherlands: Brill Sense.

Karin, D., Nyström, M., & Dahlberg, H. (2008). *Reflective lifeworld research* (2nd ed.). Lund, Sweden: Studentlitteratur.

Kemmis, S., & Grootenboer, P. (2008). Situating praxis in practice: Practice architectures and the cultural, social and material conditions for practice. In S. Kemmis & T. J. Smith (Eds.), *Enabling praxis: Challenges for education* (pp. 37-62). Rotterdam, The Netherlands: Sense.

Kemmis, S., Edwards-Groves, C., Wilkinson, J., & Hardy, I. (2012). Ecologies of practices. In P. Hager, A. Lee, & A. Reich (Eds.), *Practice, learning and change: Practice-theory perspectives on professional learning* (pp. 33-49). Dordrecht, The Netherlands: Springer.

Mahon, K., Kemmis, S., Francisco, S., & Lloyd, A. (2017). Introduction: Practice theory and the theory of practice architectures. In K. Mahon, S. Francisco, & S. Kemmis (Eds.), *Exploring education and professional practice: Through the lens of practice architectures* (pp. 1-30). Singapore: Springer.

McIlveen, P. (2018). *Defining employability for the new era of work: A submission to The Senate Select Committee on the Future of Work and Workers*. Canberra, Australia: The Senate. doi:10.13140/RG.2.2.23333.60646

Nicolini, D. (2012). *Practice theory, work and organisation: An introduction*. Oxford, England: Oxford University Press.

Ratner, C. (1991). *Vygotsky's sociohistorical psychology and its contemporary applications*. New York, NY: Plenum.

Rouse, J. (2007). *Practice theory* (Division I Faculty Publications: Paper 43). Retrieved from http://wesscholar.wesleyan.edu/div1facpubs/43

Schatzki, T. R. (2001). Practice theory. In T. R. Schatzki, K. Knorr-Cetina, & E. von Savigny (Eds.), *The practice turn in contemporary theory* (pp. 1-14). London/New York: Routledge.

Schwartz, B., & Sharpe, K. (2010). *Practical wisdom: The right way to do the right thing*, New York, NY: Riverhead Books.

Sternberg, R. J. (2003). *Wisdom, intelligence, and creativity synthesized*. Cambridge, England: Cambridge University Press.

Taylor, R. B. (2010). *Medical wisdom and doctoring: The art of 21st century practice*. New York, NY: Springer.

Joy Higgs AM, PhD (ORCID: https://orcid.org/0000-0002-8545-1016)
Emeritus Professor, Charles Sturt University, Australia
Director, Education, Practice and Employability Network, Australia

DAVID CARR

2. WISDOM, (MORAL) VIRTUE AND KNOWLEDGE

THE UTILITARIAN EDUCATION OF THOMAS GRADGRIND

The opening page of *Hard Times* by the 19th century English novelist Charles Dickens is often quoted in discussions of the nature of education and teaching. In this opening, the Victorian schoolmaster Thomas Gradgrind insists that we should teach young people nothing but facts: "Facts alone are wanted in life. Plant nothing else, and root out everything else. You can only form the minds of reasoning animals upon facts: nothing else will ever be of any service to them" (Dickens, 2003, p. 1). This noted, it should also be said that Gradgrind is by no means the major villain of this novel or himself a cold or heartless man. As the story proceeds to show, Gradgrind is the very soul of not only charity, but genuine warmth and kindness, towards others in the narrative – not least towards the abandoned circus child Sissy Jupe.

Still, Gradgrind is clearly in thrall to an emerging modern Western rational-empiricist mindset entirely driven by fairly basic socioeconomic concerns. His educational philosophy, as Dickens is clearly concerned to highlight, is firmly rooted in the 19th century (probably largely Benthamite) philosophy of utilitarianism that reduces human value – or what humans can be reasonably said to value – to materialist cost-benefit calculation. In consequence, Gradgrind's education of cold fact-based reason effectively starves his own children of emotion, imagination and moral sense and succeeds only in alienating them and wrecking their lives. Towards the end of the novel, Gradgrind is brought to painful appreciation of the dire failure of his own philosophy and educational methods. Significantly, he confesses that though he had once been told that there is a wisdom of the heart as well as of the head, he had foolishly failed to believe this.

Dickens' novel, along with much other 19th century literature in the so-called "romantic" tradition (one is reminded of similar normative themes in the poetry of William Wordsworth and William Blake), mounts a devastating critique of a Western post-industrial conception of human knowledge and reason that had already gained ascendance in Dickens' day and which continues to wield much influence in today's world of modern and postmodern free-market capitalism and globalisation. In this regard, it is notable that the Gradgrind quote from *Hard Times* continues to reappear in much literature of educational theory that is critical of the test-based examination and assessment of much contemporary (global) schooling. It is an education that prizes the evidence-based knowledge of scientific research and enquiry over sources of insight that cannot be empirically validated or "proved" – as seems evident from widespread global side-lining of literature, arts and humanities in such latter-day schooling.

(On this view, Darwin's *Origin of Species* [1859] would count as a more valid source of knowledge or wisdom than Dickens' *Hard Times*.) It seems also to be an education that, in Oscar Wilde's famous definition of a cynic, "knows the price of everything and the value of nothing" (Wilde, 2000, p. 48) and takes life to be primarily concerned, in the words of the poet William Wordsworth, with "getting and spending" (Nichol-Smith, 1921, p. 146).

What, however, of Gradgrind's eventual rejection of the rationalist grounding of all value in empirically measurable and/or utilitarian benefit and his late conversion to "wisdom of the heart"? On the face of it, this seems to suggest some "either-or" dichotomy that might (or might not – since some things are just dichotomous) well arouse philosophical suspicions. At any rate, if "head" here is meant to signify reason, and "heart" refers to feeling, emotion or passion, then it would seem that the heart cannot be quite sufficient for wisdom. Socrates and Plato, the great founders of Western philosophy, warned of the moral hazards of blindly following our feelings and desires, and great tragic poetry from the Greeks to Shakespeare is full of stories of human disaster and suffering when agents are swayed by passion rather than reason. Indeed, the philosophers of Greek antiquity generally agreed that reason or rationality is the defining feature of human nature and that which distinguishes us from other animals.

So, the truth seems to be that human agents may fail to do well by lacking feeling or reason and that both of these are needed for wisdom. But this, of course, is not to deny that reason and feeling (or passion or emotion) are different or that there may be some tension or opposition between them. The key question seems more that of how reason and feeling are conjoined or implicated in wisdom.

We have already observed a kind of reason – namely, the empirical or evidence-based rationality of Gradgrind's factual education – that does appear to be somewhat at odds with the wisdom we might expect to be conducive to a well lived or flourishing human life. Dickens' *Hard Times* is a literary case study of how such an education can drain the soul and life-blood out of human life better than Count Dracula. In that case, the task would seem to be that of conceiving or discerning a type or mode or reasoning or rationality that is differently situated in the psychic, moral or spiritual economy of human life and conduct from any such more rationally calculative capacity. In the view of many ancient and modern philosophers and moral theorists the most promising perspective on this issue ever given is that of the ancient Greek philosopher Aristotle (349 BC/1941) in his account of virtue and virtues (such as honesty, self-control, courage, justice, compassion) as the powers required for genuine human (moral and other) flourishing.

In the account of virtue he offers in his *Nicomachean Ethics*, Aristotle departs significantly and conspicuously from his great teacher Plato. According to Aristotle, the trouble with the conception of moral reason pioneered by Plato under the influence of Socrates, lay in its simultaneously uniform and abstract character. While Plato certainly did – in his "divided-line" *epistêmology* (see Republic, 380 BC/1961) – recognise a distinction between higher (intelligible) and lower (sensible) kinds of reasoning, he denied any real *epistêmic* validity to forms of reflection tied to the largely corrigible deliverances of sensible appearance and regarded only the higher contemplation of abstract forms as rationally justified. While fundamentally at odds with Aristotle's metaphysical naturalism – the view that any accurate knowledge of the world of human experience would need to be grounded on observable evidence and experiment – the Platonic view also fails to appreciate that different forms of reasoning may be needed for different human purposes. As the great theorist of logic and rationality of the ancient world, Aristotle argues that while the "higher" forms of theoretical reasoning identified by Plato may be needed for mathematics and science, a quite different sort of reasoning is needed for deliberation regarding the more experientially and contextually shifting concerns of human practical affairs.

Thus, in his *Nicomachean Ethics*, Aristotle distinguishes between diverse forms of reason and understanding associated with five different "intellectual virtues". These, however, are (roughly) divisible in terms of a further distinction between capacities of more theoretical and practical nature; and the two key forms of practical deliberation – *phrónêsis* and *tékhnê* – are yet further differentiated in terms of the very different ends or purposes of these. The capacity to which Aristotle refers as *tékhnê* – often glossed as "productive deliberation" – is that employed by artists and crafts-persons for the acquisition, cultivation and/or exercise of practical skills: "the art of making by the aid of a right rule" (Aristotle, 349 BC/1941, book 6, section 4). However, for Aristotle, the power that governs the cultivation of virtue is the species of reason he calls *phrónêsis* and which is usually translated as "practical wisdom".

The modern founder of neo-Aristotelian virtue ethics, Elizabeth Anscombe, described this mode of human reasoning as "one of Aristotle's best discoveries" (Anscombe, 1959) and established a central place for it in the development of post-war philosophy of action – though post-war action theorists did not always distinguish clearly between the precise concerns of *phrónêsis* and *tékhnê*. Still, whilst Aristotle himself did (in the present view) incline to some misleading comparison between the practical acquisition of skills on the one hand and the virtues of human flourishing on the other, he is no less often clear enough that the defining feature of *phrónêsis* is its more particular concern with the proper ordering of natural feelings, passions and appetites for the individual and common good. As the present author has elsewhere put it: virtues may be understood as more or less equivalent to states of emotion, feeling or appetite ordered in accordance with some deliberative ideal of practical wisdom (Carr, 2009).

Actually, this way of putting things is a little less than precise, since a significant difference needs to be observed between *feelings* – construed as the natural states of affect that all sentient creatures, non-human no less than human, may undergo – and the *emotional* states that are more characteristic of human experience. So, for example, while one may sensibly ascribe fear, rage, panic or sexual attraction to non-humans, it is more difficult (if not impossible) to attribute such states as envy, pride, love, disgust, vanity or gratitude to such creatures as spiders, bats, dogs, cats or even monkeys. While this distinction is a bit rough-hewn and human dog lovers are likely to bridle at it ("of course, Rover loves and is grateful to me: he shows it all the time"), the clear enough difference between these affective states is that the latter require a level of language-mediated cognition that is simply not available to animals that lack this – which arguably, though not uncontroversially, means all other than human agents.

From this viewpoint, a broadly Aristotelian approach to understanding virtue also seems to have made a major contribution to modern philosophy of emotion by showing that what is distinctive about those human affective states commonly called "emotions" is that they are inherently "intentional". Emotional states such as envy, pride, vanity, love and jealousy involve reference to events or states of affairs in the world whereby they may be judged right or appropriate, or mistaken or inappropriate. Thus, while a non-human animal cannot be pronounced correct or incorrect in its fear or rage, proud or jealous human agents may be judged mistaken or unwarranted in their pride or jealousy. So we may say that Othello should not have felt jealousy regarding Desdemona, since his jealousy was groundless – and, of course, some human emotions such as arrogance and vanity, in and of themselves, imply some such lack of good normative warrant: to feel vanity or arrogance is *ipso facto* to have a false estimate of oneself. So one might here usefully observe a rough and ready distinction between *feelings* – as forms of raw affect that all sentient creatures can experience – and *emotions* as forms of rationalised or cognitive affect (though these are not quite the same thing) that are only very accurately ascribable to human agents. At all events, such observations have evident implications for any account of wisdom, and we shall return to them in due course.

Still, in these terms, there can be no Aristotelian practical wisdom of *phrónêsis* in the absence of the feelings, passions and appetites it seeks to order and no wisely ordered passions and feelings in the absence of practical reason. In this light, Aristotle clearly distinguishes not only the rationally ordered emotions and passions of (moral and other) virtue from the frequently disordered natural passions, but also the emotionally grounded reason of (moral or other) virtue from the clever but cold and self-interested utilitarian calculation of Gradgrindian education. Further, it is notable that Aristotle (departing conspicuously from Plato) seems to have held that the cultivation of the practical wisdom of virtue might be greatly assisted by attention to the human issues and dilemmas depicted in tragic poetry and other literature: in short, that a reading of (say) Dickens' *Hard Times* might be of more value for the development of human wisdom than attention to (say) Darwin's *Origin of Species*.

At all events, there has been much recent appreciation of the educational significance of Aristotle's practical wisdom – not least in recognition that this quality has been rather neglected in latter-day institutionalised schooling and professional education (see especially, Dunne, 1997) – for helping young and old to live virtuous and flourishing lives. In this regard, much pioneering work continues to be done to this end in the Jubilee Centre for Character and Virtues of the University of Birmingham (United Kingdom). Indeed, a broadly Aristotelian conception of practical wisdom has been widely employed for understanding not only the general human development of such qualities of moral character as honesty, courage, justice, self-control and compassion, but also the role and operations of such qualities in the conduct of a wide variety of professional practices such as teaching, medicine, law, business, nursing and social work (see, for example, Carr, 2018). In this regard, it has been widely held that while practical wisdom is a requirement of any and all virtuous agency, it is a very particular requirement of morally wise and virtuous public and professional service. But the *phrónêsis* of Aristotelian virtue ethics has lately become very much the theory of choice in contemporary attempts to understand the nature of human moral and other wisdom. In the present view, however, this is far from conceptually and normatively unproblematic.

WISDOM AND KNOWLEDGE

In the present view, a major difficulty is that while Anscombe and other contemporary virtue ethicists are right to regard Aristotle's conception of *phrónêsis* or practical wisdom as a discovery of large significance for our general understanding of moral life and character, the notion is – at least in Aristotle – *epistêmically* anomalous. To be sure, the main claims made for practical deliberation are substantial. To begin with, it is widely and rightly held by latter-day theorists of moral education and professional ethics that the more theoretical or universalistic conception of the wisdom of virtue to which Plato seemed inclined is not helpful towards understanding or addressing the complex and messy particularities of actual practical human moral life. From this viewpoint, deliberating to moral decisions is indeed very different from the deductive reasoning of mathematics or the inductive or empirical reasoning required for the formulation of scientific hypotheses.

To be fair, it should be said that Plato also clearly appreciated this in his divided-line *epistêmology* but was still inclined to locate the reflective goal of distinctively moral thought – his "form of the good" – at the universal (absolute certainty) rather than the (less certain) local or particular pole of speculation. It is to this that Aristotle precisely and explicitly objects in the early sections of his *Nicomachean Ethics*: Plato's abstract and absolute form of the good can be of no earthly (literally as well as metaphorically) use to us in addressing the more practical day-to-day details of moral (or other) life and conduct which vary with context and circumstance and are not readily amenable to or resolvable by the application of general rules. For one thing, while the virtue of honesty may counsel general truth-telling, and that of compassion generally sparing others' feelings, there may well be a problem in circumstances of conflicting virtues where we may need some "economy" with the truth in order to avoid hurting others (Carr, 2003).

But another much rehearsed apparent difficulty with any universalistic or absolutist conception of moral virtue or good is that it is not always clear in particular practical circumstances what the virtuous expression of honesty, justice, self-control or compassion might be. To begin with, what counts as virtuous may seem to shift from one situation to another. Thus, for example, while it may sometimes be (wisely) courageous for an individual to take up arms against a sea of troubles and by opposing end them, it may be less so in circumstances in which resistance is futile and one cannot but resign oneself to the slings and arrows of outrageous fortune. In that case, as the common English saying goes, discretion – or some reasonable accommodation with opposing circumstances – may be the better part of valour. Further to this, somewhat more worryingly, it would also appear that what counts as virtuous on a given occasion would appear to vary from person to person. Thus, for example, someone who is naturally timid and needs much effort to be brave may be considered more virtuously courageous on occasions when she stands up to the insults of a bully, whereas the more naturally confident or self-assured person who (perhaps more wisely) ignores or shrugs these off as beneath contempt may be regarded as less so. Or vice versa; it is simply far from easy to tell.

To be sure, Aristotle's own highly influential way of addressing such issues – his celebrated "doctrine of the mean" – is to advise that virtuous agency should aim for a middle course between excess and deficiency of feeling, passion or appetite. On this view, the virtuously courageous should aim to avoid too much fear (cowardice) and too little (recklessness); the self-controlled should seek a course between too much appetite (gluttony) and too little (self-denial); the generous should aim between too much giving (profligacy) and too little (miserliness); and so on. Again, however, the trouble is that Aristotle does not seem to provide very precise criteria for the identification of particular instances of virtue in any of the indeterminate cases lately noticed. Indeed, he has commonly been interpreted as holding that in the absence of any such precisely determining measure, what counts as virtuous in this or that circumstance can only be a matter of case-by-case judgement. But whose judgement?

Clearly, it could hardly be that of a fool or simpleton and would need to be the judgement of someone who counts as knowledgeable or wise in the circumstances. But who might this be other than the practically wise agent of virtuous character? Aristotle does indeed suggest that virtuous deliberations and judgements are just those that a virtuous agent – one possessed of practical wisdom – would be inclined to make.

But while this may not be an unintelligible position – we might well understand what it means – its unhelpful circularity is no less apparent. From the practical viewpoint of general or professional education in moral virtue, it is obviously hard to know how to proceed if one has to know what the virtuously wise would judge in order to know how to become virtuously wise oneself or to teach wisdom to others. Indeed, this is the evident problem with the philosophically influential neo-Aristotelian virtue ethics of John McDowell (1997): his inherently agent-privileged view of virtue – whereby becoming virtuous requires acquiring a virtuous agent's perspective – makes it hard to see how this perspective could be shared with or communicated to the not yet virtuous. But this problem is clearly exacerbated by the lately noted consideration that there is at any rate no obvious way to determine who counts as a virtuous agent and/or that there may be diverse and potentially conflicting ways of counting as (or at least appearing) virtuous. Is virtue, then – and the wisdom through which virtue is exhibited – just a subjective free-for-all?

On the face of it, Aristotle is no moral relativist. Indeed, the neo-naturalist or ethical descriptivists, responsible for the revival of Aristotelian virtue ethics in the late 20th century, argued in the name of their master for a natural sense of moral good as an antidote to what they perceived as various forms of subjective and relativist moral prescriptivism and constructivism (see Foot, 1978; Geach, 1977). The ethical return to virtues, as Aristotelian states of good character, was to focus on acquired human properties or characteristics that are nevertheless naturally and objectively conducive to what he calls *eudaimonia* or flourishing. Precisely the claim was, that just as there is a perfectly straightforward and unproblematic sense of "good" that serves to identify the proper functions of such ordinary objects as knives and shoes, so there is a no less descriptive sense of good that serves to identify the proper moral functioning of human character traits. Put simply, the claim is that character traits such as honesty, courage and self-control conduce to – are, as it were, naturally productive of – objective human flourishing or wellbeing in the same way that sharp edges and water-tightness are contributory if not essential to the goodness of knives and shoes.

While correct up to a point, however, this perspective falls well short of doing the ethical work that Aristotelian neo-naturalists and descriptivists supposed it to do. To be sure, the Aristotelian position shows why such human qualities of character as honesty, courage, self-control, justice and kindness are commonly regarded as virtues or "excellences", insofar as they do generally appear more conducive to (personal and social) success and wellbeing than their opposites of dishonesty, cowardice, intemperance, unfairness and meanness. To this extent, such qualities do – as neo-naturalists promised – seem to bridge the infamous fact-value distinction of much classical ethics (including that of Hume and Kant and, probably, Plato).

Precisely, it is clear enough why humans value – or evaluate more highly – honesty over dishonesty, justice over unfairness and self-control over intemperance, insofar as such qualities are on the whole productive of more admirably successful lives. If evidence is needed, it is clearly such character virtues rather than vices that are celebrated in classical human cultural narratives such as Greek and Shakespearian tragedies. It is for the same reason that child rearing and education in most if not all human cultures have sought to encourage and reinforce such qualities in the young.

But there is a major difficulty – to which some modern Aristotelian naturalists have not themselves been blind. This is that the human virtues or "excellences" of Greek ethics were not clearly moral virtues in anything like the modern sense of this term. Indeed, while the latter-day sense of virtue is often taken to be synonymous with morality, it is also far from contradictory in modern usage to regard such qualities as courage, self-control and loyalty *as* virtues while admitting that they may often be directed to morally disreputable ends. In short, it is not only saints and heroes who are courageous and self-controlled in pursuit of noble goals, but villains and criminals in pursuit of ignoble ones.

Indeed, it is here worth observing that though Aristotle himself offers a complex and detailed account of the virtue of justice, this is not only at odds with any modern sense of justice but at considerable variance with anything that could be regarded as morally acceptable justice. For while, on the one hand, Aristotle's just agents might count as virtuous by (say) avoiding extremes of fear or favour, they would, on the other hand, be permitted to regard slaves and women as inferior beings unworthy of the respect of free male citizens. So Aristotle's virtuously just (people) might well be less than morally just in any ethically defensible sense.

Of course, one immediately tempting way out of this impasse is precisely to have recourse to Aristotle's notion of *phrónêsis* or practical wisdom. For surely, we might say, the trouble with "courageous" criminals or "just" misogynists is that they simply could not in the light of practical wisdom *really* count as courageous while being oblivious to the wickedness of their goals, or as truly just without due respect for women. However, the trouble is that there is nothing in Aristotle's notion of practical wisdom that clearly precludes such partial virtue. To the extent that criminals judiciously avoid too much and too little fear (cowardice and recklessness), they may be counted as virtuously courageous. To the extent that the citizens of Aristotle's slave economy are scrupulous in giving others their (albeit locally prescribed) due – say, by avoiding bribes or favouritism – there is no reason either not to consider them *virtuously* just or fair, even if we also want to say that they are not *morally* so.

The trouble with Aristotle's *phrónêsis* or practical wisdom is that its main purpose seems to be that of ordering an agent's natural affections and appetites for the formation of good character conceived as conducive to the best interests (*eudaimonia*) of the individual or the local group of which she or he is a member. But character traits such as honesty, courage, self-control and even fairness may do this to perfection without such interests looking particularly moral – that is, in any sense of moral that significantly extends beyond local personal or social advantage. Put another way, there seems to be nothing in Aristotle's ethics that would adequately support – indeed, the idea seems quite foreign to Aristotle – the powerful normative intuition that treating the enslaved or women as human inferiors is unjust in the sense of simply *morally wrong*.

VIRTUE, WISDOM AND HONESTY

Such considerations bear strongly on a previous observation that Aristotle's concept of *phrónêsis* or practical wisdom is *epistêmically* anomalous. The chief difficulty is that if *phrónêsis* is supposed to be a kind of *wisdom*, then it seems natural to expect it to be grounded in or to draw on some sort of *knowledge*. This is the issue that is addressed head on by Aristotle's philosophical predecessor and mentor Plato in the Socratic dialogues. In various places, Plato (380 BC/1961) clears the ground by showing that any knowledge of moral life and understanding could not be either the knowledge of scientific enquiry or the practical know-how of productive skills: the morally wise person is not someone who has grasped some body of factual information or theory or mastered the skills of joinery or painting. So of what would such knowledge consist? Plato, seeing (rightly in the present view) that it is not derivable from the deliverances of sense experience, seeks it in the intellectual stratosphere of pure empirically unsullied ideas. Aristotle rejects this as unhelpful and seeks it in a kind of practically focused deliberation that is, however, itself separated from the *epistêmic* concerns of science. He explicitly separates what he calls the *epistêmic* or truth-seeking virtues of scientific enquiry from those virtues concerned with the practical ordering of the natural affect and appetite of human agents for their effective functioning.

To be sure, Aristotle would not deny the obvious fact that rational agents do need to possess much everyday knowledge for such functioning: the courageous need some clear idea of the dangers they are in; the temperate need some idea of what pleasures are good or harmful; the compassionate need some idea of the needs of others and so on. The key difficulty, however, is that such knowledge is neither the goal nor the substance of *phrónêsis* – and one might well have all available information of this general circumstantial kind and yet lack practical wisdom. Indeed, insofar as the key goal of Aristotle's practical wisdom seems to be the effective personal or interpersonal functioning of *eudaimonia* – more than knowledge or truth seeking – the development of one's character for flourishing might best be secured by some *epistêmic* economy.

Indeed, this is something that is brought into sharp relief in contemporary *eudaimonistic* developments of virtue ethics that focus much on Aristotle's analogy between the cultivation of virtues and the development of more practical skills. But in that case, it could be that the goals of virtue are best served by *less* rather than *more* knowledge or information. A good example of this is to be found in the utilitarian virtue ethics of Julia Driver who has recently argued that modesty – which she actually calls a "virtue of ignorance" – should be conceived as a matter of agents' deliberate understatement or false estimate of their talents and achievements (Driver, 1989, 2001). Such understatement is held to be conducive to or a condition of – not appearing arrogant or big-headed – and so consequently congenial to the company of others.

However one might regard this (variously objectionable and contestable) view, it underscores the more general *epistêmic* indeterminacy of Aristotle's notion of *phrónêsis* or practical wisdom and its relations to anything that we would ordinarily count as rational knowledge. On the one hand, there seems to be a requirement for *phrónêsis* to be anchored in some clearly identifiable knowledge or principle determining what should count as virtuously right in this or that situation. On the other hand, as highlighted in previous examples, Aristotle gives us little in the way of such knowledge or principle beyond the judgement of some ideal *phrónimos* – perhaps in principle beyond the ken of the not yet wise – based on some fairly evasive notion of mean avoidance of excess and deficiency of affect and appetite, to the end of some no less clearly determinable (or particularly moral) conception of personal or social wellbeing.

But perhaps there is not quite *nothing* in Aristotle. As such modern virtue ethical commentators as John McDowell have pointed out, there is a striking passage of *Nicomachean Ethics* in which Aristotle compares so-called *akratic* or weak-willed agents – those who know (in some sense) what they should do, but yet fail to do it – as like the drunken who may know their way home but fail to grasp it in their inebriated state. While this does not contribute much clarification to what might here be meant by "knowledge" (is this, after all, a kind of "knowing that" or "knowing how"), it does suggest that the moral error or failure of the *akrates* is a kind of misperception or clouded vision – a glass through which things are seen only darkly. While there seems little elsewhere in Aristotle's *Nicomachean Ethics* to square his discussion of *akrasia* with his broader view of practical wisdom, it at least suggests a rather different *perceptual* model of virtuous knowledge from anything suggested by his comparison of virtues to skills (Aristotle, 349 BC/1941, book 2, section 1). On this view, those who fall short of virtue, go wrong not because they make a practical mistake but because they fail to *see* clearly – and they fail to see clearly because their vision is clouded.

But clouded by what? In fact, Aristotle's discussion at this point seems closer – and may well be directly indebted – to the views of his philosophical predecessors Socrates and Plato than to his own revisionary account of the deliberations of *phrónêsis* or practical wisdom. Throughout his dialogues (non-Socratic no less than Socratic) Plato defends a conception of (moral) wisdom – more or less attributed to the historical Socrates – as essentially a kind of freedom from passion-induced error or ignorance. In short, it is not that the wise agent has acquired information or techniques after the fashion of a scientist who has formed a new hypothesis or learned a new theory, or a craftsman who has learned a new skill.

It is rather that virtuously wise agents have managed to rid themselves of or correct fundamentally mistaken perspectives on the world that – whilst no doubt rooted in unrestrained natural desire – are also liable to reinforcement in the course of faulty socialisation and upbringing. In previous exploration of the relationship of human affect to reason, we have already noticed some of the states from which the wise agent needs liberation in this way. Indeed, these are the kind of states – such as vanity, (excess) ambition, arrogance, avarice, envy, jealousy, vengefulness – named in traditional lists of the deadly sins. All of these follow from agents' mistaken beliefs about themselves, ultimately grounded – as Plato explicitly argues in the *Laws* – in a kind of immature egotism that places self above all else and all others in the world.

Literature is, of course, full of dramatic illustrations of the disastrous consequences that are liable to follow from such self-attachment. For example, in the tragedies of Shakespeare: Othello's downfall is a direct consequence of his unfounded jealousy regarding Desdemona; the havoc wrought by Macbeth follows from his selfish ambition; the ill fortune of King Lear is traceable to his childish petulance and distorted conceptions of human love and attachment; and so forth. Indeed, the distinguished 20th century philosopher and novelist Iris Murdoch (1970, 1993) argued explicitly under the influence of Plato – though somewhat at odds with Plato's own mistrust of the moral value of the arts – that serious literature may and should be regarded (more than philosophy) as the most promising route to human appreciation of the errors and delusions of self-attachment into which human agents are liable to fall and as a potent means to liberation or emancipation from the Platonic cave of false and vain appearance. On this view, such clarity of vision or perception – coming to be able to see the world, ourselves and our relations with others without the fog of self-obsession – would be a necessary if not a sufficient (as Socrates seems to have thought) condition of human moral or other wisdom.

If all this is so, then there is clearly an *epistêmic* – knowledge or truth seeking – dimension to the wise deliberations of virtue. So, while Aristotle was clearly correct to regard the kind of reasoning and deliberation as distinctively concerned with the ordering of human natural affect, passions and appetites for good character – and therefore, to this extent, as not reducible to the knowledge of scientific enquiry or skill acquisition – it seems ill-advised to separate it completely from the *epistêmic* virtues and effectively to deny any concern of practical wisdom with the discernment of truth.

For feelings, passions and appetites to be correctly ordered to the end of good or honourable character, they must above all be consistent with an honest perception or assessment of the world, ourselves and our relations with others in the world. This is again, why the *Nicomachean* account of appropriate feeling, passion and appetite in virtue is unhelpfully couched in terms of reason's determination of the right *amount* of such states. For it is not the *amount*, but the *quality* – specifically the *epistêmic* content in the terms of honesty – that matters: vanity is not too much self-interest, but the wrong (dishonest) kind of self-interest; envy is not too much regard for the possessions of others, but the wrong (egotistic) sort of regard; lust is not too much sexual passion, but the wrong sort of (other-demeaning) sexual passion; and so on.

That said, there seems an outstanding problem about this Platonic-Socratic perspective on practical wisdom. For just as it is difficult on the Aristotelian conception of the operations of reason in practical wisdom to perceive any standard or principle that might help us to determine what precise ordering of feeling, passion or appetite amounts to moral virtue – so that it is consistent with regarding genuinely courageous, self-controlled or even just acts as nevertheless not morally good – neither is any such principle more conspicuously evident on a Socratic-Platonic account of such wisdom as correct perception. More precisely, while coming to clear perception of things may well reveal that I am treating myself as vainly or arrogantly superior to others (women, slaves, those less well-off, etc.), what might show me that I am (morally) wrong to treat them in this way? Can I just not consider my relations to others – as might the great-souled Aristotelian man – to be properly ordered by nature and circumstance in this fashion?

Against this, however, it seems reasonable to hold that any wise agent should or would be a *moral* agent, and that moral agency should be compatible with justice, conceived – not merely as conformity to local convention – but in more *universal* terms. In this light, we might refuse to regard someone as wise who discriminated against others on grounds of race, skin pigmentation, gender, class or religious faith. However, it is significant that no knock-down argument or grounding principle for any such universal conception of justice as equal moral regard is clearly discernible in the work of either Plato or Aristotle – though both, in their different ways, seem to have sought some kind of rationally objective basis for a more morally distinctive form of deliberation and judgement. Still, while we have

25

noticed that Aristotle's particularistic practical wisdom of *phrónêsis* – or the notion of *eudaimonia* on which he grounds this – is not entirely helpful in this regard, the Platonic universalism of ideal forms (of good, virtue and justice) that Aristotle rejects in his ethics may seem to be more promising.

From this viewpoint, there are two general Platonic themes which, taken together, do point strongly towards the wider conception of justice as equal moral regard that would seem needed here. The first, as we have seen, is the basically Socratic idea that the "knowledge" of moral wisdom is mainly a matter of liberation from the vanity and egotism of the prisoner in the Platonic cave of delusion. The second, largely just further to this, is precisely Plato's anti-naturalist (moral) *epistêmology*. Unlike his pupil Aristotle, Plato did not believe that moral deliberation and judgement could be derived from, properly grounded in or founded upon the deliverances of sense experience. Hence, his *epistêmology* of the divided line aspires to a *normative* grounding of moral judgement – of even greater rational certitude than the formal reasoning of mathematics – entirely beyond the Platonic cave of false opinion.

Interestingly, the early modern thinker whose work most conspicuously embodies these two Platonic themes – and who explicitly acknowledged debt to Plato – is the 18th century French social philosopher Jean-Jacques Rousseau. Essentially, Rousseau (1977) argued that the widespread, largely class-conditioned, injustice of his time should be understood as a direct consequence of the division of labour of advanced economies which had fostered widespread inequality and encouraged the privileged and propertied to regard themselves as superior to others. Rousseau referred to such perspectives as *amour propre* (self-love), took them to be basically delusional in much the manner of the vain beliefs of the prisoners in Plato's cave, and – above all – to be inimical to the universal moral regard needed to sustain liberal-democracy. Consequently, he argued for a radical or progressive form of education designed to counter the more socially divisive effects of human socialisation to the end of promoting more unprejudiced and egalitarian human regard (Rousseau, 1991).

However, in addition to his influence on modern progressive education, Rousseau's ideas had a profoundly formative effect on broadly "romantic" literature from the 17th century onwards – which is also much concerned with human emancipation from various forms of social and ideological conditioning and indoctrination – but, above all on the deontological ethics of the 18th century philosopher Immanuel Kant (1967) who also grounded morality in a form of justice as universal moral respect unhindered by local individual and social biases. And, while it has commonly been held – especially by modern naturalist or neo-Aristotelian virtue ethicists (in the wake, notably, of Anscombe 1959, 1981) – that the ethics of Kant and Aristotle are fundamentally incompatible, this is by no means clearly so.

For while the modern return to Aristotle has been salutary with regard to the revival of a notion of virtuous wisdom that well enough shows how personally and socially beneficial character traits are rooted in natural conditions of human advantage, it yet lacks – as previously indicated – clear grounds for distinction between virtuous deliberation and conduct of local benefit and a *moral* virtue that requires grounding in some conception of more inclusive or universal human benefit. Modern Kantian deontology – directly influenced by an anti-naturalistic Rousseauian conception of universal moral regard that has deep resonances with Platonic *epistêmology* – offers such grounds without being problematically incompatible with Aristotelian location of the roots of virtue as good character in human nature.

While persons of wisdom certainly require Aristotelian *phrónêsis* or practical deliberation to negotiate the local and particular contingencies of prudent human agency, they also need the unclouded vision of wider moral regard for which Socrates and Plato both sought via an empirically transcendent and universal form of normative enquiry of a kind later developed by modern deontologists. While wise agents certainly need to be Aristotelian *phrónimos*, they also need to be morally so in a way that cannot be exclusively derived from the idea of *phrónêsis* in itself.

REFERENCES

Anscombe, G. E. M. (1959). *Intention*. Oxford, England: Blackwell.
Anscombe, G. E. M. (1981). Modern moral philosophy. In G. E. M Anscombe (Ed.), *The collected philosophical papers of G. E. M. Anscombe: Volume III: Ethics, religion and politics*. Oxford, England: Basil Blackwell.
Aristotle. (1941). Nicomachean ethics. In R. McKeon (Ed.), *The basic works of Aristotle* (pp. 935-1111). New York, NY: Random House. (Original work published 349 BC)
Carr, D. (2003). Character and moral choice in the cultivation of virtue. *Philosophy, 78*(2), 219-232.
Carr, D. (2009). Virtue, mixed emotion and moral ambivalence. *Philosophy, 84*(1), 31-46.
Carr, D. (Ed.). (2018). *Cultivating moral character and virtue in professional practice*. London and New York: Routledge.
Darwin, C. (1859). *On the origin of species by means of natural selection, or the preservation of favoured races in the struggle for life*. London, England: John Murray.
Dickens, C. (2003). *Hard times*. Harmondsworth, England: Penguin Classics.
Driver, J. (1989). The virtues of ignorance. *Journal of Philosophy, 86*(7), 373-384.
Driver, J. (2001). *Uneasy virtue*. Cambridge, England: Cambridge University Press.
Dunne, J. (1997). *Back to the rough ground: Practical judgement and the lure of technique*. Notre Dame, IN: Notre Dame Press.
Foot, P. (1978). *Virtues and vices*. Oxford, England: Blackwell.
Geach, P. T. (1977). *The virtues*. Cambridge, England: Cambridge University Press.
Kant, I. (1967). *The critique of practical reasoning and other works on the theory of ethics* (T. K. Abbott, Trans.). London, England: Longmans.
McDowell, J. (1997). Virtue and reason. In R. Crisp & M. Slote (Eds.), *Virtue ethics* (pp. 141-162). Oxford, England: Oxford University Press.
Murdoch, I. (1970). *The sovereignty of the good*. London, England: Routledge and Kegan Paul.
Murdoch, I. (1993). *Metaphysics as a guide to morals*. Harmondsworth, England: Penguin.
Nichol-Smith, D. (Ed.). (1921). *Wordsworth: Poetry and prose*. Oxford, England: Clarendon Press.
Plato. (1961). Symposium, republic and laws. In E. Hamilton & H. Cairns (Eds.), *Plato: The collected dialogues* (L. Cooper & others, Trans.). Princeton, NJ: Princeton University Press. (Plato's *Republic* originally published 380 BC)
Rousseau, J.-J. (1977). *The social contract and other discourses*. London, England: Dent Everyman.
Rousseau, J.-J. (1991). *Emile: Or, on education*. Harmondsworth, England: Penguin.

Wilde, O. (2000). *Lady Windermere's fan.* In *The importance of being Earnest and other plays* (pp. 1-64). Harmondsworth, England: Penguin Classics.

David Carr PhD
Emeritus Professor, University of Edinburgh, United Kingdom

BERNARD MCKENNA

3. SOCIAL PRACTICE WISDOM

A wisdom-based approach begins with the fundamental question facing most humans: what is the ultimate purpose of my existence, or what Aristotle calls "the final cause" or the *telos*. Aristotle answered this question with the notion of *eudaimonia,* translated as "human flourishing" by Martha Nussbaum (1994). A wise person, says Aristotle, combines intellectual and moral virtues, which produces *aretè*, or excellence, which in turn contributes to human flourishing for society at large. Intellectual virtues allow one to acquire knowledge and to reason logically.

According to Aristotle (349 BC/1984), we achieve human flourishing by behaving virtuously. The essence of virtuous behaviour is to place the good of humanity and the longer term good ahead of one's own self-interest, notwithstanding the prudence to ensure that one primarily cares for oneself and one's family. To behave virtuously, says philosopher Nancy Snow (2009), one needs "an enduring disposition incorporating practical reason, appropriate motivation, and affect" (p. 1). Because our virtues, or lack of them, are important components of our personality and character, Snow says, they are stable over time and regularly evident in the way that we behave in a wide range of situations.

Moral virtue is "a settled disposition of the mind determining the choice of actions and emotions, consisting essentially in the observance of the mean relative to us", which is determined "as the prudent man would determine it" (Aristotle, 349 BC/1984, 1107a, pp. 1-5). The "golden mean" is commonly misunderstood as though it were an arithmetic mean between two extremes; however, to apply this to virtuous behaviour would simply mean that the mediocre or central tendency was always chosen. By contrast, there are times when extreme conditions require extreme responses (such as reporting toxic waste dumping) rather than the mean ground of inaction. The Aristotelian mean might be better understood as "balance". As explained by wisdom psychologist, Robert J. Sternberg (2004), wisdom is the application of intelligence and experience as mediated by values toward the achievement of a common good through a balance among diverse interests, over the short and long terms, to achieve a balance among adaptation and change. Despite the diversity of cultures globally, there is considerable agreement about the important virtues. A study by Dahlsgrad, Peterson, and Seligman (2005) found six core virtues shared across the major religions and spiritual traditions (Confucianism, Taoism, Buddhism, Hinduism, Athenian philosophy, Judaism, Christianity and Islam). The most strongly shared virtues are justice and humanity. Temperance and wisdom are also strongly shared virtues. Transcendence ("the notion that there is a higher meaning or purpose to life" [Dahlsgrad et al., 2005, p. 209]) was at least implicit in all the surveyed traditions. However, courage did not appear in all. Thus, it can be said that most adults would not be ignorant of the established virtues of their society.

DEFINING WISDOM

Unsurprisingly, definitions of wisdom vary considerably. I will consider only those definitions of wisdom that occur in the secular, not religious or spiritual literature, particularly in psychology. Two approaches have been adopted to theorise wisdom: integrative approaches and cognition-based approaches. Integrative theories are those that identify various components of wisdom. The three core components of integrative wisdom are cognition, reflection and affect.

The cognitive component is not so much about knowledge. In Sternberg's (2003) edited book, *Why Smart People Can Be So Stupid,* several researchers explain why talking about "smart" and "stupid", "intelligent" and "unintelligent" is often not very helpful. The reasons for this include the fact that academic and practical intelligence are not highly correlated. This is largely because, unlike reality, academic problems are usually presented as "closed" problems with conclusions emerging from agreed knowledge and assumptions. Issues we face in reality are not clearly defined, that is, are ambiguous, and without relevant information and knowledge at hand despite insurmountable amounts of data being available. As well, "gifted" children who are used to being praised, on growing to adulthood learn that they do not need to exert as much effort as the less gifted and so become arrogant, fail to listen to advice, lose touch with reality, lack resilience when the going gets tough, and fail to acknowledge their mistakes. Another potential weakness of smart people is *akrasia*, or a lack of willpower and moral weakness.

The reflective aspect of wisdom is vital to making sense of our experience and learning from it. It is by reflecting on our successes and our failures that we gain insight into ourselves, and thereby better prepare to meet future challenges. As a result we achieve greater balance, enhance our self-efficacy, and develop coping skills (Webster, 2007). Canadian researchers, Webster and Deng (2015), claim that traumatic life events are correlated with growth in wisdom. The third element, affective capability, refers to compassion and benevolence. In her three-dimensional scale to measure wisdom, Monika Ardelt (2003) incorporates an affective dimension which assesses "the presence of positive emotions and behavior toward other beings, such as feelings and acts of sympathy and compassion, and the absence of indifferent or negative emotions and behavior toward others" (pp. 278-279).

More cognition-focused approaches define wisdom as knowledge and reflection about fundamental life issues and skill in dealing with them. This approach has been largely developed by German theorists such as Ursula Staudinger (Staudinger & Glück, 2011). Her dominant characteristics of General Wisdom are rich factual knowledge about the fundamental pragmatics of life and fundamental pragmatics for dealing with life. Rich factual knowledge incorporates knowledge about human nature and life conditions (mortality, self-perception, social relationships, normative rules) and knowledge about the life course (how we change as we age). Rich procedural knowledge about dealing with the fundamental pragmatics of life includes insightful decision making, cost-benefit analysis of various options, and flexible planning of alternative options. The cognitive-based approach also incorporates relativism of values and life priorities as a component of wisdom. Wise people know that people differ in their values and life goals from their own which are embedded in different cultural and social expectations and evaluations (Mickler & Staudinger, 2008).

The most recent attempt at defining and measuring wisdom has been provided by Thomas et al. (2017) who identified six characteristics of wisdom: social advising, emotional regulation, pro-social behaviours, insight, tolerance for divergent views and decisiveness. Rather than argue the strengths and weaknesses of various components for inclusion in a wisdom definition or measurement scale, the next section provides a range of characteristics for what has been defined as Social Practice Wisdom. This is a refinement of a set of principles first devised by Rooney, McKenna, and Liesch (2010) to be applied in management and organisation.

SOCIAL PRACTICE WISDOM

Social practice wisdom (SPW) refers to the type of wisdom that is needed in dealing with social situations (e.g. balancing corporate social responsibility with profit requirement) rather than personal situations (e.g. helping a person who is depressed by a life crisis). Essentially SPW involves deliberative judgement to make decisions and takes actions in any organisational context. SPW draws its principles from Aristotle's theory of practical wisdom, and is also influenced by Buddhist theories of wisdom. It takes into account the rich empirical wisdom research for the past 20 years which has been published in philosophy, management, psychology, neuroscience, spirituality and education publications. SPW incorporates four integrating principles to guide and assess the degree of wisdom that is evident in social practice, where social practice may be a manufacturing company, a hospital, a government department or a professional sporting team. These principles guide the disposition of people who enact decisions they have made.

Qualities of mind and spirit. Wise people have certain characteristics that create a virtuous disposition. These characteristics include being aware, compassionate, humble and keeping an actively open mind. Wise people are equanimous, meaning that they are composed and display calmness in difficult situations. People with such a disposition are more likely to be insightful and virtuous, thereby revealing sound leadership capability. Underpinning these characteristics is humility, which Tangney (2000) defines as "a rich, multifaceted construct that entails an accurate assessment of one's characteristics, an ability to acknowledge limitations, and a 'forgetting of the self'" (p. 70). This involves a de-centreing of the ego, which has been shown to be valuable in decision making because such people are able to distance themselves emotionally and in terms of self-advancement, thereby producing better decisions (Kross & Grossmann, 2012). People with self-awareness are better able to understand uncertainty and relativities in life brought about by conflicting values, identities, cultures and politics, and knowledge imperfection (Glück & Bluck, 2013).

Agile and transcendent reasoning. It is important that a wise organisational member has deep knowledge relevant to that organisation. However, the larger the organisation the less likely it is that even the most senior organisational members will have knowledge depth in certain areas. For example, an engineer may rise to senior management but lack extensive knowledge about financial accounting or human resources policies. Thus, it is important that they have the humility to "know what they don't know" and to seek quality advice. Book knowledge based on fluid intelligence becomes less important the longer one is in an organisation. Instead, tacit knowledge about how things work and how to get things done based on crystallised knowledge becomes more important (Zacher, 2015).

There are two other vital elements in wise reasoning: one is the capacity for "gut instinct"; the other is the capacity for ontological acuity. Intuition is particularly important in situations where the facts are unclear, the problem lacks clarity, or the issues cannot be decomposed (broken into sequential parts). Intuition can be defined as "a non-sequential information processing mode, which comprises both cognitive and affective elements and results in direct knowing without any use of conscious reasoning (Sinclair & Ashkanasy, 2005, p. 357). A neuroscientific account of intuition is that a person has the ability to understand or know something without conscious attention by recognising "patterns in the stream of sensations that impinge upon them ... The result is a vague perception of coherence which is not explicitly describable but instead embodied in a 'gut feeling' or an initial guess, which subsequently biases thought and inquiry" (Volz & von Cramon, 2006, p. 2077).

In other words, applied knowledge and reasoning is insufficient to arrive at some decisions, forcing us to draw on a feeling about the right course of action, which is largely based on accumulated experience. However, relying on gut instinct alone, often borne out of laziness or arrogance or both, will produce bad decisions. It is known that gut instinct has a greater success rate the greater one's expertise within the domain under question (Dane, Rockman, & Pratt, 2012). Judgements arrived at intuitively are difficult to articulate because they occur as a sense of coherence that develops subconsciously; decisions arrived at through insight can be articulated because they manifest as an unexpected solution that is brought about by consciously restructuring the representation of a problem.

The second vital element of wise reasoning is ontological acuity (McKenna & Rooney, 2008). To understand this concept requires understanding of Foucault's (1972) notion of *epistêmê*. Applied to an organisation, it is assumed that organisational knowledge is articulated in organisational discourse. This "knowledge" is an *epistêmê*, a framework of relationships between what is understood to be true (e.g. that markets behave in a certain way) and the practices that emerge from that assumed knowledge about the way things are. The clearest example of this is in medicine where a doctor gathers together the symptoms, formulates a diagnosis according to the knowledge available at the time, and prescribes a treatment. While this is relatively straightforward, a large amount of "knowledge" is based on *epistêmic* grounds that can be questioned. This is because all knowledge claims are based on our human capacity to understand things as they are "out there" in the world. There are two problems with this. First, knowledge changes over time and it takes time for new knowledge to be widely applied.

The second problem is that knowledge is frequently based on ideological assumptions about what *should* be the case. Thus, for example, economic and monetary practices since the 1980s have been founded on two fundamental neoliberal principles that economies work best when governments lower taxes and expenditure, and that market mechanisms should be used to make most decisions. This period was ushered in because of problems with the old Keynesian economic order. Instead of altering the application of Keynesian theory which accompanied a "welfare state" model that provides subsidised or free education and health as well as pensions for the elderly, the sick and the unemployed, many governments simply switched to a hard-line neoliberal model, leading to massive shifts in wealth and income distribution in favour of those in the upper levels. Those who are most responsible for setting the global rules are often incapable of understanding their own ideological bias such as in the Global Financial Crisis in 2008 when the Western capitalist system was brought to the brink of collapse. At this time the Chairman of the US Federal Reserve, Alan Greenspan, responded in testimony to the US Government Oversight Committee (23 October 2008):

Greenspan: I made a mistake in presuming that the self-interests of organizations, specifically banks and others, were such as that they were best capable of protecting their own shareholders and their equity in the firms...

Waxman: In other words, you found that your view of the world, your ideology, was not right, it was not working.

Greenspan: Absolutely, precisely. You know, that's precisely the reason I was shocked, because I have been going for 40 years or more with very considerable evidence that it was working exceptionally well.

Within an organisation, managers can apply ontological acuity by questioning the often unwritten, or tacit, assumptions that guide what is taken to be true "out there". This so-called "objective knowledge" most often rests on assumptions that can be challenged in terms of their facticity and their underlying ideology and in terms of what knowledge is excluded and included. Thus, for example, in schools, the notion of "student-centred learning", which is a useful educational principle, often gets misapplied when teachers do not challenge students to get outside their comfort zone and do something that is initially challenging but may ultimately be rewarding.

A good way to look at the knowledge and ideological assumptions underlying organisational practice is to consider an organisation's KPIs, and ask why these are valourised. For example, a university's current strategic plan states that one of its focus areas will be to increase investment in digitisation and active learning. Implied in this is a binary that non-digitised technologies (such as a paper-based book or writing with a biro or pencil) are inactive or passive. This KPI implies that increasing a university's digital capability is, by implication, linked to a better form of learning. But how do we know that students learn better this way? What evidence is there?

Embodiment. This characteristic draws both from ancient philosophy and from contemporary sociology. The ancient philosophy from the Stoics proposed that the proper disposition for a good life was to be intellectually and morally humble: their aim was to be the "least bad person" (Brouwer, 2014, p. 105). To achieve this required "simplicity, humility and reflectiveness in pursuit of the common good" (McKenna, 2017, p. 43). By embodying proper values, wise people develop a particular habitus, which is a concept that comes from the French sociologist, Pierre Bourdieu. Whereas a habit "denotes mechanical behaviour, a stimulus–response reflex" (Crossley, 2013, p. 139), the habitus incorporates a disposition that is enacted and represented by our body, bodily actions, and interactions with people and situations. In his book, *Distinction*, Bourdieu (1984) showed how the enactment of habitus reproduces social patterns of behaviour whether it be a peasant farmer in the provinces or a middle-class person in Paris. Bourdieu (1990) explains it this way:

> structures constitutive of a particular type of environment ... produce habitus, systems of durable, transposable dispositions, structured structures ... as principles of generation and structuring of practices and representations which can be objectively 'regulated' and 'regular' without in any way being the product of obedience to rules. (p. 72)

So habitus is a "structuring structure" that "organizes practices and the perception of practices" (Bourdieu, 1984, p. 170) in the body of a person. Habitus structures how we do things, wear things, eat things, etc., but it also sends a message to other people about where we locate ourselves. These dispositions expressed as habitus are largely unconscious: in fact, we unconsciously pick up the cues about how to behave from infancy through to adulthood. However, at certain times as adults we become acutely conscious of adopting the habitus proper to a particular site, such as a non-religious person attending a church wedding or even when we go to a dinner party with guests we do not know. One of the significant times that we are conscious of adapting our habitus is when we begin work with a new organisation. However, after some time, we simply act "normally", consistent with the patterns of behaviour within an organisation.

An example of this occurred when Australian car workers were laid off after the industry was shut down around 2015. Predominantly a male industry, the usual behaviour was to good-naturedly "take the piss", that is, make fun of other people who were expected to "take it" and hopefully respond with a reciprocal insult which was accepted by the other person without being offended. Crude language was commonplace. The men in particular prided themselves on their physical strength and their technical knowledge. When they were re-trained for new jobs, however, it was mostly in the hospitality and caring industries where there was considerable sensitivity about the clients' needs and great importance placed on politeness. Thus, many men after 20 or 30 years exhibiting a tougher working-class habitus had to now assume an entirely new persona with the appropriate habitus.

Once embedded in an organisation, we become less conscious of our habitus because we enact what are considered to be normal practices. This is what makes it difficult to be consciously aware of the knowledge assumptions and embedded ideology that guides our daily practices at work. However, those with ontological acuity have the capacity to identify and question the norms and the knowledge assumptions. This is not something that one would do on a daily basis as this would lead to "paralysis by analysis". However, if intuitively or objectively things just do not seem right or poor outcomes are common, then rather than re-arranging positions or creating new rules, a wise organisational member will go back to basics to challenge assumptions.

To sum up then, a wise organisational member is conscious that their habitus of dispositions operates within a set of norms, beliefs and values that precede them. To operate effectively within that organisation, all organisational members must conform to varying degrees with those norms, values and beliefs. If we wish to act with a Stoic sense of values then we choose simplicity, humility and reflectiveness in pursuit of the common good to guide our behaviour. If the norms of the organisation are at odds with those values then one has to decide to what extent it is possible to try to have an impact in order to change those norms. For example, an experienced scrub nurse at a large Australian hospital was appalled at the throwaway mentality that operates in most hospital operating theatres. While there is a lot of common sense in these practices to ensure sterile practices and patient safety, little thought had been given to contributing to the massive problem of urban waste. She campaigned successfully to sort disposables into those that could be recycled and those that could not. As a result, the amount of material going to landfill was reduced. Instead of simply conforming her habitus to the throwaway culture, she questioned the ontological assumptions about the disposable practices, raised the issue with the management and gained sufficient support to change the practices.

In summary, embodying wise practice means to creatively and decisively enact wise performative skills in a situation, based on experience, understanding, timing and judgement in order to responsibly apply knowledge and power. This involves sensing and knowing why, how and when to adapt to the surroundings and why, how and when to change them, and how to astutely make necessary trade-offs.

Ethical commitment. Although a person might be smart, intelligent, creative and successful, they may not necessarily be wise. The most vital element of wisdom is virtue. Thus, without virtuous intent our actions cannot be deemed wise. The virtues have been discussed above, but at the core is compassion. On the other hand, compassion without the ability to understand could simply make us a likeable Forrest Gump. We need sound knowledge about the domain of activity in which we work whether it be finance, engineering or government. Such a disposition requires the capacity for ego transcendence, or humility. We need to align our values with our social behaviour and embodiment, and with insight into the human condition. We choose the right and virtuous thing to do at the right time.

EMOTIONAL INTELLIGENCE

So far, we have seen that emotions are an important consideration in moral virtue, in wisdom, and in leadership. That is, moral virtue includes having a settled disposition that allows one to choose the right emotions. Aristotle's prescription is now classified by psychologists as emotional regulation, which is a characteristic included in at least two wisdom scales (Thomas et al., 2017; Webster, 2003). We also saw that emotional regulation is vital in being able to distance oneself when making decisions (de-centreing of the ego). However, there is another aspect of emotions that is important in wisdom. Ardelt's definition of wisdom included having positive emotions in relation to others. This involves to a large degree a capacity for empathy: "the ability to recognize and understand the emotions and feelings of others, and this interpersonal skill can make it easier to develop a cooperative relationship of mutual trust" (Mahsud, Yukl, & Prussia, 2010, pp. 562-563). Empathy is a vital component of emotional intelligence (EI) (Law, Wong, & Song, 2004). There is evidence that EI is positively related to wisdom. A large German study using a sample of 318 participants from three age groups (young adults; middle-age; and older adults) asked participants how they would respond to a difficult life problem, with the responses being coded by experts. The results of this study by Kunzman and Baltes (2003) corroborated the proposition that "wisdom-related knowledge is related to indicators of psychological functioning in three realms: affect (subjective affective experiences), motivation (value orientations), and interpersonal behavior (strategies of conflict management)" (p. 1114).

Empathic emotion in a leader is shown predominantly through individualised consideration, which means that a leader displays a caring and nurturing disposition particularly in supporting followers' personal development. In a study of 75 religious leaders and 158 employees of each leader, that linked leaders' personal wisdom with transformational leadership, Zacher et al. (2014) showed that personal wisdom positively predicted the transformational leadership dimension of individualised consideration. Furthermore, individualised consideration mediated the relationship between leaders' personal wisdom and leader member exchange (LMX) quality. That is, leaders' personal wisdom predicted the quality of LMX, which is the effectiveness of a leader's relationship with subordinates, but only by being connected to individualised consideration. Given that LMX is essential to leader effectiveness (Mahsud et al., 2010), it makes sense that an organisation would want to choose leaders who are predisposed through wisdom and EI attributes to behave in such a way. EI can be defined by four characteristic dimensions:

1. Appraisal and expression of emotion in oneself (self-emotions appraisal), that is, "an individual's ability to understand his or her deep emotions and to be able to express emotions naturally".
2. Appraisal and recognition of emotion in others (others-emotions appraisal), defined as "an individual's ability to perceive and understand the emotions of the people around them".

3. Use of emotion to facilitate performance (use of emotion), defined as "the ability of a person to make use of his or her emotions by directing them toward constructive activities and personal performance".
4. Regulation of emotion in oneself (regulation of emotion), that is, "the ability of a person to regulate his or her emotions, enabling a more rapid recovery from psychological distress". (Zacher, McKenna, & Rooney, 2013, pp. 1698-1699)

This empirical evidence reinforces one of the themes of this chapter, namely that wisdom is a set of moral and personal attributes that are embodied in people's habitus, their everyday practice. EI, which emerges out of values and behaviours, is positively related to transformational leadership in a current study by Greaves et al. (2014), and transformational leadership produces positive organisational cultures.

A FINAL WORD

Finally, it is reassuring to note that empathic-based wisdom is positively correlated to happiness (Bergsma & Ardelt, 2012; Zacher et al., 2013), which enhances the quality of people's lives.

REFERENCES

Ardelt, M. (2003). Empirical assessment of a three-dimensional wisdom scale. *Research on Aging, 25*(3), 275-324.
Aristotle. (1984). *Nicomachean ethics* (H. G. Apostle, Trans.). Grinnell, IO: The Peripatetic Press. (Original work published 349 BC)
Bergsma, A., & Ardelt, M. (2012). Self-reported wisdom and happiness: An empirical investigation. *Journal of Happiness Studies, 13*, 481-499.
Bourdieu, P. (1984). *Distinction: A social critique of the judgement of taste* (R. Nice, Trans.). London, England: Routledge and Kegan Paul.
Bourdieu, P. (1990). *The logic of practice* (R. Nice, Trans.). Stanford, CA: Stanford University Press.
Brouwer, R. (2014). *The Stoic sage: The early Stoics on wisdom, sagehood, and Socrates.* Cambridge, England: Cambridge University Press.
Crossley, N. (2013). Habit and habitus. *Body & Society, 19*(2-3), 136-161.
Dahlsgrad, K., Peterson, C., & Seligman, M. E. P. (2005). Shared virtue: The convergence of valued human strengths across culture and history. *Review of General Psychology, 9*(3), 203-213.
Dane, E., Rockman, K., & Pratt, M. (2012). When should I trust my gut? Linking domain expertise to intuitive decision-making effectiveness. *Organizational Behavior and Human Decision Processes, 119*(1), 187-194.
Foucault, M. (1972). *The archaeology of knowledge.* London, England: Tavistock.
Glück, J., & Bluck, S. (2013). The MORE life experience model: A theory of the development of personal wisdom. In M. Ferrari & N. M. Weststrate (Eds.), *The scientific study of personal wisdom: From contemplative traditions to neuroscience* (pp. 75-97). Dordrecht, The Netherlands: Springer.
Greaves, C., Zacher, H., McKenna, B., & Rooney, D. (2014). Wisdom and narcissism as predictors of transformational leadership. *Leadership & Organization Development Journal, 35*(4), 335-358.
Kross, E., & Grossmann, I. (2012). Boosting wisdom: Distance from the self enhances wise reasoning, attitudes, and behavior. *Journal of Experimental Psychology: General, 141*(1), 43-48.
Kunzmann, U., & Baltes, P. B. (2003). Wisdom-related knowledge: Affective, motivational, and interpersonal correlates Personality & Social Psychology Bulletin, 29(9), 1104-1119.

Law, K. S., Wong, C. S., & Song, L. J. (2004). Construct and criterion validity of emotional intelligence and its potential utility for management studies. *Journal of Applied Psychology, 89*(3), 483-496.

Mahsud, R., Yukl, G., & Prussia, G. (2010). Leader empathy, ethical leadership, and relations-oriented behaviors as antecedents of leader-member exchange quality. *Journal of Managerial Psychology, 25*(6), 561-577.

McKenna, B. (2017). Business schools' role in embodying a wise graduate disposition. In W. Küpers & O. Gunlaugson (Eds.), *Wisdom-learning: Perspectives on wising-up business and management education* (pp. 41-61). London, England: Gower.

McKenna, B., & Rooney, D. (2008). Wise leadership and the capacity for ontological acuity. *Management Communication Quarterly, 21*(4), 537-546.

Mickler, C., & Staudinger, U. M. (2008). Personal wisdom: Validation and age-related differences of a performance measure. *Psychology and Aging, 23*(4), 787-799.

Nussbaum, M. (1994). *The therapy of desire: Theory and practice in Hellenistic ethics*. Princeton, NJ: Princeton University Press.

Rooney, D., McKenna, B., & Liesch, P. (2010). *Wisdom and management in the knowledge economy*. New York, NY: Routledge.

Sinclair, M., & Ashkanasy, N. M. (2005). Intuition: Myth or a decision-making tool? *Management Learning, 36*(3), 353-370.

Snow, N. E. (2009). *Virtue as social intelligence: An empirically grounded theory*. New York, NY: Routledge.

Staudinger, U. M., & Glück, J. (2011). Psychological wisdom research: Commonalities and differences in a growing field. *Annual Review of Psychology, 62*, 215-241.

Sternberg, R. J. (2003). *Why smart people can be so stupid*. Harvard, MA: Yale University Press.

Sternberg, R. J. (2004). What is wisdom and how can we develop it? *Annals of the American Academy of Political and Social Science, 591*(1), 164-174.

Tangney, J. P. (2000). Humility: Theoretical perspectives, empirical findings and directions for future research. *Journal of Social & Clinical Psychology, 19*(1), 70-82.

Thomas, M. L., Bangen, K. J., Palmer, B. W., Martin, A. S., Avanzino, J. A., Depp, C. A., Glorioso, D., Daly, R. E., & Jeste, D. V. (2017). A new scale for assessing wisdom based on common domains and a neurobiological model: The San Diego Wisdom Scale (SD-WISE). *Journal of Psychiatric Research, S0022-3956*(17), 30751-30753.

Volz, K. G., & von Cramon, D. Y. (2006). What neuroscience can tell about intuitive processes in the context of perceptual discovery. *Journal of Cognitive Neuroscience, 18*(12), 2077-2087.

Webster, J. D. (2003). An exploratory analysis of a self-assessed wisdom scale. *Journal of Adult Development, 10*(1), 13-22.

Webster, J. D. (2007). Measuring the character strength of wisdom. *International Journal of Aging and Human Development, 65*(2), 163-183.

Webster, J. D., & Deng, X. C. (2015). Paths from trauma to intrapersonal strength: Worldview, posttraumatic growth, and wisdom. *Journal of Loss and Trauma: International Perspectives on Stress & Coping, 20*(3), 253-266.

Zacher, H. (2015). Successful aging at work. *Work, Aging and Retirement, 1*(1), 4-25.

Zacher, H., McKenna, B., & Rooney, D. (2013). Effects of self-reported wisdom on happiness: Not much more than emotional intelligence? *Journal of Happiness Studies, 14*(6), 1697-1716.

Zacher, H., Pearce, L. K., Rooney, D., & McKenna, B. (2014). Leaders' personal wisdom and leader-member exchange quality: The role of individualized consideration. *Journal of Business Ethics, 121*, 171-187.

Bernard McKenna PhD (ORCID: https://orcid.org/0000-0001-7092-4944)
UQ Business School
University of Queensland, Australia

DIANE TASKER AND JOY HIGGS

4. MINDFULNESS AND PRACTICAL WISDOM

"Mindfulness and wisdom can be thought of as phenomena ... as aspirations to be pursued, as lived experiences and, particularly, within professional life, as practices" (Higgs & Tasker, 2017, p. 188). Mindfulness, in particular, can be considered as both an attitude and a practice, linking thoughts and feeling with practical action. As a primary example, the concept of mindfulness as it developed within Buddhism occurred through the practical experiences of Buddha himself as he sat beneath a tree contemplating life and how to best address its vicissitudes.

> Wisdom is not just a way of thinking about things; it is a way of doing things. If people wish to be wise, they have to act wisely, not just think wisely. We all can do this. Whether we do is our choice. (Sternberg, 2003, p. 188)

The art of binding together what we think and how we carry out activities within our lives presents opportunities for a high level of achievement for people, with radiating effects for families, communities and society. Success in this process can be considered *practical wisdom*, a highly prized state of being that not everyone achieves. Wise people often become revered, listened to, learned from and remembered long after they have left us. What is practical wisdom and how did these people become wise? How can we as individuals become practically wise in our living and in our work, to better take care of our society and its people?

In this chapter, we explore how mindfulness of individuals but also between people can contribute to gaining practical wisdom. We argue that such "mindful wisdom" is practised through the timely and careful use of dialogue and narrative within reflection and interaction to better manage the human spheres of thought and action, bridging the different perceptions of time. Such processes are becoming increasingly important because modern society places increased demands on individuals to manage higher expectations of responsibility and performance in communication and human interaction in work and personal life – all within the constraints that time imposes.

PERCEPTIONS OF TIME AND ITS MANAGEMENT

Great expectations are laid upon the shoulders of a wide variety of practitioners to make ethically good, sound and wise decisions for individual clients as well as for institutions and communities – making *the right decision at the right time* (Schwartz & Sharpe, 2010). Time has become a difficult and rare commodity. Everywhere we go, we feel pressured not to waste time, especially that of the busy people we interact with – our doctors, professionals and educators plus community and family members. Increasingly, people and the organisations that govern our society seek advice and help in addressing enormously complex issues. Examples include climate change, the promotion of peace between peoples and increasing levels of both professional and technological insertion into our society. People feel increasing dissatisfaction with *their lot in life* and even a growing fear that other people don't know us, what has meaning for us or how to help us achieve our personal goals (Schwartz, 2011). Such an uneasy situation is inherent in what it means to be human; however, in daily life, everyone needs to be aware of and sensitive to the needs of the people they communicate with. Such interaction can be quite difficult but it is essential if we are to succeed in promoting harmony.

Perceptions of time and its management present essential differences in form and experience. Any professional practitioner will recognise the tension that inevitably occurs between the need to listen to and hear their clients, and the need to manage the imperative of completing time-limited/pressured appointments. Development of a productive relationship obviously needs time to be spent in listening and reciprocating, but completing an interaction also demands attention to the clock. Such conflict requires much emotional energy expenditure and skill. Management of time must be balanced with validation of the more experiential and narrative nature of clients' contributions. As the number of people and expectations increase, so too does time pressure in the face of a bewildering array of activities that need to be carried out. Maintaining a wise presence within relationships that seek to combine these different perceptions of time becomes a practical necessity for practitioners in modern day practice.

MINDFULNESS FOR OURSELVES AND OTHERS

> Mindfulness is the basic human ability to be fully present, aware of where we are and what we're doing, and not overly reactive or overwhelmed by what's going on around us. (Foundation for a Mindful Society)[1]

There is great need for people to make time and space for reflection and consideration within their busy lives. Most people recognise this need but many find it very difficult to manage a comfortable balance between thought and activity. Agitation, stress and fatigue accumulate within individuals as they strive to live and work well and ethically. This can cause great distraction and lack of prolonged focus for longer-term goals. Such difficulty naturally becomes amplified when there is a need to interact with others to provide or receive help, solve problems or collaborate on ongoing complex situations. Ego can rise to the surface as people try to keep control of time and circumstances, and create change for and with other people. Hierarchical structures so often seen within our society encourage such egoistic strategies and do not always achieve desired outcomes in the presence of complexity and rapid change.

Individually, people search for some means to manage their work and personal life in ways that will engender health, emotional balance and clarity of thought. Great interest has emerged in meditation as it was discovered in Eastern philosophy, particularly Buddhism. The term "meditation" refers to a range of practices designed to cultivate a calm, concentrated and absorbed state of mind.

Meditation can describe both a practice and a state of mind and derives from the Latin word *meditari* which means "to reflect upon" (Meditation Association of Australia, 2018). Western practitioners and managers came to realise that even small periods of meditation can help establish balanced thinking and energy renewal for busy people. Within healthcare, mindfulness practices have proved useful for patients with pain and illness as well as for students and practitioners. For example, within law practice, increasing attention has been given to mindfulness as a way to promote mental health and enhance sustainable practice (Orenstein, 2014). "The result is better balance, increased understanding and clarity in our thinking, improved relationships and empathy with others, and an improved overall sense of wellbeing. This is going to result in better outcomes for our clients and for ourselves" (ibid, p. 109).

Ann Webster-Wright (2013), a mindfulness practitioner, draws on narrative research methodology and existential phenomenological philosophy to explore how people make sense of their lived experiences by focusing on learning, wellbeing and authenticity. She contends that "mindful inquiry" acts like "a reflective journey from the chatter of the world, through the heart of stillness, to sit with paradoxes and uncertainties, emerging, refreshed and revived at the very least, and on occasions with a new spark of an idea" (ibid, p. 564) – seeing our world with fresh eyes. This idea, she argues, is worth pursuing for many reasons: philosophical considerations, empirical research and practical experience. She argues that mindfulness supports subjective wellbeing and offers a tool for developing mental resilience and equanimity.

Meditation practices can be said to provide a dislocation of time for people to be able to better consider themselves and their actions in relation to each other and to develop more considered perspectives of their thoughts and actions.

> By being aware of our thinking and mental patterns, we are able to observe with greater clarity, cutting through the distortions and reactions that habitually form the basis of our thinking. Mindfulness helps us to be fully present, to be aware of our own thoughts and reactions and more in tune with those of others. Consequently we are able to listen with more presence, space-out less, and remain focussed for greater periods of time. (Orenstein, 2014, p. 107)

Diane (our first author) experienced this time effect first-hand after seriously considering mindfulness and applying it to her community-based practice.

> *Only recently, the wife of a client followed me out to the car to thank me for spending so much time with her husband to explore what was important for him. As I drove away, I realised that I had actually been there for a shorter time than I would normally have allowed.* (Tasker, 2013, p. 229)

We could explain this phenomenon as *making the best of the time available* and indeed it is; but it is also a case of *making the best of a relationship* by being fully present in a deep but relaxed way as well. Such relaxation and ease for the participants in the interaction is particularly important. In times of stress and when endeavouring to accomplish difficult and complex professional practices, it is tempting to use a lot of energy to try and alter power balances or change systems and cultures. The use of mindfulness as an attitude and a practice provides a different approach to such endeavours.

> Mindfulness is a completely different approach to our habitual ways of dealing with life's ups and downs. It does not involve attempting to eliminate difficulty from our lives by running from a stressful situation or imagining ourselves in a better place. In fact, mindfulness is simply about noticing what is happening in each moment without attempting to change anything. (Orenstein, 2014, pp. 108-109)

Such a shift in our attitude can open up resources previously unexplored or used. *Noticing rather than acting* and *noticing before acting* can be powerful ways of negotiating difficult situations and complex issues. It also allows better management of our energy and access to other types of emotional energy (for example, compassion) to support both thought and action. Compassion is an emotion that can provide strength and resilience. It is closely linked to mindful practice and a mindful attitude in its ability to enable people feeling compassion to extend their care beyond self to others, individuals and the wider community.

As can be seen from the definition of mindfulness at the beginning of this section, meditation can certainly be considered a mindful practice or preferably a set of practices, aiming to develop awareness through relaxation and attention management. Mindfulness as a broader concept would seem to incorporate a pausing or paralleling of time in an attitude of consideration to better plan for future action or reflect on past action. Both are needed in different ways, if thought, feeling and practice are to be well integrated into people's work and personal lives. Looking within ourselves is essential if we are to successfully interact with other people, both for their good and the good of the community. We argue that bringing such mindfulness into relationships through engagement and dialogue is necessary if we are seeking to develop real practical wisdom.

DIALOGICAL MINDFULNESS

When mindfulness or careful attention is brought to bear upon a dialogical interaction in the interest of deepening understanding or producing useful and ethical action, there is a much greater chance of its intent being realised. Indeed "intention" is a major contributing factor to this process.

> *Practice wisdom has more of an intention around it – you're actually organising the way in which you're going about things. You absolutely need to understand the strategic intent of where you're going but with an eye on the client, then I think you never lose sight of what it is that you need to do and how you need to do something [quote from a professional practitioner].* (Higgs & Tasker, 2017, p. 193)

In Diane's doctoral studies of community-based physiotherapeutic relationships (Tasker, 2013), mindful dialogical activity was explored and explained within the model of "Mindful Dialogues" (see Figure 4.1). Community-based physiotherapists were seen to intentionally build mindful and narrative dialogues with their clients and clients' families and carers through strongly dialogical and narrative means. By being mindful, staying engaged and becoming responsive, in an iterative style of interaction, therapists skilfully merged the needs and concerns of those involved and assisted their clients to build productive lives. Relationship-based approaches help to promote wellbeing for the people concerned.

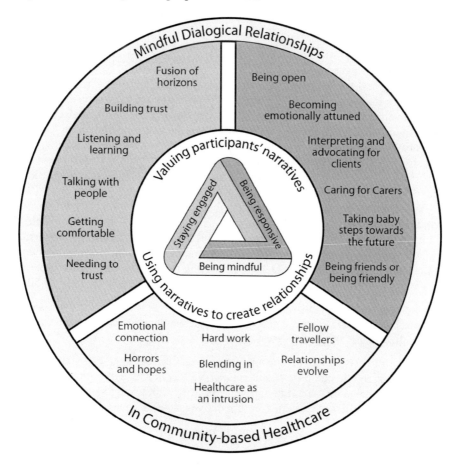

Figure 4.1. Mindful dialogic relationships (Tasker & Higgs, 2017, p. 54, reprinted with permission).

Mindful, wise practice is more than just simple intention to carry out planned action. Rather, it involves grounding of informed intent to meet the expectations of the practitioners' own practice model, to fulfil their professional reasons for practising, and to uphold their basic ethical responsibility in contracting with clients to provide a quality and genuine service that has an outcome beneficial to clients (Higgs &

Tasker, 2013 p. 190). Deliberate intention in dialogue can set the scene for the process and outcome that is wished for and expected. It allows a strengthening of focus, which can become a mindful activity in itself, promoting sensitivity to what is happening around that person and highlighting awareness of peripheral influencing factors. Intention can then be a highly mindful activity. Watson (2001), in her work about intentionality and consciousness in transpersonal nursing practice, argued that this should rather be called intentionality – a philosophical expansion of the term "intention", which links our "intentions" within a broader context of "caring consciousness".

NARRATIVE HELPS CREATE "SHAPES OF TIME"

Practitioners and the people they try to help, know that meaning must be made of experiences if anything is to be gained and the problems are to be solved. This need applies to all people taking part in an interaction. Satisfaction or dissatisfaction with a human interaction can occur as a direct result of the understanding that is built (or not built) between the people participating in the dialogue. Such understanding will be deepened and better accepted if it can be remembered and reviewed as required.

Narrative helps us to talk about our human experience, interpreting it in order to understand it. Using Aristotle's *Social Poetics* conceptualisation, Ricœur (1983) suggested that people make sense of their experience by organising it via "emplotment": that is, by telling their story. He argued that such narratives help us to integrate different aspects of time: cosmic (chronological) and phenomenological (experienced) through the process of mimesis (quoting Augustine's treatises on time, written between AD 397 and AD 398). According to St Augustine, "the measure of time is not to be found in things, but in the human mind" (Hausheer, 1937, p. 506).

> Wherever we look in this world, we seek to grasp what we see not just in space but in time as well. Narrative gives us this understanding; it gives us what could be called shapes of time. (Porter Abbott, 2008, p. 10)

The term "mimesis" refers to "the act of representation of human experience, where time is configured to compose an imaginatively ordered whole of events, agents and actions that makes activity intelligible" (Kearney, 2009, p. 58). Ricœur (1983) proposed three different mimetic (representative) stages or moments of time:

- Prefiguration (mimesis 1) – pre-existing knowledge and pre-understanding of the world (allowing action to take place)
- Configuration (mimesis 2) – the way in which narrative constructs a story through emplotment (interpretation occurs)
- Refiguration (mimesis 3) – the process by which we redefine ourselves through narrative (the story appears).

Ricœur (ibid) argued that the moment of interpretation ("configuration") was particularly important in telling the story. People re-enact their everyday activities as they tell someone else about them.

Meaning has to be communicated before it can become meaningful, implying that the teller of and the listener to a story must reach a common understanding of the content of the story to communicate. (Alsaker & Josephsson, 2009, p. 66)

Such interpretation and representation of human experience realised and articulated through dialogue requires ongoing mindfulness and engagement if real meaning is achieved between people, setting the basis for further communication and action.

CODA

We set out in this chapter to highlight a connection between mindfulness and practice wisdom. In doing so we have made this connection more vivid. We end with a poem to extend this reflection.

Walking mindfully
through life and practice
I am aware
of where I tread in the world
and how I interact with others.
This choice of life and work is wise
through minds that are open
and mindful
of my purpose and impact.
I cannot be wise
without being mindful
and being mindful
of self and others
I draw wisdom from what I do
and how I am with others.
Being wise
in dealing with life's challenges
requires mindfulness
of many views and possibilities
and an openness to life's
subtleties and nuances
as well as a vitality and awareness
of how we are being-in-the-world.
Practice wisdom requires of us
the mindful pursuit of ethical practices
the highest form of practice wisdom –
it encompasses consideration of others
as does practice wisdom
and wise practice
the highest form of professional practice.

NOTE

1. https://www.mindful.org/foundation/

REFERENCES

Alsaker, S., & Josephsson, S. (2009). Occupation and meaning: Narratives in everyday activities of women with chronic rheumatic conditions. *Occupational Therapy Journal of Rehabilitation, 30*(2), 58-67.

Hausheer, H. (1937). St. Augustine's conception of time. *The Philosophical Review, 46*(5), 503-512.

Higgs, J., & Tasker, D. (2017). Pursuing practice mindfulness and wisdom. In D. Tasker, J. Higgs, & S. Loftus (Eds.), *Community-based healthcare: The search for mindful dialogues* (pp. 187-196). Rotterdam, The Netherlands: Sense.

Kearney, P. (2009). *Reconfiguring the future: Stories of post-stroke transition* (Unpublished doctoral dissertation). University of South Australia, Adelaide.

Meditation Association of Australia. (2018). *What is meditation.* Retrieved from http://meditationaustralia.org.au/

Orenstein, J. (2014). Mindfulness and the law: A different approach to sustainable and effective lawyering. *QUT Law Review, 14*(1), 106-109.

Porter Abbott, H. (2008). *The Cambridge introduction to narrative* (2nd ed.). Cambridge, England: Cambridge University Press.

Ricœur, P. (1983). *Narrative and time* (Vol. 1). Chicago, IL: The University of Chicago Press.

Schwartz, B. (2011). *Using our practical wisdom.* Retrieved from https://www.ted.com/talks/barry_schwartz_using_our_practical_wisdom#t-122946

Schwartz, B., & Sharpe, K. (2010). *Practical wisdom: The right way to do the right thing.* London, England: Penguin.

Sternberg, R. J. (2003). *Wisdom, intelligence, and creativity synthesized.* Cambridge, England: Cambridge University Press.

Tasker, D. (2013). *Mindful dialogues in community-based physiotherapy* (Unpublished doctoral dissertation). Charles Sturt University, Australia.

Tasker, D., & Higgs, J. (2017). A model for mindful dialogues in community-based practice. In D. Tasker, J. Higgs, & S. Loftus (Eds.), *Community-based healthcare: The search for mindful dialogues* (pp. 53-66). Rotterdam, The Netherlands: Sense.

Watson, J. (2001). Intentionality and caring-healing consciousness: A practice of transpersonal nursing. *Holistic Nursing Practice, 16*(4), 12-19.

Webster-Wright, A. (2013). The eye of the storm: A mindful inquiry into reflective practices in higher education. *Reflective Practice: International and Multidisciplinary Perspectives, 14*(4), 556-567.

Diane Tasker PhD
Wentworth Falls, Australia
Member, Education, Practice and Employability Network, Australia

Joy Higgs AM, PhD (ORCID: https://orcid.org/0000-0002-8545-1016)
Emeritus Professor, Charles Sturt University, Australia
Director, Education, Practice and Employability Network, Australia

ANGIE TITCHEN

5. PRACTICE WISDOM AND PROFESSIONAL ARTISTRY

Entering a Place of Human Flourishing

ENTERING THE MYSTERY

Poems in the sky
Trees whisper ancient wisdom
Yes, I can hear you

Figure 5.1. Walking in the wood.

Entering the wood,[1] I am breathless with the beauty of luminous, backlit leaves of vibrant green. I walk silently, aware of my breath, relaxing the tension in my shoulders and neck and opening all my senses into the pathless dark. Smelling mossy earth mounds, tasting wild garlic, feeling the texture of bark, the mystery, magic and myths of trees. In wonder, I stand motionless in a ring of ancient trees. My mind empties and stops wrestling with how to bring together the breadth and depth of what I want to share in this chapter. I am at one with the wood. I am the wood, in awe, fully present, soulful. I feel encircled by wisdom.

© KONINKLIJKE BRILL NV, LEIDEN, 2019 | DOI: 9789004410497_005

My Path

For much of my professional life I have explored ways of lighting up, through professional artistry, the embodied and embedded *background* and *underground* of person-centred healthcare practice. This has been important to me because the background enables us to see and perceive the foreground of practice, but usually without us being conscious of it. Moreover, underground, tacit professional craft knowledge or practical know-how is held in our bodies and embedded in our practices, in addition to our bodies having an innate wisdom to which we often do not listen. I have come to see this background–underground interplay as deeply embedded and embodied in our *praxis* (mindful doing with moral intent enabled by professional artistry) and, although it can sometimes be felt and experienced, its largely non-cognitive nature makes it seem mysterious and difficult to put into words. But tacit and innate wisdom can be put into words, if we uncover and listen to it, then intentionally articulate it to ourselves and others. If we also meld and blend it with explicit, cognitive knowing and multiple intelligences, we can deepen, practise and take enhanced wisdom back in our body and way of being. When this happens, something magical happens and we flourish (see Figure 5.2).

Figure 5.2. Painting my chapter.

I sit at the foot of a huge oak. In a flash, I remember the ecosystem of Elder (mature) trees providing sugars, via underground networks of fungi, for saplings to grow and flourish. Trees also connect with each other through these networks to alert each other to dangers. The trees' communication and nurturing resonates with me and brings to mind the way "Elders" or Indigenous *wise people* listen to, and learn from, the embodied wisdom of Nature. I am minded too of how they share this wisdom with younger members of their tribe or community. I begin to frame the chapter as an inquiry to better understand the role of professional artistry in learning, and helping others to learn, how to embody practice wisdom. I pull my journal, paint box and brushes from my backpack, gaze with soft eyes at the swirling leaves above me and eventually, dip my brush into the lake and start to paint this chapter.

I write in my journal, "Practice wisdom sits within professional artistry and professional artistry is essential for helping us embody practice wisdom. It is an intimate, hidden relationship or ecosystem, but am I doing enough to help people develop the professional artistry side of the relationship?" I am aware of intentionally working with the *dimensions* of professional artistry and pointing them out to my young companions, but my *painting* now has made me aware that I do not so often point out the more hidden *processes* of professional artistry in my practice and in their practices. Arising from my painting and reflections, I decide that this is what I will do now more intentionally here. I will reflect about if and how *background* professional artistry lights up and nurtures practice wisdom and consider how *underground* networks and flowing rivers of practice wisdom and professional artistry can be brought into the *foreground/above ground* through particularised practice with service users, clients, patients, colleagues and students and therapeutic love in the form of loving-kindness. The chapter provides guidance for Elders (i.e. practitioners with expertise, facilitators, critical-creative leaders, companions, educators and researchers) working with "saplings" and "young trees".

HUMAN FLOURISHING

Human flourishing occurs when we bound and frame naturally co-existing energies, when we embrace the known and yet to be known, when we embody contrasts and when we achieve stillness and harmony. When we flourish we give and receive loving-kindness. (McCormack & Titchen, 2014, p. 19)

Within the critical creativity landscape (see Chapter 17), human flourishing and professional artistry lie at the heart of transformational practice, development, learning, leadership, education and research in an intimate philosophical relationship. The ultimate purpose and moral intent of working in this landscape is human flourishing. It is brought about through a *praxis* spiral of mindful knowing, doing, being and becoming enabled by professional artistry. Professional artistry can be discerned in the elements of human flourishing definition above, especially the element of non-judgemental loving-kindness when learning to embody practice wisdom through professional artistry. My circular painting at the centre of Figures 5.3 and 5.4 symbolises human flourishing.

THE HIDDEN PRACTICE WISDOM–
PROFESSIONAL ARTISTRY RELATIONSHIP

Practice wisdom is widely held to be a meld of three dimensions within professional artistry, i.e. multiple knowledges, intelligences and ways of knowing (see Figure 5.3, top drawing). My work suggests that this is achieved through the other dimensions in this figure and supported by professional artistry processes (see Figure 5.3, bottom drawing). Unlike two key bodies of research into professional artistry in caring professions, one that links with the Arts in terms of aesthetic appreciation and connoisseurship for instance (e.g. Fish 1998) and the other with reflection in and on action and professional judgement (e.g. Schön, 1983), my work is derived from studies of the professional craft knowledge of practitioners with expertise and has focused on enabling others to develop their professional artistry. This artistry in the form of synchronicity, balance, interplay and attunement processes emerged in my study of a nurse with expertise in patient-centred nursing (Titchen, 2001) and of myself helping her to become a facilitator of others' experiential learning (Titchen, 2004). I added further dimensions through scholarly research (e.g. Titchen, 2009; Titchen & Higgs, 2001) and, over many years, further processes through my personal development and self-inquiry into my own practice wisdom of person-centred facilitation in action research projects, an International Practice Development Collaboration and with colleagues, work with Master of Science and doctoral students and workshop and conference participants. Through this inquiry, I revealed, developed, evaluated, practised and refined, in continuous cycles, what I now re-present as the two frameworks in Figure 5.3 and the strategies in Figure 5.4.

Figure 5.3. Professional artistry dimensions of self (top drawing) and more hidden processes (bottom drawing) developed from Titchen (2009).

WISDOM AND ARTISTRY

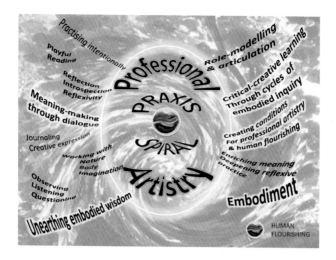

Figure 5.4. Learning cycle of inquiry to access, develop, refine, embody practice wisdom.

My experience of walking alongside saplings and young trees has shown me the need to pay attention to growing the dimension of multiple intelligences, in particular, emotional and spiritual intelligences, as well as the artistic qualities of courage and the audacity to step over established boundaries. Moreover, Elders may not be familiar with articulating their intelligences. I italicise processes when they come into play within the practice wisdom-professional artistry "ecosystem".

Multiple Intelligences

Intelligence is taken to mean a capacity for, and quickness of, understanding or sagacity. Embodied, emotional, artistic and spiritual intelligences provide the capacity and background wisdom that facilitate different ways of knowing. They contribute to the rapid blending of different knowledges and the ability to switch quickly and effortlessly from one level of knowing to another (e.g. from pre-cognitive to cognitive or metacognitive or reflexive) as appropriate to the context and situation. Multiple intelligences work closely together in a beautiful ecosystem or *interplay* of professional artistry processes such as *attunement, balance, synthesis, synchronicity, energy* and *flow* in their melding with each other.

Embodied intelligence is wisdom of the body that people can access when they are trying to understand themselves and engage in reflexive analysis of their understanding and practice. The body holds hidden knowing or insight that is usually overshadowed by cognitive knowing and can be accessed and expressed to gain understanding of pre-cognitive knowledge of ourselves and others. Helping saplings and young trees to develop embodied intelligence through embodied learning (Lawrence, 2012), particularly in Nature, by paying attention to the body and imagination is very powerful (see Figure 5.4).

51

Emotional intelligence gives people an awareness of, or *attunement* to, their own and others' feelings, appropriate responses to pain or pleasure, facilitating social adeptness, empathy, compassion, motivation and caring. A capacity and quickness in picking up emotional cues, in ourselves and others, is central to practice with a concern for human flourishing and transformation. Emotional intelligence therefore comes into play when we encounter difficult emotions that endanger our capacity to provide particularised care with loving-kindness or when we feel unsure, afraid, vulnerable, angry, a failure, rejected, unvalued, unloved, hurt and when ego kicks in hard and diminishes our Greater Self.

Artistic intelligence is the capacity to create, perform and appreciate artistic expression. Artistic intelligence helps us, in a heartbeat, to judge whether, as an Elder, one has rapidly synthesised an embodied learning experience for a young tree in that moment, in a way that is right for that person, at that time. It also shows us whether the learning experience is sufficient, pleasing, nourishing and fulfilling and whether, there is beauty and form created through *balance, flow, interplay, synchronicity, attunement, synthesis* and *energy*. Whereas embodied and emotional intelligences help us to work within the boundaries of our situation and context, artistic and spiritual intelligences enable us to work with and beyond the boundaries and the known to shape and transform the situation. In this sense, they are future-oriented. When we are "alone on the edge" the professional artistry dimension of *artistic qualities,* particularly courage, audacity and the disposition to do good, are vital. We also invoke spiritual intelligence when we are creative, using our deep, intuitive sense of meaning and value to guide us at the edge of order and chaos and thus our comfort zone. On the edge, we call on all our intelligences, but it is spiritual intelligence that enables us to address and work out problems of meaning and value, and to place our actions, lives and pathways in wider, richer, meaning-giving contexts. It guides mindful practice, imbued with loving-kindness and the moral intent of human flourishing (*praxis*) as we become wiser, more open to the beauty and wisdom of Nature and the universe and aspire, dream and uplift ourselves.

Professional Artistry Processes

The professional artistry processes (see Figure 5.3, bottom drawing) enable the practitioner, facilitator, leader, educator and researcher to create particularised care and embodied learning experiences, interventions and responses that are right for the patient, service user, colleague, student, team or co-inquirer within the particular context, situation and time, because they create unique configurations (shapes/patterns) of the dimensions. So in one situation, a meld or blend of experiential and propositional knowledge, intuitive and cognitive ways of knowing, embodied and spiritual intelligences and creative imagination might come together, whilst in another, the configuration would be completely different. The processes are so familiar in our lives and in the natural world (like my wood) that perhaps we tend not to pay enough attention to them in our practices.

- *Attunement:* picking up cues, signals from the context, or person being helped; using intuitive and rational "antennae"; sensitivity to, and in connection/ alignment with these cues (e.g. sounds, smells, signs, feelings, touch, energies); being alert, aware
- *Interplay:* generally, interplay of all aspects of self (our being, knowing, doing and becoming) creates unique configurations and interplay between the professional artistry dimensions and processes
- *Flowing:* moving in and out of metaphysical,[2] metaphorical and physical spaces; between different energies and dimensions, e.g. different knowledges, ways of knowing, *praxis*, being, becoming, as well as physical *movement*
- *Energy*: lyrical, staccato, chaos, flowing and stillness energies or rhythms necessary for our vitality and flourishing; we work with energies of emotion, life force, positive, negative, low, high, directed and non-directed in fruitful ways for our own and others' flourishing; we need to acknowledge the beauty of each energy and see its potential for human growth and for loving-kindness (McCormack & Titchen, 2014)
- *Balance*: achievement of balance between dimensions and processes of professional artistry, as well as methods used to facilitate embodiment of practice wisdom, e.g. movement (through meditative walking, dance, exercise and writing) and stillness (reflecting, silence, painting, body sculpture, visualisation and meditation)
- *Synchronicity*: perceived meaningful coincidence in which happenings in the wider context align with personal experience, perhaps mirroring or resonating with one's own concerns or thoughts
- *Synthesis*: melding, blending and harmonising of any of the above to create something new and unique.

I have attempted so far to bring embodied practice wisdom from underground to above ground (from unconscious to conscious) and to show it up through the backlight of professional artistry. Now the focus shifts to showing how to help others learn to embody practice wisdom, thus bringing the continuous learning cycle in Figure 5.4 to life as a guide for Elders (practitioners with expertise, critical-creative companions and facilitators). Key components of the cycle are italicised. This focus has been present implicitly above and explicitly in Chapter 17 where I accompanied Niamh Kinsella towards a place of human flourishing as she inquired into her practice wisdom of particularised care and loving-kindness.

LEARNING TO EMBODY PRACTICE WISDOM THROUGH *PRAXIS* ENABLED BY PROFESSIONAL ARTISTRY

In our artistic and cognitive critique of learning to embody practice wisdom of particularised practice and loving-kindness, Niamh and I showed the presence of concepts underpinning such practice. Also made visible were the dimensions of professional artistry as a melding, blending and harmonising of different knowledges, multiple ways of knowing, discourses and intelligences, creative imagination and expression; all through the therapeutic and transformative use of self. Artistic qualities, such as discrimination and discernment, were present, as were the professional artistry processes. The key *praxis* spiral skills (see Figure 5.4) for this melding and blending are the abilities to interplay, unravel, reveal, interweave, imagine, symbolise, harmonise, balance and make meaning. These skills enable Elders to disclose what has been observed, perceived and done and to imagine and achieve particularised, unique outcomes for those they care for and help to learn. In the spiral, they intertwine four ways of knowing – that is, pre-cognitive, cognitive, metacognitive and reflexive – as these ways influence and challenge each other during peak performance and integration. Thus, practice wisdom is the capacity to engage in mindful doing, being and becoming with the moral intent of human flourishing. In this engagement, the professional artistry dimensions and processes are lived critically, creatively, ethically, morally and with loving-kindness for the purpose of making the right decisions (with the person being helped) and carrying them out effectively within the particularities of the person's life and circumstances.

So learning to embody such practice wisdom is a tall order for practitioners, educators (see Lawrence, 2012) and researchers using embodied research approaches (see Finlay, 2014). Undertaking *continuous cycles of critical-creative learning through embodied inquiry* (see Figure 5.4) and *creating the conditions for professional artistry and human flourishing* takes time. Vital to both learning and developing practice wisdom is first being able to *articulate it to oneself and others*. Elders who embody particularised practice and loving-kindness can use the *observing, listening and questioning strategy* within critical-creative inquiries to put this wisdom into words, so that they can go on to develop and refine their practice wisdom. In a beautiful, reciprocal, eco-systemic relationship, young saplings and young trees also help Elders articulate their practice wisdom, using the same strategy, as the Elder nurtures the beginning of the sapling's learning journey. This reciprocity and interplay can happen even in workplaces where reflective and conversational spaces and places are not yet easily available, because they can occur during work itself. Short *walks* in nature, with intentional opening up of the body senses and awareness to still the mind and nourish the heart, body and soul can be taken. These can be alone or with a colleague or critical-creative companion, in workplace grounds or gardens or nearby parks or even inside the workplace, providing opportunities for *reflection, introspection and reflexivity*. The power of such walks for unearthing practice wisdom and creating the conditions for human flourishing is clearly shown in Chapter 17, as well as my faction above.

Interplaying and flowing between *walking, journaling, creative expression, dance, body sculpture, playful reading, practising intentionally* and *meaning-making through dialogue,* prepares saplings and young trees for critical-creative learning through cycles of embodied inquiry. These cycles enrich meaning and deepen *reflexive* practice. For example, working synergistically with embodied intelligence, Elders can *role-model and articulate* artistic intelligence for saplings and young trees to show how the unconscious can be brought to consciousness through artistic expression.[3]

Elders can facilitate *meaning-making through dialogue* and *artistic and cognitive critique* of newly emerging wisdom – their own, as well as that of the person they are helping to learn. If role-modelling is combined with articulation, the learning experience will be much more powerful. Learning about self, as an Elder developing these skills or as a sapling or young tree, working alone on the edge of our known is sometimes painful and attention must be paid to developing one's emotional and spiritual intelligences to be able to cope with, to learn from, turbulence and existential pain and to flourish. So we may have to learn to do particularised practice and loving-kindness for ourselves, so we can do it for others. Moreover, we have to *articulate* practice wisdom to ourselves and others in order to develop it and then, we do for ourselves and others (those inquiring with us or those we are helping to learn), *what* we are learning to embody, i.e. particularised practice and loving-kindness. In such a way, *meaning is enriched and reflexive practice is deepened. Embodiment is achieved when we really effortlessly know we know something without having to recall it cognitively.*

CONCLUSION

As I re-enter the wood, I take a new path. The ancient body motion of walking connects me to the earthy footprints of ancient wisdom. Yes, by resonating with the forest ecosystem, I have been able to go some way to unearthing the embodied wisdom of professional artistry. To the best of my ability, I have shown readers something of how practice wisdom is embedded within professional artistry and how professional artistry is essential for helping us embody practice wisdom. Of course, there is more to do to reveal this reciprocal relationship or ecosystem. My hope is that wise practitioners, practice developers, leaders, educators and researchers will walk alongside each other, in Nature when possible, to unearth their practice wisdom. My dream is that they will engage in critical-creative learning through embodied inquiry; learning how to role-model and articulate their practice wisdom and professional artistry to less experienced practitioners, colleagues, teams, students and co-inquirers. I imagine those who are less experienced entering a place of human flourishing and engaging with the learning cycle of inquiry to access, develop, refine and embody practice wisdom that I have presented here. I urge them to seek out wise colleagues and observe, listen and question them as they go about their everyday work. Even when the conditions for nurturing learning at work[4] are not fully in place, this can be possible. Finally, I cannot overemphasise the importance of companionship in this work and working with the body, heart and soul, as well as the mind. Each of us, alone or with others, will find our own way. Go well.

ACKNOWLEDGEMENTS

Love and light to my "young trees" with whom I have walked over the last several years and to those who helped me with this chapter – Alex Fink, Donna Frost, Karen Hammond, Niamh Kinsella, Mary Mulcahey and Lorna Peelo-Kilroe.

NOTES

[1] This section is a "faction" or fiction based on the empirical facts that informed the growth of this chapter. The first line of my opening haiku is inspired by one of Kahlil Gibran's sayings (Gibran, 1995, p. 19).

[2] Metaphysical space is "outside the cognitive mind" in the realms of "being", imagination and embodied, instinctual, archetypal knowing of the body and soul. For example, it might be associated with the flow of human grace in helping relationships (Tasker & Titchen, 2016). In metaphorical spaces, we work with metaphors that arise and resonate with how we are feeling, thinking, being and becoming. So we work with the cognitive mind, as well, in this kind of space. My opening faction is a metaphorical space.

[3] Examples of metaphorical spaces and use of creative imagination and expression can be found in Higgs et al. (2011).

[4] See Dewing et al. (2014) for help into creating the conditions for learning at work.

REFERENCES

Dewing, J., McCormack, B., & Titchen, A. (2014). *Practice development workbook for health and social care teams.* Oxford, England: Wiley-Blackwell.

Finlay, L. (2014). Embodying research. *Person-Centred & Experiential Psychotherapies, 13*(1), 4-18.

Fish, D. (1998). *Appreciating practice in the caring professions: Refocusing professional development and practitioner research.* Oxford, England: Butterworth-Heinemann.

Gibran, K. (1995). *Sand and foam: A book of aphorisms.* New York, NY: Alfred A. Knopf.

Higgs, J., Titchen, A., Horsfall, D., & Bridges, D. (Eds.). (2011). *Creative spaces for qualitative researching: Living research.* Rotterdam, The Netherlands: Sense.

Lawrence, R. L. (2012). *Bodies of knowledge: Embodied learning in adult education.* San Francisco, CA: Jossey-Bass.

McCormack, B., & Titchen, A. (2014). No beginning, no end: An ecology of human flourishing. *International Practice Development Journal, 4*(2), Art. 2.

Schön, D. A. (1983). *The reflective practitioner: How professionals think in action.* Aldershot, England: Ashgate.

Tasker, D., & Titchen, A. (2016). Through mindfulness and grace towards embodied practice. In J. Higgs & F. Trede (Eds.), *Professional practice discourse marginalia* (pp. 153-160). Rotterdam, The Netherlands: Sense.

Titchen, A. (2001). Skilled companionship in professional practice. In J. Higgs & A. Titchen (Eds.), *Practice knowledge and expertise in the health professions* (pp. 69-79). Oxford, England: Butterworth-Heinemann.

Titchen, A. (2004). Helping relationships for practice development: Critical companionship. In B. McCormack, K. Manley, & R. Garbett (Eds.), *Practice development in nursing* (pp. 148-174). Oxford, England: Blackwell.

Titchen, A. (2009). Developing expertise through nurturing professional artistry in the workplace. In S. Hardy, A. Titchen, B. McCormack, & K. Manley (Eds.) *Revealing nursing expertise through practitioner inquiry* (pp. 219-243). Oxford, England: Wiley-Blackwell.

Titchen, A., & Higgs, J. (2001). Towards professional artistry and creativity in practice. In J. Higgs & A. Titchen (Eds.), *Professional practice in health, education and the creative* arts (pp. 273-290). Oxford, England: Blackwell Science.

Angie Titchen DPhil (Oxon)
Independent Practice Development & Research Consultant

ALLAN PITMAN AND ELIZABETH ANNE KINSELLA

6. A PLACE FOR PHRÓNÊSIS IN PROFESSIONAL PRACTICE

A Reflection of Turbulent Times

In this chapter we consider the question of *phrónêsis* and its place in professional practice in complex and changing times. It is our position that the core of professional practice involves the exercise of situated wise judgement and that a fruitful way of exploring this dimension is through a revitalisation of an Aristotelean understanding of the nature of knowledge. For Aristotle, there were three forms of knowledge: *epistêmê*, *tékhnê* and *phrónêsis*. The first two of these have come down to us in the present age in the form of epistemic and technical knowledge. *Epistêmê* is characterised as scientific, invariable, context-independent knowledge; while *tékhnê* is characterised as context-dependent, pragmatic, variable, craft knowledge, oriented toward practical rationality and governed by a conscious goal (Flyvbjerg, 2001; Kinsella & Pitman, 2012a). The third, *phrónêsis*, has tended to drop from the public consciousness as a subject for scrutiny. It has, however, been gaining attention and has been reinvigorated in recent years. *Phrónêsis* is that form of knowledge – one of Aristotle's virtues – which is enacted in situated wise judgement, incorporating a moral purpose in order to act for the best. It involves deliberation based on values and is concerned with practical judgement and informed by reflection; it is pragmatic, variable, context-dependent and oriented toward action (Kinsella & Pitman, 2012a).

The irony is that despite the re-emergence of calls for *phrónêsis* in multiple fields of professional practice such as nursing, healthcare, social care, business and education, the grounds for growing *phrónêsis* appear to have become more complex and increasingly hostile to its cultivation (Pitman, 2012). In this chapter we consider the tension between the changing contexts of contemporary professional practice and growing calls for *phrónêsis* and the implications for the professions. Our aim is to reinvigorate the concept of *phrónêsis* as a concept of crucial importance to professional citizenship and the social good.

THE PROMISE OF PHRÓNÊSIS

Although elusive in nature, and difficult to define, the promise of *phrónêsis* (or practical wisdom) for professional life is frequently elucidated in the narratives that professionals convey about their practices (see Frank, 2012; Schwartz & Sharpe, 2013). An illustrative example is noted in the words and wise actions of a hospital janitor: "Sometimes I might start waxing and a patient comes out and he wants to walk up and down the hall. He wants to exercise. As soon as I get ready, he'll start.

I don't bother him. I'll just wait 'cause I know I can't tell them to go sit down. They need to build themselves up and that's what I have to tell my supervisor: Couldn't do it, 'cause (of) the patient" (Schwartz & Sharpe, 2013, p. 172). This example reflects Schwartz and Sharpe's description of *phrónêsis* or practical wisdom as "the capacity to know the right thing to do in a particular circumstance and the motivation and courage actually to do it", and as involving "good judgement or horse sense or ethical intelligence" (ibid, p. 176).

As another narrative example, a family physician shared a story in a recent workshop that speaks to what some might consider *phrónêsis*. The physician was working with a family whose child had terminal cancer with only a few months to live. The child was enrolled in numerous therapies and special educational programs including oncological appointments, occupational therapy, speech therapy, physiotherapy, recreation therapy and special programs at school. The parents were weary with the demands of attending a relentless line up of appointments with their child, and worried that quality of family life and relationships were being severely impacted and strained due to their exhaustion levels. The physician said to the parents, *"Technically I can't tell you not to continue with treatments, however to be honest if I were in your shoes, I would focus instead on making memories, spending time with your child – this will be her last Christmas – read books, make cookies, play games, have fun, travel together ... there is not much time"*.

Paul Kalanithi (2016) in his reflections on becoming a physician speaks to the experiential dimension of *phrónêsis*, and the ways it informs action: "Reading books and answering multiple choice questions bore little resemblance to taking action with its concomitant responsibility. Knowing you need to be judicious when pulling on the head [during a birth] to facilitate delivery of the shoulder is not the same as doing it. What if I pulled too hard? (*Irreversible nerve injury...*)" (p. 63). Enacting *phrónêsis* in practice, is not the same as possessing the epistemic knowledge (*epistêmê*), or learning the technical skills (*tékhnê*); it is frequently born out of and developed through experience and a consideration of context, and it is closely related to praxis – the *doing* of actions infused with practical wisdom (Kemmis, 2012; Kinsella & Pitman, 2012c). Kemmis (2012) suggests that *phrónêsis* is a strange attractor for those who seek to fill a void in understandings of professional practice; he suggests that the longing for *phrónêsis* is born out of a recognition of the limits of technical rationalities to respond to the problems that professionals encounter. *Phrónêsis* springs from a desire to find concepts to grasp the elusive forms of professional knowledge necessary for understanding and acting with good judgement as required by of the practical situations in which practitioners find themselves (Eikeland, 2006; Hibbert, 2012; Kemmis, 2012; Kinsella & Pitman, 2012a).

Sometimes *phrónêsis* is best recognised through its absence; we know it when we see it and we know it when it is absent (Kemmis, 2012). A striking example of the absence of *phrónêsis* is evident in the vignette below:

An occupational therapy student, Mark, was asked by his preceptor to provide education to a client (Mary), regarding wound care following bilateral amputations of her legs above the knee. The surgery would require Mary to use a wheelchair for mobility after surgery, and likely for life, as she was not a candidate for prosthetic legs. Mark had recently learned about wound healing and was eager to share his new knowledge. Mark's preceptor provided educational material with a checklist of topics to cover, as well as a video about amputation wound care. Mark was instructed by his preceptor to carry out the education in his next meeting with Mary. When Mark met with Mary, he began by telling her what they would do, and then proceeded to turn on the video. Mary began to cry. Mark was worried about having adequate time to complete the education, so he did not respond to her tears. She continued to cry; she sobbed, she wept. Mark let the video run and stood awkwardly by. At the end of the video, Mark told Mary that it was important that they talk about wound care, and he proceeded to talk through the ten points on his checklist. Finally, having accomplished his tasks, Mark asked why Mary was crying. She said that she had not heard a word of the video or a word of what he said because she was worried about her situation. As a sole parent she was overwhelmed with concern about how she would work and care for her five children. She could not even begin to think about 'wound care' because all she could think about was: How would this change her life? Who would pay the bills? How could she care for her children in the years to come? (Adapted from Kinsella, 2010)

In this example the student had carried out the technical dimensions of his job, he was up to date on the latest scientific knowledge, yet his intervention had not served Mary's needs. While this example points to the absence of *phrónêsis* enacted by Mark, it raises the question "Why didn't he respond when he witnessed Mary's distress?"; and also points to the tensions that practitioners and students may experience in the face of the pervasive technical rationalities, or what Stein (2001) has referred to as the "cult of efficiency", in health and social care settings. In an analysis of this situation one wonders: What were the institutional pressures and expectations that Mark and his preceptor were facing? How might Mark's institutional pressures, and Mary's lived experiences be in conflict with one another (Kinsella, 2010)? While such narratives point to illustrative examples of *phrónêsis*, or its absence, in practice, they may also illuminate tensions that practitioners experience in their efforts to enact *phrónêsis*, and underline the moral courage required at times to invoke it. Below we explore some of the tensions, in light of the changing conditions of professional practice, the basis of professional knowledge, applications of *phrónêsis* in contemporary times and the incongruent obligations that professional practitioners face.

THE CHANGING CONDITIONS OF PROFESSIONAL PRACTICE

Any discussion about the professions and professional action should be placed in the context of time and place. The social-political landscape in which professionals practice is changing rapidly as a consequence of various factors including economic and organisational rationalities guiding practice, technological advances in communications, changes in required work capabilities, and increased organisational modalities of control and surveillance. Politically, we are seeing the continuation of the assertion of neoliberal policies and a corresponding evolution of new management regimens in which the role of technology is more predominant than ever. As the economies and technologies surrounding professional occupations exert their impact, a question arises as to how the nature of professional work is being transformed, not least as to how it affects what lies at the core of professional practice. A central concern lies in the apparent shift from an emphasis on individual *responsibility in practice* to a focus on *accountability for one's practice*.

A story from nursing told by Arthur Frank (2012) illustrates the distinction:

> An experienced dialysis nurse described a patient who did not speak English and was both especially apprehensive about dialysis treatment and in pain. He was agitated and pulling at the dialysis lines, so he was given a breakthrough dose of narcotic, according to protocol. He fell into a calm sleep. As the treatment progressed, a floor nurse came by, noted on the patient's chart that the protocol called for him to receive an oral pill, and proposed to wake him up to administer the dose. The dialysis nurse objected that this was ridiculous – the patient was already asleep. She also pointed out that the patient's chart indicated a choking hazard. The floor nurse returned with a supervisor; the patient was woken and given the pill, by mouth despite the choking hazard that was charted and written on a sign over the bed. (pp. 57-58)

The dialysis nurse in this instance was attempting to invoke *phrónêsis*, to see the big picture of what was in the best interests of the patient, and to take *responsibility* for actions in light of her professional judgement; the floor nurse on the other hand was acting in response to the documented protocol, she was acting with *accountability* to the orders on the chart; her actions however were not responsive to the specific situation at hand, or it could be argued to the best interests of the patient. Frank (2012) calls this a story of "anti-*phrónêsis* because it's about overriding the claims of practical wisdom in favour of routines that have been decided on without reference to the situation at hand" (p. 58).

When one takes "responsibility" in practice one is concerned with using one's professional judgement to act toward the greatest good in professional life. When the focus is on "accountability" for one's practice, the concern is shifted to practitioners being held accountable to external codified practices, and regulatory mechanisms to whom the professional must "account" for their professional decisions and actions. The concern is with the change in emphasis: both are necessary in the professions, however the shifting emphasis toward accountability and away from responsibility provides a context in which the very nature of what it means to act professionally is called into question. An emphasis on accountability, for instance, may create pressure for practitioners to operate from defensive or fear-based postures in order to avoid reprimand; this is opposed to proactive and creative positions of responsibility informed by the qualities and characteristics of *phrónêsis*, i.e. ethical, wise, reflective and deliberative practice. These changing contexts of professional practice are occurring at a time when technologies are enabling tighter surveillance of practice and contributing to increasingly efficient modes of monitoring accountability to professional and corporate demands (Tatnall & Pitman, 2002, 2003). They leave us with questions related to the application of *phrónêsis*. First, in what ways do the changing socio-political grounds in which professional practitioners work create conditions that might be seen as challenging to the cultivation of *phrónêsis* and the exercise of wise judgement in professional practice? Second, if *phrónêsis* continues to hold promise, how might the application of *phrónêsis* as core to practice be accomplished in these changing times?

THE BASIS OF PROFESSIONAL KNOWLEDGE AND PRACTICE

What is a profession and what is professional practice? It is important to separate the institutional structure of a profession from the nature of the work and the practices of its members. The dilemmas of professional practice and of acting professionally can be found in the tensions between a profession's codified regulations and claims for best practices on the one hand, and the situated judgements of the practitioner on the other (Pitman, 2012). An additional tension may be introduced by the organisations that employ professional practitioners and the extra dimensions of accountability that are introduced through such organisations.

What constitutes good practice is best summarised as applying one's knowledge, both formal professional and codified knowledge and knowledge generated through experience, in unique situations which are, to a degree, within the bounds of a community of fellow practitioners. There is a moral imperative and teleology involved: to act for the best – that is, in the interests of one's "client". The need exists to make informed decisions in the best interests of the client/service user/ patient/student as the practitioner understands just what "for the best" actually means in situated contexts. Yet, practice takes place in social and organisational contexts that are also important to consider when making situated ethical judgements in practice. It could also be argued that there is a moral imperative for practitioners to act in the best interests of the organisation that employs them.

What happens when these two dimensions come into conflict? As an example, this may occur when a physical therapist is treating a client in the community following a motor vehicle accident, and the treatment is being paid for by a private organisation such as an insurance company. The therapist may recommend daily treatment for an extended period and release from the workplace for a minimum of six months. Yet the mandate of the insurance company may come into conflict with a mandate to provide basic care and focus on return to work of the client as quickly as possible. At times the therapist's allegiance to the client for whom they are responsible may come into conflict with the therapist's allegiance to the dictates of the employer to whom they are accountable. The issue is one of the problems being wrestled with in Ontario regarding the potential requirement of financial advisors to act in the best interest of the client rather than of the employer (Maley, 2018).

At the heart of practitioners' situated judgement is the knowledge that a professional practitioner possesses and how this knowledge is related to practice. While the dominant discourses of professional practice and education centre upon epistemic and practical domains, we argue that a broader view founded on all three of Aristotle's forms of knowledge – *epistêmê*, *tékhnê* and *phrónêsis* – points to the general exclusion of practical wisdom – *phrónêsis* – from explicit consideration in professional education and practice, despite its necessity in everyday professional life. Yet, in the situation above, with the economic rationalities that guide professional practice, we can see that the ground for practitioners to use their situated judgement and practical wisdom may at times be experienced as hostile. On the other hand, it could be argued that *phrónêsis* is required to find what Aristotle identified as the *balance point*, the *mean*, between competing interests (Jenkins, Kinsella, & DeLuca, 2019).

At a time when populist movements call the value of expertise into question, and where legitimate perspectives can be dismissed as so-called "fake news" or in the interest of political-economic agendas, it is more important than ever to draw out, and make explicit, the place of professional judgement and the basis of professional knowledge and practice. In the interest of advancing *phrónêsis*, Arthur Frank (2012) identifies six claims that are made upon professionals, that practitioners must consider, and that inform professional action in practice. These are practical claims, professional claims, scientific claims, commercial claims, ethical claims and moral claims. In what ways might *phrónêsis* be advanced, and the middle path be found, if practitioners recognise each of these claims as shaping their situated professional judgements in practice? Further, it is necessary to consider the ways in which one may respond to the objection that society can rely on so-called "common sense" as a route to solutions. Taking the characterisation of "common sense" from Gramsci (1971), as "the incoherent set of generally held assumptions and beliefs common to any given society" and "good sense" as meaning "practical empirical common sense" (p. 323), Hoare and Smith (editors of Gramsci's writing), describe common sense as "linked to many beliefs and prejudices" and "to almost all popular superstition" (Gramsci, 1971, p. 396). A danger of the appeal to only common sense is that it kills off the possibility of debate. An irony lies in Gramsci's claim that common sense as it emerged in the 17th century was linked to the rise of scientific thinking. Yet, the present sees "common sense" being turned against scientific claims, professional claims, practical claims, ethical claims and moral claims, in the interests of political-economic agendas.

APPLICATIONS OF PHRÓNÊSIS IN CONTEMPORARY TIMES

Despite the promise and potential of taking up the tripartite view of knowledge – *epistêmê*, *tékhnê* and *phrónêsis* – espoused by Aristotle, it must be recognised that he conceptualised his framework in a world alien to our own and as a consequence, it is necessary to rethink applications of *phrónêsis* for contemporary times. As discussed in earlier work (Ellett, 2012; Kinsella & Pitman, 2012a), Aristotle lived in a different world:

> comprised of freemen and slaves. Races were deemed superior or inferior. Men and women were seen to have intrinsically different capacities that precluded women from involvement in serious intellectual work. The world was viewed as stable and eternal. The object of the intellect was to gain knowledge and,

through knowledge, wisdom (*sophia*) and to develop a love for knowledge (*philos*). (Kinsella & Pitman, 2012c, p. 3)

In Aristotle's times "philosophy was the pursuit of the elite: the object was a society ruled by the wise 'philosopher king'" (Kinsella & Pitman, 2012c, p. 3). This is juxtaposed with current times, where we may desire wise, thoughtful political leaders, yet we do so in a fundamentally different social and philosophical world. To elaborate:

> The social constructions surrounding class, ethnicity, and gender with which we live differ vastly from those taken into consideration in the Athens of Aristotle. This difference has implications for thinking about professional practice in respect to the teleology of 'the good' and of 'doing the good,' as well as for assumptions about what that might mean, about who can take part in the practice, and for whom such practice is intended. The concern here is on two levels: one in which the focus is on *phrónêsis* as it relates to professional practice and its practitioners, the other on those engaged in meta-discussions about *phrónêsis* itself. Recognition of the social constructions surrounding class, ethnicity, and gender is, it would appear, key to any reconstitution of the notion of *phrónêsis*. Indeed, the whole understanding of what is 'the good' – the teleological objective of the whole exercise – must be reconsidered in light of the different positions and the situatedness of those engaged in professional practices. (Kinsella & Pitman, 2012c, p. 3)

Further, in this world, in which theoretical work has been differentiated from the practical and technical, and a post-Enlightenment framing of science dominates our world view, new understandings of the tentative nature of our law-like claims call into question, for example, the eternal verity of Aristotle's *epistêmê* (Kinsella & Pitman, 2012c).

As the work of Kuhn (1970), and sociologists of scientific knowledge point out, *epistêmê* and *phrónêsis* may be much more intertwined than previously recognised. *Epistêmê* itself may be viewed as constituted in the social practice of science, and as involving practices of *tékhnê* and *phrónêsis* (Chishtie, 2012).

Ellett (2012) argues that what cannot be recovered in applications of *phrónêsis* for contemporary times "is a moral essentialism of humankind's nature, purpose, and function, or a first philosophy that is fixed, timeless, and universally necessary. The naturalness of sexism, classism, and racism is emphatically rejected" (Kinsella & Pitman, 2012c, pp. 3-4). Ellett (2012) proposes four aspects of *phrónêsis* as recoverable in contemporary times. First, he points out that *phrónêsis* typically involves judgement that is deliberative; second, *phrónêsis* can still be viewed as a virtue, as a positive aim for democratic citizenship; third, *phrónêsis* is an embodied social practice that typically has internal goods and excellences – that is, those goods that come from *engaging in the practice itself*, such as satisfaction, bonding or the advancement of what is considered excellent; and finally, *phrónêsis* may be seen to involve complicated interactions between general and practical states of affairs.

Further dimensions of *phrónêsis* relevant for contemporary times are highlighted by Eikeland (2006, 2014). He describes *phrónêsis* as a way of using *logos*, a way of reasoning about what to do. He describes *phrónêsis* as deliberative but notes that deliberation is not a characteristic of *phrónêsis* alone, for instance cleverness is also deliberative but it is lacking in virtuous ends. *Phrónêsis*, on the other hand, is oriented toward virtue; it is intellectual but also ethical. Eikeland (2014) suggests the ethical dimension of *phrónêsis* is especially important for a number of reasons:

- because one would blame someone for *forgetting* or *neglecting* to do these intellectual exercises in dealing with others, treating everyone exactly the same regardless of circumstances, preconditions, and so on;
- because *abstaining consciously and voluntarily* from deliberating for and against on what to do would be considered an ethical deficiency; and
- because one would blame someone for deliberating merely cleverly for other – unethical – purposes in dealing with others, or even manipulating others technically. (p. 625)

The centrality of reflection in the process of deliberation and the development of practical, situated wisdom is a further dimension that may be recovered for contemporary times, given that "whatever else *phrónêsis* might be, we can safely say that it involves reflection" (Kinsella, 2012, p. 37). Kinsella (2012) proposes an elaboration of ways of thinking about reflection in the interests of *phrónêsis* through a continuum of reflection. This continuum invokes a range of ways of applying reflection, such as: intentional practical reflection (reflection on practical experience), embodied reflection (reflection that occurs through doing – without a prior intellectual operation), critical reflexivity (examination of the social conditions in which knowledge is produced and used) as well as receptive forms of reflection or what some refer to as mindfulness or contemplation (insights that arise through a receptive or contemplation orientation).

Phrónêsis involves a disposition toward certain kinds of judgements, which are informed by processes of reflection. While the question is frequently raised as to whether an orientation toward such *phrónêtic* judgements may be taught, Kinsella (2012) questions "if by making more explicit the criteria by which practitioners make judgements, and by encouraging the conscious adoption of criteria oriented toward *phrónêtic* ideals, practitioners might move toward *phrónêtic* judgements in professional practice" (p. 37). Kinsella (2012) highlights six criteria – pragmatic usefulness, persuasiveness and aesthetic appeal (implied in Donald Schön's theory of reflective practice), as well as ethical imperatives, dialogic intersubjectivity and the potential to positively transform the situation (proposed by Kinsella) that practitioners could consider in cultivating judgements oriented toward *phrónêsis* in professional life. Her work raises the question: "What criteria might we consider when using reflection to make judgements and to discern action oriented toward *phrónêsis*? If *phrónêsis* cannot be explicitly taught, might the disposition toward *phrónêsis* be encouraged, and the modes of thinking that work against it be revealed?" (Kinsella, 2012, p. 37).

Such an approach would surely incorporate the ambiguities and conflicts for those aspiring to *phrónêtic* practice *in situ*. Not least of these is the uncertainty as to whether a particular wisely determined action is in fact the best. This is what Green (2009) is concerned with in his invocation of Derrida's concept of *aporia*:

> the fundamental dilemma of professional practice, enacted constantly and even unceasingly, at all levels: the impossibility of having enough information on the basis of which to make the right decision, in all the urgency and drama of the moment; and yet, the necessity of doing so, of acting, of moving on – the imperative to act, and doing so, but without guarantees. (pp. 4-5)

INCONGRUENT OBLIGATIONS:
ETHICAL TENSIONS AND THE CALL FOR PHRÓNÊSIS

The work of a professional generally takes place within the confines of an associated regulatory professional organisation, such as the College of Physicians and Surgeons, the College of Teachers or the College of Occupational Therapists, etc. The modern professions as they have emerged under the jurisdiction of regulatory bodies may be seen as secular models that parallel religious orders of the past. As such, the professions are governed by sets of rules and practices codified by organisations established by the State, in a similar way in which governance was overseen in the past by the Church and its members (Pitman, 2012).

It can be seen how the intent of the individual to practise for the best, exercising wise judgement, can potentially come into conflict with codified rules of conduct and the prescripts of the state. It is at this juncture that we see regulatory policies of accountability intersecting and potentially coming into conflict with policies of institutionally delegated mandates and being played out in respect to pressures on the individual practice of members within a profession. Further, these two dimensions have the potential to come into conflict with a third dimension involving the practitioner's enactment of *phrónêsis* – ethical, situated judgements, oriented toward the greatest good – in practice. An example is found in a case in Ontario in which the government mandates that a system-wide test be administered to all Grade 3 students in the Province, under stringent test conditions. There are several instances in Ontario in which teachers and principals have encouraged some students to miss the test or have deviated from the protocols for the test administration. In some instances, this has resulted in these professionals being disciplined and stripped of their licences to teach by the College of Teachers (see Pitman, 2012).

Yet if one listens to the narratives of teachers there may be convincing moral justification for a teacher to deviate from the protocol. For instance, if a teacher's professional judgement discerns that it may be best for the identity and wellbeing of a newcomer, second-language student, to forego the potentially debilitating experience of sitting through a test of little educational value to the child, should the teacher act to avoid that situation or follow the strictures of the authorities (Pitman, 2012)? Attending to *phrónêsis* might dictate one pattern of behaviour whereas attending to regulatory policies of accountability, or institutionally delegated mandates, might dictate another altogether. We can see in this instance the ways in which the organisation of professional practices may come into conflict with and potentially be extremely hostile to the enactment of the ideal of *phrónêsis*.

If one is to argue for *phrónêsis* – ethical wise reflective judgement – as a core dimension of professional practice, then we must address the dilemma this conception has the potential to pose for members of formally regulated professional occupations who have in recent years "had to satisfy an increasing number of incongruent obligations to different stakeholders" (Freeman & Jauvin, 2018, p. 1). Ethical tensions have the potential to arise when professions are organised with control over the behaviour of their members and when such control is set down in codified form. Ethical tensions may be characterised (drawing on Jameton, 1984) in different ways, and as involving:

> *ethical dilemmas*, situations in which ... professionals face two mutually exclusive possible courses of action, each having costs and benefits; *ethical distress*, situations in which ... professionals are constrained from acting in the way they believe to be most appropriate; and *ethical uncertainty*, situations in which ... professionals are unsure about whether or not a situation is an ethical issue, and if so, which principles may be in conflict. (Durocher et al., 2016, p. 216)

Such tensions occur regularly in professional practice, not least in healthcare practice and in education. While sources of these tensions vary, practice issues related to systemic constraints "have been reported to be a prevailing source of ethical challenge" for practitioners in many fields (Durocher et al., 2016, p. 216). As these authors elaborate, "[S]uch tensions can have significant implications ... and may set up situations that may be experienced as forms of injustice" (p. 216), or as environments that create challenging conditions for the enactment of *phrónêsis*.

Given the tensions that professional practitioners face, Freeman and Jauvin (2018) have called for a rethinking of a sole emphasis on accountability mechanisms as a dominant view in professional practice, arguing that other lenses such as an ethical lens and a lens that recognises the professional as a worker in a particular context are also essential to consider. Such a view is consistent with what *phrónêsis* would call for in practice; situated judgements that attend not only to one's accountabilities, but also to a bigger picture view, that considers ethical and moral imperatives, and analysis of the contexts of practice, as a means to discern with practical wisdom the best action that is of the greatest good for the client, in professional practice.

CONCLUSION

Despite, the challenges that practitioners face in climates that might be seen as hostile to *phrónêsis*, we are filled with hope by the stories of *phrónêsis* we hear from professional practitioners in a range of fields, and the emergence of attention to practice wisdom in contemporary scholarship. As we've noted elsewhere (Kinsella & Pitman, 2012b):

> Perhaps one of the primary attractions to *phrónêsis* is the possibility it offers of a discourse for practitioners, individually and collectively, to resist the moral compromise and despair that a focus solely on external goods may invoke, and that the trend toward pervasive technicism, instrumentalism, and manager-

ialism may fuel. Perhaps *phrónêsis* represents a beacon of light, hope, and belief that there might be, indeed must be, a way for practitioners to negotiate the internal goods of their professional practices with wisdom, integrity, and authenticity and on morally respectable grounds amidst the *aporias* of uncertainty and in contexts where external goods such as money, prestige, and power are at play. (pp. 166-167)

What possibilities might be offered if educational practices oriented toward *phrónêsis* were to inform our democratic ideals and constitute a moral imperative within the social imagination of what it means to be a professional? What benefits might be accrued at a societal level if *phrónêsis* were recognised as a social good, and woven into the fabric of professional education and practice? What is the benefit of recognising the contemporary professional practice conditions that both foster and create tensions for the enactment of *phrónêsis*? How might such tensions be overcome and counterbalanced in productive ways? We argue that attention to *phrónêsis* as an organising framework for what it means to be a professional offers considerable promise as a way forward, particularly if it is embraced widely in the socio-cultural imagination of democratic societies. We propose that *phrónêsis* offers a potential antidote or at least a counterbalance to the limitations invoked by a failure of emphasis on situated professional judgement in the face of technical rationality, new technologies, punitive surveillance and accountability mechanisms, and the economic-political rationalities that are shaping our times.

REFERENCES

Chishtie, F. (2012). Phronesis and the practice of science. In E. A. Kinsella & A. Pitman (Eds.), *Phronesis as professional knowledge: Practical wisdom in the professions* (pp. 101-114). Rotterdam, The Netherlands: Sense.

Durocher, E., Kinsella, E. A., McCorquodale L., & Phelan, S. (2016). Ethical tensions related to systemic constraints: Occupational alienation in occupational therapy practice. *OTJR: Occupation, Participation and Health, 36*(4), 216-226.

Eikeland, O. (2006). Phronesis, Aristotle, and action research. *International Journal of Action Research, 2*(1), 5-53.

Eikeland, O. (2014). Phronesis. In D. Coglan & M. Brydon-Miller (Eds.), *The SAGE encyclopedia of action research* (pp. 624-626). London, England: SAGE.

Ellett, F. (2012). Practical rationality and a recovery of Aristotle's 'phronesis' for the professions. In E. A. Kinsella & A. Pitman, A. (Eds.), *Phronesis as professional knowledge: Practical wisdom in the professions* (pp. 13-33). Rotterdam, The Netherlands: Sense.

Flyvberg, B. (2001). *Making social science matter: Why social inquiry fails and how it can succeed again.* Cambridge, England: Cambridge University Press.

Frank, A. (2012). Reflective healthcare practice. In E. A. Kinsella & A. Pitman (Eds.), *Phronesis as professional knowledge: Practical wisdom in the professions* (pp. 53-60). Rotterdam, The Netherlands: Sense.

Freeman, A., & Jauvin, N. (2018). Analyzing the professional practice context using three lenses: An essential step in responding strategically. *Occupational Therapy in Health Care.* Retrieved from https://doi.org/10.1080/07380577.2018.1553086

Gramsci, A. (1971). *Selections from the prison notebooks* (Q. Hoare & G. Smith, Trans. & Eds.). New York, NY: International Publishers.

Green, B. (2009, December 1). *The (im)possibility of the project* (Radford Lecture). Delivered to the Annual Conference of the Australian Association for Research in Education, Melbourne, Australia.

Hibbert, K. (2012). Cultivating capacity: Phronesis, learning and diversity in professional education. In E. A. Kinsella & A. Pitman (Eds.), *Phronesis as professional knowledge: Practical wisdom in the professions* (pp. 61-71). Rotterdam, The Netherlands: Sense.

Jameton, A. (1984). *Nursing practice: The ethical issues*. Englewood Cliffs, NJ: Prentice Hall.

Jenkins, K., Kinsella, E. A., & DeLuca, S. (2019). Perspectives on phronesis in professional nursing practice. *Nursing Philosophy, 20*(1), 1-8, e12231.

Kalanithi, P. (2016). *When breath becomes air*. New York, NY: Random House.

Kemmis, S. (2012). Phronesis, experience, and the primacy of practice. In E. A. Kinsella & A. Pitman (Eds.), *Phronesis as professional knowledge: Practical wisdom in the professions* (pp. 147-161). Rotterdam, The Netherlands: Sense.

Kinsella, E. A. (2010). The art of reflective practice in health and social care: Reflections on the legacy of Donald Schön. *Reflective Practice, 11*(4), 565-575.

Kinsella, E. A. (2012). Practitioner reflection and judgement as phronesis: A continuum of reflection and considerations for phronetic judgement. In E. A. Kinsella & A. Pitman (Eds.), *Phronesis as professional knowledge: Practical wisdom in the professions* (pp. 35-52). Rotterdam, The Netherlands: Sense.

Kinsella, E. A., & Pitman, A. (2012a). Engaging phronesis in professional practice and education. In E. A. Kinsella & A. Pitman (Eds.), *Phronesis as professional knowledge: Practical wisdom in the professions* (pp. 1-11). Rotterdam, The Netherlands: Sense.

Kinsella, E. A., & Pitman, A. (2012b). Phronesis as professional knowledge: Implications for education and practice. In E. A. Kinsella & A. Pitman (Eds.), *Phronesis as professional knowledge: Practical wisdom in the professions* (pp. 163-172). Rotterdam, The Netherlands: Sense.

Kinsella, E. A., & Pitman, A. (Eds.). (2012c). *Phronesis as professional knowledge: Practical wisdom in the professions*. Rotterdam, The Netherlands: Sense.

Kuhn, T. (1970). *The structure of scientific revolutions* (2nd ed.). Chicago, IL: University of Chicago Press.

Maley, D. (2018, December 5). Do advisors act in investors' best interests? A tussle over terminology. *The Globe and Mail*, p. B7.

Pitman, A. (2012). Professionalism and professionalisation: Hostile ground for growing phronesis? In E. A. Kinsella & A. Pitman (Eds.), *Phronesis as professional knowledge: Practical wisdom in the professions* (pp. 131-146). Rotterdam, The Netherlands: Sense.

Schwartz, B., & Sharpe, K. (2013). The war on wisdom and how to fight it. In M. Jones, P. Lewis, & K. Reffitt (Eds.), *Toward human flourishing: Character, practical wisdom and professional formation* (pp. 167-192). Macon, GA: Mercer University Press.

Stein, J. (2001). *The cult of efficiency*. Toronto, Canada: House of Anansi Press.

Tatnall A., & Pitman A. (2002). Issues of decentralisation and central control in educational management. In D. Passey & M. Kendall (Eds.), *TelE-learning. IFIP WCC TC3 2002. IFIP – The International Federation for Information Processing, 102*. Boston, MA: Springer.

Tatnall A., & Pitman A. (2003). Information technology and control in educational management. In I. D. Selwood, A. C. W Fung, & C. D. O'Mahony (Eds.), *Management of education in the information age. ITEM 2002. The International Federation for Information Processing, 120*. Boston, MA: Springer.

Allan Pitman PhD
Faculty of Education, Western University, Canada

Elizabeth Anne Kinsella PhD
Faculty of Health Sciences, Western University, Canada

RACHAEL FIELD

7. RESILIENCE, SELF-MANAGEMENT AND AGENCY

Living Practice Wisdom Well

Practice wisdom is critical to effective practice and to achieving excellence in practice because it supports creativity, breakthrough thinking and is the foundation for effective discernment, good judgement and appropriate decision making. This chapter argues that in the contemporary neo-liberalist society, practitioners need resilience, self-management and agency for practice wisdom to be possible and achievable. That is, in order to practise creatively, ethically and with good judgement, practitioners need to be psychologically well, and supported by positive workplace and societal structures and cultures.

Resilient practitioners who have self-management skills and agency will be better able to enact practice wisdom because they will be better able to cope with the realities, challenges and stressors of modern workplaces. On this basis, the support of practitioners' wellbeing – and in particular, their resilience, self-management and agency – is a significant professional imperative.

RESILIENCE, SELF-MANAGEMENT AND AGENCY IN THE CONTEXT OF PRACTICE WISDOM

Resilience, self-management and agency are elements of wellbeing. Wellbeing is a complex and subjective notion; however, a significant amount of theoretical and empirical research exists to help understand it. In particular, Self-Determination Theory (SDT) (Deci & Ryan, 1985), an important meta-theory of positive psychology, identifies elements of wellbeing, and provides predictors of "social conditions that promote high quality development and performance" (Deci & Ryan, 2000, p. 263).

SDT establishes that human beings have an inherent orientation towards growth, adaptation and development, but also are vulnerable to amotivation and psychological ill-health when they experience unsupportive conditions (Niemiec, Ryan, & Deci, 2010, pp. 174-175). An important sub-theory of SDT is Basic Psychological Needs Theory (Vansteenkiste, Niemiec, & Soenens, 2010), which identifies the three key basic psychological needs for wellbeing as autonomy, competence and relatedness (Ryan & Deci, 2008).

Sheldon and Krieger (2007) summarise the three basic needs as follows:

> According to SDT, all human beings require regular experiences of autonomy, competence, and relatedness to thrive and maximise their positive motivation. In other words, people need to feel that they are good at what they do or at least can become good at it (competence); that they are doing what they choose and

want to be doing, that is, what they enjoy or at least believe in (autonomy); and that they are relating meaningfully to others in the process, that is, connecting with the selves of other people (relatedness). These needs are considered so fundamental that Ryan (1995) has likened them to a plant's need for sunlight, soil, and water. (p. 885)

If the three basic needs are absent from a person's life, there are adverse consequences and implications for mental health, persistence and achievement. If the needs are satisfied, however, wellbeing is supported, intrinsic motivation is satisfied and intrinsic goal setting is encouraged (Ryan & Deci, 2000).

In supporting wellbeing, the three basic needs are also relevant to the development of wellbeing's sub-elements – including resilience, self-management and agency. A resilient person has skills and attitudes that create capacity to "adapt and grow in response to adverse events" (Stallman, 2011, p. 121). Resilient people can "self-right" (Werner & Smith, 1992) and "bounce back" (Christiansen, Christiansen, & Howard, 1997) when faced with stressors or adversity (Coutu, 2002; Mandleco & Peery, 2000). Ungar (2008) argues that people with resilience experience wellbeing because they are able to navigate a range of resources, including psychological, social, cultural and physical. Seligman (2004) links resilience with high motivation, success and optimism.

A lack of resilience is associated with pessimism, depression and learned helplessness (Satterfield, Monahan, & Seligman, 1997). Resilient people are able to self-manage because they are socially competent, have good problem-solving skills, and are autonomous with a strong sense of independence and an internal locus of control. They have a positive sense of purpose and hope about the future and personal characteristics such as creative problem solving, an ability to gain positive attention, optimism in the midst of adversity and a sense of having a meaningful life. For these reasons resilient, self-managing people also experience a sense of agency.

Resilience, self-management and agency are all positive supports for practice wisdom. Conversely, practice wisdom is a positive support for wellbeing, particularly in terms of addressing the basic needs of autonomy, competence and relatedness. Practice wisdom is a form of inductive and intangible professional knowledge which is difficult to categorically define (Chu & Tsui, 2008; Samson, 2015). Elements of practice wisdom include knowledge arising out of practical experience, reflective practice (Litchfield, 1999), embodied and analytical reasoning (Chu & Tsui, 2008; O'Sullivan, 2005) and professional values (Klein & Bloom, 1995).

Practice wisdom goes beyond knowledge obtained through education and training, bringing together life experiences, belief systems and professional expertise (Higgs, 2012). Whilst intuitive, practice wisdom certainly has a foundational basis in experience, professional knowledge and theory, and reflection. DeRoos (1990) refers to the development of practice wisdom as "evolutionary epistemology" – an accumulated integration and synthesis of knowledge and ideas from multiple sources that is always in development as an influence on practice decisions.

Samson (2015) argues that practice wisdom involves "knowing-in-action" and "reflecting-in-practice" (p. 123) in order to arrive at new professional knowledge, that also assists practitioners to recognise and respond to personal and professional limitations.

Practice wisdom is a critical aspect of professional mastery and artistry because it supports discernment, good judgement and appropriate decision making. The argument of this chapter is that in the context of the stressors arising from the modern neo-liberalist society (see Giroux, 2015, 2018), wellbeing in the form of resilience, self-management and agency, will make practice wisdom possible and achievable. Practitioners who have their wellbeing supported will be better able to practise creatively, ethically and with good judgement. The relationship between practice wisdom and wellbeing works conversely as well. Practice wisdom addresses the key basic needs of autonomy, competence and relatedness because it supports the development of authentic beliefs, goals and values.

A person with practice wisdom is able to identify intrinsic professional goals and – through intrinsic motivation – is able to experience enjoyment from their professional practice. Practitioners with practice wisdom therefore have potential to practise more professionally and ethically, and they will have a deep self-understanding which can enable continuous professional development and improvement. The potential beneficial flow-on effects are manifold: positive interpersonal relationships, being better able to help others and build community; achieving honesty, integrity, cooperation, respect and altruistic behaviour in professional work.

Clearly, then, the relationship between wellbeing and practice wisdom is symbiotic. For this reason, supporting practitioners' wellbeing becomes a professional ethical imperative because practitioners who are well will be more likely to be able to develop practice wisdom. The next section discusses how a range of ethical philosophical perspectives support the imperative to promote the well-being of practitioners to enable practice wisdom.

ETHICAL PERSPECTIVES ON THE IMPERATIVE TO FOSTER PRACTITIONER WELLBEING TO ENABLE PRACTICE WISDOM

Ethical professional justifications for the promotion of practice wisdom through the support of practitioner wellbeing have not yet been explored in detail in the literature. However, as this chapter establishes, this is an area worthy of detailed exploration. There are a number of possible ways to explain and justify an ethical obligation for the promotion of practitioner wellbeing to support practice wisdom, each of them adding to the persuasiveness of a need to act on this imperative for the efficacy of contemporary professional practice.

Parker (2004) defines an ethical question as relating to "what is the good or right thing to do in particular circumstances", and to "the moral evaluation of a person's character and actions" (p. 51). In professional contexts of practice, our professional ethics provide the principles and values that regulate our moral behaviour and define our professional identity. These ethical principles guide us to ensure that, as far as possible, when faced with challenging dilemmas about what is fitting, appropriate or proper, we "do the right thing" and pursue what is just.

It is through our ethical principles that we know how we ought to act. Our ethics are therefore our bedrock benchmark of what is right and moral – foundational to what we do as professional practitioners and fundamental to the efficacy of our personal and professional identities. Practice wisdom is critical to ethical professional conduct.

The ethical question of what we should do, given what we know about the importance of practice wisdom, is evident – practice wisdom should be supported and one way to do that is through the promotion of practitioner wellbeing. It is simply fundamental that the ethical thing to do in this context, the good and right thing to do, or in other words, what we ought to do, is to act to promote practitioner wellbeing so that practice wisdom is fostered.

Why is the ethical nature of the imperative to act so clear? There are in fact numerous and diverse ethical theories, conceptual frameworks and practical ethical decision-making models that offer distinct support for this position – teleological, deontological, as well as models based in virtue and ethic of care perspectives. In addition, both the concept of a moral compass and deliberative ethical decision-making models, offer applied ethical frameworks, providing practical guidance on how ethical decisions in this context involve responsible action. The intention of the exploration in this chapter of the ethical justifications for working to promote practice wisdom through wellbeing is to establish the efficacy of the proposition by illustrating that the imperative is supported from a diverse range of ethical angles.

Philosopher Elizabeth Minnich (1994) has argued that professional responses to ethical challenges should start with the question: "What is at stake?". This consequentialist question brings ethical decision making back to a fundamental issue of impact, requiring a preliminary ethical cognitive process to inform whether or not action is called for. If practice wisdom is "what is at stake", then clearly action is needed to ensure practice wisdom is possible – and this supports the imperative to foster practitioner wellbeing.

This argument can be assisted by articulating some of the dichotomous practical realities of action as compared with inaction. That is, a choice as to whether to enable practice wisdom through the support of practitioner wellbeing – or not – could mean the difference between the capacity for practitioners to: alleviate suffering or allow suffering to occur; support fulfilled and meaningful lives, or contribute to a compromised life; prevent a death, or be complicit in failing to prevent a death; succumb to the negative impact of the broader, neo-liberalist, social contexts in which professional practice now operates, or challenge and push back against those contexts; give up and give in, or take control and empower professional practice to make a significant difference in society.

Professional practitioners are daily put in a position of making moral and ethical decisions, working in contemporary postmodern contexts which disavow binary thinking, but which can also be experienced by practitioners as increasingly polarising. Professional practice occurs within the macro globally dominant paradigm of neo-liberalism, a context that confirms the importance of engagement with the moral obligations we have as practitioners, as a way of resisting the potential injustices and de-humanising tendencies of this paradigm.

Next, this chapter briefly canvasses some of the major ethical paradigms to illustrate that each of them supports the professional imperative of fostering practitioner wellbeing to enable practice wisdom.

Deontological ethical perspectives are rule-based approaches to ethics that focus on the existence of duties, obligations and rights, and ask us to do the right thing simply because it is the right thing to do (Preston, 2007). Immanuel Kant offered one of the most influential articulations of deontological ethics as a form of absolute moral science based on rationality, consistency and logic (ibid).

In Kantian ethics, rational reasoning results in a universally applicable categorical imperative to operationalise the principle of respect for others, and to "do unto others as you would have them do to you" (ibid). According to Kant, individuals exercise their autonomous authority through their rational application of universal rules, or maxims, to dictate the ethical course of action.

A deontological approach to identifying the ethical thing to do about the issue of promoting practice wisdom through wellbeing requires us to ask what rule, arrived at rationally, with universal categorical application, and grounded in the principle of respect for persons, should we follow? The answer possibly lies in the maxim to "do no harm"; a maxim which applies to all professional practice contexts.

Practice wisdom is something that can assist practitioners to "do no harm". Therefore, it follows that enabling practice wisdom is a professional ethical imperative, and if the support of practitioner wellbeing can help to achieve this, then logically it is also an ethical imperative to support practitioner wellbeing.

Teleological ethical approaches also support this argument. Teleological ethical approaches are consequentialist ethical theories which focus on the greater good and in which the end justifies the means (Preston, 2007). Through this lens, the greater good is undoubtedly fulfilled through promoting the possibility of practice wisdom through the wellbeing of practitioners.

Further, an ethic of response adds additional weight to the position. Preston comments: "If teleology is a theory of 'the good', and deontology a theory of 'the right', then the ethics of response is one of 'the fitting'" (Preston, 2007, p. 61). An ethic of response requires

> A response to all facts relevant to a moral situation, all moral agents involved, all alternative actions available, all the possible consequences of those actions and consequences of those consequences (including whether these actions would be acceptable if they were universalisable); all this is to be interpreted within a framework of social solidarity and life's interconnectedness, after consideration of appropriate values, principles, and the character disposition of the moral agent; and then a fitting decision is made for which the responsible self remains accountable. (Preston, 2007, p. 63)

Through the lens of an ethic of response a responsibility arises to enable practice wisdom because this is professionally "fitting" and as a consequence the imperative to support practitioner wellbeing is again justified.

Intuitive ethics offer another ethical theoretical perspective that supports the imperative to enable practice wisdom through supporting practitioner wellbeing (Haidt & Joseph, 2004). Intuitive ethics see basic moral propositions as self-evident; that is, evident in and of themselves. Intuitive ethics recognise relationality, social constructedness and the connections that exist between the cognitive and emotional aspects of our daily lives.

Haidt and Joseph (2004) propose that "human beings come equipped with an intuitive ethics, an innate preparedness to feel flashes of approval or disapproval toward certain patterns of events involving other human beings" (p. 56). Acting to enable practice wisdom through this ethical lens can be seen as intuitively something that is the right thing to do because practice wisdom is such an important aspect of excellence and efficacy in practice.

Contextual ethics are an additional way of conceiving of ethical responsibilities that support the imperative to act to enable practice wisdom through the support of practitioner wellbeing (Fletcher, 1966; Morris, 1927; Niebuhr, 1963). Contextual ethical approaches connect with, and to some extent draw from, the work of the postmodern ethicists, such as Levinas (1969), Lyotard (1984) and Bauman (1993, 1995).

Contextual ethics are ethical approaches, sometimes referred to as contextualism, occasionalism, circumstantialism and actualism (Fletcher, 1966, p. 29) that are not rule-based, but that require the ethical agent to engage with, assess and take account of, the context of the situation in which a decision must be made in order to come to an ethically justifiable position, and to determine the ethically "fitting action" (ibid, p. 72). In other words, contextual ethics are about determining what is ethically appropriate and justifiable for the circumstances of a given situation (ibid). There is little doubt that enabling practice wisdom through fostering practitioner wellbeing is fitting and apt in contemporary professional practice.

In relation to understanding the imperative to promote practice wisdom through supporting practitioner wellbeing, virtue ethics is perhaps one of our most obvious guides (Macintyre, 2007). Virtue ethics helps to explain how we are motivated at a deeply personal level. This view of the issue of wellbeing emphasises virtues, or moral character, compared with emphasising duties or rules, or the consequences of actions. "Virtue ethics shifts the focus ... to the quality or character of the actor" (Parker, 2004, p. 54). A morally virtuous person appreciates the importance of practice wisdom for excellence in professional practice and thereby appreciates the importance of promoting practitioner wellbeing.

Finally, an ethic of care perspective provides further clear support for the imperative to enable practice wisdom through supporting practitioner wellbeing. Gilligan (1977, 1982) identified a feminist ethic of care in her work in the early 1980s. Through the lens of "an injunction to care", the support of practice wisdom can be seen as ethical from both the practitioner and client perspective.

That is, the relationship between practice wisdom and wellbeing indicates that it is the self-caring thing to do for practitioners to empower themselves by developing practice wisdom. In addition, where practitioners are in caring professional roles, their development of practice wisdom will enable them to better fulfil that caring role. From each of these perspectives supporting practice wisdom is the caring, compassionate, and therefore right, thing to do.

Having established the ethical imperative to support practice wisdom through fostering practitioner wellbeing, the next section turns to consider who bears the responsibility of response to this ethical imperative.

Figure 7.1. Resilience.

WELLBEING FOR PRACTICE WISDOM: WHOSE RESPONSIBILITY?

The question of who bears the responsibility of responding to the ethical imperative to support practice wisdom through fostering aspects of wellbeing such as resilience, self-management and agency has professional and political complications. Imposing an imperative on individual practitioners to ensure their own wellbeing so that practice wisdom is possible ignores the wider complex socio-political and neo-liberal context in which professional work occurs in contemporary times.

Whilst an individual practitioner may ethically acknowledge that it is the right thing to do to build their resilience, self-management skills and agency to enhance their capacity to enact practice wisdom, there is a danger that imposing the imperative on individual practitioners buys into the neo-liberal agenda of efficiency and productivity for profit-making.

Parker (2014) has asserted that there is "a danger that the wellbeing discourse will be co-opted by powerful interests that seek to confine change to the individual and not the collective social, economic and political levels" (p. 1105). Responsibility for devising ways to operate optimally in the structurally and culturally challenged context of the neo-liberal workplace should not rest with individuals. Rather, the responsibility for creating humane workplaces, in which practice wisdom is possible because practitioners are well and enabled, lies at a more macro organisational and societal level.

This is ultimately a matter for leadership, both at a political level nationally and globally, but also within the diverse professions and areas of practice. Practitioners, as human beings, deserve the support of their profession and colleagues in building capacity, both individually and collectively, to cope with the challenges of the neo-liberalist work environment; not with the intention to increase their individual productivity or profitability, but rather to enable a professional life well-lived, and professional practice for the public good. This requires the prioritisation of psychological health over economic productivity, for public policy and public education to emphasise this focus, and for professions, institutions and communities to harness their significant influence.

CONCLUSION

Recognition of the symbiotic relationship between practice wisdom and resilience, self-management and agency helps with thinking about how practice wisdom can be made possible. The wellbeing of practitioners is clearly linked to the efficacy of professional practice because wellbeing enables the achievement of practice wisdom. This chapter argues that the relationship between practice wisdom and wellbeing creates an ethical imperative for the support of the wellbeing of practitioners.

Practitioners who are well will be better able to achieve effective and excellent practice, they will be creative, discerning, have good judgement and be able to make appropriate decisions. Resilient practitioners who have self-management skills and agency will also be better able to enact practice wisdom because they will be equipped with the skills and attitudes that enable them to cope with the realities, challenges and stressors of modern neo-liberal workplaces.

A diverse range of ethical philosophical perspectives have been shown to support the imperative in practice contexts to promote the wellbeing of practitioners to enable practice wisdom. The chapter argues, however, that whilst individuals bear some responsibility to care for their own wellbeing, thus making practice wisdom possible, in fact, in the context of the current neo-liberal environment, the ethical imperative to support practice wisdom through wellbeing sits concomitantly at a more macro level with workplaces, professions, institutions and society more broadly.

REFERENCES

Bauman, Z. (1993). *Postmodern ethics*. Oxford, England: Blackwell.
Bauman, Z. (1995). *Life in fragments: Essays in postmodern moralities*. Oxford, England: Blackwell.
Christiansen, J., Christiansen, J. L., & Howard, M. (1997). Using protective factors to enhance resilience and school success for at-risk students. *Intervention in School and Clinic, 33*(2), 86.

Chu, W. C. K., & Tsui, M. S. (2008). The nature of practice wisdom in social work revisited. *International Social Work, 51*(1), 47-54.
Coutu, D. L. (2002). How resilience works. *Harvard Business Review, 80*(5), 46-55.
Deci, E. L., & Ryan, R. M. (1985). *Intrinsic motivation and self-determination in human behaviour*. New York, NY: Springer Science+Business Media.
Deci, E. L., & Ryan, R. M. (2000). The 'what' and 'why' of goal pursuits: Human needs and the self-determination of behavior. *Psychological Inquiry, 11*(4), 227-268.
DeRoos, Y. S. (1990). The development of practice wisdom through human problem-solving processes. *Social Service Review, 64*(2), 276-287.
Fletcher, J. (1966). *Situation ethics*. London, England: SCM Press Ltd.
Gilligan, C. (1977). In a different voice: Women's conceptions of self and morality. *Harvard Educational Review, 47*(4), 481-517.
Gilligan, C. (1982). *In a different voice: Psychological theory and women's development*. London, England: Harvard University Press.
Giroux, H. A. (2015). *Against the terror of neoliberalism: Politics beyond the age of greed*. New York, NY: Routledge.
Giroux, H. A. (2018). *Terror of neoliberalism: Authoritarianism and the Eclipse of Democracy*. New York, NY: Routledge.
Haidt, J., & Joseph, C. (2004). Intuitive ethics: How innately prepared intuitions generate culturally variable virtues. *Daedalus, 133*(4), 55-66.
Higgs. J. (2012). Realising practical wisdom from the pursuit of wise practice. In E. A. Kinsella & A. Pitman (Eds.), *Phronesis as professional knowledge: Practical wisdom in the professions* (pp. 73-85) Rotterdam, The Netherlands: Sense.
Klein, W. C., & Bloom, M. (1995). Practice wisdom. *Social Work, 40*(6), 799-807.
Levinas, E. (1969). *Totality and infinity: An essay on exteriority*. London, England: Kluwer.
Litchfield, M. (1999). Practice wisdom. *Advances in Nursing Science, 22*(2), 62-72.
Lyotard, J.-F. (1984). *The postmodern condition: A report on knowledge* (trans. G. Bennington & B. Massumi). Minneapolis, MN: University of Minnesota Press.
Macintyre, A. (2007). *After virtue: A study in moral theory* (3rd ed). Notre Dame, IN: University of Notre Dame Press.
Mandleco, B. L., & Peery, J. C. (2000). An organizational framework for conceptualizing resilience in children. *Journal of Child and Adolescent Psychiatric Nursing, 13*(3), 99-111.
Minnich, E. (1994). *What is at stake? Risking the pleasures of politics*. Washington, DC: Society for Values in Higher Education.
Morris, C. W. (1927). The total-situation theory of ethics. *International Journal of Ethics, 37*(3), 258-268.
Niebuhr, H. R. (1963). *The responsible self: An essay in Christian moral philosophy*. San Francisco, CA: Harper & Row.
Niemiec, C., Ryan, R., & Deci, E. (2010). Self-determination theory and the relation of autonomy to self-regulatory processes and personality development. In R. H. Hoyle (Ed.), *Handbook of personality and self-regulation* (pp. 169-191). Malden, MA: Blackwell Publishing.
O'Sullivan, T. (2005). Some theoretical propositions on the nature of practice wisdom. *Journal of Social Work, 5*(2), 221-242.
Parker, C. (2004). A critical morality for lawyers: Four approaches to lawyers' ethics. *Monash University Law Review, 30*(1), 49-74.
Parker, C. (2014). The 'moral panic' over psychological wellbeing in the legal profession: A personal or political ethical response? *UNSW Law Journal, 37*(3), 1103-1141.
Preston, N. (2007). *Understanding ethics* (3rd ed). Leichhardt, Australia: Federation Press.
Ryan, R. M., & Deci, E. L. (2000). Self-determination theory and the facilitation of intrinsic motivation, social development and well-being. *American Psychologist, 55*(1), 68-78.
Ryan, R. M., & Deci, E. L. (2008). Self-determination theory and the role of basic psychological needs in personality and the organization of behaviour. In O. P. John, R. W. Robins, & L. A. Pervin (Eds.),

Handbook of personality: Theory and research (3rd ed., pp. 654-678). New York, NY: The Guilford Press.

Samson, P. L. (2015). Practice wisdom: The art and science of social work. *Journal of Social Work Practice, 29*(2), 119-131.

Satterfield, J. M., Monahan, J., & Seligman, M. E. (1997). Law school performance predicted by explanatory style. *Behavioral Sciences & The Law, 15*(1), 95-105.

Seligman, M. E. (2004). *Authentic happiness: Using the new positive psychology to realize your potential for lasting fulfillment.* New York, NY: Simon & Schuster.

Sheldon, K. M., & Krieger, L. S. (2007). Understanding the negative effects of legal education on law students: A longitudinal test of self-determination theory. *Personality and Social Psychology Bulletin, 33*(6), 883-897.

Stallman, H. M. (2011). Embedding resilience within the tertiary curriculum: A feasibility study. *Higher Education Research & Development, 30*(2), 121-133.

Thompson, L. J., & West, D. (2013). Professional development in the contemporary educational context: Encouraging practice wisdom. *Social Work Education: The International Journal, 32*(1), 118-133.

Ungar, M. (2008). Resilience across cultures. *The British Journal of Social Work, 38*(2), 218-235.

Vansteenkiste, M., Niemiec, C. P., & Soenens, B. (2010). The development of the five mini-theories of self-determination theory: An historical overview, emerging trends, and future directions. In T. C. Urdan & S. A. Karabenick (Eds.), *The decade ahead: Theoretical perspectives on motivation and achievement* (pp. 105-165). Bingley, UK: Emerald Group Publishing Limited.

Werner, E. E., & Smith, R. S. (1992). *Overcoming the odds: High risk children from birth to adulthood.* New York, NY: Cornell University Press.

Rachael Field PhD (ORCID: https://orcid.org/0000-0003-3264-6933)
Law Faculty
Bond University, Australia

PART 2

PRACTICE WISDOM AND SOCIETY

Gathering resources together
to construct
a message
of hope
of balance
of endeavour
of shared purpose.

Enduring sentinel
Looking back
into the past
Looking forward
to future possibilities
Inviting reflection
and imagination.

Joy Higgs
Lakeside, Canada. 2017

NITA L. CHERRY

8. CONTESTED PRACTICE

Being "Wise" in an Age of Uncertainty

Between them, science and technology have allowed people to experience relatively high levels of agency in dealing with the world. Techno-rationalism and evidence-based practice have served enterprise and government in getting things done. Being an *expert* means being credentialed *and* being able to participate effectively in the projects of enterprise and government. But rapidly changing contexts challenge us to look again at our understandings of wise and responsible professional practice. Paradoxical and unresolvable issues are created by multiple and diverse stakeholders. Public and academic authority are also increasingly challenged by social media, the contesting of facts and claims of "false news". Uncertainty abounds.

Commentators have offered stimulating descriptions of emergent practice complexity, framing it as fuzzy and ambiguous, a fertile but potentially dangerous *terrain vague* (van Schaik, 1999) informed by troublesome knowledge that generates serious new problems in the process of solving existing ones. *Wicked problems* produce dilemmas that emerge only when we try to engage with them, when trying to *do* something useful triggers unexpected and unwanted consequences. There can be serious consequences whether one takes further action or no action at all.

Briggs (2007) argues that intractable wicked problems are now so commonplace that they are accepted as inevitable, characterised by chronic failure of government policy and by decades of academic failure to appropriately explore them. But while the "death of truth" might be accepted by some politicians, philosophers and academics, the sheer scope and scale of social media suggest that many people remain furiously attached to particular views of how the world works and how we should deal with its problems. As Stacey (2012) has observed, uncertainty is just as likely to produce rigid thinking, divisive morality and rage, as it is to produce learned helplessness and resignation. These outcomes could make practitioners struggle to accept accountability for even trying to engage with uncertainty and complexity.

In this context, what does it mean to be a wise practitioner? What is the responsibility that professional practitioners have in trying to be effective and helpful? And how is wise and responsible practice to be developed and sustained in the face of both public cynicism and aggressive social commentary? This chapter explores how professional practitioners might examine the ways in which their own sense of wise and responsible practice is being tested, and dimensions of wise *being* and *becoming* that they can cultivate.

© KONINKLIJKE BRILL NV, LEIDEN, 2019 | DOI: 9789004410497_008

THE DIMENSIONS OF PRACTICE UNDER CONDITIONS OF UNCERTAINTY

Over the last three decades, the conceptual framing of geo-political, social, economic and technological issues as complex has been developing more momentum. Peters (1990) predicted that organisations, as practice environments, would resemble a "floating crap game" of projects embedded amid multiple and ambiguous networks. This thinking resonates with Bauman's (1992) framing of a *liquid modernity*, suggesting several dimensions of modern uncertainty that follow when economies are globalised, privatised, deregulated and mobile. One is the speed with which many social structures that appear to be entrenched and enduring can "decompose and melt faster than the time it takes to cast them" (Bauman, 2000, p. 1). Seemingly strong borders become penetrable, as when information considered secure to high standards of commercial and military integrity is regularly hacked. Bauman also described rapid shape-shifting, such as capital raising that trashes currencies and assets overnight, triggering boom and bust cycles. As a result, national governments struggle to protect citizens and workers from dynamics that impact their jobs, assets and standard of living. In theory, individuals are free to make choices but this freedom is not matched by their capacity to understand and live with the decisions they make. Even so, they must accept responsibility for them. This has significant moral as well as practical consequences:

> The ethical paradox of the postmodern condition is that it restores to agents the fullness of moral choice and responsibility while simultaneously depriving them of the comfort of the universal guidance that self-confidence once promised. (Bauman, 1992, p. xxii)

Bauman (2007) also described the replacement of long-term thinking with "swift and thorough forgetting" (p. 3); the undermining of stable interpersonal connections and social capital; avoidance of accountability by both government and corporations; diminishing human agency; and lack of transparency in power and control dynamics.

> What is valued today ... is the ability to be on the move, to travel light and at short notice. Power is measured by the speed with which responsibilities can be escaped ... Power is increasingly mobile, slippery, shifty, evasive, and fugitive. (Bauman, 2000, p. 14)

This fluid and rapid cycle of stabilising and de-stabilising, of construction and re-construction, discourages attachment to anything and continually questions notions of commitment and trust. This applies as much to professional practitioners as anyone else. Contemporary dynamics of both traditional and social media reflect that nothing is sacred, that *everything* can be either defended or discredited, that *fake news* is one of the catch cries of the day and that *the truth of the matter* is infinitely malleable. The paradox paradigm (Lewis, 2000) now frames human experience as inherently involving unresolvable tensions. Barnett (2012) suggest an even more uncompromising practice world of super-complexity that is essentially unknowable. Contentions that problem solving creates problems, that troublesome knowledge produces uncertainty, that both professional and life practice are essentially paradoxical and unresolvable, and that super-complexity renders the practice world unknowable, collectively presents serious provocations for wisdom and responsibility in contemporary practice. So how is the practice world responding?

BEING PROFESSIONALLY "WISE" AND RESPONSIBLE IN A CONTESTED WORLD

Human beings often have limited tolerance for dilemmas that can't be resolved through decisive intervention. Instead, we often prefer to simplify the complexities of *what* and *how*, retreating to strongly held ideological positions, emotional indignation and high moral ground when the *what* is elusive, and clinging strenuously to rules, technical prescriptions and existing logic when the *how* is unclear (Stacey, 2012). But emergent and unresolvable issues don't go away, coming back to confront us, sometimes when and where we least expect. This produces its own anxieties, the projection of fears onto others, blaming and anger, on the one hand, or entrenched cynicism, apathy and helplessness, on the other.

Practice communities dealing regularly with disaster and distress develop shared ways of limiting anxiety when even the best care and technique can't make things better. For example, police and nursing cultures have characteristic ways of dealing with unconscious anxiety in the face of complexity. Pervasive use of the *managerial calculus* (Evans, 2010) in modern organisational life also provides a powerful way of engaging with contemporary uncertainties. The calculus works by providing detailed descriptions of problems and opportunities. Wise and responsible practice comes down to serious calculation of risk on behalf of those who own and invest resources. The calculus is essential in assessing situations, planning and executing action, and defending those diagnoses and actions if they go wrong.

Evans (2010) argued that it is now impossible to imagine organisations – and therefore professional practice – without the managerial calculus. It underpins global practices of decision making and governance in almost every area of collective human effort, extending beyond business to public administration, health services, the arts, sports and the non-profit sector. Its success rests on widely shared understanding and expectations of managerial and professional practices that can be rationally explained and defended, no matter where or when, and irrespective of who happens to be involved. Wise and responsible practice, in this scenario, invites individuals to participate in a continuous negotiation of what should be done, between people from different professional and cultural backgrounds, in ways they can all understand. This has had profound implications for the ways in which we conceive of skilled professional practice. Wilensky (1964) saw the writing on the wall when he pronounced that in modern organisations "everyone is a professional".

To participate in the calculus, practitioners must possess the intellectual skills to turn data into workable options and undertake ongoing risk management. They must also be able to communicate with multiple stakeholders and colleagues across the room and across the globe. Thanks to the global proliferation of business schools over the past 60 years, a homogenised universal language of organisational practice now exists. Its success in shaping dominant modern organisational processes is one of the great modern academic successes. It is certainly a very powerful form of the enactment of wisdom and responsibility. At its very best, the calculus provides an organised and speedy way of mobilising thinking from all around the world.

The calculus also has serious implications for professional agency and influence. More and more people participate in the assessment of what can and should be done. But individual practitioners cannot expect an automatic right to be heard on the grounds of their qualifications and expertise alone. Professional wisdom involves sustained enactment with many other players. Linehan and Kavanagh (2006) have noted that even the more benign language of *communities of practice* and *collegiate learning* can't disguise the potential for dumbing down of professional practice and responsibility in these contexts, as the actors learn to play the game, withdrawing from risk, resisting change and becoming marginalised.

Other aspects of modern organisation also undermine individual and collective agency: boundary-less careers, temporary and casual jobs, and virtual teams (Kotter, 1995). Gabriel (2002) invokes the "glass cage in which many people work, where external surveillance combines with continual self-surveillance and discipline, through total exposure to the eye of the customer, the fellow employee, the manager" (p. 176). A continually *becoming* professional self, routinely scrutinised by self and others, becomes *fragile*, to use Gabriel's term, or even *corroded*: a "pliant self, a collage of fragments unceasing in its becoming, ever open to new experience ... these are just the psychological conditions suited to short-term work experience, flexible institutions and constant risk-taking" (Sennett, 1998, p. 133).

The speed and reach of social media exacerbate these dynamics. Their power in building identities of convenience for self and others, then destroying them, extends from cyber-bullying through to constant questioning of professional credibility. A boundary-less world means the professional self becomes a site for endless negotiation that can progress over months or overnight. These media don't force us to re-think the context of practice alone, but also what individual or collective practices actually represent. The challenges presented to practitioners and educators who seek to be *wise* and *responsible* in their practice are especially poignant.

WISDOM AND LEARNING AS COMPLEX PRACTICE:
THE CALL FOR PEDAGOGIES OF LIQUIDITY, BEING AND BECOMING

These perspectives undermine many of the stable and generalisable mappings previously assumed (Lineham & Kavanagh, 2006). Barnett's (2012) assertion of the world as essentiality unknowable kicks away a solid viewing platform from which to observe the flow. In a liquid world, the effective agency of individuals, organisations and nations is seriously compromised. For some thinkers, mastery, wisdom and accountability are illusions and the individual disappears altogether. Even the managerial calculus can struggle in this context, oversimplifying public messages about what is possible and creating distorted expectations about what organisations will actually take responsibility for when circumstances change. Organisations look substantial, trustworthy and wise, right up to the moment they fail, when their identity, assets, accountabilities and liabilities become liquid and blurred. Most public commentary blames government and corporations for failures of regulation and governance, while others point to more shadowy agents, less easily named and shamed. Some have noted the failure of business schools to anticipate the Global Financial Crisis, arguably one of the greatest manifestations of a lack of *knowing* recently.

But while daunting at first glance, the implications of a volatile, uncertain and even unknowable modernity suggest exciting opportunities for transformations in how we understand and enact wise and responsible practice. For many, these provocations have been a clarion call to avoid simplification and denial, and to explicitly acknowledge the uncertain and unresolvable nature of many issues. Barnett has been even more emphatic, inviting practitioners and educators to reclaim and refresh their professional agency, wisdom and responsibility through direct and deliberate engagement with the existential dilemmas for learning, practising and educating that are posed by uncertainty:

> Under these conditions of uncertainty, *the educational task is, in principle, not an epistemological task*; it is not one of knowledge or even knowing per se. It is not even one of action, of right and effective interventions in the world. For what is to count as a right or an effective intervention in the world? Amid super-complexity, *the educational task is primarily an ontological task*. It is the task of enabling individuals to prosper ... amid a situation in which there are no stable descriptions of the world, no concepts that can be seized upon with any assuredness, and no value systems that can claim one's allegiance with any unrivalled authority. This is a curricular and pedagogical challenge that understands, therefore, that terms such as 'fragility', 'uncertainty' and 'instability' are as much ontological terms as they are epistemological terms. Accordingly, this learning for uncertainty is here a matter of learning to live with uncertainty. (Barnett, 2012, p. 69, italics in original)

A range of nuanced ways of understanding and engaging with the challenges of contemporary uncertainty and complexity have emerged. These are based on explorations of the ways in which things become problematic in the first place. The emerging complexity literatures differentiates *first and second order complexity*: that is, the properties of the system under study as compared with the way we experience, construct and represent that complexity as human beings. This distinction goes to the heart of the ontological debates between objectivist, subjectivist and radical understandings, and for the ways in which they frame agency and wisdom. There have been several significant shifts in ontological thinking about human agency and practice. The *practice* turn, *discursive* turn, *paradoxical* turn, *transdisciplinary* turn, and *virtual* turn have all provided stimulating ways of engaging with uncertainty. Significant agency is created by understanding that how we frame issues and what we do about them, are inextricably *part of* those issues.

In a masterful summary of the *practice* turn, Schatzki (1996) cites the contention of philosophical thinkers like Wittgenstein (1958), that practices underlie both subjects and objects, and transcend rigid, action-structured oppositional thinking. Cultural theorists referred to *practices* in order to depict language as discursive activity, in opposition to structuralist and poststructuralist conceptions of language.

These were important contributions that radically questioned the idea of individual action and agency and their status as building-blocks of social phenomena.

While taking several paths, influenced by several lines of ontological thinking, the *discursive* turn is a distinctive paradigm focused on the performativity of language (Bozatzis, 2014). Like other turns, it has implications for ways of understanding the dynamics of practice wisdom and responsibility. The cognitive view that language is a precursor to action is replaced with the notion that language *is* action, constructive rather than representative. The longstanding position that it takes experience and practice to recognise and engage with opportunities for innovation is turned upside down: such opportunities are thought to emerge through experience and practice, not the other way around (Schatzki, 1996).

The *paradoxical* turn (Lewis, 2000) questions "either-or" ways of understanding things that oversimplify the dynamics of practice. Dilemmas suggest that the risks and consequences of choices can be separated, calculated and managed. Paradoxes, on the other hand, pose dynamics that are contradictory, interdependent, self-reinforcing and perpetual. Action inevitably triggers opposing reactions, just as making a choice resolves nothing. Paradoxical tensions are inevitably created when human beings attempt to mobilise collective energy and skills to get things done. Smith and Lewis (2011) suggest that the paradox perspective operates at the level of meta-theory or paradigm, and contrast it with the contingency paradigm so dominant in management disciplines. The Taoist symbol of yin and yang captures the essence of paradox: boundaries don't just include some things and exclude others; rather, what is included is defined by what is excluded.

Some fundamental and recurring paradoxes are suggested. *Paradoxes of learning* can occur when past practice wisdom is challenged. When the familiar needs to be left behind, the familiar fights back: the more things change, the more they stay the same. Wisdom that was a source of strength in the past can limit fresh engagement with the new. *Paradoxes of organising* involve the contradictions of encouraging trust, empowerment, commitment and creativity while maintaining control, efficiency, discipline and order. The dynamics of this paradox produce Foucault's (1977) panopticon: practices that make visibility a means of control, producing compliant and docile populations. Lineham and Kavanagh (2006) note the paradoxical commitment to preserving human rights, safety and privacy through regulations, protocols and relentless tracking through electronic surveillance. *Paradoxes of belonging* highlight tensions inherent in a group becoming cohesive, influential and distinctive while maintaining separate identities, values, roles and worth. This last is essentially the paradoxical challenge created through the managerial calculus, as it makes everyone a professional and simultaneously undermines individual agency and responsibility. The fundamental connections between mutually reinforcing cycles are not easy to recognise, the key indicators being separated in time and space. Skilled practitioners might believe they are dealing with contingencies of specific situations that call for discerning assessment of the pros and cons of certain actions, unaware that whatever they do, they are likely to add to the problem. Awareness of paradoxes opens up different options.

The *transdisciplinary turn* encourages multiple and blended disciplinary perspectives, and the use of macro, meso and micro analyses. One of these is the capability of modern neuroscience to map many aspects of human awareness, sense-making and behaviour. Others have revived interest in older ways of understanding human behaviour such as psychodynamic theory, which painted a vivid picture of unconscious battles playing out to defend people from the flood of anxiety that would otherwise overwhelm them if their true vulnerability were to be fully realised.

Meanwhile, the *virtual turn* (Savin-Baden, 2007) asks how digital practices, including social media, challenge existing theories of identity (actual and virtual personalities) and practice (plugging individuals into virtual worlds and plugging others into *them*). Schön (1987) recommended *virtual worlds* as contexts for experiments in which usual blocks to reflection recede. He cited hand-drawn architectural sketches that reveal dimensions that could not have been imagined until the pen engaged. However, the distinction between the imagined world of Schön's era and the world of social media which constructs and entraps, creates and destroys, is very clear. The capacity for *accurate rehearsal* and *experimentation with the possible* have very different meanings now. Privacy and safety in any online environment cannot be guaranteed. Its riskiness, however, is what makes it fertile.

There are many other intellectual, aesthetic and spiritual disciplines that try to fully engage with the frailty and uncertainty of human life, with its intrinsically unresolvable dimensions. Any one of the perspectives mentioned here offers profoundly interesting possibilities for our understanding of wise and responsible practice. All of them reinforce Barnett's (2012) fundamental question for practitioners: what *is* the ontological premise on which your practice thinking and intervention is based? Wisdom and responsibility involve consideration of how particular ontologies are privileged, what we are attached to, and what our frames make figural, marginal, normal, problematic: a joke, a disaster, a storm in a teacup (Lineham & Kavanagh, 2006). As a result, living and practising wisely and responsibly in a state of uncertainty require ontological humbleness, acknowledgement of the possibilities opened up and those ignored. That means living with the idea that everything we think we know about ourselves and the world is contestable. But, central to this chapter, it *does not* mean living without confidence in personal and collective agency and accountability. How, then, is the capacity and confidence to act wisely and responsibly reclaimed and enacted? Barnett (2012) has suggested that this reclamation requires a state of *being-for-uncertainty*, based in human dispositions of carefulness, humility, criticality, receptiveness, thoughtfulness, courage and stillness. His notion of *learning in-and-with-uncertainty* requires people to thrive in situations where there are deeply contested value systems.

PRACTICE OF PRACTICE: FRAMING AGENCY IN PRACTICE AND EDUCATION

The quest is for practices for engaging with uncertainty and complexity without dumbing them down. Many pitfalls are implied in this endeavour. Indeed, when it comes to learning, a liquid modernity challenges many understandings of what education is and what it can achieve.

present-day challenges deliver heavy blows to the very essence of the idea of education ... they put in question the invariants of the idea, the constitutive features of education that have thus far withstood all the past challenges ... (Bauman, 2003, p. 19)

Obvious questions arise. How does one prepare and educate for an unknowable future? Can uncertainty be engaged with only in terms of situated local practice? If mastery is defined in local or individual terms, what happens to the idea of wisdom that can be generalised, or helpful to others? And what sort of practices are sustainable in the face of the vulnerability entailed in being-for-uncertainty? As noted, Gabriel (2002) has described the tensions to which the continually re-negotiated, *continually becoming self* is subject, and the resulting fragility and corrosion of personal and professional identity.

The idea of the *practice of practice* (van Schaik, 2003) opens up interesting possibilities for exploring wisdom and responsibility in the light of these questions. This is a multi-layered idea, used in music to convey that mastery requires insightful and skilled approaches to practising for performance, beyond repetition. It is also familiar in the development of performance in sport, where disciplines like interval training are continually reviewed and refined by specialists. And in professions that have taken up the work of reflective practice.

Schön (1987) suggested that many skilled professional behaviours cannot be taught. Wise practice is not just the application of technical prescriptions, or about one person simply handing to another a blueprint or vision of effective performance. The vision – if it exists – is often difficult to articulate, let alone to share or prescribe. Practice is about crafting something which emerges gradually, is enacted, supported by disciplined *reflection*. Schön's examples were the masterclass in musical performance and the architectural studio. They illustrate the deep *attention* paid to what is being done, and the skilled facilitation that helps to turn the intrinsic uncertainty of the process into a source of energy and joy. Architecture and design not only illustrate this but add the dynamics of *paradox*. Their key challenge is to resolve the conflicting and contradictory requirements of the things we use and our life and work spaces. We mostly want these things to be functional, safe, sustainable in their manufacture and use, as well as affordable and aesthetically pleasing. To *resolve* these issues in a wise, masterful way is not to fall into easy polarisation, to prioritise one thing over another or to compromise, but to find a robust way to hold conflicting expectations and physical parameters in permanent tension.

The practice-of-practice embodies and embraces paradox and uncertainty. In design terms, it acknowledges the skills we develop as individuals simply do to make ourselves "comfortable" (which might include resourceful bricolage in its most basic forms), and at the same time entertains the possibility that our efforts might be useful to others in different circumstances. Universal uncertainties that are tackled locally can create *microcosms of knowledge* and wise practice (Linehan & Kavanagh, 2006) arising through individual or small group experience. Indeed, the practice-of-practice can be thought of as *paradoxical practice* in its own right. Lewis (2000) has paid attention to dynamics of engagement and learning that both *empower* people and at the same time *render them ontologically humble and emotionally vulnerable*.

This is consistent with the Jungian view that only paradox comes anywhere near to comprehending the fullness of life and work, enabling deeper awareness of one's being and creating generative spaces for becoming (Schneider, 1990). The famous paradox of change embedded in the gestalt tradition of learning and therapy asserts that only when I fully encounter things as they are and myself as I am, can I change. The gestalt view is that full appreciation and contact with what currently is, immediately triggers the energy for movement towards what might be.

Kelly's (1970) *personal construct* theory also exemplifies the paradoxical dynamics of the practice-of-practice. Kelly's contention was that complete understanding can only be accomplished by engaging with opposites. The starkest universal example of this is the existential paradox that *being alive* can only be fully appreciated if we allow ourselves to contemplate its opposite: *non-being*. Seen paradoxically, *loneliness* is experienced individually in many different ways: physical isolation, feeling invisible in a crowd or not having a lover. To *resolve* loneliness can mean very different things. The same principle is in play in Lewis and Dehler's (2000) assertion that the way to challenge an existing either/or mindset is "immersion with the extremes" (p. 712), not to synthesise those extremes but to identify and hold their antithetical qualities. Most of us would have seen the figure and ground conundrum that presents us with an image that alternates the faces of an older and younger woman. The point is not to merge them but to see both clearly.

Taken together, these dimensions and possibilities of the practice-of-practice offer much but also demand much. The ambiguous, volatile, paradoxical, unknowable, wicked and unresolvable, can represent challenges that can be unbearable. Taking action can create or contribute to a wicked problem, with serious consequences whether one takes further action or no action at all, leaving practitioners to struggle with the ethical and moral dimensions of engagement, as well as the emotional, spiritual, analytical and operational ones. Denial, simplification, rigid logic, righteous indignation, helplessness, apathy and withdrawal, in all the forms they can take in professional practice, are understandable. For individuals, direct experience of uncertainty can be extremely uncomfortable: issues that seemed manageable when kept apart can become absurd and irrational when experienced together. Modern organisation mostly serves to maintain boundaries, but when boundaries become fuzzy and permeable, psychodynamic anxiety that is usually suppressed can be painfully visible in sudden episodes of emotional breaching or extended bouts of depression and withdrawal.

Any sustainable practice-of-practice must employ practical ways to cope with the patterns of behaviour that both practitioners – and those who help them – can readily default to under pressure. Fortunately, there are many powerful and delightful examples in the literature. They include *holistic understandings of reflexivity* based on radical reflexive phenomenology (Bleakley, 1999); *appreciative and humorous post-modernism;* of *scaffolding (hanging over the precipice in a harness)*; the creative energies of *liminal spaces and marginalia*; the possibilities of *story* and *enactment*; and even an explicit *pedagogy for paradox* (Lewis & Delher, 2000). Bleakley (1999) has offered rich ontologically based perspectives on the business of reflective practice, meeting in advance the challenge laid down years later by

Barnett. His contribution is outlined in some depth here because it is a masterful example of how notions of agency, and possibilities for wisdom and responsibility, can be enriched, rather than undermined. He explored how the development of reflective practices have been dominated by a number of the great ontological paradigms. He argued that reflective practice has been hijacked by *techno-rational thinking* and appropriated by human resources departments. When reflective practice is understood as a desirable functional competence, it becomes a:

> technical-rational way of learning, with its developmental programs, progressivism, stages, steps, skills and knowledge hierarchies, spiral curricula, and overarching dogma that one must always proceed from the simple to the complex. Such developmental-ism denies the value of suffering the complex right from the start, perhaps relishing open-endedness, chaos, or unpredictability in learning, and valuing its ambiguities, paradoxes and twists. (Bleakley, 1999, p. 318)

In the *humanistic* paradigm, reflection has been framed as a critical stance on the status quo, and therefore a means of emancipation, autonomy and empowerment. Bleakley had a fundamental objection to this position, citing the dangers when reflection becomes a narcissistic cultural obsession with self:

> thanks to our Cartesian legacy, [we] see reflectivity as an introspective bending in, to review mental life ... Where reflection becomes a purely cognitive event – a fundamental mode of increasing or raising consciousness – this denies its grounding in sense, intuition and passion. As we get more sophisticated with this narcissistic pondering, so we may be less sensitive to the world around us, anaesthetised to other species, to deteriorating environments and ... to the needs of others – less able to discriminate and tolerate 'otherness' and 'difference'. (Bleakley, 1999, pp. 320–321)

Postmodern perspectives also questioned liberal humanism, but from a different position. Postmodernism sees personhood and subjectivity as being culturally constituted, and meaning as being constructed linguistically. Seen in this way, liberal humanism transforms recognisable outer control by external authorities into something more subtly insidious: self-control, made dangerous because it takes the form of self-surveillance and self-discipline while posing as emancipatory self-development (Foucault, 1977):

> Normative ... procedures formalised in the outer social and cultural life are reproduced in psychological life as a regulative self-discipline, thus paradoxically maintaining the status quo through a different set of discursive practices ... (Bleakley, 1999, p. 320)

The problem is that postmodernism directly challenges the idea that self-hood, as usually experienced, involves personal agency and responsibility. To be wise and responsible on its terms is very challenging, Bleakley points out. We are asked to question our whole experience of ourselves as autonomous identities capable of purely personal agency, and to deconstruct the social and cultural process through which our subjective experience of ourselves as a *self* is constructed. It requires the capacity to *think against* one's self: to go beyond the personal and question the very conditions under which our particular notions of identity, autonomy, personal agency and responsibility have developed within a particular culture. Ultimately, Bleakley himself proposed *holistic reflexive practices* that aren't limited or lost in the privileging of language as the primary means of sense-making, nor absorbed by an essentially human-centric preoccupation. This moved him to an ontology of radical phenomenology, a view in which the agency and responsibility of the individual does not disappear but is not narcissistic, either. Rather, our own selves are *presenced into being* through interaction with things, a formulation in which reflection is not detached thought but rather a "critical, reflexive, ethical, aesthetic act of participation in the world, and one which is ecological, or sensitive to difference" (Bleakley, 1999, p. 328). In this way, Bleakley reclaimed the notion of agency in the ontological and existential terms demanded by Barnett (2012). Bleakley saw the practice-of practice not simply as an act of personal agency *on a world* (emancipatory empowerment), nor just as *world-making* through cultural construction and thinking against oneself (postmodern deconstructivism), but thinking with the world. It is a state of engaged agency with an outside-in, rather than an inside-out, focus:

> Importantly, the reflective act can then be framed as a sensitivity ... an aesthetic event rather than a functional or technical adjustment ... This would give further meaning to Schön's notion of 'professional artistry' – it is not just a 'doing' but a 'being', an apprehension' ... a play of sensitivity within a habitat, based on immediacy ... It is ... a mode of being grounded in passion and body rather than cognition and mind, with an outside-in, rather than inside-out, focus. Primarily it is eco-logical, rather than ego-logical: worldly rather than personal ... reflection as action may be described as a thinking with the world, as an engaged agency. (Bleakley, 1999, pp. 323–324)

Bleakley offered the concept of *reflection-as-action*, enriching Schön's notions of *reflection-on-action* and *reflection-in-action*. Reflection, he suggests, "needs body, passion, sensitivity to context, and, above all, begs for style ... a 'hands-on' business, rooted in the immediacy and heat of practice, the sticky moment of indecision, feeding on sudden shifts in circumstances" (Bleakley, 1999, p. 319). Together these notions of the practice-of-practice and holistic reflexivity are invigorating, enriching our conceptualisation of possibilities for practice wisdom.

PRACTICES AND PEDAGOGIES OF BEING AND BECOMING

Bleakley's account of reflexive practices in terms of agency is echoed in the work of Cunliffe (2002) who has argued that "critical approaches often dehumanise and disempower people by viewing them as occupants of discursive space, or products of systems of control" (pp. 40–41). She suggests that between tacit knowing and explicit knowledge is what she describes as "muddy water". She highlights the moment in which we are *struck*, when things don't add up, or we suddenly realise we are out of our depth, in a lonely or excitingly different place. In this moment of being struck, wise and responsible practice-of-practice doesn't mean walking away, but jumping in to explore new possibilities, to make connections between tacit and explicit knowing. and to engage with problem framing rather than problem solving.

Lewis (2000) offers further insights into how wise and responsible professional agency might be enacted in the face of uncertainty. As a first step, people need to be able to recognise when paradoxical dynamics are in play. She has offered a number of suggestions as to how paradoxes can be conceptually "located and bracketed" (p. 771) drawing on narrative, psychodynamic and multi-paradigm perspectives. The objective in using these approaches is to help people *read* complexity, to see everyday life differently, notice contradictions and surface conflicting views, stories and feelings. By "critiquing oversimplified explanations and taken-for-granted, often nonsensical, conventions, students can be inspired to seek and accommodate opposing views, to creatively make sense of contradictions by transcending either/or logic and overcoming fears of sounding absurd" (Lewis, 2000). And in gestalt terms, *contact* with what *is* creates energy for creating *what can be*.

Agreeing that "the underlying aspects of daily work are rich with clues to cultural meaning and processes of sustaining social construction" (Hatch & Ehrlich, 1993, p. 251), Lewis suggests techniques borrowed from *narrative* analysis, such as using humour and irony as signs of paradox, which would otherwise be difficult to articulate. Humour helps to expose conflicting emotions, and the *duplicity of meaning* from which paradoxes arise, such as the example that "accepting a position as a guard makes one a prisoner" of a larger system (Hatch & Ehrlich, 1993, p. 517). *Multi-paradigm* approaches explicitly ask people to adopt different lenses to view a situation. Such lenses, Lewis suggests, can be contradictory, fragmentary or integrative, surfacing contradictions in ways that can be absurd, weird and fascinating. Lewis also draws on *psychodynamic* approaches, suggesting imagery techniques (drawing, mapping); construction of artefacts, modelling; and enactment (performance, role-play, psychodrama) that offer pathways to catching what is subtle, tacit, latent, interrupted, denied or absent from talk.

Usually people try to ignore, trivialise or rationalise the discomfort of paradox. This might work for some time, but ultimately makes things worse as tensions fester, sometimes producing dramatic eruptions in anger, blame and denial, or, in contrast, helplessness and withdrawal. So there is intrinsic paradox in educating for paradox: it involves intentionally creating some level of uncertainty and confusion, while maintaining sufficient comfort for learning to be possible. Lewis and Dehler (2000) developed a *pedagogy for ambiguity and paradox* which fosters this creative tension. People are supported to recognise the paradox for what it is, then to engage with the tension rather than struggle against it. Explorations might be gradual and even playful, drawing on the three approaches already mentioned. Randall and McKim (2008) suggest appreciative rather than de-constructive postmodernism, in which humorous and ironical playfulness allow the construction of alternative stories of our lives and professional practices. Others have tackled this challenge, suggesting ways for educators and mentors to work with their own anxieties, defences and need to control what is happening. Barrett's (1998) framing of the *Paradox Mind-Set* asks educators to be open, sceptical, contrary, para-logical, imaginative and courageous, as they encourage students to do likewise. But this is easier said than done, and "it takes nerve not to flinch from or be crushed by the sight of one's shadow, and it takes courage to accept responsibility for one's inferior self" (Whitmont, 1991, p. 15).

This realisation has prompted ideas about *holding environments, provisional resting places* and *scaffolding* which protect us while still allowing us to engage in the midst of what puzzles, enrages or scares us. Holding environments and provisional resting places can be deliberately created apart from, or right in the midst of, action. They can often be articulated and enacted as a collective responsibility, as when a facilitator asks a group to ensure that all voices are listened to. Provisional resting places allow people to immerse themselves in a particular set of assumptions or ways of framing things, while knowing full well that it is a temporary state of affairs. Serious play and humour can offer comfort and create energy in the midst of uncertainty and risk. Creating and occupying liminal and marginal spaces (Higgs, 2016) also facilitate immersion in alternative ways of thinking, acting and feeling.

If, paradoxically, possibilities are revealed even as we discover and realise what *is*, the recognition of possibility can emerge through sharing vivid stories of practice, sensitively searching for weak signals, experimenting on a small scale and bricolage. Experimentation and improvisation entail getting the *feel* of things, using *enactment* as a way of rediscovering professional agency. This can range from role-playing and simulations to hearing your own voice and appreciating *your self* as conveyed through your voice. These approaches resonate with Schön and Bleakley's sense of the importance of *immersion* and *attending*.

By way of conclusion to this section and to the entire chapter, the intention has been to share pathways for turning uncertainty into a source of energy, confidence and delight, as well as of wisdom and responsibility. We live in times that demand that we all find such pathways.

REFERENCES

Barnett, R. (2012). Learning for an unknown future. *Higher Education Research & Development, 31*(1), 65-77.
Barrett, D. (1998). *The paradox process: Creative business solutions where you least expect to find them.* New York, NY: AMACOM.
Bauman, Z. (1992). *Intimations of postmodernity.* London, England: Routledge & Kegan Paul.
Bauman, Z. (2000). *Liquid modernity.* Cambridge, England: Polity Press.
Bauman, Z. (2003). *Liquid love.* Cambridge, England: Polity Press.
Bauman, Z. (2005). Education in liquid modernity. *Review of Education, Pedagogy and Cultural Studies, 27*(4), 303-317.
Bauman, Z. (2007). *Liquid times: Living in an age of uncertainty.* Cambridge, England: Polity Press.
Bleakley, A. (1999). From reflective practice to holistic reflexivity. *Studies in Higher Education, 24*(3), 315-330.
Bozatzis, N. (2014). Introduction. In N. Bozatzis & T. Dragonas (Eds.), *The discursive turn in social psychology* (pp. 15-24). Chagrin Falls, OH: Taos Institute Publications.
Briggs, L. (2007). *Tackling wicked problems: A public policy perspective.* Canberra, Australia: Australian Public Service Commission. Retrieved from https://www.apsc.gov.au/tackling-wicked-problems-public-policy-perspective
Cunliffe, A. L. (2002). Reflexive dialogical practice in management learning. *Management Learning, 33*(1), 35-61.

Evans, T. (2010). *Professional discretion in welfare services: Beyond street level bureaucracy*. Surrey, England: Ashgate.

Foucault, M. (1977). *Discipline and punish: The birth of the prison*. Harmondsworth, England: Penguin.

Gabriel, Y. (2002). Glass palaces and glass cages: Organisations in times of flexible work, fragmented consumption and fragile selves. *Ephemera, 3*(5), 16-84.

Hatch, M. J., & Ehrlich, S. B. (1993). Spontaneous humour as an indicator of paradox and ambiguity in organizations. *Organization Studies, 14*(4), 505-526.

Higgs, J. (2016). Marginalia and core discourse: Shaping discourse and practice. In J. Higgs & F. Trede (Eds.), *Professional practice discourse marginalia* (pp. 17-26). Rotterdam, The Netherlands: Sense.

Kelly, G. A. (1970). A brief introduction to personal construct psychology. In D. Bannister (Ed.), *Perspectives in personal construct psychology* (pp. 1-30). San Diego, CA: Academic Press.

Kotter, J. (1995). Leading change: Why transformation efforts fail. *Harvard Business Review, 73*(2), 59-67.

Lewis, M. W. (2000). Exploring paradox: Toward a more comprehensive guide. *Academy of Management Review, 25*(4), 760-776.

Lewis, M. W., & Dehler, G. E. (2000). Learning through paradox: A pedagogical strategy for exploring contradictions and complexity. *Journal of Management Education, 24*(6), 708-725.

Linehan, C., & Kavanagh, D. (2006) From project ontologies to communities of virtue. In D. Hodgson & S. Cicmil (Eds.), *Making projects critical* (pp. 51-67). Houndsmill, England: Palgrave Macmillan.

Peters, T. (1990). Prometheus barely unbound. *Academy of Management Executive, 4*(4),70-84.

Randall, W. L., & McKim, A. E. (2008). *Reading our lives: The poetics of growing old*. New York, NY: Oxford University Press.

Savin-Baden, M. (2007, March). *Second life PBL: Liminality, liquidity and lurking*. Keynote address presented at the Reinventing Problem-Based Learning Conference, Republic Polytechnic, Singapore.

Schatzki, T. R. (1996). *Social practices: A Wittgensteinian approach to human activity and the social*. Cambridge, England: Cambridge University Press.

Schneider, K. J. (1990). *The paradoxical self: Toward understanding of our contradictory nature*. New York, NY: Insight Books.

Schön, D. A. (1987). *Educating the reflective practitioner*. San Francisco, CA: Jossey-Bass.

Sennett, R. (1998). *The corrosion of character: The personal consequences of work in the new capitalism*. London, England: W.W. Norton.

Smith, W. K., & Lewis, M. W. (2011). Toward a theory of paradox: A dynamic equilibrium model of organizing. *Academy of Management Review, 36*(2), 381-403.

Stacey, R. (2012). *The tools and techniques of leadership and management: Meeting the challenge of complexity*. London, England: Routledge.

van Schaik, L. (1999). *Terrain vague: A Melbourne reflection on sites of abandonment*. Melbourne, Australia: Faculty of Constructed Environment, RMIT University.

van Schaik, L. (2003). The practice of practice: Practice based research in architecture. In L. van Schaik (Ed.), *The practice of practice: Research in the medium of design* (pp. 12-18). Melbourne, Australia: RMIT Publishing.

Whitmont, E. (1991). *The evolution of the shadow*. In C. Zweig & J. Abrams (Eds.), *Meeting the shadow: The hidden power of the dark side of human nature* (pp. 12-18). New York, NY: Tarcher/Putnam.

Wilensky, H. (1964). The professionalization of everyone. *The American Journal of Sociology, 70*(2), 137-158.

Wittgenstein, L. (1958). *The Blue and Brown Books*. New York, NY: Harper and Row.

Nita L. Cherry PhD
Adjunct Professor, Faculty of Business and Law
Swinburne University of Technology, Australia

JAN FOOK

9. PRACTICE WISDOM AND THE SOCIOLOGICAL IMAGINATION

Some decades ago, when I was a newly graduated social worker, I recall how the idea of "practice wisdom" was taken up enthusiastically by social work practitioners (see Carew, 1979). The concept of practice wisdom placed value on learning derived from practice experience, and in this sense, offered an alternative source of legitimate knowledge to that gained through formal knowledge or theory learned in the classroom. Now, some years later, I believe even more strongly that we need to value the learning of professionals from their own practice experience, and am convinced that learning gained through taking on knowledge from sources outside oneself (from books, formalised theoretical perspectives, etc.) must indeed be complemented by self-reflective learning. However the picture is not as simple as this sounds.

I have learned a lot more about the complex nature of knowledge creation over several decades in which I have worked extensively with practitioners, from many different countries and fields, in practising how to critically reflect. I see critical reflection as a process of deep learning from experience. (I will define this in more detail later in the chapter.) In the process of reflecting, people are able to unearth and examine some fundamental, and usually hidden, assumptions about themselves, their expected roles in relation to other people, and their place and power in their social and professional worlds. More often than not, these assumptions seem to reflect a fairly generic popular culture, made up of ideas which most of us take for granted, often partly because we assume other people around us think the same. It is always useful to uncover these taken-for-granted ideas, and to examine them for relevance and accuracy in current contexts. In most cases, these ideas are so deeply ingrained that they have never been examined systematically. Sometimes people do not change their ideas through this process of examination, but mostly they do.

What this tells me is that without deep critical reflection on experience, most practitioners would not necessarily question ideas which, after critical reflection, they would actually opt to change. If they are not reflecting deeply on their experience, it is likely that the "practice wisdom" which results, will remain within the limits of popular culture, or at least within the limits of what has come to be taken-for-granted within their profession. This means they are less likely to challenge pre-existing ideas which might frame or limit their practice; or they might simply derive reasonably superficial learning from limited contexts of practice which may be less transferable to different settings.

Early in my career I also studied the work of C. Wright Mills (1959), that famous sociologist who coined the term *the sociological imagination*. I became totally intrigued with this perspective, as it seemed this type of analysis was vital to the profession of social work which claimed to work with *person in situation* (Hamilton, 1951). But what concerned me about the sociological imagination was that it did not appear very easy to develop this consciousness which linked personal troubles and public issues. I found that many social workers had difficulty in translating structural analyses of society into how to understand personal experiences, and even harder, how to work on an individual level with these. The view which seemed to predominate was that we needed to turn to psychological theories and therapies in order to work with individual people. This struck me as very polarised and "siloed" thinking, antithetical to the vision of social work as a socially oriented profession. I examined these issues in detail, writing a major book which critiqued the "psychological deluge" of the times and proposed an approach to working with individual people based on an understanding of them within a social and structural context (Fook, 1993).

Given the possibility that "practice wisdom" might simply reflect popular and taken-for-granted and psychologically informed views about the world, then it also seems likely that thinking derived in such a way will not necessarily reflect a sociological imagination. If this is the case, there is a vast amount of important analysis which might be omitted from a professional's thinking and ways of working. Certainly this omission is reflected in contemporary literature which, for example, decries the lack of awareness of the influence of poverty in peoples' lives and strategies in social workers' practice with children and families in Britain (Gupta, Blumhardt, & ATD Fourth World, 2018) and indeed in other countries as well (Krumer-Nevo, 2016).

There has been a lot more writing and thinking over the last few decades which has a bearing on our understanding of practice wisdom and the sociological imagination. I want to update our thinking in order to propose links between practice wisdom and a sociological imagination and how developing such an imagination can contribute to practice wisdom. I illustrate my points with examples of hidden assumptions which have emerged through critical reflection by participants from workshops I have conducted. I show how these assumptions, indicative of taken-for-granted professional cultures, can benefit from a more sociological imagination. I end the chapter by describing some ways in which critical reflection can enhance our sociological imagination and how practice might be improved, or transformed, accordingly. I will start by discussing the concepts of practice wisdom, the sociological imagination and critical reflection.

PRACTICE WISDOM

The idea of practice wisdom entered common discourse in social work several decades ago. It appears to have been mostly used in the early days by social workers (Powell, 2008), not social scientists or other professionals, and over the decades it has been coupled with concepts like "felt knowledge", "tacit knowledge", "intuition" and "common sense" (Zeira, 2010). Each of these terms implies a kind of secondary status, as opposed to *knowledge* which is derived from either theory or research (Zeira, 2010). Such a definition of knowledge implies that all these ways of knowing (or, as many would now argue, *types* of knowledge) are difficult to pinpoint, are not empirically verifiable, and the process by which such more practice-based (rather than research or theory driven) knowledge is derived, is difficult to articulate.

It is understandable that "practice wisdom" has been characterised in this way, given that attempts to give legitimacy to the idea arose out of recognising the limits of overly positivist approaches to theorising and researching social work practice (Cheung, 2016; Chu & Tsui, 2008). The term practice wisdom can be seen as a way of valuing what is not or less empirically measurable, in an age of evidence-based practice. Some of the attempts to define "practice wisdom" reflect these debates.

For example, Klein and Bloom (1995) define practice wisdom as the "personal and value-driven system of knowledge which emerges out of the transaction between the phenomenological experience of the client situation and the use of scientific information" (p. 79). Note the implied split between "knowledge derived from experience" and "scientific information", with practice wisdom defined as arising out of an interaction of the two. This idea is echoed in Samson's definition (2015) which characterises practice wisdom as bridging the gap between theory and practice, or the "art" and "science" of social work. In some ways a type of split is also implicit in Dybicz's (2004) conclusions about practice wisdom as "the application of values, over that of efficacy of interventions, is what lies at the heart of practice wisdom" (p. 197). Yet to characterise practice wisdom on the basis of such polarised ways of conceptualising professional practice is to oversimplify the nature of practice, and the nature of the types of knowledge upon which it is based, and the types of knowledge which emerge from it. Powell (2008) puts it beautifully in a framework based on narrative knowing.

> Practical, or practice, wisdom that is peculiar to our profession develops through the experience of doing our craft in the context of our professional relationships and the social circumstances in which they are played out (Lave & Wenger, 1991). The foundation of wisdom, generally, is acquired by keen students of the whole of life and enhances our cognitive capacity for making sense of things – for narrative knowing ... Our minds consciously and unconsciously weave stories based on the circumstances of our work and our lives. Experience, narrative knowing, and shared associations inform us, in our present and our hindsight, how circumstances shape the trajectories of lives and events. Wisdom utilizes that experience and knowledge as we seek the best paths to the best ends and weave our way into the future. (Powell, 2008, p. 95)

Practice wisdom (from a narrative perspective) involves

> complex habits of mind. It is an eminently practical cognitive ability, a means of 'seeing' courses of action through a lens of knowledge, pattern recognition, and experience. It improves and substantiates our judgment, complements our thought and knowledge, hints at preferred courses of action, and improves the outcomes of our work. It uses conscious and unconscious mental processes or deliberation with and without attention (Dijksterhuis, 2006). (Powell, 2008, p. 95)

In the above quotes Powell emphasises the different types of cognitive activity which are involved in developing wisdom from practice experience. Practice wisdom is essentially a holistic experience which integrates our pattern recognition capabilities, interpretations (conscious and unconscious), personal predilections and judgements in a narrative format which helps make meaning of experiences. In this sense, the knowledge developed in practice wisdom may incorporate all other types of knowledge, mediated by personal and professional experience and values. It is little wonder then, that reflection is regarded as an essential capacity in developing practice wisdom (Samson, 2015; Scott, 1990). What needs attention if valuable practice wisdom is to be developed through reflection, is some scrutiny of the bases of "felt knowledge", "tacit knowledge", "intuition" or "common sense", and whether these sorts of knowledge are relevant to the situations at hand. I will return to this theme in the later section on critical reflection.

THE SOCIOLOGICAL IMAGINATION

> The sociological imagination enables its possessor to understand the larger historical scene in terms of its meaning for the inner life and the external career of a variety of individuals ... The first fruit of this imagination ... is the idea that the individual can understand his [sic] own experience and gauge his own fate only by locating himself within this period ... The sociological imagination enables us to grasp history and biography and the relations between the two within society. That is its task and its promise. (Mills, 1959, pp. 5-6)

Perhaps the most memorable of the concepts associated with the sociological imagination are those of "personal troubles" and "public issues" (Mills, 1959, p. 8). Mills argued that it was essential to understand the distinction between the two. "Troubles" are to do with the private milieu of an individual: their inner life and areas of social life of which they are directly aware. "Issues" are concerned with matters which transcend the private milieu, but are to do with how many social milieux are organised to form a larger structure of social and historical life (ibid. p. 8). "Troubles" and "issues" both arise when either personally or socially held values are felt to be threatened. The key to a sociological imagination, for Mills, is the ability to grasp the connection between private troubles and public issues. And the key to beginning to pinpoint the major troubles and issues of our time is to appreciate what values are being supported or threatened by major social trends. This is an important point for critical reflection.

Today we have many more theories from which to analyse the connections between personal and social worlds, yet Mills' basic concept of the sociological imagination still stands as a call to all those of us who wish to make a difference in the lives and worlds of the people we strive to help. Unfortunately, despite this clear call, the capacity to make meaningful connections between "troubles" and "issues" is actually quite difficult. I would argue that what we often see as "common sense" or unconsciously uphold as accepted ways of thinking, echoes a more polarised way of thinking; that is, we tend to favour individualised ways of understanding phenomena, or plump for more structural analyses, often finding it difficult to marry the two. This is certainly how our major disciplinary thinking is organised, into either psychological (individual) or structural (sociological) frameworks. Therefore, there is a need to spell out some of the theoretical orientations which make connections between personal and structural worlds explicit, as discussed further below.

CRITICAL REFLECTION

Defining Critical Reflection

I define my approach to reflection as a process of learning from experience by unsettling deep-seated assumptions (embedded in stories of personal experiences) in order to examine them. It becomes critical if the assumptions unearthed are fundamental; have to do with power and aspects of the social or structural context; and enable transformational change. (I have discussed this in much more detail elsewhere: see Fook, 2002; Fook & Gardner, 2007, 2013.)

Learning from experience also involves the ability to make greater meaning of experience, so that if deeply held ideas, which are often initially hidden, are exposed and changed, then new frameworks for understanding are developed. These new frameworks provide guidelines for action which are usually transferable beyond the type of situation in which the original experience occurred. For example, if someone reflects on an experience of having an angry interaction with a colleague at work, they may unearth assumptions about how people should behave generally towards each other (e.g. being respectful). This may lead them to (re)formulate their beliefs about what behaviours are acceptable and in what types of settings. Thus, their original learning from a work situation might turn into learning which is applicable in a broader range of settings.

What I have found over the years though, is that many people unearth assumptions which, although firmly held by them, do not necessarily originate from their own experience. In short, they often hold assumptions which they have taken on, unquestioningly, from the broader social or cultural fabric in which they were raised, live and work. I have therefore designed my approach and model for practising critical reflection using a number of theoretical frameworks which provide different ways of understanding the connections between personal ways of thinking, and aspects of the social, cultural, historical and structural environment. In brief, there are three main theoretical perspectives which are useful here: the concept of reflexivity; the linguistic turn; and critical social theories.

The Concept of Reflexivity

Reflexivity involves personal awareness of our social place, and how it has formed who we are, and continues to inform our awareness and how we relate in the world. Being reflexive means that we are aware of who we are as whole people: through personal biography; physical entity; the historical and cultural period in which we were raised and are now influenced; our psychological and emotional makeup; our social identity (e.g. gender, age, ethnicity); and our structural and material conditions (e.g. class, influence of social policies and institutions) (Fook, 1999). Being reflexive therefore involves an ability to identify how our own assumptions and interpretations can be influenced by who we are, socially and personally; and, therefore, how we create the knowledge we believe to be important. Indeed, being reflexive makes us aware of what knowledge we do not even notice, or factor in as important, because of the peculiar lenses we create for ourselves from the amalgam of who we are as an individual person. Reflexivity is useful in critical reflection as it draws attention to how we are involved in making choices about what we notice and privilege, and therefore what we believe to be relevant and important knowledge. Armed with this understanding of how we have a role in constructing what we see, it becomes easier to question and change some assumptions which we may not have actively considered or evaluated before.

The Linguistic Turn

The linguistic turn in social theorising draws further attention to the way we create knowledge through our language use, and what this has to do with power. The concept of discourse is now regularly used. This refers to how ways of talking about phenomena, the actual phrases and terms used, and indeed what terms are *not* used, frames how a phenomenon is understood or valued. This leads us to understand how power is created through our use of language. Usually it is argued that the major discourses which are accepted are the discourses of people in power, and that the way less powerful people see things is often not recognised, or indeed is missing from public discussions. The concept of discourse is eminently useful in analysing why some ways of thinking become unconsciously embedded or taken-for-granted. This is a very useful concept for helping to pinpoint what is "common sense", or culturally accepted ways of thinking and doing things in particular environments. In this way, understanding how knowledge, and indeed some realities, are constructed through our social fabric, is vital to critical reflection. Not only does language articulate the connection between knowledge and power, it also helps us to become aware of the language we use, where it comes from, and what it values and excludes. Such understanding allows us to make more informed choices about our interpretations of the social world and our engagement with it.

Critical Social Theories

The term "critical social theories" refers to a broader category of theorising which principally posits connections between personal and social worlds, and how these connections create and maintain power through these connections. Such connections essentially support the idea that knowledge is created through personal experience, as well as through other means (e.g. research), and that often socially created ideas are internalised by individual people (who may believe that these ideas are their own). In this way, individual people are "socialised" to conform to the main social ideas, which may be generated by more powerful groups, and therefore in turn, may not necessarily work to the advantage of the person who holds the belief. For example, if I am a person from a working-class background, I may believe that going to university is just about avoiding going to find a "real" job. This idea, of holding beliefs which function as self-defeating is sometimes referred to as "false consciousness".

Critical reflection can be aided by this concept, because we can become aware of how the beliefs we hold, about ourselves and other people, can be self-defeating, may work against other ideas we hold, or may not in fact even be our own ideas. For example, if I believe my managers are all-powerful (this is a common belief which comes out in critical reflection sessions) then I tend to believe that I (as a front-line practitioner) am not powerful, and therefore I will not attempt to work in the way I think best if it contravenes the way I believe I am being told to work.

Another common idea is a self-belief that if I am powerless, there is not any point in trying to change things. A related assumption is that managers, being "all-powerful" are not "human beings" trying to live lives like the rest of us. Everything they do therefore, is inflicted on "us" intentionally because of their power (rather than the fact that they might have made a mistake, had a misunderstanding, not communicated very well, been misinterpreted, had a bad day, etc.). Critical social theories are crucial to reflection and transformative learning. In particular, an analysis of how and what social beliefs are internalised and unquestioned, can lead to pinpointing different ways of interpreting and seeing the social world and our place in it. Social theories can enlighten us as to what assumptions we have unconsciously assumed, and alert us to possible different interpretations.

SOME PRACTICE WISDOMS WHICH EMERGE THROUGH CRITICAL REFLECTION

One of the things I find particularly intriguing about critically reflecting with many practitioners, is the learning which they have derived from their experiences before they critically reflect on them using the above approach. This gives me some insight into what we sometimes assume about the "taken-for-granted", "common sense" or the tacit knowledge we believe that everyone in the profession believes. This insight is part of the model of critical reflection I have devised (see Figure 9.1).

In my model participants typically critically reflect in a small group and in two stages. They begin by identifying an example of their practice experience which they believe is significant to their learning in some way. Mostly they choose experiences which they find puzzling or unsettling, and often at the heart of these is some perceived threat to the values they hold dear. For example, a common incident identified is one in which a practitioner has felt, and sometimes expressed, anger towards a client. They feel they have contravened their own personal and professional ethical code in doing this. Each member of the group is helped, through dialogue, to uncover what they believe to be some of their fundamental assumptions embedded in their story of their experience. (Stage 1). In Stage 2, the focus is on assisting the person to rebuild the meaning of their experience and to devise a new way of understanding it and practising on this basis, going forward.

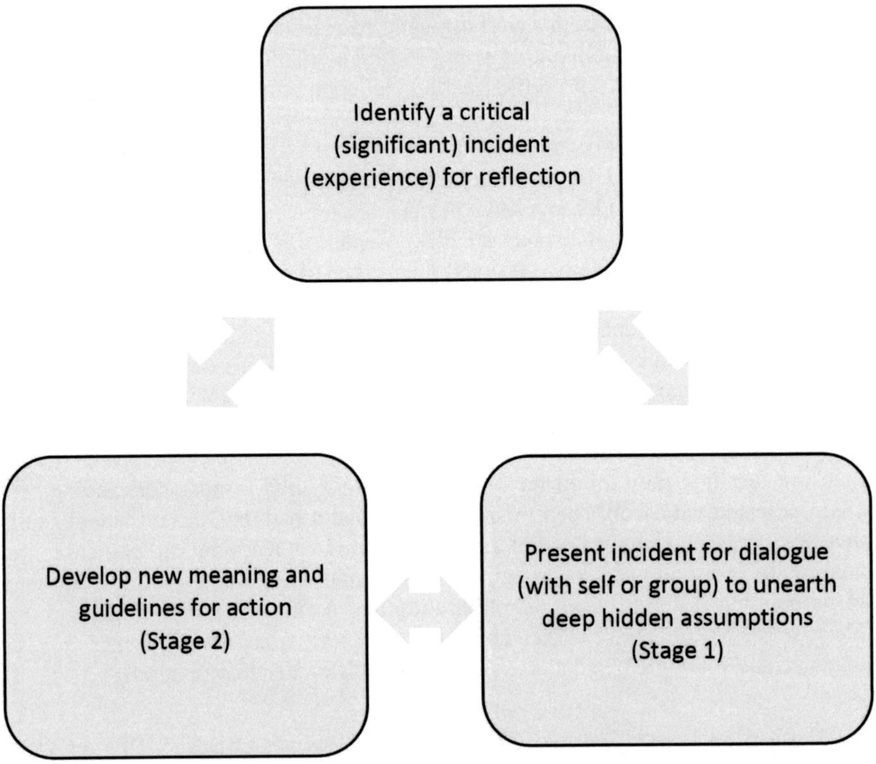

```
┌─────────────────────────┐
│   Identify a critical   │
│   (significant) incident│
│  (experience) for       │
│       reflection        │
└─────────────────────────┘
         ↙        ↘
┌──────────────────┐   ┌──────────────────────┐
│ Develop new      │   │ Present incident for │
│ meaning and      │⇄  │ dialogue (with self  │
│ guidelines for   │   │ or group) to unearth │
│ action           │   │ deep hidden          │
│ (Stage 2)        │   │ assumptions          │
│                  │   │ (Stage 1)            │
└──────────────────┘   └──────────────────────┘
```

Figure 9.1. A model of critical reflection.

In this section I want to focus on some of the practice wisdoms which emerge in Stage 1, in order to illustrate how these might benefit from the application of a more sociological imagination. First is the example I alluded to above, in relation to the way front-line practitioners often characterise their managers or sometimes supervisors. There is a tendency to see managers as quite omnipotent, as beings who should be able to be fully competent, and able to control their environments and so be focused fully on the welfare of the staff they manage or supervise. I am aware this sounds like a gross exaggeration, but I have also encountered this assumption from managers themselves.

An example I am thinking of here is of a very experienced manager in a local authority in London. This person (let's call him Ken – not his real name) managed about 20 people, and he presented to the group an experience in which he felt he had failed his staff, because he had failed to prevent a particular case, over which there was concern, from proceeding to a formal inquiry. In critically reflecting on this experience, Ken unearthed an assumption that managers should be able to protect staff, no matter what. When he said this out loud, he laughingly characterised himself as "wearing a cape" (i.e. thinking of himself as a superhero). His practice wisdom, developed over his years of experience, led him to believe that he should be omnipotent. When he unearthed this idea, he saw, of course, that what he was thinking was impossible for any manager. It did not take much examination for him to want to change this belief, yet it was a belief which had been built up over many years of managing staff, and it was, until then, a very firmly held belief. Fortunately, Ken decided to reframe his "superhero" idea, but he would not have done this if it weren't for his experience in reflecting deeply enough to unearth very influential ideas which had remained hidden. His practice wisdom in this case had not helped him in coping with the expectations of his job, as he had constructed them. It was only when Ken considered the context of his work, and the construction of his role as a team manager, with all its policy, resourcing and organisational constraints, that he realised what he was setting himself up for was unrealistic. Once he understood his experience within the social and structural contexts of his job, he was able to reframe his expectations of himself in relation to this. Seeing the connections between "private troubles" and "public issues" helped him gain a more balanced sense of what he could reasonably expect of himself in a manager's role.

There are also, of course, issues about power embedded here, about how individual practitioners see their own power, especially in relation to those they think have more or less power than themselves. Assumptions about power play a significant role in practice wisdom. For instance, it can often be the case that practitioners, if they feel powerless, will construct power as something which is static, and which can only be gained through a formal job position (Fook, 2011). These common assumptions can very much function to ensure that individual practitioners do not step outside the power they believe is conferred by their position. However, if practitioners can begin to appreciate, through critical reflection, that these assumptions about power can function to keep them powerless, they may begin to build the foundations for changing these beliefs. Again, developing a more sociological way of understanding power and its operation, using a critical social theory analysis, can assist in helping practitioners to feel empowered to practise in ways which they believe are more congruent with their values.

A second example is provided by Jane, who was working as a manger in a local authority in London (Fook, Royes, & White, 2017). Jane's experience involved an aging client who died in a house fire. Although Jane was only the supervisor of the social worker whose client it was, she still felt perturbed and distressed by the incident, and could not put these feelings to rest, despite repeated attempts to discuss the experience with the worker and other colleagues. Colleagues simply assured her that she had done nothing wrong, but this did not make Jane feel any better. When she critically reflected on the incident, Jane realised that much of her continued distress was based on an assumption that she should have prevented the incident. A more fundamental assumption was that in fact she believed that managers were able to control events by simply filling in the right forms!

Whilst she realised that this sounded ridiculous, she began to appreciate that this type of thinking was encouraged by the culture in her organisation, where following correct bureaucratic procedure was highly valued. Again, in this instance, Jane's "practice wisdom" before critical reflection, involved feelings of self-blame. When she reflected, and became aware of how these ideas were endemic to the bureaucratic culture of where she worked, she was able to make this connection between her own private trouble (i.e. personal experience) of self-blame, and the public issue of the broader workplace culture. Jane went on to reflect how this realisation led her to understand much better the experiences of colleagues in feeling defensive within this workplace culture, and how this helped her become a better supervisor.

There are many other examples of potentially erroneous or damaging assumptions which can arise from uncritical practice "wisdom" of practitioners. Cosier (2008) analysed her assumptions about the objectivity of the medical role; Kicuroski (2008) discussed his realisation that assumptions about professional boundaries played into the stigma directed at people labelled with borderline personality disorder; and Rubensohn (2008) discussed her disempowering assumptions of social work as "the saviour" and clients and communities as "the saved" (p. 80). These examples all illustrate how our everyday practice may in fact be embedded with what seem like "common sense" ideas which can be believed to be good practice wisdom. In the following section I discuss briefly how, by being aware of a sociological imagination, we can guard against our practice "wisdoms" unwittingly preserving some taken-for-granted ideas which are not necessarily desirable, and may work against the interests of ourselves and our clients.

CONCLUSION: PRACTICE WISDOM AND THE SOCIOLOGICAL IMAGINATION

The examples outlined above illustrate how deep reflection may be needed in order to turn "practice wisdom" ideas and assumptions into more helpful learning. A possible problem with practice wisdom, especially if the process for deriving it is unclear, is that the learning derived may simply mirror taken-for-granted ideas which are embedded in already established cultures. Rather than allowing for new perspectives, "practice wisdoms" might simply perpetuate existing ways of thinking or practising. This can of course be a problem in our current workplaces, where much is characterised by change and uncertainty.

I have argued in this chapter that coupling a sociological imagination with wisdoms derived from practice experience, can provide more holistic and nuanced ways for practitioners to understand themselves, their work roles and their capacities for influencing change within these contexts. Unfortunately, a sociological imagination, or the ability to appreciate individual experience within a broader social context, does not necessarily occur naturally. Our broader societal context often tends to polarise psychological or sociological perspectives, rather than encouraging a more complex and nuanced way of appreciating personal experience and its interaction with social contexts.

Mills (1959) offers some very helpful intellectual exercises to stimulate the sociological imagination. For example, he suggests trying to re-classify the "files" in your own head; looking for comparative examples; having an attitude of playfulness towards the terms or ideas you use or hold; and considering the extreme opposite of what you are inclined to think. These strategies can indeed be helpful in making us aware of the socially conditioned way in which we think, and invite us to consider perspectives we may not even have been aware of before. I would argue that a process of deep critical reflection also assists us to do something similar. By actively attempting to consider and re-examine the assumptions inherent in many examples of practice wisdom, we might enhance them by through connecting them with social influences, and thereby improve our professional practice. A clear and intentional process of critically reflecting on our experience, which is based on theoretical frameworks which allow us to make direct connections between individual lives and social conditions, can enliven our sociological imaginations. In doing this, we can also reconnect with the values which we may perceive as being threatened by current social conditions (which Mills alerted us to above), as being one of the fundamental ingredients of "private troubles" and "public issues". In this way, deep reflection on our experiences might allow us to develop an "ethical and compassionate engagement with the word and its dilemmas" (Socrates, as cited by Nussbaum, 1997).

REFERENCES

Carew, R. (1979). The place of knowledge in social work activity. *British Journal of Social Work, 9*(3), 349-364.

Cheung, J. C.-S. (2016). Researching practice wisdom in social work. *Journal of Social Intervention, 25*(3), 24-38.

Chu, W. C. K., & Tsui, M.-S. (2008). The nature of practice wisdom in social work revisited. *International Social Work, 51*(1), 47-54.

Cosier, W. (2008). What part of 'no' don't you understand: Social work, children and consent. In R. Pockett & R. Giles (Eds.), *Critical reflection: Generating theory form practice* (pp. 45-61). Sydney, Australia: Darlington Press.

Dybicz, P. (2004). An inquiry into practice wisdom. *Families in Society: The Journal of Contemporary Social Services, 85*(2), 197-203.

Fook, J. (1993). *Radical casework: A theory of practice.* St Leonards, Australia: Allen & Unwin.

Fook, J. (1999). Reflexivity as method. *Annual Review of Health Social Sciences, 9*, 11-20.

Fook, J. (2002). *Social work: Critical theory and practice.* London, England: Sage.

Fook, J. (2011). Critical reflection and power in social work. In T. Okitikpi (Ed.), *Social control and child and families social work practice in the 21st century* (pp. 126-140). Lyme Regis, England: Russell House Publishing.

Fook, J., & Gardner, F. (Eds.). (2013). *Critical reflection in context: Applications in health and social care.* Oxford, England: Routledge.

Fook, J., & Gardner, F. (2007). *Practising critical reflection: A resource handbook.* Maidenhead, England: Open University Press.

Fook, J., Royes, J., & White, A. (2017). Critical reflection. In M. Chambers (Ed.), *Psychiatric and mental health nursing: The craft of caring* (3rd ed., pp. 117-126). London, England: Routledge.

Gupta, A., Blumhardt, H., & ATD Fourth World. (2018). Poverty, exclusion and child protection practice: The contribution of the politics of recognition and respect. *European Journal of Social Work, 21*(2), 247-259.

Hamilton, G. (1951). *Theory and practice of social casework.* New York, NY: Columbia University Press.

Kicuroski, T. (2008). Borderline personality disorder and binary thinking: Challenging power dynamics and practice In R. Pockett & R. Giles (Eds.), *Critical reflection: Generating theory from practice* (pp. 62-76). Sydney, Australia: Darlington Press.

Klein, W. C., & Bloom, M. (1995). Practice wisdom. *Social Work, 40*(6), 799-807.

Krumer-Nevo, M. (2016). Poverty-aware social work: A paradigm for social work practice with people in poverty. *British Journal of Social Work, 46*(6), 1793-1808.

Mills, C. W. (1959). *The sociological imagination.* New York, NY: Oxford University Press.

Nussbaum, M. (1997). *Cultivating humanity: A classical defense of reform in liberal education*. Cambridge, MA: Harvard University Press.

Powell, W. (2008). Sophia's window: Practice wisdom and selecting better paths. *Portularia, VIII*(2), 91-102.

Rubensohn. R. (2008). International social work vs local practice: The moral dilemma of knowing where to give aid. In R. Pockett & R. Giles (Eds.), *Critical reflection: Generating theory from practice* (pp. 77-92). Sydney, Australia: Darlington Press.

Samson, P. L. (2015). Practice wisdom: The art and science of social work. *Journal of Social Work Practice, 29*(2), 119-131.

Scott, D. (1990). Practice wisdom: The neglected source of practice research. *Social Work, 35*(6), 564-568.

Zeira, A. (2010). Testing practice wisdom in child welfare. In S. B. Kamerman, S. Phipps, & A. Ben-Arieh (Eds.), *From child welfare to child well-being: An international perspective on knowledge in the service of policy making* (pp. 49-63). Dordrecht, The Netherlands: Springer.

Jan Fook PhD
Department of Social Work
University of Vermont, United States of America

SANDY O'SULLIVAN

10. A LIVED EXPERIENCE OF ABORIGINAL KNOWLEDGES AND PERSPECTIVES

How Cultural Wisdom Saved My Life

This is a chapter in a book on practice wisdom. I was invited to write a chapter on practice wisdom from two perspectives: my Indigenous culture as practice, and my life as an individual experience of this culture in my living practice. Each of us brings many perspectives and experiences to how we practise; and none of us fail to bring our unique selves as well as our community belonging into our life and work practices. I take this opportunity to uncover wisdom from within my culture and celebrate the way this wisdom has helped me and others face challenges in our life practices.

I'm a queer Aboriginal person who performs drag. That is, drag *king*, rather than the better-known *queen*. I am also, what has become known in recent years, as *genderqueer*. I deploy the term because it assists in challenging a binary gender assignation that has proven problematic. I am also a lesbian. Are you confused yet? You shouldn't be; across all of our cultures, the body individually experienced is complex and formative regardless of our outward facing behaviours and societal commitments. The impact of the colonial project cast First Nations' Peoples as objects to be managed by the state and church. This external management has frequently denied us the subtle complexities of sexuality and gender claimed by mainstream culture in Australia over recent decades (O'Sullivan, 2015).

I use the terms "Indigenous", "First Nations' Peoples" and "Aboriginal" interchangeably, and always capitalised to indicate that they form the short form for a proper noun, i.e. Aboriginal Australia, Indigenous Australian, etc. I capitalise Community and Elders as a sign of respect, and as an indication that they also operate as a short form for a proper noun, i.e. Aboriginal Elder, Wiradjuri Elder, Aboriginal Community, etc.

If asserting our complex identities as Indigenous people in all forms is an anti-colonial act of resistance and remonstrance, then it will only be through our own agency over the presentation of the diversity of our lives that we will truly be free of the shackles of colonial oppression. The premise of integration and the removal of the complexity of Aboriginal People was historically framed within the "smoothing the pillow of a dying race" paradigm (Shannon, 2002), in the quiet erasure of our distinctive characteristics. The following discussion reflects on several events that drew me back to some important wisdoms provided from within our Community, that will help us – with the support of mainstream Australia – to challenge the diverse understandings of who we are and who we can be, as we robustly refuse to have our identities erased and homogenised. I'd like to mention that mainstream Australia is not homogenised either and in reflecting on personal and practice wisdom, lack of sameness is a reality to be acknowledged, liberated and valued.

REPRESENTATION MATTERS

For First Nations' Peoples, the externally imposed, narrowed understanding of our identity has frequently shaped our survival. At times, members of our Community have actively participated in the resulting erasure. In 2013, the ABC TV drama, *Redfern Now* featured an episode showing a gay man and his relationship with his family and the Community. After the episode aired, Aboriginal boxer Anthony Mundine delivered a series of statements through social media and across the news media where he expressed homophobic views and indicated that historically we would have been killed for being gay. He further claimed that his religion and his Aboriginality forbade homosexuality, that positive representation was unacceptable, and made the broad claim that this would not be tolerated in our Community and that it was not cultural ("Anthony Mundine says", 2013).

There was substantial outcry from within the Community, by the producers, in social media and from mainstream media organisations. Wamba man, Steven Ross (2014), presented a view of both Mundine's comments and the impact that they would have on queer people living in smaller Communities. In a piece in *The Guardian*, titled, *Not in Our Culture? Open Hearts Helped Me Grow Up Indigenous and Gay*, Ross shares the painful experience of both support and abuse that he received as a young man coming to terms with his sexuality. He speaks of the extreme danger in which Mundine's words intentionally places young people who may be queer or questioning, but also speaks of how this incident – and the television series that prompted the discussion – have galvanised support for better understanding. Ross also asserted that many queer Indigenous people were and are strong leaders across the Community, and that we are accepted by many and we do important work across the Community more broadly, while being visible and "out". Ross was not the only one to challenge Mundine's views. A number of presenters on IndigenousX, the national rotating Twitter account followed by some 20,000 Aboriginal and Torres Strait Islander People devoted several weeks and stories to challenging these perceptions and providing positive stories.

These multiple challengers took on Mundine's unsubstantiated views that homosexuality was a colonising influence. His claims were both impossible to prove – and he took no steps to prove them beyond the assertion that it is not cultural. Mundine's words erase every queer Aboriginal person's life. Perversely, his views buy into the colonial fiction that fails to account for our internal diverse expression as a people. To believe his theory that queer people did not exist in Aboriginal culture prior to invasion, suggests that Aboriginal queers are either not Aboriginal, or our presentation is only a presentation of the colonial mindset. Fortunately, many people are actively challenging these ideas. For example, the work of Yugambeh person, Maddee Clark, who argues extensively not only against the reductive view of Mundine, but also strongly for our capacity to resist categorisation and these notions of authenticity (Clark, 2014).

Like Steve Ross and others, I was concerned about the impact that these statements would have on young people who may be struggling with acceptance within themselves or their families and Communities. Aboriginal people have inordinately high levels of suicide and suicidal ideation; statistics across the mainstream population show higher levels for LGBTIQ+ people across the wider population, and Indigenous suicide rates are also higher than the mainstream population (Bonson, 2017). While there are currently no statistics on the impact of these converging figures, it is reasonable to assume that there is a higher risk in the queer Aboriginal population than for the rest of the country.

All of this was a cause for concern, and this was the tone of most of the community redress, reminding people that the vulnerable should be supported. But as the debate continued – in fact Mundine has stated these views as recently as 2018 – there was also continuing discussion across our Community, often visible across social networking, in everyday conversations and across the media, and it was hard to hear; to have our very existence debated. There were few programs or activities except those existing in isolation to help members of our Community who may be vulnerable to being subjects and objects of these debates. It was during a further spike of this kind of activity that I experienced – after decades of being out and proud, and very clear about my sexuality and Aboriginality – an event that shook me to the core.

In 2017 at the height of a further difficult debate in Australia that would result in marriage equality passing into law, my brother, David Hardy, had a massive stroke. He has since fully recovered, but at the time he was gravely ill and wasn't expected to live, so friends, colleagues and extended family relied on his social media account to keep updated on his progress. Two years before the stroke, David, who is gay, had authored a book (Hardy, 2015) that detailed the lives of more than 50 older LGBTIQ+ people – *Bold*. It included a number of First Nations' Australians and was the first book of its kind. David has a national profile as a leader in the queer community, and so many people were following his profile to see how he was doing and how they could help.

An Aboriginal woman we vaguely knew that David had friended on Facebook, began to write horrifically homophobic posts, and she tagged dozens of people in them. Naturally many people removed the tags and reported her. Her account remained intact and she continued to post. David's name was tagged to all of her posts. He was, as he lay unconscious, incapable of removing them; neither could I.

A fervent marriage equality advocate, two days before he had the stroke, David was calling constituents urging them to vote "yes" in the national survey. I wrote about this in an IndigenousX post (O'Sullivan, 2017) in an effort to both call out this behaviour, as well as to correct any perception that he was a willing supporter of these homophobic rants. But in spite of this action, I found it shocking and disabling.

GUNYA

In the same way that many of us became galvanised against the words of Anthony Mundine, for me this social media attack drew an important perspective into view: Gunya. Gunya is the Wiradjuri word most frequently translated in English to mean home, but the meaning reaches beyond a location or tangible place in the physical world. While terms like "safe harbour" or "haven" invoke some aspects of the meaning in English, Gunya more directly locates an encompassing space of safety than any word found in English. Understanding Gunya, for me, has been a journey of considering the trust I place in my body and in the way that Elders and leaders have supported me in navigating the complexities of identity in a world that often says it wants to understand but does this superficially, without listening.

But it was that moment of the Facebook tagging, that had compounded the commentary around Mundine's words on our right to exist, that Gunya felt the most threatened. At an essential level, Gunya represents the place where we can be who we are, and it is where we should expect the support of those across our community. Gunya supports lived, real and diverse experiences and it is something and somewhere that we can both demand and expect. It underscores our most essential right to sovereignty over our own bodies, thoughts and lives. Remembering this grounded me, it created an opportunity to locate the challenges and provided opportunities for redress.

> I am hurt
> and need a place
> to heal
> to be safe
> I am Wiradjuri,
> I have Gunya
> here I belong
> here I find strength
> here tomorrow's path
> becomes clearer to me.

Gunya suggests a strategy to locate Mundine's comments, as well as those actions and rhetoric leading up to the same sex marriage debate; it provides a way to understand the frequent absence of queer representation in mainstream understanding of First Nations' Peoples. Gunya creates a space where the centralising ontology – who we are, who I am, is centred in my body and my experience. In doing so, Gunya challenges reductive views that are as various as each member of the Community.

Recently (Whittaker, 2015), more than 20 academics and Community members came together to write a book on our experience of being queer: *Colouring the Rainbow, Blak Queer and Trans Perspectives: Life Stories and Essays by First Nations People of Australia*. This text is powerful, like many more that show our diversity, because it was written by us.

The agency of the text provides a literary Gunya from which to challenge these views as it speaks to the success, struggles and challenges within the community, and to the power of our diverse identities. It provides a lexicon of expression and ideas for community members and those who seek to work with our community. While the text was, in part, written as a direct challenge to the Mundine diatribe, it is more than a protest against the containment of our identity, instead providing markers for engagement, understanding and a commitment to taking back the space that we deserve (Hodge, 2015).

SYMBOLIC ANNIHILATION

Tell them who you are, don't let them tell you

In *Colouring the Rainbow*, Gomeroi woman, Alison Whittaker (2015), uses her essay to worry the idea of erasure, suggesting that many queer people already rejected by their family further compound their sense of alienation from community by failing to identify as Aboriginal, lest they are subject to further rejection. While this exclusion is not explicitly stated in any of our communities or organisations outside of organised and Westernised religious affiliations, she argues that the perception of rejection from a Community has long-lasting effects. The failure to actively include can also result in the kind of symbolic annihilation that we can only challenge by ensuring that our whole Community is supported and included.

Decades ago, I was fortunate to have had someone help me understand the impact of presenting my diverse self. A female Elder, who has since passed away,[1] could tell that I struggling with my own sense of identity and direction. When I expressed my concern that others might not see me as authentic, she explicitly stated that I should always "tell them who you are, don't let them tell you". "Them" probably meant something specific to her, but her advice has provided an enduring legacy in my life across a lot of "thems". It has guided my sense of Gunya, my sense of safety and belonging in my Community, and my right to have a complex identity and be an authentic Aboriginal person. Her advice helped me challenge the internal bickering that sometimes happens in Communities and in families, and it helped me ground my work on identity and my work as an Aboriginal academic who has a responsibility to others to support the complex presentations of our identities.

For young people, or people questioning their sexuality, it is essential that we provide them with their own Gunya and their own sense of safety. We can only do this if we challenge the symbolic annihilation of our diverse presentation, challenge people who present direct threats and demonstrate that they cannot kill off what makes us strong: our diversity and our complexity.

As a senior Aboriginal person, who has never been capable nor interested in being gender-conforming, I have a responsibility to speak my own truth and to challenge others who would seek to speak for me.

> This is what an Aboriginal person looks like.
> My identity isn't narrowed to a single marker.
> I am Wiradjuri,
> queer,
> genderqueer,
> and a senior Aboriginal person.
> I am a member of a large and diverse family,

a musician and performer,
an advocate for the rights of all First Nations' Peoples.
This is what an Aboriginal person looks like.

NOTE

[1] The Elder has since passed away, and I don't have permission to use her name. It is common to remove the names or use name replacements as a sign of respect for people who have passed away.

REFERENCES

Anthony Mundine says homosexuality and Indigenous culture don't mix. (2013, November 1). *ABC News Online*. Retrieved from https://www.abc.net.au/news/2013-11-01/anthony-mundine-aborigines-homosexual-gay/5063836

Bonson, D. (2017). *Voices from the Black Rainbow: The inclusion of the Aboriginal and Torres Strait Islander LGBQTI, Sistergirls and Brotherboys in health, well-being and suicide prevention strategies*. Sydney, Australia: Indigenist.

Clark, M. (2014). Against authenticity CAL-Connections: Queer Indigenous identities. *Overland, 215*, 30.

Hardy, D. (2015). *Bold: Stories from older lesbian, gay, bisexual, transgender and intersex people*. Panton Hill, Australia: The Rag & Bone Man Press.

Hodge, D. (Ed.). (2015). *Colouring the rainbow, Blak queer and trans perspectives: Life stories and essays by First Nations People of Australia*. Mile End, Australia: Wakefield Press.

O'Sullivan, S. (2015). Stranger in a strange land: Aspiration, uniform and the fine edges of identity. In D. Hodge (Ed.), *Colouring the rainbow, Blak queer and trans perspectives: Life stories and essays by First Nations People of Australia*. Mile End, Australia: Wakefield Press.

O'Sullivan, S. (2017, September 24). An open letter to our community about marriage equality. *IndigenousX*. Retrieved from https://indigenousx.com.au/sandy-osullivan-an-open-letter-to-our-community-about-marriage-equality/

Ross, S. L. (2014, October 31). Not in our culture? Open hearts helped me grow up Indigenous and gay. *The Guardian*. Retrieved from https://www.theguardian.com/commentisfree/2014/oct/31/not-in-our-culture-open-hearts-helped-me-grow-up-indigenous-and-gay

Shannon, C. (2002). Acculturation: Aboriginal and Torres Strait Islander nutrition. *Asia Pacific Journal of Clinical Nutrition, 11*, S576-S578.

Whittaker, A. (2015). The border made of mirrors. In D. Hodge (Ed.), *Colouring the rainbow, Blak queer and trans perspectives: Life stories and essays by First Nations People of Australia*. Mile End, Australia: Wakefield Press.

Sandy O'Sullivan (Wiradjuri) PhD (ORCID: https://orcid.org/0000-0003-2952-4732)
School of Communication and Creative Industries
University of the Sunshine Coast, Australia

KAROLINA ROZMARYNOWSKA

11. PRACTICAL WISDOM AND ETHICAL ACTION

Ethics is a reflection birthed by the question: How should I live? In everyday practice, people keep asking themselves: What action is right? How ought I to behave? What should I do? In developing their ethical concepts, ethicists try to answer these questions looking for universal norms, principles and rules which people should follow in their actions. "Normative rules and principles say what things are required, or permitted, or good or bad. In other words, normative rules and principles say what agents ought to do or what agents are allowed to do; or what deserves to be promoted, praised, or approved; or what deserves to be opposed, criticized, or disapproved" (Hooker, 2006, p. 382). Moral norms are thus the rules of conduct which express an imperative or a prohibition (e.g. "do not steal", "do not lie", "respect others", "do not humiliate others", "keep your promises"). They are defined content-wise in line with the generic specification of the basic categories of human action (Ślipko, 2002) and are the basis of moral obligations which become their detailed actualisation. Obligation is, in fact, the moral necessity of a particular action which the subject experiences as a duty (moral constraint).

With regard to the realisation of norms, of particular importance is the answer to the question why a norm makes a particular action imperative and not another, i.e. what substantiates its content. In very general terms, we may say that the norm which is experienced as an obligation in a particular situation makes imperative an action which contributes to the achievement of a good or avoidance of an evil; or, in axiological terms, which realises or protects values. Thus, it is good as such that provides substantiation for the binding power of norms. Such assertion, while theoretically correct, does not remove all problems and doubts, of course. Often the acting subject does not know whether the actualisation of a particular norm will most contribute to a good, or, as in the case of a conflict of norms, does not know which one to choose when the actualisation of one norm means betraying another.

The obligation to take a specific action appears when the subject encounters someone or something that is valuable, precious or important, and that is under threat at a particular moment. This means that the objects of obligations include not only persons, but also animals, or the natural environment, the world of culture, or anything else which, being valuable, needs to be protected in a particular situation. Thus, the subject experiences an obligation when, to use Józef Tischner's (1982) expression, they encounter something which should not be (e.g. when another person suffers, is harmed, or wronged), or when they know that the failure to act or taking an action in defection from a particular norm will cause something which should not be (e.g. if I fail to return a thing I have borrowed, or do not keep my promise). The subject experiences an obligation in a concrete situation, as it refers to a particular condition which should be protected or remedied. It therefore represents the experience of the necessity of a particular action. Consequently, the obligation is expressly defined, e.g. "you should take care of your mother/father when they are ill", "you should help your child", but, importantly, the ways in which it may be actualised are multiple, i.e. the form in which care or help is provided may be diverse. Consequently, there is often a lack of certainty which results from the difficulty in determining what action would be most appropriate, i.e. what the optimum actualisation of a particular obligation would be. The subject is faced with the difficult task of adjusting norms to the specific requirements of a particular situation.

The above assertions lead to the conclusion that of key importance as far as moral norms are concerned is not only their recognition and acknowledgement, but also the ability to actualise them. The realisation of moral norms should be understood as making the right choices about actions which contribute to the achievement of a goal, or, in other words, to the actualisation of the content of a particular norm in a concrete situation. It thus requires a certain kind of wisdom, namely the ability to adjust the means to the ends. Aristotle called this ability "practical wisdom".

PRACTICAL WISDOM AS EXCELLENCE OF PRACTICAL ACTION

In accordance with the definition provided by Aristotle, "practical wisdom is concerned with things human and things about which it is possible to deliberate" (Aristotle, 349 BC/2009, p. 1141b). It is therefore "good deliberation" whose object is that which "is capable of being otherwise", or an aim which can be obtained through action. Practical wisdom, by the very fact that it is concerned with a specific action in specific circumstances, requires recognition of the particulars. A practically wise person thus judges well what should be done in a particular situation. To this end, they need both knowledge, or the understanding of that which is general, and experience, or knowledge of the particular.[1] Practical wisdom, the Stagirite[2] explains, is a kind of sense ("perception") which is the result of knowledge and experience. Knowledge is concerned with moral principles, while experience provides us with knowledge of that which is particular, referring both to specific individuals and to certain types of situations and to appropriate choices, behaviours and attitudes. In a way, it is therefore a general kind of knowledge – knowledge of facts which is founded on experience, and which provides guidelines for specific action (Devereux, 1986).

Practical wisdom understood by Aristotle as "good deliberation" consists of contemplating and reasoning, and is concerned with "things just and noble and good for man [sic]" (Aristotle, 349 BC/2009, p. 1143b). Practical reasoning takes the form of syllogism in which the major premise is the general principle, i.e. refers to that which the agent desires (that which is good);[3] the minor premise refers to the manner in which the major premise can be achieved or its necessary pre-conditions, and the conclusion is the action which puts that general principle into operation. The right way of applying general knowledge to a particular situation requires good deliberation and experience. Deliberation is good when it leads to achieving the right ends with the deployment of the right means. The choice of the right means is the work of practical wisdom, as it allows one to consider "means to achieve happiness", while choosing the right end is the function of moral virtue.[4] That statement emphasises the complementariness of both virtues and the fundamental role they play in moral action. Aristotle expresses that saying: "the work of man [sic] is achieved only in accordance with practical wisdom as well as with moral virtue; for virtue makes us aim at the right mark, and practical wisdom makes us take the right means" (Aristotle, 349 BC/2009, p. 1144a). The criterion of what is right or appropriate results, of course, from anthropological premises; that is, from Aristotle's view of human nature and the assumption that any action is teleological in nature, and the ultimate end of man's life is happiness understood as "an active life of the element that has reason" (ibid, p. 1098a).

The complementariness of moral virtue and practical wisdom is achieved because, by working together, they make actions we perform both good and right. The goodness of an action depends on its intentions. An action is referred to as "good" in view of its aim. The criterion here is moral virtue, which is a state of character and which determines our desiring that which is good and expedient. Moral virtue, like Kant's good will, consists not only of acting in accordance with what is right, but first of all, acting for the sake of what is right. The excellence of our character thus refers to the subjective, and not the objective dimension of human actions and requires something we might call a desire for good. Practical wisdom, in turn, makes our actions right. The rightness of an action depends on the way we act, on the right choice of means we deploy to achieve our end. Thus, moral virtue makes our actions morally good, while practical wisdom gives our actions the right form, making us choose the most appropriate course of action. This internal relationship means that "without wisdom, excellence of character would be like a man [sic] groping in the dark and not knowing where to go; without the desires of an excellent character, wisdom would have nothing to do" (Urmson, 1988, p. 84).

The object of practical wisdom is to find a good solution for difficult dilemmas, or such situations in which there are several alternative ways to proceed, and among which an inexperienced man finds it hard to choose the right one[5] (Hursthouse, 2006; Polansky, 2000). That which makes us capable of judging correctly in untypical situations is discernment. It enables us to solve difficult dilemmas involving a conflict of virtues, e.g. between kindness and honesty. Such conflict results from the fact that the requirements of both virtues substantiate opposite behaviours. On the one hand, there are reasons for which one should tell a lie, on the other – it appears to be requisite to tell the cruel truth. Such a dilemma can only be solved if the virtues are interpreted correctly. *Phrónimos*[6] is aware of the fact that in some situations, kindness consists precisely in telling the cruel truth, and that acting with discretion or passing over certain matters in silence is not always the same as dishonesty (Hursthouse, 2006). *Phrónimos* actions differ from those of a virtuous but inexperienced person in that s/he does not perceive virtues from the perspective of conventional generalisations, following acquired, drilled, schematic ways. In order to recognise a conflict between virtues and find the correct solution, or recognise where an exception is appropriate, one must possess all virtues and "have an overall conception of how each of the various virtues do fit together with one another to make up the final end of life, *eudaimonia*" (Bostock, 2006, p. 88). It is only then that the development of a more sophisticated understanding which comes with practical wisdom will be possible.

Another constitutive element of practical wisdom is the ability to get the situation right. It is not possible to act right without understanding the situation in which we find ourselves, without being aware of it in minute detail. Right judgement is the work of comprehension, which, Aristotle explains, refers to "things which may become subjects of questioning and deliberation" (Aristotle, 349 BC/2009, p. 1143a). Comprehension, as an intellectual capacity, comes not only from experience, but is also the result of learning. People learn, for instance, in what circumstances it is advisable to be suspicious and mistrustful, what people most often lie about, who can and who cannot be relied on. They learn that a different account is most often rendered by each person participating in an event. They thus become suspicious about the opinions and accounts of others, which forces them to ask appropriate questions about the reliability of the persons they listen to (Hursthouse, 2006).

This is also related to perceptiveness, which is a condition of passing correct judgements. It supplies us with practical knowledge about people, and is necessary to recognise and understand what is involved. For instance, judgement requires the ability to correctly interpret people's emotional states, allowing us to judge whether a particular expression we observe in another person corresponds to the emotions it is supposed to represent, or whether it is an attempt at concealing that person's true feelings. In order to develop that capacity, apart from participating in social interaction one also needs memory, imagination and experience. In the broader sense, perceptiveness refers to understanding the world around us: the circumstances of life, social reality and the ability to perceive a hierarchy of goods. Understood that way, perceptiveness is a component of practical wisdom, as it is an element of getting the situation right, of understanding the practice circumstances in which we find ourselves (Hursthouse, 2006). Even if there are things I cannot change, by being aware of them I may, through deliberation, change my attitude towards them.

Another essential element of practical knowledge is cleverness, which is the ability to identify the most effective means leading to a desired end. Interestingly, it is an ability which *phrónimos* has in common with a vile, unscrupulous person. Just like a capable crook, a practically wise person must be able to deliberate well (Hursthouse, 2006). Cleverness, understood as a certain type of "intelligence without any sense of the good" (Demos, 1961, p. 155) is not the same as practical wisdom, however. The difference between them results from the fact that in the case of practical wisdom, the criterion set for choosing the means leading to a given end is not concerned merely with the effectiveness of the action. Deliberations concerned with the choice of right (correct) means also include moral reflection and side effects. Therefore, practical wisdom sometimes calls for rejecting even such means as are the only possible way of achieving a desired end. Consequently, practical wisdom should take into account a broad perspective and include the element of imagination and the ability to foresee potential consequences and create possible scenarios of various alternative courses of action. In order to choose the right action, it is necessary to evaluate those various possibilities and their elements. Thus, choice is a kind of judgement based on rational premises. James Urmson (1988) points out that cleverness is not the ability to plan actions, but it is necessary "after deliberation has terminated and the plan has been made" (p. 82). As an executive ability, cleverness is a condition of putting the plan into effect. Urmson emphasises the difference between planning and execution: they are two separate stages of an action, and each requires different abilities. "Part of knowing how to get things done is ... a matter of having the requisite information" (ibid, p. 82) requiring comprehension and sagacity which allow us to get the situation right. To successfully put the plan into operation, in turn, we need cleverness, and often courage.

Based on the above deliberations, we can conclude that practical wisdom is not inborn, given to us by nature, but it is acquired by human practice. The conviction that such intellectual excellence can be developed means that the wickedness of character isn't a valid excuse for wrongdoing (Demos, 1961). Practical wisdom is an ability, like moral virtues, which is achieved by effort and experience (even though it is not available to everyone in the same degree). As a capacity which develops with practice, it is concerned with how to act and what to be like. Thus, it combines two areas: that of action and that of character. Even if not all of our respective elements can be developed, such as our temperament or certain circumstances of life, everyone may, to such degree as is available to each of us, develop and strive at perfection in both our actions and character.

Practical wisdom means excellence of practical action. It is the most important virtue with respect to the moral dimension of action in view of the nature of human *praxis*. When we come to consider right human conduct, there are no "fixed definitions". This means any attempt at defining precisely how to act in particular situations is doomed to failure. General assertions on how we should behave lack precision, as they do not take into account the particular circumstances which to a large extent determine the success or failure of our actions. Even the golden mean principle is not a recipe which can be applied "as instructed". For the mean "is neither one nor the same thing for all". This is due to the fact that "behaviour is concerned with particulars". In view of the diversity and lack of stability in the sphere of human actions, it is impossible to formulate "universal rules which we can rely on in making practical decisions" (Devereux, 1986, p. 501). Consequently, it is "the agents themselves [who] must in each case consider what is appropriate to the occasion" (Aristotle, 349 BC/2009, p. 1104a). That, however, is not easy to do.

Unlike the arithmetic mean, which is descriptive, the mean measure is normative (or axiological) in that it defines what is right, appropriate or due (Brown, 1997). That in turn is relative, as it means the experience of passions "at the right times, with reference to the right object, towards the right people, with the right motive, and in the right way" (Aristotle, 349 BC/2009, p. 1106b). Thus, the right conduct is different in each situation, depending on a number of circumstances. Practical wisdom allows us to apply the mean measure understood that way by enabling us to choose the correct course of action in particular circumstances; that is, such action as is consistent with the right judgement. It may thus be inferred that practical knowledge related to practical wisdom differs from theoretical knowledge. The latter deals with invariable things, or such as cannot be otherwise, while practical knowledge deals with that which may undergo change, or to human *praxis*. And while there is the "final principle that one should always act in a way that promotes eudaimonia", for obvious reasons it may never "give guidance in practical situations" (Urmson, 1988, p. 86). There are also certain general rules which say what actions are worthwhile in the pursuit of happiness;[7] they do not, however, tell us how to act in a particular situation. "They do not obviate the need for a final judgement, in the light of all the facts, which does not follow automatically from any simple principle or principles" (Urmson, 1988, p. 86). Consequently, a "wise person's judgement about how to act in a particular case is perfectly determinate and appropriate to the situation" (Devereux 1986, p. 496). Therefore, practical wisdom is not a set of practical rules of conduct, but comprises a number of "various subordinate excellences of intelligence" (Urmson, 1988, p. 81) such as: sagacity, comprehension, shrewdness, good deliberation. These abilities allow us to recognise what course of action will promote happiness, or not.

PRACTICAL WISDOM AS MORAL JUDGEMENT IN SITUATION

Similar significance is assigned to practical wisdom by the contemporary French philosopher Paul Ricœur. He emphasises its relevance in "the hard cases of law, medicine or everyday life" (Ricœur, 1998, p. 92). In view of the possibility, inherent to human life, of "facing hard cases", he asks: "How can one decipher one's own life in situations of uncertainty, of conflict or of risk?" (ibid, p. 92). In order to identify the essence of conflict, he refers to Greek tragedy. He believes the best example is provided by Sophocles' *Antigone*, where

> conflict emerges as soon as Antigone and Creon identify entirely with a particular norm and become blind to everything else: Antigone, for whom the obligation to bury her brother's body, arising from imprescriptible law, cannot see the fact that the reason of state, the state's law sees her brother as an enemy …; Creon, to whom power in the state subordinates family relationships to the distinction between friend and enemy, exemplifies another kind of blindness. (Drwięga, 1998, p. 169)

Ricœur points out that the two protagonists draw the line between friend and enemy in an entirely different way. The tragedy is born against the conflict of roles. The conception which both Creon and Antigone develop about their duties does not exhaust the wealth of their meanings, and does not take into account the variety of different situations in which they may arise (Ricœur, 1992). The source of conflict, therefore, is the "narrowness of viewpoint" which results from the meaning the protagonists attach to norms defining what they ought to do in view of the value of the act. For Creon, "Alone is 'good' that which serves the city, 'bad' that which is harmful to it; the good citizen alone is 'just' and 'justice' commands only the art of governing and being governed" (ibid, p. 244). Also, Antigone's view of the world is impoverished and simplified, with only family relationships counting, and friend being only the deceased relative. Ricœur concludes that "[t]hese are indeed two partial and unilateral visions of justice that are set in opposition by the protagonists" (ibid, p. 244).

Such a limited, inherently contradictory axiological view of the world and the "strategy of simplification", to use Martha Nussbaum's expression, leads to the emergence of conflicts between different views of the same values (e.g. justice), or between different values (e.g. truthfulness and kindness). The analyses he performs lead Ricœur to the conclusion that the source of conflict, aside from the one-sidedness of the characters, is first of all "the one-sidedness of the moral principles which themselves are confronted with the complexity of life" (Ricœur, 1992, p. 249). This is why practical wisdom is needed. As Ricœur explains, "in the conflicts to which morality gives rise, only a recourse to the ethical ground ... can give rise to the wisdom of judgment in situation ... that can shelter moral conviction from the ruinous alternatives of univocity or arbitrariness" (ibid, p. 249). In *Intellectual Autobiography* he adds:

> The peculiarity of instances, conflicts between the obligations attached to living in a society – where the choice is most often between shades of grey rather than between black and white – and situations which I call situations of despair – where the choice is not between good and evil, but between bad and worse – require practical wisdom. (Ricœur, 2005, p. 52)

Ricœur claims that the source of conflicts is morality. We must therefore explain how he understands morality and how it differs from ethics. Ricœur (1992) describes ethics (ethical aim) as the "aiming at the 'good life' with and for others in just institutions" (p. 172). Emphasising and defending the primacy of ethics over morality, he also points out that it is necessary for the ethical aim to pass through the restriction of moral norm. Ricœur links the moral dimension with formalisation and universalisation of the ethical aim. It includes that which imposes itself as obligatory, and means the relationship of the aim of good life to "norms characterized at once by the claim to universality and by an effect of constraint" (ibid, p. 170). Morality, Ricœur explains, is therefore "an attempt at incorporating the ethics of the aim of good life into a universal norm, at subordinating this aim to the imperative" (Lubowicka, 2000, p. 143). The passage of the ethical aim through the restriction of moral norm gives rise to conflicts, however, and thence the need for practical wisdom. The three main moments of Ricœur's morality, i.e. the formalism of institutions, respect for another, and autonomy, correspond to the three spheres of possible conflict.

Conflict in the sphere of institutions is caused by a purely procedural approach to justice. Many concepts of distributive justice fail to take into account the diversity of goods to be distributed. The qualitative difference between them is wiped out, and consequently their distribution becomes unjust. If, however, the emphasis is shifted from the procedure of distribution to the difference between goods to be distributed, new problems emerge. The first one is related to the return of the teleological perspective which brings that which is just and that which is good back together again. As Ricœur points out, John Rawls (1971) opens up this issue himself when he refers to the idea of social primary goods. The question about what qualifies these goods as such gives rise to conflict, as they are related to heterogeneous estimations. Another problem arises in view of the historical and cultural nature of such estimations. Michael Walzer (1983), whom Ricœur refers to, takes into account the diversity of goods to be distributed and the diversity of their estimations, and introduces the idea of spheres of justice. Each sphere, e.g. security, welfare, offices, money and merchandise, is governed by particular rules. The conflict that arises is related to the competition between these spheres and the threat of one being trampled by another. Yet another problem is the question about which of the spheres is to be given priority for its claims (Ricœur, 1992).

Abstract right, which lacks the capacity of creating relationships between people, as it "is limited to separating what is mine from what is yours" (Ricœur, 1992, p. 254), will not solve these problems, Ricœur believes. In his opinion, a solution should be sought on the grounds of the political society. Capacities which determine people's actions (e.g. discussion, co-deciding, cooperation) may only develop in the institutional environment (ibid). Therefore, only in political practice is it possible to take up conflicts arising from the idea of just distribution. In everyday discussion in a state of law, the conflict focuses around deliberations about social goods of primary importance. Disputes are aimed at creating a temporary order of such goods. In democratic states, this is done through reasonable political discussion and decisions in the form of choice. Historical experience shows that there is no rule capable of establishing an order of values as primary as freedom, security and the rule of law (ibid). For it is not possible to scientifically settle what social good consists of. Consequently,

> only a public debate, whose outcome is always arbitrary, may give rise to an order of priority. Such order will only have value for one nation, however, during a certain period in its history, and will never be irresistibly compelling to all people and in all times. (Ricœur, 1991, p. 48)

This is why conflicts in democracy are unavoidable, and political discussion remains un-concluded. The lack of conclusion does not mean a lack of decision, however. Decision is a political "judgment in situation, which advanced democracies identify essentially with majority vote" (Ricœur, 1992, p. 258). On the institutional plane, it becomes an equivalent of Aristotle's *phrónêsis*. Practical judgement is also necessary when looking for and choosing a "good constitution" and a "good government". Ricœur emphasises that "historical realization of one set of values can be obtained only at the expense of another set" (ibid, p. 259). And when we cannot serve all values at the same time, only the legislators' conviction is left, their sense of justice which is actualised in a political judgement in situation at the time of "historical" choices (ibid).

Concluding his reflections on the role of practical wisdom in the sphere of institutions, Ricœur refers to equity. He understands it, like Aristotle, as a correction of law which is excessively universal. When a situation occurs for which no decided cases exist, equity commands a solution which is consistent with the legislator's intention. Ricœur (1992) explains his understanding of equity by saying that public debate and the decision making that results from it constitute the only agency qualified to 'correct the omission' that today we call the 'legitimation crisis.' Equity ... is another name for the sense of justice, when the latter traverses the hardships and conflicts resulting from the application of the rule of justice. (p. 262)

The other area of conflict is related to the dialogic dimension of morality, and results from the application of the second Kantian imperative which says that humanity in one's own person and in the person of others should be treated as an end in itself rather than simply as a means. In the form of this imperative Ricœur finds a line dividing the universalist aspect, represented by the idea of humanity, and the pluralist aspect, represented by the idea of persons as ends in themselves. The possibility of conflict emerges when the otherness of persons proves to be incompatible in certain circumstances with the universality of the rules that underlie the idea of humanity. As Ricœur (1992) explains:

respect then tends to split up into respect for the law and respect for persons. Under these conditions, practical wisdom may consist in giving priority to the respect for persons, in the name of the solicitude that is addressed to persons in their irreplaceable singularity. (p. 262)

A situation of conflict may arise when a maxim is applied to a concrete situation in which the otherness of persons calls for recognition. Ricœur analyses this problem using the example of a false promise. Kant, considering this case, allowed for exceptions from the rule, but only for the sake of one's own benefit. Ricœur points out that he failed to account for exceptions made for the sake of another. For Kant, the source of duties towards others is upholding one's own personal integrity, wherefore a false promise is an expression of contempt for oneself. The wrong done to the other is not taken into account. Such argument only appears when the maxim is submitted to the test of circumstances and consequences. The promise is then transferred to the area of reciprocity, governed by the Golden Rule. Ricœur emphasises the difference between making promises and being obligated to keep them. He calls this obligation the principle of fidelity, stressing its dialogic structure. By making a promise, one responds to an expectation, to a request coming from another. One is more faithful to another than to oneself. If the commitment to uphold one's own identity in keeping one's promises were not accompanied by the condition of responding to an expectation of another, this commitment, Ricœur points out, could turn into simple constancy and a silly wager. Therefore, he believes that self-constancy which is manifested in being faithful to one's word is a response to the expectation of another, the one to whom an obligation is owed (Ricœur, 1992).

This structure of reciprocity in promising entails the possibility of conflict which consists of a "split" between respect for the rule and respect for persons. If fidelity consists of responding to the expectation of another, is it not necessary at times to make an exception from the rule on behalf of the other? Ricœur claims that in conflict situations, practical wisdom is manifest in conduct "that will best satisfy the exception required by solicitude, by betraying the rule to the smallest extent possible" (Ricœur, 1992, p. 269). He analyses an example concerning the end of life, related to the dilemma of telling or withholding the truth from the dying, i.e.:

> telling the truth without taking into account the capacity of the dying to receive it, out of sheer respect for the law ...; or knowingly lying, out of fear ... of weakening the forces in the patient struggling against death and of transforming the agony of a loved one into torture. (Ricœur, 1992, p. 269)

He decides that "practical wisdom consists here in inventing just behavior suited to the singular nature of the case. But it is not, for all that, simply arbitrary" (Ricœur, 1992, p. 269). Practical wisdom should, in his opinion, take the form of meditating on the relation between happiness and suffering. He concludes that "in such cases, one must have compassion for those who are morally or physically too weak to hear the truth. In certain other cases, one must know how to communicate this truth" (ibid, p. 269). Even if we believe the sick person is capable of receiving the truth, we must be able to see that "it is one thing to name an illness, it is another to reveal the degree of seriousness and the slight chance of survival, and yet another to wield the clinical truth as a death sentence" (ibid, p. 269).

The significance of practical wisdom results, in Ricœur's opinion, from the fact that it is the only tool available to a person facing a moral dilemma. He says that one should not "legislate in an area where the responsibility for difficult choices cannot be made easier by laws" (Ricœur, 1992, p. 269). In the sphere of interpersonal relationships, in making such difficult choices one should rely on practical wisdom which takes the form of "critical solicitude". It makes one aware that: 1) it is advisable to consider whether the adverse positions call upon the same principle of respect and differ only with regard to its field of application; 2) it is wise to look for the "just mean", the Aristotelian middle way; 3) the counsel of persons most competent and the wisest should be sought. Then the conviction will become the result of a debate by many persons (ibid).

The last area of conflict arises, according to Ricœur, when a clash occurs between the "universalist claim attached to the rules claiming to belong to the principle of morality and the recognition of positive values belonging to the historical and communitarian contexts of the realization of these same rules" (Ricœur, 1992, p. 274). The most significant conflicts arise from the restrictive criterion of universalisation which considers a maxim immoral if, when raised to the level of a universal rule, it proves to be internally contradictory. In most general terms, it may be reduced to a conflict between universalism and contextualism. The tragedy of action resulting from this antinomy may only be overcome, according to the French philosopher, by the practical wisdom of moral judgement in situation.

The solution proposed by Ricœur consists in embracing an ethics of argumentation that would "integrate the objections of contextualism, while allowing the latter, at the same time, to take seriously the requirement of universalization in order to focus on the conditions for placing this requirement in context" (Ricœur, 1992, p. 287). Argumentation should play the role of a critical agency operating inside the convictions in order to carry them to the level of *considered convictions*. This "reflective equilibrium between the requirement of universality and the recognition of the contextual limitations affecting it ... is the final issue in the judgement in situation" (ibid, p. 288). Reflective equilibrium is reflected well in the notion of universals in context. It is about a dialogue between the ethics of argumentation and convictions. Ricœur (1992) believes that

> only a real discussion, in which convictions are permitted to be elevated above conventions, will be able to state, at the end of a long history yet to come, which alleged universals will become universals recognized by all the persons concerned, that is, by the representative persons of all cultures (pp. 289-290)

Summing up the above reflections, it should be stressed that in Ricœur's opinion, practical wisdom is a tool for solving conflicts resulting from morality. These conflicts may be reduced to the tension between universalism and contextualism. The universalist nature of morality requires the adoption of universal, unchangeable laws. Their universality, however, does not account for the otherness of persons and uniqueness of situations. This is why we need practical wisdom which puts the individuality of persons before the law. By taking circumstances into account, it allows for exceptions required by solicitude, while departing from the rule to the least extent possible. Ricœur proposes an ethics of argumentation whose goal is to arrive at "considered convictions" in concrete situations. Ricœur emphasises the need for balancing the requirement of universality against the concrete circumstances which give rise to limitations.

Ricœur clearly points to the primacy of ethics (good) over law or rule. Law does not take into account the context of situations or feelings of the subject, while every human decision requires personal involvement and reflection. Therefore, one should not apply the rules of law without reflection, as they do not take into account the uniqueness of persons and situations; instead, they should be treated as general guidelines.

The significance of practical wisdom which can be inferred from Ricœur's concept reflects the outcome that practical wisdom not only allows us to understand that each universal principle has its limitations, but also to go beyond them. The unlimited scope of principles prevents moral judgement from being reduced to that which is acceptable or practised in a society. Thus, practical wisdom requires and at the same time develops our imagination and moral sensitivity. It is essentially the opposite of an instrumental treatment of moral principles or ethics in general.

It is Ricœur who points out that the need for practical wisdom is related to the fact that life is complex to the extent we cannot subordinate it to a single principle, attitude or value. Only a "moral judgment in situation and the conviction that dwells in it" (Ricœur, 1992, p. 241) can measure up to the complex circumstances of a conflict. This is why it is so important to mutually renounce prejudice, and to expand and deepen axiological identity. Practical wisdom makes us aware that ethical conflict is unavoidable, and sometimes also irresolvable. There are circumstances in life, which Karl Jaspers (1970) calls borderline situations, in which one does not and cannot know how to act, because whatever action is taken, its consequences will be tragic. Therefore, practical wisdom incorporates tragic wisdom which manifests itself in the awareness that conflicts are unavoidable, and in the ability to recognise that which is doubtful and irrational.[8]

In his few remarks on practical wisdom, Ricœur answers the question about the causes of diversified moral judgements. He shows that due to the unilateral nature of rules and the diversity of human characters, our practical experience of values and our estimation of actions is different. Practice is much more complex than the ideal sphere of values. In this context, we may ask whether the fact that conflicts are unavoidable is a good thing for the moral subject? It seems that it depends, on the one hand, on the type and subject matter of the conflict, and on the other – on how the subject approaches the conflict they experience. Depending on these factors, conflict may be creative or destructive; that is, it may widen and deepen the subject's moral awareness (and sensitivity), or evoke a sense of powerlessness and lack of belief in the meaningfulness of moral choices.

CONCLUSIONS: THE PLACE AND ROLE OF PRACTICAL WISDOM IN THE SPHERE OF HUMAN ACTIONS

For both Aristotle and Ricœur, practical wisdom is related to the sphere of practical action. Without this capacity, moral norms and general rules of conduct would become useless. Rules do not determine the justness of our choice of means – this is the role of practical judgement. It is thanks to practical wisdom that the subject may know not only what norms they should refer to in a particular situation, but first of all how (by what means) these norms should be implemented. This implementation cannot be reduced merely to practical guidelines, however, about how to behave in a given situation; it also includes the ability to explain why we are supposed to behave one way and not another, and why we are supposed to do anything at all.

Practical wisdom has its applications mainly where the solution of a given problem does not fit within any theoretical paradigm or common experience (Podrez, n.d., pp. 3, 33). In the case of a conflict, moral dilemma or borderline situation, when rules and moral norms are no longer clear and obvious, the subject realises that the powerlessness, helplessness and irrationality resulting from the incidental conditions of human life are unavoidable elements. This role of practical wisdom must not be disregarded. The ability to recognise tragic situations as tragic, when we must choose between two competing norms or values, allows us to avoid a pointless and futile search for a non-existing morally good solution at any cost. Therefore, even though practical wisdom as moral knowledge includes the awareness of universal moral norms, it also encompasses knowledge about the world, other people, and oneself, and helps us recognise that not every action yields to simple judgement. Human life is complex, unpredictable and abounding in various dilemmas.

With practical wisdom, the subject can know – apart from that which is certain and obvious – also that which is doubtful and irrational (Podrez, n.d., p. 4). Even if this knowledge does not release the subject from responsibility, it does protect them from self-hypocrisy and a false moral picture of the world. This way, practical wisdom becomes an antidote to arrogance, which is "an attitude based on self-righteousness" (Jakubowski, 2014, p. 91). It makes the subject realise that every ethical system is relative, and may serve, at the most, as a general guideline which does not, however, provide ready-made solutions about how to behave in a particular situation. Ultimately, the decision and the responsibility for making it always rests on the subject. This results from the fact that "the relationship between a concrete choice and the value to which it is subordinated is unavoidably that of interpretation" (ibid, p. 93), and in this effort of interpretation the subject cannot be replaced by anyone else. Moreover, often "the making of a choice must be preceded by choosing between values – by arranging them into a hierarchy, sacrificing one value for another" (ibid, p. 93), and this choice is always made by the subject, even if they rely on someone else's advice. People who have practical wisdom are able to make these choices, because they have both the knowledge of what is good and the ability to act in compliance with this criterion, i.e. the ability to make judgements in situations. They are able to correctly interpret the hierarchy of values and obligations, as they have the capacity for critical deliberation. Practical wisdom thus combines moral knowledge with a properly developed attitude, character and abilities. It also includes practical knowledge about people, and an understanding of where the differences in people's convictions, attitudes and judgements come from. With such knowledge, people are cautious in their evaluations – instead of passing hasty judgements, they try to understand the motives behind other people's actions (Podrez, n.d., pp. 9, 11).

ACKNOWLEDGEMENT

Fragments of this chapter have been published in the following articles: Rozmarynowska, K. (2015). The ethical dimension of practical wisdom. *Organon F, 22*(1), 34-52; and Rozmarynowska, K. (2015). Mądrość praktyczna jako zdolność do realizowania norm moralnych. In P. Duchliński & T. Homa (Eds.), *Z problematyki norm, zasad i mądrości praktycznej* (pp. 109-119). Kraków: Akademia Ignatianum, Wydawnictwo WAM.

NOTES

[1] Daniel Devereux explains that "knowledge of particulars ... could be understood as knowledge of the specific types of action appropriate for specific types of situation: 'situations of this type call for such and such action'. Or, it could be understood as knowledge of individual acts and circumstances: 'this situation I find myself in calls for this particular response'" (Devereux, 1986, p. 485).
[2] Name for Aristotle.
[3] Aristotle identifies these two categories with one another: that which is good is the object of desire, and the object of desire is that which is good (Aristotle, c. 400 BC/2014).
[4] That conviction differs from the view of Hume who claimed that the aim is the result of feelings, and the reason is only able to calculate what means should be deployed to achieve it.
[5] Polansky defines practical wisdom as a calculative and problem-solving capacity.
[6] *Phrónimos*: practically wise, sensible.
[7] Having a concept of the goal of happiness is a necessary element of practical wisdom. It refers to universal assumptions and is the basis for the major premise in practical reasoning. And yet, as David Bostock has pointed out, Aristotle "does not make any real attempt to spell out just how the practically wise man conceives of the ultimate end, *eudaemonia*". He only says that a practically wise person is capable of deliberating on that which is good for him with reference to the "right way of living in

general". He must, therefore, know what is the ultimate end, that is, happiness (Bostock, 2006, pp. 82-100).

[8] "We are doomed to struggling with the notorious ambiguity of the concept of good as the aim of striving, and with the undecidable aporia of evil and the very real, as we have been taught by experience, possibility of making bad choices" (Wolicka, 2010, p. 139).

REFERENCES

Aristotle. (2009). *Nicomachean ethics* (W. D. Ross, Trans.). Oxford, England: Oxford World's Classics. (Original work published 349 BC)
Aristotle. (2014). *Metaphysics* (W. D. Ross, Trans.). Adelaide, Australia: The University of Adelaide. (Original work published c. 400 BC)
Bostock, D. (2006): *Aristotle's ethics*. New York, NY: Oxford University Press.
Brown, L. (1997). What is 'the mean relative to us' in Aristotle's Ethics? *Phronesis, 42*, 77-93.
Demos, R. (1961). Remarks on Aristotle's doctrine of practical reason. *Philosophy and Phenomenological Research, 22*, 153-162.
Devereux, D. T. (1986). Particular and universal in Aristotle's conception of practical knowledge. *The Review of Metaphysics, 39*, 483-504.
Drwięga, M. (1998). *Paul Ricœur daje do myślenia*. Bydgoszcz: Homini.
Hooker, B. (2006). Moral rules and principles. In D. M. Borchert (Ed.), *Encyclopedia of philosophy* (Vol. 4, p. 382). Detroit, MI: Thomson Gale/Macmillan Reference.
Hursthouse, R. (2006). Practical wisdom: A mundane account. *Proceedings of the Aristotelian Society: New Series, 106*, 285-309.
Jakubowski, P. (2014). Odnaleźć phronesis w aesthesis: Paul Ricœur wobec samotności wyboru i działania. *Zeszyty Naukowe Centrum Badań im. Edyty Stein, 12*, 91-103.
Jaspers K. (1970). *Philosophy* (E. B. Ashton, Trans.). Chicago & London: The University of Chicago Press.
Lubowicka, G. (2000). *Sumienie jako poświadczenie: Idea podmiotowości w filozofii Paula Ricœura*. Wrocław: Wydawnictwo Uniwersytetu Wrocławskiego.
Podrez, E. (n.d.). *Mądrość praktyczna jako podstawa działania moralnego w ujęciu Arystotelesa, Kanta i Ricœura* [typescript].
Polansky, R. (2000). 'Phronesis' on tour: Cultural adaptability of Aristotelian ethical notions. *Kennedy Institute of Ethics Journal, 10*, 323-336.
Rawls, J. (1971). *Theory of justice*. Cambridge, MA: Harvard University Press.
Ricœur, P. (1991). Osoba: Struktura etyczna i moralna. In *Zawierzyć człowiekowi. Księdzu Józefowi Tischnerowi na sześćdziesiąte urodziny* (J. Fenrychowa, Trans.). Kraków: Znak.
Ricœur, P. (1992): *Oneself as another* (K. Blamey, Trans.). Chicago, IL: University of Chicago Press.
Ricœur, P. (1998). *Critique and conviction: Conversations with François Azouvi and Marc de Launay*. New York, NY: Columbia University Press.
Ricœur, P. (2005). *Refleksja dokonana. Autobiografia intelektualna* (P. Bobowska-Nastarzewska, Trans.). Kęty: Antyk.
Ślipko, T. (2002). *Zarys etyki ogólnej*. Kraków: Wydawnictwo WAM.
Tischner, J. (1982). *Myślenie według wartości*. Kraków: Znak.
Urmson, J. O. (1988). *Aristotle's ethics*. Oxford, England: Basil Blackwell.
Walzer, M. (1983). *Spheres of justice: A defence of pluralism and equality*. New York, NY: Basic Books.
Wolicka, E. (2010). *Narracja i egzystencja: 'Droga okrężna' Paula Ricœura od hermeneutyki do ontoantropologii*. Lublin: Wydawnictwo KUL.

Karolina Rozmarynowska PhD
Institute of Philosophy, Faculty of Christian Philosophy
Cardinal Stefan Wyszynski University in Warsaw, Poland

BERNARD MCKENNA

12. DEVELOPING WISE ORGANISATIONS

THE WISE ALTERNATIVE

As organisations try to cope with varying stakeholder demands and with the internal paradoxes of organisations, the tendency is simply to add more and more regulations, processes and internal auditing processes based on metrics such as key performance indicators (KPIs). The result is often an overwhelming sense of busyness and inadequacy with people working excessive hours, experiencing stress and burnout. In contrast to this ever-intensifying process, organisational wisdom theory seeks to provide guiding principles rather than mandated practices. In reflecting on organisational wisdom we need to remember that we cannot be two different people (in life and work) for the most fundamental life questions: who am I and how do I go about shaping the world of which I am part?

Essentially, current organisational theory and best organisational practices now understand that the idea of *homo economicus* is totally inadequate in describing the motives of human beings. The idea of the "economic man" was first devised by economic philosopher, John Stuart Mill, as a parsimonious assumption about people's motivations: accumulation, leisure, luxury and procreation. In fact, the "father of modern management", Peter Drucker, in 1939 wrote *The End of Economic Man,* and following World War Two, *The Future of Industrial Man,* in which he provided a desirable social vision of a harmonious world in which management and workers collaborated and in which socially desirable outcomes rather than simply profit were presented as the responsibility of management.

However, although it is highly respected and taught widely in business schools, Drucker's vision has been at odds with the practices in much of economic society. This has been particularly so since the 1980s era of "destructive capitalism" promoted by economist Joseph Schumpeter: this is a time when global competition and the primacy of shareholder value has led to organisations globally outsourcing work to cheaper sources of labour, stock markets rewarding short-term profits not long-term stability, expanding micro-management, and the move to a gig economy of short-term contracts and insecure unemployment. Clearly the result has not been a good one with many "developed" economies experiencing high unemployment, zero or declining wage growth, and vast disparities of wealth and income. The global environment, too, must be accorded the strongest emphasis given the parlous state of fragility the world currently faces.

Organisations, therefore, need to be understood as simply the meso-level encased like a Russian doll in a larger macro-level (knowledge, technology, social practices, and dominant beliefs, values and ideologies understood as "common sense") in which they operate as part of a complex system. As well as operating in a complex system, organisations have to cope with complex data. However, humans have only bounded rationality (Simon, 1991). This is because the behaviour of many phenomena is incomprehensible through observation or measurement because they are transient, unique, unstable or evolving into other forms. According to Simon this boundedness limits the extent to which agents can make a fully rational decision, and people are forced to make decisions by "satisficing"[1,2] not by "maximisation".

In order to cope with the complexity, people use heuristics to assess, predict and make judgements. These heuristics are often highly economical and usually effective; however, they can lead to systematic and predictable errors (Tversky & Kahneman, 1974). Acknowledging that we are boundedly rational and that we frequently make complex decisions not by using lots of data, instead, we must acknowledge the role of good judgement based on experience, reflection, intuition, heuristics and distributed cognition. Good judgement is an outcome of being wise, so it stands to reason that for an organisation to operate as effectively as possible it needs to have processes that encourage wise judgement.

A further problem faced by contemporary organisations is that they encounter incommensurable discourses, which means that there is confusion about goals and practices. This is because many organisational members now have to deal with a multiplicity of stakeholder expectations and increasing external regulations such as professional and occupational standards, occupational health and safety, as well as auditing and reporting. This leads to a knee-jerk response to multiple pressures in the form of ever-increasing internal rules, standards and procedures and ever-increasing forms of surveillance.

THE NATURE OF ORGANISATIONS IN BRIEF

Modern organisations can be understood by acknowledging their behaviour as institutions, which can be explained by (neo-)institutional theory and the nature of paradox. Institutional theory does not look at organisations primarily in terms of sections outlined in organisation charts and ostensible lines of authority that produce rational, "objective" decision, but from the perspective of culture and cognitions. Culture and cognition underlay one of the earliest critiques of organisational practices in the watershed article by Meyer and Rowan (1977) which drew attention to the development of isomorphism within organisational structures as they sought legitimacy by conforming to the dominant practices in the external environment. This is why understanding the macro-context is vital to understanding internal practices of organisations.

This isomorphism materialised in the dominant discourses that were primarily concerned with maximising profit by creating "leaner" structures which in reality often meant that workers took on more responsibility without necessarily being compensated at the same level as the managers whose jobs had been "flattened". The dominant ideology was that workers needed to be more entrepreneurial and to align their personal identity with that of the organisation. Perhaps the most used discursive term was "change" with preferences given to change managers.

While firms must change internal practices in order to adapt to changing circumstances, the notion of change simply became an unquestioned mantra of managerialist discourse "representing 'knowledge' or 'received wisdom' ... about what constitutes effective management" (Zorn, Page, & Cheney, 2000, p. 517). Applied unthinkingly, the notion of change was increasingly resisted, even resented, by workers who experienced a succession of new, often messianic, managers who promised a new, more effective approach.

The impact was often negative, with people feeling insecure about their employment and economic security, having their status reduced, and losing a sense of identity. Even teamwork, which was claimed to replace hierarchical structures in order to provide more democratic, participatory and creative systems, was found to be restrictive, and, in the words of Barker (1993), what really happened in organisations was as follows:

> I began to notice that the way the team members talked, both informally and at team meetings, had changed. They did not talk so much about the importance of their teamwork values as they did about the need to 'obey' the team's work norms. Team meetings began to have a confrontational tone, ... Team meetings became a forum for discussing norms and creating new rules. (p. 425)

Barker called this "concertive control", which is more insidious. While they appear to be more open and democratic than traditional bureaucracies, team-based systems in fact can be highly controlling with team members being unaware of how the system controls their actions. This happens because workers invest themselves through their strong identification with the value-based system and workers socially construct their identity (a psychological term) or their subjectivity (a poststructural sociological term) as members of a system they have created. Consequently, they develop "groupthink" where team members readily control their own actions.

Although this neo-institutional approach to organisations has been helpful, it is important not to overlook two aspects. First, we need to remember that organisational members have some degree of agency, and they should not be regarded as automatons who simply enact organisational practices. Second, it should not be assumed that there is one unitary organisational logic that guides practice. More recently, organisation theorists have shown how organisations can have multiple, even inconsistent logics, internal tensions or paradoxes (Lewis, 2000). It is now assumed in organisation theory that paradoxes and tensions are naturally inherent in organisations (Smith & Lewis, 2011).

However, in practice, such paradoxes are often denied or hidden. Managers need to face the challenge of reconciling contradictory expectations. As well, organisational divisions that operate according to different logics may conflict or compete: for example, finance seeking increased gross sales despite unethical outcomes; HR setting up unattainable performance targets symbolic of a lack of trust; while those concerned with promoting the socially responsible organisation may feel that they are simply "greenwashing" practices like exploitative supply chains and greenhouse emissions that are at odds with their publicly espoused values.

Furthermore, because many organisational members have their personal identity so closely aligned with their organisational practice, particularly their primary group affiliation within an organisation, they can become extremely agitated when that identity is threatened.

CAN AN ORGANISATION BE WISE?

There is considerable criticism about the way that organisations are being administered. A book by two senior business academics, André Spicer and Mats Alvesson, *The Stupidity Paradox: The Power and Pitfalls of Functional Stupidity at Work*, outlines the many ways in which organisations have lost their way by forcing people into increasingly manic and mindless routines. Most of the criticism can be summarised as comprising isomorphism, "technophilia", increasing regulation and control, and management fads.

Omar Aktouf, a Canadian professor of management, urged management practitioners and researchers to eschew the technical, control-obsessed, short-sighted approach, and turn to more people-oriented humanistic values in organisations (Aktouf, 1992): in other words, he called for organisational wisdom. Isomorphism has been discussed above. Technophilia is the belief that significant problems will be resolved by applying scientific theory and technique. Donald Schön, one of the most significant contributors in the 20th century to the theory of organisational learning, identified a crisis of confidence in the professions because of its reliance on technical rationality to solve problems.

Henry Mintzberg (2000), a renowned professor of management strategy, warned that many organisational practices are founded on "pseudo-scientific" fallacies and are over reliant on formalised procedures. Integrated into increasingly formalised procedures are various monitoring and evaluation processes that are based on the assumption that all things can be measured and thereby controlled.

This was the concern raised by Michael Power, a Professor of Accounting at London School of Economics in his book, *The Audit Society* (Power, 2000). He argues that, while we can easily regulate and audit trivial matters, to attempt to do so with more complex matters leads to increasingly manic behaviour, evident in work stress and excessive working hours. The assumptions of an audit society are founded on functionalist and instrumentalist views of knowledge, science and technology that are inadequate.

A growing criticism about contemporary organisations is the erosion of ethical values leading to a loss of public trust. Warren Bennis, another 20th century giant of organisational theory as both an academic and practitioner, identified a leadership crisis based on the growing disparity between rich and poor, declining trust, reduced employment and lack of empowerment. Purely financial concerns are destroying the foundations of good organisational life leading to chronic anxiety: "American big business's obsession with the bottom line in the last decade and its continuing inability to see that its workers are its primary asset has gotten it into big trouble", he argued, and called for a re-assertion of humane values such as "integrity, dedication, magnanimity, humility, openness, and creativity" (Bennis, 1997, pp. 19-

20). Egregious examples of poor behaviour were aired in the 2018 Australian Royal Commission into Misconduct in the Banking, Superannuation and Financial Services Industry.

Rather than acting prudently and conservatively to protect people's livelihoods, the major Australian banks set up internal mechanisms that rewarded approving loans beyond clients' capacity to pay, using unqualified "introducers" that even included gym managers to bring in clients, and charging excessive amounts for services that cost the banks very little. One can see that this not only causes grief to clients forced into economic hardship, but also undermines the stability of the whole financial system, and reduces public trust in the pillars of our society. It stands to reason then that a wise organisation does not participate in such reprehensible behaviour.

WISE PRINCIPLES

Wise principles to underlie organisational practice have been provided by the Ancients. In particular, Aristotle's distinction between *epistêmê*, *tékhnê* and *phrónêsis* provides a strong foundation. Aristotelian wisdom reminds us that the *epistêmê*, or knowledge base, is founded not so much on objective knowledge, but on knowledge that mutates over time and is quite often infused by ideological assumptions. In his *Posterior Analytics*, Aristotle differentiates between an infallible *epistêmê* from fallible *doxa* (Barker, 2005), where *doxa* is defined as a "spontaneous belief or opinion [that] ... would seem unquestionable and natural" (Thompson & Bevan, 2013, p. 112) or "things people accept without knowing" (p. 114). On the other hand, *nous* is an intuitive capacity that accounts for those things "for which there is no reasoning" (Aristotle, 349 BC/1984, Bk 6, pp. 1142b: 9, 25-28). *Nous* is the "the insightfulness that makes up for the imprecision of rationality" (Dunne, 1997, p. 15).

Tékhnê is the expert competence that is guided by "rational" accounts of organisational activity that leads to the production of a good or service. Clearly, organisational members need specific skills sets based on agreed knowledge whether they be the air conditioning mechanic or the chief accountant. However, such "expert" skills and knowledge, which are developed over time, do not in themselves produce wise outcomes as is evident in the clever tactics of the Enron management or the Wall Street financiers who created the 2008 Global Financial Crisis.

In addition to technical competence, a wise person must display *phrónêsis*, which Aristotle defines as giving due "regard to things that are good or bad for man [sic]" (Aristotle, 349 BC/1984, pp. 1140 a1124-b1112). This means that there must always be an axiological perspective to human action such that a manager must use knowledge (*epistêmê*), technology and skills (*tékhnê*), and *phrónêsis* to do right in each particular situation.

Such a capability is crucial in the complex, contradictory and changing world that managers contend with (Smith & Tushman, 2005). Displaying *phrónêsis* would be evident in "habitually acting in ways that fulfill the highest human potentialities", by using courage, self-restraint, generosity, magnificence, magnanimity, sociability, justice and prudence in actions (Bragues, 2006, p. 342).

It is quite misguided to think that a person who acts according to the highest human values is somehow naïve and incapable of being a sophisticated organisational operator. This is erroneous because a wise organisational person uses their organisational knowledge and intuition to bring about desirable outcomes. To do this involves knowing how power really operates in an organisation and how processes actually work in practice. To achieve this, wise organisational members need to use the capability known as *mētis*, a concept that comes from Greek philosophy. *Mētis* means living by one's wits by negotiating with those in power and navigating through administrative processes when trying to achieve an outcome. In ancient Greek philosophy it was understood as cunning intelligence, which was widespread in large sectors of Greek social and spiritual life and valued highly within their religious system, according to Detienne and Vernant (1991).

Mētis does not mean to be sly and devious. It means instead to use one's practical intelligence to guide actions towards a desirable outcome. This could mean knowing sufficient information about regulations and laws to navigate effectively, knowing whom to deal with and whom to avoid, and understanding their motivations, their modes of operation, their worldviews. It means using available discretion to interpret laws, rules and guidelines, and which sets of rules to apply.

Activating *mētis* is appropriate in fluid situations where variables and the environment are constantly changing (Detienne & Vernant, 1991, p. 13). In this way, a capacity for *mētis* enables us to deal with the unexpected and with those situations where the attempt to simply apply rules or procedures does not bring about an effective outcome.

What separates the wise person's application of *mētis* from the Machiavellian opportunist is that a wise person uses *mētis* to bring about a greater good guided by noble virtues. Thus, *phrónêsis*, "the ability to find some action in particular circumstances which the agent can see as the virtuous thing to-do" (Hughes, 2001, p. 105), completes the circle in terms of achieving *eudaimonic* outcomes that this chapter began with. In considering embodiment, we understand that *eudaimonic* virtue is expressed "not merely in fine action but in fine emotions as well" (Sherman, 1997, p. 24). An organisational commitment is both an ethical commitment, and a commitment to community wellbeing, which organisations claim in their corporate social responsibility statements.

SEVEN STEPS TO DEVELOPING THE WISE ORGANISATION

Any organisation that wishes to act wisely in order to achieve the best possible outcomes for the organisation and the society within which it operates should implement these seven steps.

STEP 1   *Wise organisations do not rely solely on the wisdom of their leaders. Instead, these organisations create the conditions for organisational members to act wisely.*

While it is vital that an organisation directs itself to efficient and effective production of a good or service, it is a mistake to arrange the organisation into a totally mistake-free zone. This is because it limits creativity and doesn't allow people to learn in practice. Of course, there are some areas where zero mistakes must be the only policy. One of these is flying a passenger airline. The pilot and cockpit crew have to ensure that all routines, which have been tested as the best practice, are scrupulously followed.

An example of the near disastrous outcome of a failure to do this occurred in March 2009. An Emirates Airbus passenger jet with 257 passengers and 18 crew aboard nearly crashed on take-off from Melbourne Airport because a flight crew member had entered the wrong plane weight.[3] He had entered 100 tonnes less than the actual weight of 362 tonnes. This data is vital for the airline's computers to estimate the take-off power needed.

Because its weight was drastically understated, the aircraft could barely lift off by the end of the runway. Emirates learned from this mistake and installed a backup computer for all future flights. However, the point is that the cockpit crew should have taken care that this vital data was correctly entered. Of course, a similar mistake-free policy is vital in hospital surgeries to ensure that the right patient is entering the right operating theatre for the right surgery by the right surgeon. Of course, once that has been established, the outcome will be determined by the skill and precision of the surgeon.

Notwithstanding this, a wise leader must allow for two types of competencies to avoid learning errors. The first, technical competence with new technologies, should be supported with appropriate expert help and sufficient time to gain mastery. The second competence is less clear-cut because it involves acquiring tacit and intuitive knowledge in learning effective routines and dealing with people in difficult situations.

Wise leaders are also aware of the typical responses to mistakes by organisational members. A study of medical interns by Mizrahi (1984) found three social defences that organisational members, particularly in hospitals, use to deal with mistakes:

Denial: "justifying mistakes on the basis that medicine is a judgement-based art or a 'grey' practice rather than a black and white science, forgetting mistakes or redefining them as non-mistakes";

Discounting: "blaming circumstances beyond the doctors' control such as bureaucracy, superiors, subordinates diseases or patients";

Distancing: "arguing that mistakes are inevitable for all doctors".

(from McGivern & Fischer, 2010, p. 599)

A wise leader can understand these natural reactions to making mistakes that can be motivated by self-concept and fear of repercussions.

STEP 2   Alongside the normal organisational aims (growth, profit, service, quality, etc.), must be the primary aim of eudaimonic outcomes for all stakeholders now and in the future.

The concepts of sustainability, corporate social responsibility and stakeholders are now well established in organisational discourse. However, for too many organisations this is simply another box to tick like the annual audit.

Indeed, it is now widely agreed that business acceptance of corporate social responsibility has largely been a means of ensuring that governments do not introduce regulations on the grounds that businesses are effectively self-regulating. However, these codes of conduct have been revealed as relatively ineffectual (Shamir, 2010). Sustainability must be seen in the broadest context of social as well as environmental sustainability.

For example, it's of little use in maintaining a socially cohesive society if companies publicly sponsor a local sporting team or make a contribution to cancer research while at the same time they exploit their workers by underpaying them or using tax loopholes to evade and minimise their tax. As the gap in the distribution of wages and profits widens in many countries, those whose lives are characterised by continual poverty and fear of job loss lose their commitment to the institutions of society. This resentment can often be expressed in choosing to vote for populist politicians who offer authoritarian remedies based on scapegoating and blaming.

STEP 3   Organisations must place as much emphasis on ensuring that their members, particularly those in key management roles, possess high levels of technical knowledge and skill (tékhnê) as they do on their possessing or acquiring experience, intuition, imagination, creativity and an understanding of emotions (phrónêsis).

Phrónêsis essentially means that a person's habits are such that they seek to enhance the highest human potential. They do this in their self-restraint, generosity and prudence. However, a vital element is frequently having foresight, vision and courage. Although often criticised, the Whitlam Government of 1972–1975 brought about massive positive changes in Australian society, the effects of which reverberate today. Externally, Prime Minister Gough Whitlam ended soldier conscription, withdrew Australian forces from Vietnam, and recognised China's government.

At the time, he was criticised for being soft on communism. As the Chinese economy has grown (with a mixture of capitalism and communism) so has the economic benefit to Australia. In future, our forces were directed much more to peacekeeping roles that built relationships in the region creating goodwill. Internally, Whitlam introduced universal health insurance, now known as Medicare, against enormous opposition from doctors and insurance funds.

Yet now the medical profession endorses Medicare and the Australian voters overwhelmingly support it. He introduced equal pay for women against furious employer opposition and provided money for women's shelters assisting those suffering domestic violence. He created the first ministries for the environment and regional planning, which was unheard of but now commonplace.

In these and other cases Whitlam left an enormous legacy to the nation because he had a vision of a fairer, more creative, tolerant and adaptable Australia. He had the courage do this by declaring a "crash through or crash" approach, which did not mean that he was reckless, rather that he had the courage to fight for the vision even if it meant that he might be voted out. Although Whitlam was voted out in a landslide loss in 1975, many of his changes could not in the longer term be reversed – free university education was one that was reversed – because people came to see and experience the good sense of the change.

STEP 4   Organisations must encourage in their most senior management levels ontological acuity rather than isomorphism and conformity to doxa.

Established organisations tend to be conservative in two ways. First in relation to other organisations in similar industries, organisations tend to be isomorphic, which, say Dimaggio and Powell (1983), produces "startling homogeneity of organisational forms and practices" (p. 148), which is quite at odds with many organisations' claims to be innovative and creative. Dimaggio and Powell (1983) identify three types and sources of isomorphism.

- Coercive isomorphism occurs because of regulatory requirements.
- Mimetic isomorphism is self-imposed in that, when faced with environmental ambiguity, organisations "model" themselves on other organisations using particular cues that they believe will help them be successful.
- Normative isomorphism emerges largely from professionalisation, which means that to be classified as, say, an accountant or engineer one has to obtain degrees from universities and observe codes established by the relevant profession.

While the standardisation of education and regulatory codes promotes good practice, it also tends to maintain static knowledge and limits the range of actions that a "professional" is allowed to do, and thus is another form of coercion.

The second conservatising tendency is created by internal institutional logics (Friedland & Alford, 1991), which "shape rational, mindful behaviour" (Thornton & Ocasio, 2008, p. 100). To properly understand individual and organisational behaviour requires locating it "in a social and institutional context, and this institutional context both regularises behavior and provides opportunity for agency and change" (Thornton & Occasion, 2008, pp. 101-102). Senior management leaders have the capacity to analyse normal behaviours in an organisation in terms of their context and isomorphic tendencies, which are then evaluated by asking whether these "normal" behaviours are producing the most *eudaimonic* outcomes or whether they simply mimic and conform.

Challenging the fundamental assumptions of well-established beliefs and practices is unlikely to make wise managers popular; however, it can be seen as a vital element in achieving substantial and enduring change. A good example of this capability is the Australian General Sir John Monash. During World War One,

Monash largely served under the British Command. The tactic used on both sides was the same as that employed for hundreds of years by European armies, which was full scale frontal assaults. However, with the development of heavy artillery and machine guns, this tactic led to appalling casualties in this war. Yet the same assumptions and logic that had been handed down in British military history was maintained even in the face of its ineffectiveness and appalling mortality rates.

Perhaps it was the fact that Monash was primarily an engineer, not a professional soldier (he had been a reservist for many years), and that he was Jewish, a faith that was considered inferior by the dominant Christian churches, that led him to take a different path. By 1917, the war had become a stalemate with both sides fighting from trenches for small advances and losses, and the death toll just mounted. The Australians suffered appalling losses in the French Western Front.

However, at the battle of Hamel in 1918, Monash implemented a totally new strategy based on careful planning and trying to think the way that the Germans would (his grandparents emigrated from Germany). He used a "rolling barrage" method which crept towards the enemy after plane and tank attack, and he designed artillery shells to cut the barbed wire to enhance the speed of the soldiers across the disputed territory.

He used intelligence officers to determine exactly where enemy artillery was located, which was then precisely shelled. Perhaps another differing factor for Monash was that he had been a musician. Thinking like a musician, he called his tactics "an orchestral composition", he composed a precise and carefully prepared score. The outcome was that Monash repelled the German army in his sector. Despite being vilified in some quarters as an Australian Jew, his tactics were later adopted as a more appropriate way to conduct modern warfare.

STEP 5 *Senior organisational members must be able to deal with complexity, indeterminacy and change, which is a strong indicator of wisdom and vital for dealing with uncertain futures.*

Many organisations and business schools that train managers tend to plan or teach planning on the basis that events occur in a rational and predictable way. However, James G. March, one of the greatest thinkers about the nature of organisations, wrote after 40 years of research that this dependence on rational, logical processes is deeply flawed because "future consequences are often quite obscure", "systems being modeled and analyzed are substantially more complex than can be comprehended either by the analytical tools or the understandings of analysts"; that the measurability of anything is confounded with its importance; that values, wants or utility preferences are usually unclear and inconsistent; and that "the outcomes and choices of an organisation depend on the choices of other organisations" (March, 2006, pp. 203-204).

Many organisations try to cope with the uncertainty of change by compiling huge amounts of data, and developing complex models to guide behaviours. Instead of expending energy on compiling data and generating complex models, wise managers know that intelligent adaptability rather than chasing fads, and creative solutions rather than imposing old paradigms on new realities, are going to be more productive. When this approach is used, data and information usage is more focused and directed.

In their study of doctors, psychiatrists and medical regulators, McGivern and Fischer (2010) found that many of these intelligent practitioners simply submitted information that would not draw attention, and "ticked the box" so that they superficially complied with established procedures. This was to avoid "mistakes", which were mostly procedural rather than medical, and being identified, which could lead to disciplinary procedures. In other words, static, linear, micro-managed procedures simply produce apparent compliance not creativity and positive energy.

STEP 6   *Wise organisations are deeply aware of and responsive to the macro-environment particularly the profoundly threatening potential of environmental damage that has already been wrought largely as a result of Western industrialisation and unequal sharing of the earth's resources.*

As stated in Step 2, contemporary practices implementing corporate social responsibility are largely instrumental, that is, they are done for strategic and marketing reasons rather than out of a commitment to *eudaimonia*. A truly *eudaimonically* oriented organisation would be motivated by appropriate values of fairness for people and care for the earth. This may mean totally re-evaluating the profit and growth foundations of economics given that we are currently using up 1.5 Earths of consumption each year, which would be 4.4 Earths if we consumed at the US rate.[4]

In terms of producing agricultural and fishing products in future, we may need to acknowledge that the notion of sustainability is actually a negative one because it is maintaining a state that ironically is unsustainable. Instead, thinkers such as Charles Massy (2017), a farmer-scientist-philosopher, argue that we need regenerativity based on an understanding of how nature works, not on industrialised agriculture, to restore the earth and seas to pre-industrial levels.

STEP 7   *Wise leaders will encourage dialogue that produces enhanced understanding of, and respect for, different wisdom traditions resulting in more complex and widely accepted codes of virtuous behaviour.*

Respecting diversity is desirable in organisations not only because it is virtuous but also because diversity offers a wider range of orientations, knowledges and capabilities that can improve organisational performance (Bassett-Jones, 2005). However, it is the role of wise managers to create dialogical spaces within which people can truly understand each other. Active understanding occurs when the dialogic participant "assimilates the word under consideration into a new conceptual system, that of the one striving to understand" (Bakhtin, 1994, p. 76).

Wise managers do this by more than listening to the words, but by trying to understand the "frames of meaning" that different people bring. A frame of meaning must necessarily be located in a culture, belief and value system. In dialogical communication, "every communicative act is contingent on prior understandings" (Barge & Little, 2002, p. 378) that induces "new insights and divergent thinking" (p. 379). When we talk of dialogic communication, then, we should understand that we use our whole body, our cognition and our emotion. It is through dialogism that organisations are more likely to produce cooperative, mutual and non-exploitative relationships.

CONCLUSION

Drucker's vision of a harmonious social and economic world in which management and workers collaborate to produce socially desirable outcomes as well as profit has unfortunately not eventuated. Attempts at instilling a moral and humane ethic in organisational practices has now been taken up in notions of corporate social responsibility; however, this has proven to be overwhelmingly for instrumental reasons and to limit government regulation.

By understanding people and organisations from a micro-meso-macro perspective we are more likely to see the value of a wisdom-based approach to organisations. Incorporating the institutional concepts of culture and cognition within an organisation also contributes to a better understanding of good practice.

It is clear that organisations are generally framed in an isomorphic way that reinforces conformity rather than creativity, agency, and individual moral responsibility. In contrast to this conformity is the reality that organisations are characterised by inconsistent logics, internal tensions and paradoxes. An overarching philosophy that provides effective guidance for organisation managers and leaders is wisdom.

Using Aristotelian notions, it is vital to separate *tékhnê*, expert competence guided by knowledge and rationality, from *phrónêsis*, which means judgement and action that is directed to achieving the right outcome (*eudaimonia*) that enhances our humanity and respects our living planet.

To achieve *phrónêsis* requires having not just intellectual virtues but also moral virtues such as courage, self-restraint, generosity, justice and prudence. However, wise managers are not remote people perpetually engaged in contemplation. Rather, they must display the capacity of *mētis*, a cunning intelligence based on knowledge of power and administrative practices that can be used to produce desirable outcomes.

The seven steps provide guidance for managers and leaders to create the wise organisation that can achieve organisational aims while contributing to the good of society and the living planet.

NOTES

[1] Satisficing means setting an aspiration level which, if achieved, people will be happy enough with, and if they don't, will try to change either their aspiration level or their decision. These "rules of thumb" are the utmost agents can achieve in the "bounded" and uncertain real world.

[2] See also Foss (2001) for an application to the economics of organisation.

[3] http://www.traveller.com.au/wrong-computer-numbers-caused-emirates-jet-to-almost-crash-at-melbourne-airport-ao17
[4] https://www.internationalbusinessguide.org/hungry-planet/

REFERENCES

Aktouf, O. (1992). Management and theories of organization in the 1990s: Towards a critical radical humanism. *The Academy of Management Review, 17*(3), 407-431.

Aristotle. (1984). *Nicomachean ethics* (H. G. Apostle, Trans.). Grinnell, IO: The Peripatetic Press. (Original work published 349 BC)

Bakhtin, M. M. (1994). Speech genres and other late essays (M. Holquist & C. Emerson, Trans.). In P. Morris (Ed.), *The Bakhtin reader: Selected writings of Bakhtin, Medvedev, Voloshinov* (pp. 81-87). London, England: Edward Arnold.

Barge, J. K., & Little, M. (2002). Dialogical wisdom, communicative practice, and organizational life. *Communication Theory, 12*(4), 375-397.

Barker, E. M. (2005). *Aristotle's reform of Paideia.* Retrieved from http://www.bu.edu/wcp/Papers/Anci/AnciBark.htm

Barker, J. (1993). Tightening the iron cage: Concertive control in self-managed teams. *Administrative Science Quarterly, 38*, 408-437.

Bassett-Jones, N. (2005). The paradox of diversity management, creativity and innovation. *Creativity and Innovation Management, 14*(2), 169-175.

Bennis, W. (1997). *Managing people is like herding cats*. Provo, UT: Executive Excellence Publishing.

Bragues, G. (2006). Seek the good life, not money: The Aristotelian approach to business ethics. *Journal of Business Ethics, 67*(4), 341-357.

Detienne, M., & Vernant, J.-P. (1991). *Cunning intelligence in Greek culture and society* (J. Lloyd, Trans.). Chicago, IL: University of Chicago Press.

DiMaggio, P., & Powell, W. (1983). The Iron Cage revisited: Institutional isomorphism and collective rationality in organizational fields. *American Sociological Review, 48*, 147-160.

Dunne, J. (1997). *Back to the rough ground: Practical judgement and the lure of technique*. Notre Dame, IN: Notre Dame Press.

Foss, N. (2001). Bounded rationality in the economics of the organization: Present use and (some) future possibilities. *Journal of Management and Governance, 5*, 401-425.

Friedland, R., & Alford, R. R. (1991). Bringing society back in: Symbols, practices, and institutional contradictions. In W. W. Powell & P. J. DiMaggio (Eds.), *The new institutionalism in organizational analysis* (pp. 232–263). Chicago, IL: University of Chicago Press.

Hughes, G. J. (2001). *Aristotle on ethics*. London, England: Routledge.

Lewis, M. W. (2000). Exploring paradox: Toward a more comprehensive guide. *Academy of Management Review, 25*(4), 760-776.

March, J. G. (2006). Rationality, foolishness, and adaptive intelligence. *Strategic Management Journal, 27*(3), 201-214.

Massy, C. (2017). *Call of the reed warbler: A new agriculture – a new earth*. St Lucia, Australia: University of Queensland Press.

McGivern, G., & Fischer, M. (2010). Medical regulation, spectacular transparency and the blame business. *Journal of Health Organization and Management, 24*(6), 597-610.

Meyer, J. W., & Rowan, B. (1977). Institutionalized organizations: Formal structures as myth and ceremony. *American Journal of Sociology, 83*(2), 340-363.

Mintzberg, H. (2000). *The rise and fall of strategic planning*. London, England: Pearson Education.

Mizrahi, T. (1984). Managing medical mistakes: Ideology, insularity and accountability among internists in training. *Social Science & Medicine, 19*, 135-46.

Power, M. (2000). The audit society – second thoughts. *International Journal of Auditing, 4*(1), 111-119.

Shamir, R. (2010). Capitalism, governance, and authority: The case of corporate social responsibility. *Annual Review of Law and Social Science, 6*, 531-553.

Sherman, N. (1997). *Making a necessity of virtue: Aristotle and Kant on virtue*. Cambridge & New York: Cambridge University Press.

Simon, H. A. (1991). Bounded rationality and organizational learning. *Organization Science, 2*, 125-134.

Smith, W. K., & Lewis, M. W. (2011). Toward a theory of paradox: A dynamic equilibrium model of organizing. *Academy of Management Review, 36*(2), 381-403.

Smith, W. K., & Tushman, M. L. (2005). Managing strategic contradictions: A top management model for manging innovation streams. *Organization Science, 16*(5), 522-536.

Thompson, M., & Bevan, D. (Eds.). (2013). *Wise management in organisational complexity*. London, England: Palgrave Macmillan.

Thornton, P. H., & Ocasio, W. (2008). Institutional logics. In R. Greenwood, C. Oliver, R. Suddaby, & K. Sahlin (Eds.), *The Sage handbook of organizational institutionalism* (pp. 99-128). London, England: Sage Publications.

Tversky, A., & Kahneman, D. (1974). Judgment under uncertainty: Heuristics and biases. *Science, 185*(4157), 1124-1131.

Zorn, T. E., Page, D. J., & Cheney, G. (2000). Nuts about change: Multiple perspectives on change-oriented communication in a public sector organization. *Management Communication Quarterly, 13*(4), 515.

Bernard McKenna PhD (ORCID: https://orcid.org/0000-0001-7092-4944)
UQ Business School
University of Queensland, Australia

BARBARA HILL,
AUNTY BERYL YUNGHA-DHU PHILIP-CARMICHAEL
AND RUTH BACCHUS

13. LEARNING PRACTICE WISDOM FROM ELDERS

Wisdom Moments and How to Recognise Them

Ngiyeempaa Woman

I'm a Ngiyeempaa Woman
Fighting all the way
For my people's needs are many
And I'm growing older each day
The struggle seems to build up
No matter how hard we fight on
It's our young people we care about
When to them what we do seems all wrong
We are rejected and cursed from morning 'til night
But we must fight on regardless and try to make things alright
For I'm a Ngiyeempaa Woman standing steadfast and sure
True to my ancestors Eagle Hawk's and Crow's very strong law.
        Aunty Beryl Yungha-Dhu Philip-Carmichael (2019)

INTRODUCTION

Most of the great battles are fought in the creases of topographic maps.
        Michael Ondaatje (2018)

We are all volcanoes. When we women offer our experience as our truths, as human truth, all the maps change. There are new mountains.
        Ursula K. Le Guin (1997)

Aunty Beryl is 83 years old – a mother of 10 with five children still living. She is a grandmother and great-grandmother, and Aunty to many people from all cultures and walks of life. She is one of the last Ngiyeempaa-speaking Elders left in her community. She has fought for her Country all her life and she still does. She has always fought for education. She has fought for space in curriculum and she has fought for space in the topographic creases of our University maps. She is a tireless fighter for her people and for reconciliation between cultures. She is one of the Traditional Owners and Knowledge holders who has the cultural authority to speak for Ngiyeempaa Country.

What we can know about wisdom is that it has a geography. It is located in time – however we define it – and it is located in our connection and relationship to each other and to our connection to Mother Earth – to the places where we have learned to grow. This map – this chapter – is a story woven by the three of us: a meditation if you like on what we feel wisdom is; how we get it, how we recognise it and how we keep it alive. It is about wisdom moments and it is about reaching out for wisdom. It is about everyday wisdom practice that has been developed through our work as teachers and leaders and by our personal experience as human beings. It is a mix of many things and so is multi-layered, fluid, unfixed and both simple and complex. Every decision we make is influenced by the practice wisdom which is formed by our life experience and extends into everything we do in all our various identities: in Aunt's case as a knowledge holder, but for us all – as friends, parents, teachers, scholars and poets. Poetry and stories – indeed all narrative – is a way of interweaving ideas and thoughts and it is the love of poetry that brought us together.

At least 65,000 years of continuous Aboriginal culture in this country mean our shared stories also shape and change as we learn more about Australia's ancient past. Before western archaeologists, there were ancient ones who could read the land like a map – *and* read the creases of those topographical maps – to tell the story not only of what was/is there but of what was/is not. Billy Griffiths, in *Deep Time Dreaming: Uncovering Ancient Australia* (2018), suggests that the revelation of deep time has indeed meant a profound shift in how [non–Indigenous] Australians relate to their country. Reviewing Griffiths' book, Rebe Taylor (2018) suggests Archaeology has made deep time dreamers of us all. Griffiths quotes Indigenous activist Charlie Perkins from Peter Read's *Charles Perkins: A Biography* (1990):

> My expectation of a good Australia is when White people would be proud ... when they realise that Aboriginal culture ... is all there waiting for us all. White people can inherit ... 60,000 years of culture, and all have they to do is reach out and ask for it. (p. 315)

As Taylor (2018) suggests, the powerful thing about Charlie Perkins' offer is not only the generosity but the obligations it carries. Similarly, Mark McKenna (2018), in his essay *Moment of Truth: History and Australia's Future*, acknowledges all that has been forgotten and lost in the past 200 years since colonisation.

Where Taylor suggests the deep past has "bequeathed a living, complex Indigenous culture" that "requires a collective recognition and respect to ensure its endurance into the future" (p. 1), historian Mark McKenna (2018) writes of what Mick Dodson calls "the Australian psyche" and its fear of facing truth, as well as W. E. H. Stanner's (1968) idea of an "Australian Consciousness" that is resistant to confronting a profound historical truth: the recognition that the material successes of Australian society, with its inherent power structures, are built upon the dispossession of Indigenous Australians – and that this still "causes so many to avert their eyes" (pp. 15-16).

AUNTY BERYL'S STORY – HOW WISDOM RELATES TO COUNTRY, SPIRITUALITY; HOW WISDOM RELATES TO KNOWLEDGE AND LEARNING AND TEACHING

Guthi Guthi mookamigdar ngalia! Sacred Ancestral Being watch over us all

We must have great respect for our Ancestral spiritual beings who created the land for us along with all life forms to live in peace and harmony. Grandmothers/grandfathers have and maintain all decision-making power inside their Nations. Everything that our Spiritual beings created is very sacred, and our guidance and directions are shaped by this sacred powerful force.

It is this sacredness linked to our Spiritual self which watches over and around us at all times in today's ever-changing society. The Ancestral spiritual beings made sure all other Spiritual beings through all lifeforms kept true to their obligations to the Universe and fulfilled their Dreams. These were the keepers of water, vegetation, sun and moon, stars, animals, birds and reptiles. Special objects of stone along with the lore that was created to govern their lives for evermore were shown to Grandmothers and Grandfathers as well as law men and women to be used only for special ceremonies, about how to look after the land – our Mother – for this is where we came from and return to after death.

We should always be on alert for signs from birds, animals, ants and all life forms for these signs are imparting to us how and when we must act to protect ourselves against rough weather, floods and drought. All laws passed onto us were very strict and to break them meant banishment form the tribe.

Young people were very important and they were taught only what was right and just when very young. When old enough they would be instructed in the lore/law of their tribal lands that would govern their lives for evermore, in being good hunters and gatherers, fathers, mothers and teachers. So too men and women had various stages of the law to go through to enable them to be good hunters and gatherers, and good respectful parents to all their children, nieces and nephews.

We must teach our children from an early age to be good and kind to their family, pets, parents and grandparents and to listen carefully to sound advice whilst out walking, hunting and gathering. They are told – this will keep you from getting lost. Listen carefully whilst out gathering food and all resources that will help you survive by identifying it all. If you are thirsty a little bird called the Zebra Finch will lead you to water; he cannot survive without sucking up water. How the wind blows will also be imparting messages to you, sometimes good, sometimes sad, and likewise the whirly wind.

Grandmothers are full of knowledge and must be respected at all times. Listen to the sound advice they impart to you as it will give you great guidance, great respect for different cultural values and it will equip you for a holistic lifestyle wherever you wander. It is like a shield to you from within her Spiritual self. Guide all and advise them well.

Life on the River

The Elders I have walked with are Granny Nancy Biggs and Granny Rosie Johnston. Granny Nancy Biggs taught all us girls on Menindee Mission how to identify raw material for the manufacturing of string for making and weaving of string bags or dilly bags for carrying, as well as identifying basket grass and reeds for mats. Granny Rosie Johnston taught us how to find witchetty grubs in the ground for fishing as well as Bardi grubs from the tree trunks as bait for fishing. She also taught us where were the right places to go and fish so we would get a good feed.

Ancestral beings who created the river, waterholes and tributaries of the Murray/Darling Basin need the water to enable lifeblood to flow freely throughout the Basin. Aboriginal people who still remember the stories are saddened to know how much destruction has occurred and is still continuing along our natural waterways by blockages to stop the natural flow, for self-usage. Water is vital to our survival as a nation, and overpopulation is putting a huge strain on our water resources. This is not only the impact of people on the land and the water supply, but we must take into account the introduced species of animal and plant (cotton) life; with all of this extra strain our water supply is diminishing at an alarming rate. If we don't do anything about conservation now, we will be increasingly competing with cotton fields and animals to survive in our country. We need to look further down the track to condensing our water out of the sea. On Yam Island, people are already doing just this very thing by mixing sea water with dam water so it can be made drinkable and usable for domestic purposes. Sewerage water can be recycled back over the land and used for gardens instead of being wasted in the ocean, thereby adding nutrients back into the soil. As a nation of concerned people, we must work together now to manage our waterways so our children's children and future generations can enjoy the benefits water can provide for their lives. Only through genuine education can we hope to correct mistakes made during the past 200 years.

Identity

My Identity revolves around and within me
It makes me aware of who I am
It ties me to my country
It links me to my spiritual self
It guides me in my daily existence
It teaches me to respect different values
It teaches me to heed warning
It tells me who I am and where I fit in my family line
It teaches me to hold my head high when others persecute me
It strengthens me when I am weak
It is a powerful force linked to my spiritual self
It says Hey black girl don't worry about colour,
which is only skin deep

LEARNING PRACTICE WISDOM FROM ELDERS

> Your identity is yours to keep
> No-one can change you, if you have everything intact
> You have nothing to hide or lose
> You have nothing to hide or lose
> Because you have nothing to lack
> You are who you are, not fitting anyone else's mould
> But being my own being, through my Spiritual Self.
>
> *Kungi Giranapola norta norta – House of learning and teaching
> – achieving knowledge. Birth of Eaglehawk – Ngooringah*

*Sturt Desert Pea or Ngooringah
(Permission given by Aunty Beryl Yungha-Dhu Philip-Carmichael, 2013,
Menindee NSW Australia).*

A long time ago there were two sisters who used to live at Mount Manara Mountain on their own. Early evening they would go for a walk around the mountain ranges until late. Following a good season the land and country were covered with lots of pretty flowers. The youngest sister saw the most beautiful flower and picked it off, she broke the top off it and to her it looked like a lovely baby's face, she decided to look after it so she gathered a couple of sheets of bark, put the flower in it and left it not saying anything to her sister about her secret find. When they went out for their walk, the youngest sister went over to check on her flower in the bark and it looked more like a kid. She kept coming back and checking on it and it seemed like it was growing into a baby. One day it grew into a real baby so she took the baby in her arms and she would suckle it.

The other sister noticed how strange she was acting and also noticed her breasts had swollen, she said, "What's wrong with you, you look like you have a baby hidden?" She showed her sister who was very happy so they took it home and reared it up. It was good company for them. He was Eaglehawk and very clever, and that is the story of his birth. The flower was Nooringah, a very beautiful bell-shaped flower which is also nourishment, providing food and juice.

BARBARA'S STORY – "STILL SO MUCH WORK TO DO"

Aunty Beryl and I met as fellow poets in 1998. Since then we have seen each other once or twice a year, and we speak on the telephone every week and sometimes every day. We discuss our families, our friendship, the politics of the day, which bushes have fruited, which flowers have appeared or not appeared, and when the fish and yabbies are running. We discuss issues of water, cultural care, the Ancestor spirits, dreams and hopes and sometimes our deep despairs. We always finish these conversations laughing and Aunty Beryl says, "We still have a lot of work to do!"

Aunty Beryl Yungha-Dhu Philip-Carmichael (l) and Barbara Hill (r) at Kinchega Station National Park homestead (2000, Menindee NSW Australia).

What I have learned since I met Aunty Beryl is that you can't strain for wisdom. It comes when you are in another kind of state – walking the dogs, doing the dishes, cooking, washing and cleaning – but what you can do is acknowledge your wisdom moments and work into them. Long ago my mum used to say to me, "just get into the posture like you do when you are trying to go to sleep and you will get there". Maybe practising wisdom has an "other-worldly" feeling too – just like you are trying to spy something from the corner of your eye so you don't scare it off by your full gaze on it. I have always been struck by Director Bentley Dean's statement in the *Press Kit for First Footprints* (2013) where he quotes Wong-Goo-Tt-Oo Elder Wilfred Hicks who says:

There's a lot of spiritual issues on this land and they are alive. (p. 15)

The resonance of this over the time I have spent with Aunty Beryl in her Country is very powerful. Bentley Dean goes on to tell a story about one evening around the campfire when they were filming and Wiradjuri archaeologist Wayne Brennan explained the meaning of an ancient idea – *Birrung Burrung* – literally the moment when ripples in a pond cease, allowing one to see deep into it. I have felt similarly in Aunt's Country. Bentley says later that, "I still feel like I'm looking at ripples, but I now know the pond is deep indeed" (p. 16).

I have travelled in and through Aunt's Country for many years now. Before that I was a visitor with my family – those who also sprang from the same region, but from its surfaces rather than its depths like Aunt. I have seen two ways (and sometimes more) of looking at place; two or more sets of geography and topography – those I can be in and those that I can sometimes only sense. The latter can come to me in dreams and visions, and when it comes to teaching I draw on all this feeling of the "spiritually alive" things and the "deep ponds" because learning and teaching can have this same resonance. Aunty Beryl's generosity and that of the Elders I also work with in Wiradjuri Country have also taught me about how the still waters reflect another Universe – in a highway river and bowl lake of the stars. On quiet nights – if I look carefully enough to not see directly – you can't tell which way is up or down, Heaven or Earth, or whether it is past or present or future, now, then or before.

A Poem for Yungha-dhu

Following Auntie Beryl through
the old Menindee Mission
someone came across an old tin button.
"You can keep it," she said,
"But any 1930 pennies are mine."
The tin button belonged to one
of the kids who drank warm
milk and cocoa, heated in the
old kerosene tin, on that winter
morning years ago.

The same child puts a smile
on Auntie Beryl's face as
she tells us about the school
in a place that smells of eucalypt and sun.
Careful little fingers, soft at the ends,
had handled that button, practised
doing it up and undoing it
marvelling how good it was that
the two parts of the shirt
could meet in the middle
because of that button.

Past summer, it was also good to
have that shirt because on the cocoa
early mornings, the sun only came through
in the gaps of the moving leaves.

Months before the soft fingers
that did the button up
had carefully peeled the sticky gum
from the lolly tree, halved it
and halved it again and given
some to each child there while they
sat on the warm clay, away
from the adults, to chew.
"Better 'an sugar," the littlest one said,
although the sugar sweet tea
was good too.

As they chewed they pressed their toes
into the fine white clay, always
doing more than one thing at a time.
Later the clever man would be able to tell
the children had been there,
near the lolly tree and he would smile,
remembering his own childhood
different to the mission kind but
a childhood nonetheless,
one with a lolly tree,
before he was chosen for the
important business.

Down the track, past the schoolroom
that hovers in the mind's eye,
are the campfires of blackened clay
now rock like and exposed
like coral at low tide.
A lot of thinking went on
around campfires.

What to do about the welfare
and how to hide the kids better
especially after they took
all those little ones from

Grandmother – now mother is crazy
with sadness and dad is likely

LEARNING PRACTICE WISDOM FROM ELDERS

to do harm (more likely
to 'imself says Auntie).
"What will we do?
"Beat 'em at their own honourless game".

That's when sister says she was
digging a hole under the bed so when
the welfare came she could
hide the baby and encourage
the old dog in there too to keep
the little one warm.
"No welfare gunna take my kids," she says.
Dad says later, "When I say run
You kids, I mean it."

There are wide eyes and shifting shapes
beyond the flickering flame.
Beyond the fire is the icy
coldness of fear.
There have been children running
in this country for over 200 years.
Running into the Pilliga,
Running into the scrub, jumping into rivers,
Running, running, running

Running away from white people
with intentions, running with sister,
Brother, Auntie, Uncle or cus.
Sometimes running alone, scared,
with the heartbeats of Waratah.
On the nights the half-moon hangs
in the sky as a broad smile surrounded
by dimpled stars, the sound of feet
kissing hard clay and then soft sand
comes on something other than wind.
Run little fella run!

There's a scream (it is not clear from whose lips)
maybe even the sky cracked open
and the sun cried suddenly
sick of this witness, while the blood
sunk down into the soil around the
old River Gum, that later
the ants would drink.
Soft little pink fingers do up that button again.

The cotton cheap and not enough,
comes loose and the tin button
falls to the school house floor,
rolls languidly in an arc like the moon
and quietly disappears down the crack
between the floorboards.
It rests in white clay soil.
I'll need a new one he thinks as he
follows the button with his eyes until
it disappears.
The warm milk has reached his stomach,
filled him, made him sleepy and he sits
to watch the sun through the leaves,
thinking of the lolly tree and a spring
when he will be bigger,
when he will run faster, the dust
flying from his heels.

Barbara Hill (l) and Aunty Beryl Yungha-Dhu Philip-Carmichael (r) at Old Menindee Mission (2010, Menindee NSW Australia).

RUTH'S STORY – PRACTICE WISDOM

I have learned many things from Aunty Beryl, most of all from watching, listening and trying to absorb what I can only call her way of being. I have tried to take something of this way of being – as far as it is possible for a non-Aboriginal woman (and I acknowledge the force of arguments that it is not at all possible) – into my own life and teaching.

Learning and teaching around issues of social inequality and social justice present some of the most rewarding and also most challenging aspects of our work. There are difficulties associated with challenging white privilege while occupying it, challenging racism without simply suppressing its expression and, most importantly, making classrooms safe for all learners. Students may find it difficult to confront issues such as class, gender and race especially when it may mean acknowledging that these structures may confer privilege upon them. It is challenging for men to acknowledge the benefits conferred on men in the past and present by patriarchy. It is challenging for middle-class students to see that their advantages may come at the cost of others' disadvantages, and that poverty may not be simply a result of fecklessness on the part of the poor. But, as events and discourses in Australian politics and media would also suggest, "race" is perhaps the most confronting issue Australians face. Many school-leaver students have grown up in the shadow of John Howard's view: that colonisation was a form of "settlement" that happened long ago, that present generations of non-Indigenous Australians are not responsible for the policies and practices of past generations, and that any kind of national apology for dispossession and massacres on a scale amounting to genocide, and for the kidnapping of the many Indigenous children now known as the Stolen Generations, is unnecessary. So we continue to reap the benefits of invasion, to work, live, prosper and travel on Aboriginal country, to do so at the cost of the dispossession of the Aboriginal owners, and to dislike being reminded of it. As Aileen Moreton-Robinson (2003) puts it, "our [Indigenous] relation to land, what I call an ontological belonging, is omnipresent, and continues to unsettle non-Indigenous belonging based on illegal dispossession" (p. 24). A form of practice wisdom is needed here, to help students to acknowledge such things without, as many put it, "making me feel personally guilty".

Over the years I have asked others about the problems of racism in the classroom, and about what to do with my frustration and even anger at the comments made by students, often based upon (unreflective expressions of) their personal experiences growing up in country towns. The great Biripai educator, Associate Professor Wendy Nolan, advised me to allow students to express racist thoughts and feelings, as it was often those students who would gain the most from the subject.

And I have found this to be true: the students who were most confronting in their racism were perhaps so because they were most confronted by the material – and this was perhaps because they were most on the cusp of change. The students who had expressed racism had very often, by the end of the session, expressed a complete reversal in their thoughts and feelings, and often declared their intention of working in a remote school or community.

But there are problems with this: the most significant one arises in a space in which I've felt the most need of practice wisdom, and most lacking in it. This is a class in which at least one student might identify as Aboriginal or Indigenous, although they might be fair-skinned and thus not easily identifiable to other students. Here, any responsibility to allow one learner to "work through" their racist thinking, partly by verbalising it, is far outweighed by the responsibility to protect an Aboriginal student from such verbalisations and the damage and hurt they cause. Even if protecting those learners means shutting down the "contributions" of others, which may lead them to feel that they cannot "say what they think", that their views are not valued, and even if this plays into a discourse about so-called "political correctness" that is so lamentably prevalent in Australian politics at the moment. It is vital that Aboriginal students feel safe from both overt and covert racism in the classroom – especially given some failures of the education system which mean not as many as we might wish make it to university, and that it is all too easy to damage the resilient few who do. It is also vital that an Aboriginal learner not be asked to offer an opinion or expertise based on their Aboriginality. Something I've found to work is to begin the class by saying: "I want us to assume that there is at least one student in the room who identifies as Aboriginal or Indigenous and be sensitive to that". And I think about Aunty Beryl before I go to class and try to take a bit of her spirit with me. Aunty Beryl laughs often and loudly. She loves children and older people, and everyone between. She writes poetry and stories, and letters of protest, and telephones politicians when she feels something is not right. She knows where to find food in a landscape that looks little like a larder. She never complains. She adores her family. She has always showed the same kind of generosity as that extended by the Elders who wrote the Uluru Statement from the Heart – a willingness to reach out again and again to mainstream Australia. She belongs completely and utterly to her Country.

Tony Birch (2018) writes that a part of the invaluable cultural education he gained from long conversations with the actor and activist Jack Charles was an appreciation of "true sovereignty as an idea and practice embedded in culture, history, character and a commitment to others" (p. 8), "a psychological, metaphysical and ethical way of being" (p. 9). Aunty Beryl embodies this kind of sovereignty – sovereignty conceptualised not just in legal terms, as an imposed Western concept, but in terms of responsibility and generosity to anyone who comes to her or comes to her Country.

Aunty Beryl is a deeply committed Christian, and has an equally deep faith in the spirits of her ancestors. These spirits, both human and those ancestral beings that "created animals, plants, humans, and the physiographic features of the country associated with them" (Moreton-Robinson, 2003, p. 31), established the laws and codes by which people would live and often took the form of "elements or natural species" (ibid, p. 32). As Aunty Beryl's poem suggests, for her these were, in particular, Eaglehawk and Crow. For Aunty, there are two creation stories, two sets of Law. I'm fascinated, and in awe of, the way she can hold what may seem, in terms of Western epistemologies, to be incommensurate belief systems. And that for her, there is no tension between them.

Aunty Beryl respects all beliefs, all cultures and all peoples and asks only that this be reciprocated though, even in 2018, it may not be. She commands tremendous personal respect, among Aboriginal and non-Aboriginal communities. Because of her belonging to her Country, damage to the land, to the river, is felt by her as personal disrespect, as such a violation I think it may be as if it happens to her own body. Along with many others, I share her concerns, but also know I cannot share in

LEARNING PRACTICE WISDOM FROM ELDERS

Aunty Beryl's "ontological belonging" to Country, to Law, no matter how much I might wish or how much I might try. As Moreton-Robinson (2003) argues, "our ontological relationship to land marks a radical ... difference between us and the non-Indigenous ... [and] constitutes a subject position we do not share, and which cannot be shared" (p. 31) with non-Indigenous people.

Judith Wright's (1973/1994) poem, *Two Dreamtimes*, written for and to her friend Oodgeroo Noonuccal, celebrates the two women's ties of friendship, of sisterhood, of shared loss and grief. And, it shows that the possibility of such ties, like those we have with Aunty Beryl, are a product of the generosity of the Indigenous woman who says: "you brought me to you some of the way/and came the rest to meet me". But the poem also acknowledges the limits of this sharing, this bond; these limits lie largely, but not only, in history. Wright knows that "there is a knife between us ... the weapon made from your country's bones" and says "I turn it round/the handle to your side ... I have no right to take it". This expresses an important part of my relationship to Aunty Beryl and other Aboriginal people, including the Wiradjuri Elders of the Bathurst area. This relationship involves my listening, learning, being receptive to forms of knowledge I may never really understand and, most importantly, knowing that it is for Aunty and the Wiradjuri Elders and others to decide what this relationship will be and whether or how they wish to enter into it.

It is amazing to me that Aunty Beryl, and the Wiradjuri Elders of the Bathurst area, and so many others, continue to be willing to engage with non-Aboriginal Australians, to attempt to share their knowledge, to help us understand, to welcome us into their homes and lives, and to accept invitations to come to the houses we have built on their land. I can only be very grateful that they do.

Ruth Bacchus (l), Aunty Beryl Yungha-Dhu Philip-Carmichael (centre)
and photographer Jade Yanhadarrambal Flynn (r)
at Kinchega Station National Park homestead
(2013, Menindee NSW Australia).

ACKNOWLEDGEMENTS

Thanks to the Bathurst Wiradjuri and Community Elders and to our Biripi sister Associate Professor Wendy Nolan (retired) for your continued support in this work.

REFERENCES

Birch, T. (2018). Tony Birch on Jack Charles. *Overland, 231*(Winter). Retrieved from https://overland.org.au/previous-issues/issue-231/regular-tony-birch/

Dean, B. (2013). *Press kit for First Footprints.* Retrieved from http://www.aborigenes-australie.info/images/First_Footprints_Press_Kit_-_S.pdf

Griffiths, B. (2018). *Deep time dreaming: Uncovering ancient Australia.* Carlton, Australia: Black Inc.

Le Guin, U. K. (1997). *Dancing at the edge of the world: Thoughts on words, women, places.* New York, NY: Grove Press.

McKenna, M. (2018). Moment of truth: History and Australia's future. *Quarterly Essay, 69,* 1-86.

Moreton-Robinson, A. (2003). I still call Australia home: Indigenous belonging and place in a white postcolonising society. In S. Ahmed (Ed.), *Uprootings/regroundings: Questions of home and migration* (pp. 23-40). New York, NY: Berg. Retrieved from https://is.muni.cz/el/1421/podzim2009/AJ28084/um/Moreton-Robinson.pdf

Ondaatje, M. (2018). *Warlight.* London, England: Jonathon Cape.

Philip-Carmichael, B., with Hill, B., & Bacchus, R. (Eds.). (2019). *In the footsteps of a Ngiyeempaa Elder.* Bathurst, Australia: CSU Print.

Read, P. (1990) *Charles Perkins: A Biography.* Melbourne, Australia: Viking.

Stanner, W. E. H. (1968). *After the Dreaming: Black and White Australians – An anthropologist's view* (Boyer Lectures). Sydney, Australia: Australian Broadcasting Corporation.

Taylor, R. (2018, March 8). Deep Time Dreaming review: Billy Griffiths on exploration of the distant past. *The Sydney Morning Herald.* Retrieved from https://www.google.com.au/amp/s/amp.smh.com.au/entertainment/books/deep-time-dreaming-review-billy-griffiths-on-exploration-of-the-distant-past-20180307-h0x5q8.html

Wright, J. (1994). Two Dreamtimes. In J. Wright, *Collected Poems 1942–1985.* Sydney, Australia: HarperCollins. (Original work published 1973)

Barbara Hill PhD (ORCID: https://orcid.org//0000-0003-4878-3879)
Learning Academy, Division of Learning and Teaching
Charles Sturt University, Australia

Aunty Beryl Yungha-Dhu Philip-Carmichael PhD Honoris Causa (University of Sydney)
Ngiyeempaa Elder
Menindee, Australia

Ruth Bacchus PhD (ORCID: https://orcid.org/0000-0002-5388-0123)
School of Humanities
Charles Sturt University, Australia

JOHN WATTIS, MELANIE ROGERS,
GULNAR ALI AND STEPHEN CURRAN

14. BRINGING SPIRITUALITY AND WISDOM INTO PRACTICE

This chapter considers the way in which the split between "objective" reductionist approaches and a more "subjective" understanding of the human condition arose in the 17th century with spirituality associated with the subjective approach. The consequent difference between the biomedical and the broader biopsychosocial approaches to medicine is explored. The relationship between spirituality, religion, secularism and wisdom is explored. The concepts of a shared journey and of spiritually competent practice are used to explore how spirituality and wisdom can be integrated into truly holistic person-centred practice. Obstacles and facilitators to this kind of practice are considered including approaches to educating clinicians.

PROBLEMS WITH MODERN PRACTICE

There is much that is good in modern medical practice. Scientific and technical advances over the last couple of hundred years have been extraordinary. Yet, there is discontent about the "industrialisation" and depersonalisation of health and social care. One general practitioner recently asked how they could possibly "know" their patients when their group practice had over 11,000 patients.

Similarly, in acute hospital care, patients may be moved from one setting to another as specialists address different problems at a technical level often without attention to personal relationships. Each move brings new nursing and care staff. Throughput and pressure of work mean that nurses feel they never get to "know" their patients. In mental health, fragmentation of services with different teams looking after service users in different settings leads to a lack of continuity and a situation where the personal knowledge of the patient, that used to be an important aspect of care, is dissipated. We have produced a situation where technical abilities are advanced; but models of care are industrialised, losing the personal touch. Financial pressures in healthcare and the push for ever-greater efficiency exacerbates the situation. A target-driven system of management encourages "gaming" the statistics and does not promote good management. Parts of health and social care provision are not joined up and there is increasing likelihood of people falling through gaps in what can scarcely be described as a "system" of care.

Here, we will briefly survey some of the causes of these developments and propose some remedies. We will consider how spirituality and wisdom can be applied, contrasting materialistic (biomedical) and holistic (biopsychosocial) approaches. We will explore some aspects of evolutionary theory and consider the

© KONINKLIJKE BRILL NV, LEIDEN, 2019 | DOI: 9789004410497_014

relationship between wisdom, spirituality, culture, religion, humanism and secularism. We will conclude by reviewing the work our group at the University of Huddersfield has done on spiritually competent practice and relating this to wisdom and journeys of transformation.

BIOMEDICAL, BIOPSYCHOSOCIAL AND HOLISTIC MODELS IN MEDICINE

We share experience of practice, teaching and research in a variety of healthcare contexts. Between us, we also have experience as managers, service users and carers of people with long-term illnesses. We do not subscribe to a narrow biomedical model of practice but embrace the wider biopsychosocial model (Engel, 1977). The biomedical model (sometimes characterised as *the* medical model) is based on a reductionist view of human nature and does not allow for the interaction of social and psychological factors in the causation and treatment of disease. The biopsychosocial model was originally proposed as a new model for psychiatry. Advantages over the biomedical model seem self-evident as there are clearly psychological and social influences which impact on mental health.

Engel (1980) described a patient with a heart attack illustrating how psychological and social factors also impacted on physical health. He characterised the biomedical approach as factor-analytic, solving problems by breaking them down into their constituent parts, and contrasted this with the biopsychosocial model which recognises a hierarchy of interactive systems in medicine from the sub-cellular to the social. He asserted that medical intervention begins at the personal level and maintained that it was equally scientific to explore the psychological and social factors as it was to look at, for example, myocardial damage at the cellular level. Twelve years later, Engel (1992) was still asking "How much longer must medicine's science be bound by a seventeenth century world view?"

Epstein (2014) reviewed how the biopsychosocial model had fared nearly 40 years after it was first proposed. He believed that trainees and clinicians had not developed the capacity for resilience, self-awareness and self-monitoring needed to implement the biopsychosocial model and needed to learn how to connect with patients at the personal level by becoming more self-aware, resilient and actively compassionate. He advocated a *humanist* approach alongside the factor-analytic model of modern science. Davies and Roache (2017) presented a discussion on the biopsychosocial model in psychiatry, indicating that it was compatible with recent philosophy of mind which embraces a monist and non-reductionist approach. They argued that this liberated the (mental) health professional from choosing between a reductionist model and the Cartesian dichotomy between mind and body.

THE GREAT DIVORCE

How has the tension between a reductionist biomedical science and the subjective aspects of medicine arisen? The middle of the 17th century was a time of flux in religious and philosophical understanding. A worldview was developing which was materialist and reductionist in its approach. This came to be the dominant scientific worldview which achieved amazing advances in objective knowledge of the material world but resulted in a split with subjective understanding of the human condition. During this period of philosophical turmoil, the term *spirituality* came into the English language (McGrath, 2011), denoting direct knowledge of the divine or supernatural, roughly equivalent to what we might today term "mystical" experience. Not surprisingly spirituality (and religion) tended to be found on the subjective side of the split.

Worldviews can be considered as the cultural "spectacles" through which we view our experiences. Unless we stop and think we simply accept them as representing how things are. There are many different worldviews and variants within them though one worldview may be dominant in a particular culture. We have discussed this in more detail elsewhere (Wattis, Curran, & Rogers, 2017). For present purposes we will focus on two: the *materialist* and the *systems* worldviews. The materialist worldview understands knowledge purely in material terms addressing it by a reductionist approach, breaking everything into its component parts. This has proved invaluable in understanding organisms, cells and molecules and has made a major contribution to medical science.

Engel sees its weakness as not allowing for the understanding of systems where, for example, the patient with the heart attack may, at a personal level, not just experience sensations resulting from myocardial damage but also where psychological and social factors from higher order systems may influence the experience, the degree of myocardial damage and the eventual outcome. This might well be called a systems worldview (Laszlo, 1996) and corresponds to the biopsychosocial model.

INCREASING COMPLEXITY

Evolution is usually viewed as a process of increasing complexity. In the early 20th century the atheist scientist Vernadsky and the Jesuit palaeontologist, philosopher and theologian Teilhard de Chardin (1959) developed the idea of stages of complexity, the *geosphere* of the inanimate planet leading to the *biosphere,* the sum of all living things on earth and this giving rise to the *noosphere,* the sphere of human thought. The term *noosphere* is derived from the Greek *nous, voῦς,* meaning that which enables human beings to think rationally.

The biosphere represented a step change in complexity from the geosphere and the noosphere represented a step change from the biosphere. The systems all interacted with each other and Teilhard de Chardin believed that this would all end in an Omega point which he seems to have seen as an expression of the Divine. This idea ties in nicely with Engel's biopsychosocial approach of cosmogenesis and was explored in a short science fiction story, *The Last Question* (Asimov, 1956).

The noosphere relates to the idea of transcendence. Mind does not just exist within the individual organism but also in the noosphere. The term *transcendence* has specific meaning in theology and Kantian philosophy. The wider understanding of transcendence and the concept of the noosphere allows those who believe in God and those who don't a point of contact above the purely organismic level.

SPIRITUALITY, RELIGION AND SECULARISM

Like transcendence, spirituality is hard to define from the perspective of conventional biomedical research. We have found spiritually competent practice to be a more useful concept for research, teaching and learning purposes (Wattis et al., 2017). The difficulties in defining spirituality can lead to misunderstanding. For now, we will use Cook's comprehensive definition:

> Spirituality is a distinctive, potentially creative and universal dimension of human experience arising both within the inner subjective experience of individuals and within communities, social groups and traditions. It may be experienced as a relationship with that which is intimately 'inner', immanent and personal within the self and others, and/or as a relationship with that which is wholly 'other', transcendent and beyond the self. *It is experienced as being of fundamental or ultimate importance and is thus concerned with meaning and purpose in life, truth and values* [emphasis added]. (Cook, 2004, pp. 548-549)

At the subjective level the last sentence of this definition is vital. Here again, secular and religious understandings of spirituality can find common ground.

Spirituality as a term in the English language was born out of Christianity, but it is no longer confined to religion. Some have asserted that the terms are entirely distinct. We prefer to see them as overlapping. Some people express their spirituality through their religion; but it is possible to have a secular spirituality and some expressions of religion may be merely outward forms without any underlying spiritual engagement (Allport, 1950). We have discussed these issues more fully elsewhere (Wattis et al., 2017).

We live in a secular society. In the United Kingdom, the National Secular Society (2018) sees the separation of religion and state as the foundation of secularism. Some forms of secularism exclude religion from the public arena and confine it to the private domain. Others stress the need for mutual tolerance between those who adhere to different religions and those without a specific religious affiliation. Stammers and Bullivant (2012) discuss the issues around secularism and spirituality more fully.

WISDOM AND KNOWLEDGE

Wisdom is a (personal) quality based on experience, knowledge and good judgement. Knowledge, particularly in the "objective" materialist sense used by much post enlightenment science presents some interesting contrasts with wisdom (see Table 14.1). To be fair to knowledge we need to rehabilitate a wider understanding of the term. Swinton (2012), writing in the context of healthcare spirituality, distinguished *nomothetic* and *idiographic* forms of knowledge.

Table 14.1. Wisdom versus knowledge.

Wisdom	Knowledge
A thinking tool (and more)	A substrate of thinking
Value-based, makes judgements	Value-free
Divergent thinking and convergent thinking	Mainly convergent thinking
Broadens the options	Narrows the options
Considers the whole person	Considers the parts
Considers context (social, political, economic)	Focuses only on presenting problems
Seeks balanced "solutions"	Seeks a solution to the presenting problem
Views compassion as central	Does not of itself acknowledge centrality of compassion

NOMOTHETIC AND IDIOGRAPHIC KNOWLEDGE

Swinton (2012) described the wonder of experiencing a beautiful waterfall and the mundane experience of looking at a bucket of water taken from the waterfall. He asserted they both contain "truth"; both are made up of water (H_2O). H_2O is the nomothetic perspective. Then he asked whether the subjective sense of wonder accompanying perception of the waterfall (the idiographic perspective) is merely an artefact or something more? He asserted that healthcare practices tend to "focus on buckets rather than waterfalls", on the parts rather than the whole person in context and suggested that spirituality was needed to bridge and fill the gaps between these different ways of knowing the water and the waterfall (Swinton, 2012, p. 99).

Nomothetic (from the Greek term for lawgiving) knowledge tests hypotheses to produce general "laws". It approximates to the knowledge gained by traditional medical science utilising experiments and randomised controlled trials. Knowledge of this kind is generally based on hypothesis testing and must fulfil three criteria. It must be falsifiable, replicable and generalisable. To be falsifiable means that it must be logically possible to disprove the hypothesis.

For example, a drug trial will often be set up on the basis of a null hypothesis (that there is no difference between the active drug and placebo). The research design, including the statistical analysis ensures that any difference between active drug and placebo is unlikely to have arisen by chance and any trial, conducted according to the same design with similar subjects, would be expected to produce similar results. Finally, the results can be generalised to patients with the same characteristics and (disease) condition. This kind of knowledge is generally the main basis for evidence-based medical practice.

Application of quantitative scientific methods can be used to study the effects of religious *observance* on various aspects of health and generally there is a positive relationship between the two (Koenig, 2000). However, because spirituality involves subjective (idiographic) experience it is much harder to study. Attempts have been made to produce scales to measure spirituality in the healthcare context.

A systematic review by Monod et al. (2011) identified 35 instruments. The two most commonly used in clinical research contained subscales related to religious and existential dimensions. For example, the Spiritual Well-Being Scale (SWBS) (Ellison, 1983) has two separate scales for religious well-being (RWB) and existential well-being (EWB). When summated these give the overall SWBS score. Items which score in a positive direction in both subscales have face validity. However, the use of an RWB component assumes that all spiritual well-being must involve religious belief in God or a higher power and the EWB scale seems to correspond closely with what the positive psychology movement refer to as sustained well-being. Thus, one of the most commonly used scales to quantify "spiritual" well-being might be said to be really measuring a combination of religious and psychological/existential well-being.

Idiographic (from the Greek term for oneself, one's own) knowledge derives from unique, non-replicable experiences. It is subjective lived experience. It is no less valid than nomothetic knowledge, but it cannot be proved or disproved in the same way. Nor can it be replicated or generalised like conclusions derived from well-designed quantitative studies. It is amenable to rigorous research using qualitative methods and these can sometimes generate hypotheses that can be tested using nomothetic methods (Wattis et al., 2017).

WISDOM IN RELIGION, PHILOSOPHY, HUMANISM AND SPIRITUALITY

The main religious traditions all emphasise the importance of wisdom. In the Hebrew Bible a variety of books, including Job, Proverbs and Ecclesiastes are classified as wisdom literature. There are many references to wisdom in the Christian New Testament including a passage in the letter of James which reads:

> Who is wise and understanding among you? Let them show it by their good life, by deeds done in the humility that comes from wisdom ... [but] the wisdom that comes from heaven is first of all pure; then peace-loving, considerate, submissive, full of mercy and good fruit, impartial and sincere. Peacemakers who sow in peace reap a harvest of righteousness. (James 3:13, 17-18 NIV)

Islam also associates understanding and thought with spiritual growth and wisdom (Walker et al., 2016). Like early Christian thinking Islam incorporates ideas from Greek (Aristotelian and Neoplatonic) philosophy (El-Bizri, 2006). Various intellectual traditions of Islam emphasise ideas of personal search and wisdom through truth-seeking and self-awareness as ways of addressing spiritual aspects of religious life (Esmail, 1998; Madelung & Mayer, 2015). In Islam, wisdom and spirituality are inextricably intertwined.

Buddhism focuses on wisdom and in Mahayana Buddhism this is coupled with compassion (which not only empathises with the feelings of others but also acts to relieve suffering). Buddhism shares with early Christianity an emphasis on non-violence and loving peace. Ancient Greek philosophy recognised wisdom as one of the cardinal virtues (alongside courage, moderation and justice). Wisdom appears high in the list of virtues recognised in the modern *Values in Action Classification of Strengths* (VIA Institute on Character, 2018) which is broadly humanistic in orientation.

SPIRITUALITY AND WISDOM IN PRACTICE

How do spirituality and wisdom work together? Wisdom surely dictates that we take a biopsychosocial approach to practice embracing the spiritual dimension. As noted earlier, spirituality is *"experienced as being of fundamental or ultimate importance and is thus concerned with meaning and purpose in life, truth and values* [emphasis added]" (Cook, 2004, p. 549). Spirituality should be addressed in terms of the experience of the person with whom we are working. How can we effectively bring spirituality into practice and healthcare education?

A SHARED JOURNEY

The concept of a shared journey is useful here. This was one of the findings of Jones (2016) in her ethnographic study of how occupational therapists embody spirituality in practice. This concept of the shared journey resonates with the *Kawa* (Japanese: *River*; Iwama, 2006) model of occupational therapy, in which the patient's life is seen as a flowing river with the therapist sharing part of the journey. This puts the clinician on more even terms with the person than the more traditional expert–patient relationship. There is a need for expertise, but clinicians need to recognise the limits of their expertise and the importance of patients' expertise about their own lives. Recognising one's limitations is itself a characteristic of wisdom. Emanuel and Emanuel (1992) described four models of the physician–patient relationship: *paternalistic, informative, interpretive* and *deliberative*. The paternalistic model is the traditional model. The informative model is aligned with the idea of health as a *consumer* commodity and an emphasis on patient autonomy. The interpretive and deliberative models represent a co-operative/co-productive or partnership approach (Coulter, 1999). Wisdom and spiritually competent care both demand this approach. The clinician functions as a *limited* expert and partners with the patient in making decisions based on their own experience of illness, social circumstances, attitudes to risk, beliefs, values, preferences and spirituality.

SPIRITUALLY COMPETENT PRACTICE

Spiritually competent practice is a core concept for the Spirituality Special Interest Group at the University of Huddersfield.[1] Janice Jones' work produced a description of spiritually competent practice in occupational therapy which was subsequently modified to apply to all healthcare practitioners:

> Spiritually competent practice involves compassionate engagement with the whole person as a unique human being, in ways which will provide them with a sense of meaning and purpose, where appropriate connecting or

reconnecting with a community where they experience a sense of wellbeing, addressing suffering and developing coping strategies to improve their quality of life. This includes the practitioner accepting a person's beliefs and values, whether they are religious in foundation or not, and practising with cultural competency. (Wattis et al., 2017, p. 3)

We have identified factors which obstruct or promote spiritually competent practice. They either obstruct or promote care informed by clinical wisdom.

FACTORS WHICH OBSTRUCT SPIRITUALLY COMPETENT PRACTICE

Several factors obstruct spiritually competent care:

- fragmented patterns of working
- time and caseload pressures
- bad management systems and cultures.

Patterns of working in healthcare are increasingly fragmented. In the UK, social work input has been cut back and may be managed separately from healthcare. People with mental health issues may be supported, at different times by people from different teams, with loss of continuity. In the UK this is partly to facilitate the commissioner-provider split and ideas about market competition in healthcare; but "industrial" mechanistic, depersonalising ways of working prevail in many places as part of a political culture based on a materialistic worldview.

Doing a job well, particularly adopting a partnership rather than a paternalistic or consumer ethical stance, takes time and professionals often do not have enough time to spend with the people they work with. The number of sessions of therapy intervention may be limited, regardless of real personal need. Workers may have excessive workloads and be expected to end therapeutic relationships prematurely. Secondary pressures arise from staff stress-related sickness and demoralisation and from difficulties and delays in recruiting replacements.

Treating workers like mindless machines is unhelpful. Top-down command and control management does not free professionals to work in partnership with patients. An authoritarian, bullying culture may develop where the attitude of people at the top is "do what you're told, deliver your targets and shut up". This does not encourage workers to engage in genuine co-production, though they will no doubt tick the appropriate "patient involvement" box if required to do so. Role cultures where clinicians are seen as interchangeable "cogs" do not facilitate good personal relationships, an important foundation for ethical care within the partnership framework.

In our research around spiritually competent care by occupational therapists, advanced nurse practitioners (ANPs) and mental health nurses (Elliott, 2017; Jones, 2016; Rogers, 2016) we discovered that healthcare workers seek ways to work round constraints imposed by healthcare systems. We suspect this is common, but practitioners should not have to work against the system; the system should be working to support them.

FACTORS WHICH PROMOTE SPIRITUALLY COMPETENT PRACTICE

Several factors promote spiritually competent practice:

- team working
- good leadership and supervision
- good management systems and cultures.

Good teams where people are mutually supportive and aware of each other's special competencies and capabilities facilitate partnership working with patients. Working together in an atmosphere of mutual respect encourages members to work with patients in an equally respectful way. Acknowledgement of different and complementary but limited expertise within the team encourages recognition of the expertise of the people using services in their own subjective experience.

Good distributed leadership within teams, which recognises that different people are best equipped to lead on different issues, encourages the humility of accepting one's own limitations. This extends to working in partnership with people using services and recognising and supporting the key contributions they can make to creating new meaning and purpose when thrown off balance by illness. Peer supervision can support team members in engaging with people's spiritual needs. Beyond the team, the organisation needs to provide support through appropriate supervision and by having realistic expectations about workload.

There are alternatives to top-down command and control management. NAViGO, a social care enterprise providing mental health services uses design principles in its services (Bond, 2017), based on Social Role Valorisation (SRV), originally developed in learning disability. They are as follows:

- People who use and work in services influence design and operation
- Design facilities on domestic scale and style
- Educate staff to understand their power and influence for good or bad
- Ensure organisational design focuses on people who use services
- Language is important: "people" not patients; avoid clinical jargon
- Involve people who use services in all staff education and training
- Make clinical and security features unobtrusive in buildings
- Share common space
- Encourage public access and interaction
- Support people (staff and service users) to develop valued roles and creativity.

These principles emphasise the common humanity of staff, managers and people who use the services and reduce stigma in the wider community. They do not speak to spirituality as an intellectual abstraction but do signify spiritually competent practice.

The Virginia Mason Production System (VMPS) (Kenney, 2010) sounds very "industrial" but is based on insights originally from the Toyota Production System (TPS). This in turn was based on an adaptation of American mass production (see Dennis, 2015, for an account of Toyota's "lean production"). The key point of the TPS for present purposes is that workers are not treated as automata but as valued partners in production who contribute to the design of production systems and to continuous quality improvement. This is SRV for the workers! The VMPS similarly engages and values people who use the service, front-line clinicians and managers in ongoing service and quality improvement. NAViGO and VMPS are both discussed as examples of innovation in the second edition of *Practical Management and Leadership for Doctors* (Wattis, Curran, & Cotton, 2018).

INSIGHTS FROM WORLD RELIGIONS

The Buddhist principles of mindfulness and compassion have been used to develop approaches to resilience and therapy. Mindfulness practice and mindfulness-based cognitive therapy (MBCT) are well established fusions of ancient Buddhist ideas and pragmatic modern science.[2] MBCT is endorsed by the National Institute for Health and Care Excellence (NICE) for people who are currently well but have experienced three or more previous episodes of depression. Gilbert's (2010) *Compassion Focused Therapy* integrates techniques from cognitive behavioural therapy with insights from Buddhist psychology and neuroscience. Thus, therapies based on ancient Buddhist wisdom have proven clinical efficacy.

Other traditional wisdom has also been investigated, though at present research is at an earlier stage than for mindfulness and compassion-based therapy. One of the authors (Rogers, 2016) conducted research on applying the principles of availability and vulnerability from the Celtic Christian tradition to spiritually competent practice with ANPs. The findings suggest that the application of these principles within a professional relationship could be transformative for patient care as well as for the clinician. The Northumbria Community is a Celtic Christian Monastic community in the North of England that follows a "Rule of Life" based on two vows: availability and vulnerability (Northumbria Community, 2018). These vows imply relationship with God and other people in a non-judgemental, authentic, caring and compassionate way.

The research suggested that true availability was more than just physical presence and included emotional, spiritual and vocational aspects. All the study participants went into clinical work with an altruistic motivation and desire for their work to be vocational. Over years the changes in healthcare and push towards target-driven care had challenged their initial motivations. As they explored patient interactions, they all spoke of times which had affected them deeply. This connected to seeing the patient as a fellow human being. They recognised that to be available they first needed to be available to themselves, reflecting on their own spiritual journey and whether their own values were congruent with their practice. They recognised that to do this they needed self-acceptance, self-care and clinical supervision. Reflecting in these ways enabled them to "give" of themselves without reaching a point of burnout.

Availability also included a choice to practise in a way where patients feel welcomed and accepted (hospitality). This was integral to spiritually competent practice and included being truly present and listening attentively so that patients felt accepted, heard and cared for (Rogers & Béres, 2017). Concern for "being with" rather than "doing to" people was another key aspect of availability.

The concept of vulnerability carried negative connotations of risk of harm, whether to the patient or the clinician. However, authenticity and "giving of self" were seen as positive aspects of vulnerability involving connecting to a fellow human being. This involved genuineness, authenticity and congruence, which are well-accepted psychological approaches. One aspect of vulnerability the ANPs recognised was being open to their own limitations and being willing to be teachable. This included humility and willingness to learn from patients. ANPs viewed this as intentional vulnerability. Key was the willingness to be challenged as they gave relationships with their patients priority over professional status.

Relationships based on care, compassion and connection are the basis of holistic care and can be risky. Availability and vulnerability are deeply concerned with human connection. They are useful constructs to make spiritually competent care tangible. They necessitate a level of risk of hurt or misunderstanding but they can transform relationships with patients and make clinical practice more authentic.

DEVELOPING PRACTITIONERS TO PROVIDE WISE, SPIRITUALLY COMPETENT CARE

Spiritually competent care is supported by various aspects of wisdom, but how do we prepare people to deliver this kind of care? Research carried out by one of the authors has focused on improving the preparation of undergraduate nurses to provide spiritual care. The work is reported in more detail in her PhD thesis (Ali, 2017). An initial literature review (Ali, Wattis, & Snowden, 2015) was followed by a multiple case study, based on review of documents, interviews with educators and focus groups with students. This identified major knowledge and practice gaps in nurse education conceptualised as follows:

- lack of ontological integration
- lack in phenomenological understanding
- lack of support combined with environmental constraints
- curriculum structure and unprepared faculty.

Lack of ontological integration refers to relative inattention to the transformative experience of becoming and being a nurse. A focus on competencies to be learned and even on models for teaching about spiritual care will not be effective without work on personal development. To bridge this gap, educators need to support students in becoming self-aware and reflective in their practice through coaching, mentorship and role modelling, properly conducted.

A lack of phenomenological understanding is typified by a focus on "objective" rather than "subjective" truth. Without neglecting evidence-based practice in its narrower (nomothetic) sense people also need to embrace the evidence that idiographic person-person encounter with patients supports healing. This can be recognised in Carl Rogers' principles of *empathy, congruence* and *unconditional positive regard* (Rogers, 1959), validated in education and clinical practice (Kirschenbaum & Jourdan, 2005) and discussed in Wattis et al. (2017).

Students sometimes felt ill-prepared and under-supported in addressing spiritual issues. In addition, fragmented "industrialised" patterns of working, time and caseload pressures and bad management systems and cultures mitigated against developing skills in managing subjective, interpersonal aspects of care.

Finally, educators themselves faced similar issues of lack of support and environmental pressures, compounded by a relative lack of emphasis in the curriculum on more subjective phenomenological aspects of care. Standard-setting bodies themselves need to be persuaded to adopt a wiser, more inclusive attitude to education. These findings are summarised in Ali and Snowden (2017).

Nurturing and transforming healing approaches can accelerate the development of increased self-awareness in patients by expanding their subjective consciousness, facilitating transcendence at an intuitive level. A reflective framework, SOPHIE (Self-exploration through Ontological, Phenomenological, Humanistic, Ideological, and Existential Expressions), was developed from this work (Ali, 2017). It proposes a pedagogical shift grounded in heutagogical learning approaches. SOPHIE recognises the underlying reflective needs of a learner that are essential to develop personal authenticity, a knowledge seeking attitude and behavioural transformation. The need for a transformative approach is also reflected in the experience and education of practitioners from other disciplines, especially in palliative care (e.g. Gardner, 2012).

CONCLUSION

In this chapter we have considered the "great divorce" between materialist reductionist science and more subjective person-centred approaches to practice characterised by the contrast between nomothetic and idiographic knowledge. We have argued that wisdom and spirituality are concepts that transcend this divide. We have considered the obstacles and facilitators to spiritually competent practice which we would suggest also apply to practice wisdom. We have looked at ways of putting spirituality and wisdom into practice and of developing practitioners who are competent and have the personal qualities necessary to do this.

NOTES

[1] https://research.hud.ac.uk/institutes-centres/carh/ssig/
[2] More can be found on the Mindfulness-Based Cognitive Therapy website MBCT.co.uk including references to a variety of books: http://mbct.co.uk/

REFERENCES

Ali, G. (2017). *Multiple case studies exploring integration of spirituality in undergraduate nursing education in England* (Unpublished doctoral thesis). University of Huddersfield, England.

Ali, G., & Snowden, M. (2017). How can spirituality be integrated in undergraduate and postgraduate education? In J. Wattis, S. Curran, & M. Rogers (Eds.), *Spiritually competent practice in health care* (pp. 87-98). Boca Raton, FL: CRC Press.

Ali, G., Wattis, J., & Snowden, M. (2015). Why are spiritual aspects of care so hard to address in nursing education? A literature review (1993–2015). *International Journal of Multidisciplinary Comparative Studies, 2*(1), 7-31.

Allport, G. W. (1950). *The individual and his religion, a psychological interpretation.*, New York, NY: Macmillan.

Asimov, I. (1956). *The last question*. First appeared in the November 1956 issue of *Science Fiction Quarterly*. Retrieved from http://multivax.com/last_question.html

Bond, K. (2017). Using social role valorisation to make services sensitive to spiritual need. In J. Wattis, S. Curran, & M. Rogers (Eds.), *Spiritually competent practice in health care* (pp. 175-186). Boca Raton, FL: CRC Press.

Cook, C. (2004). Addiction and spirituality. *Addiction, 99*, 539-551.

Coulter, A. (1999). Paternalism or partnership? *British Medical Journal, 319*, 719-20.

Davies, W., & Roache, R. (2017). Reassessing biopsychosocial psychiatry. *The British Journal of Psychiatry, 210*, 3-5.

Dennis, P. (2015). *Lean production simplified.* Boca Raton, FL: CRC Press.

El-Bizri, N. (2006). Plato, platonism and neo-platonism. In *Medieval Islamic civilization, an encyclopaedia*. London, England: The Institute of Ismaili Studies. Retrieved from https://www.iis.ac.uk/academic-article/plato-platonism-and-neo-platonism

Elliott, R. (2017). *An exploration of mental health nurses' understanding of the spiritual needs of service users* (A thesis submitted in partial fulfilment of the requirements for the degree of Professional Doctorate). University of Huddersfield, England.

Ellison, C. W. (1983) Spiritual well-being: Conceptualization and measurement. *Journal of Psychology and Theology, 11*, 330-340.

Emanuel, E. J., & Emanuel, L. L. (1992). Four models of the physician-patient relationship. *JAMA, 267*(16), 2221-2226.

Engel, G. L. (1977). The need for a new medical model: A challenge for biomedicine. *Science, 196*(4286), 129-136.

Engel, G. L. (1980). The clinical application of the biopsychosocial model. *American Journal of Psychiatry, 137*(5), 535-544.

Engel, G. L. (1992). How much longer must medicine's science be bound by a seventeenth century worldview? *Psychotherapy and Psychosomatics, 57*, 3-16.

Epstein, R. M. (2014). Realizing Engel's biopsychosocial vision: Resilience, compassion and quality of care. *International Journal of Psychiatry in Medicine, 47*(4), 275-287.

Esmail, A. (1998). *The poetics of religious experience: The Islamic context* (Occasional Papers Series, Book 1). London, England: I. B. Tauris in association with The Institute of Ismaili Studies.

Gardner, F. (2012). Training and formation: A case study. In M. Cobb, C. M. Puchalski, & B. Rumbold (Eds.), *Oxford textbook of spirituality in healthcare* (pp. 451-458). Oxford, England: Oxford University Press.

Gilbert, P. (2010). *Compassion focused therapy: Distinctive features.* London, England: Routledge.

Iwama, M. (2006). *The Kawa model: Culturally relevant occupational therapy*. Edinburgh, Scotland: Churchill Livingston.

Jones, J. E. (2016). *A qualitative study exploring how occupational therapists embed spirituality into their practice* (A thesis submitted in partial fulfilment of the requirements for the degree of Doctor of Philosophy). University of Huddersfield, England. Retrieved from http://eprints.hud.ac.uk/id/eprint/27857/1/Revision_copy_of_thesis_Final23.12.15_Print_version_Turnitin.pdf

Kenney, C. (2010). *Transforming health care: Virginia Mason Medical Center's pursuit of the perfect patient experience.* Boca Raton, FL: CRC Press.

Kirschenbaum, H., & Jourdan, A. (2005). The current status of Carl Rogers and the person-centered approach. *Psychotherapy: Theory, Research, Practice, Training, 42*(1), 37-51.

Koenig, H. (2000). Religion, spirituality and medicine: Application to clinical practice. *JAMA, 284*(13), 1708.

Laszlo, E. (1996). *The systems view of the world: A holistic vision for our time* (2nd ed.). Cresskill, NJ: Hampton Press Incorporated.

Madelung, W., & Mayer, T. (2015). *Avicenna's allegory on the soul*. London, England: I.B. Tauris in association with The Institute of Ismaili Studies.

McGrath, A. E. (2011). *Christian theology: An introduction* (5th ed., pp. 108-109). Chichester, England: Wiley-Blackwell.

Monod, S., Brennan, M., Rochat, E., Martin, E., Rochat, S., & Büla, C. J. (2011). Instruments measuring spirituality in clinical research: A systematic review. *Journal of General Internal Medicine, 26*(11), 1345-1357.

National Secular Society. (2018). *What is secularism?* Retrieved from http://www.secularism.org.uk/what-is-secularism.html

Northumbria Community. (2018). *Who we are?* Retrieved from http://www.Northumbriacommunity.org

Rogers, C. R. (1959). A theory of therapy, personality and interpersonal relationships, as developed in the client-centered framework. In S. Koch (Ed.), *Psychology: A study of a science* (Vol. 3, pp. 184-256). New York: NY: McGraw-Hill.

Rogers, M. (2016). *Spiritual dimensions of advanced nurse practitioner consultations in primary care through the lens of availability and vulnerability: A hermeneutic enquiry* (Unpublished doctoral dissertation). University of Huddersfield, England. Retrieved from http://eprints.hud.ac.uk/28469/

Rogers, M., & Béres, L. (2017). How two practitioners conceptualise spiritually competent practice. In J. Wattis, S. Curran, & M. Rogers (Eds.), *Spiritually competent practice in health care* (pp. 53-70). Boca Raton, FL: CRC Press.

Stammers, T., & Bullivant, S. (2012). Secularism. In M. Cobb, C. Puchalski, & B. Rumbold (Eds.), *Oxford textbook of spirituality in healthcare* (pp. 83-88). Oxford, England: Oxford University Press.

Swinton J. (2012). Healthcare spirituality: A question of knowledge. In M. Cobb, C. Puchalski, & B. Rumbold (Eds.), *Oxford textbook of spirituality in healthcare* (pp. 99-104). Oxford, England: Oxford University Press.

Teilhard de Chardin, P. (1959). *The phenomenon of man*. New York and London: Harper Perennial.

Values in Action (VIA) Institute on Character. (2018). *The VIA classification of strengths*. Retrieved from https://www.viacharacter.org/www/Reports-Courses-Resources/Resources/Character-Strength-Fact-Sheets

Walker, P. E., Simonowitz, D., Poonawala, I. K., & de Callataÿ, G. (2016). *Sciences of the soul and intellect, Part I: An Arabic critical edition and English translation of Epistles 32-36*. Oxford University Press in association with The Institute of Ismaili Studies.

Wattis, J., Curran, S., & Cotton, E. (2018). *Practical management and leadership for doctors* (2nd ed.). Boca Raton, FL: CRC Press.

Wattis, J., Curran, S., & Rogers, M. (Eds.). (2017). *Spiritually competent practice in health care*. Boca Raton, FL: CRC Press.

John Wattis FRCPsych (ORCID: https://orcid.org/0000-0003-2991-3789)
Melanie Rogers (ORCID: https://orcid.org/0000-0002-2145-6651)
Gulnar Ali PhD (ORCID: https://orcid.org/0000-0003-4656-0882)
Stephen Curran
School of Human and Health Sciences
University of Huddersfield, United Kingdom

PART 2

PRACTICE WISDOM IN PRACTICE

Tall and strong
Yet flexible
Swaying in the breeze
While withstanding
Strong winds
And torrents

Bringing
Into the travail
of everyday building
support and structure
nature in harmony
with human endeavour

Joy Higgs
Bamboo – Dunedin, 2018

JOY HIGGS

15. PRACTICE WISDOM DEVELOPMENT

Developing practice wisdom is neither an easy task nor something that "just happens" to wise people. This chapter begins with the premise that practice wisdom is something that can be pursued through a journey of reflection and appreciation. This argument is presented in the form of a story that takes up from a tale in a previous publication: "Realising practical wisdom from the pursuit of wise practice".[1] This chapter draws links between practices like interpretation, reasoning and judgement that can be seen to relate and contribute to the use and development of practice wisdom and may form a more tangible or familiar pathway for professionals to develop and refine their practice wisdom.

PRELUDE

They came
from across the many realms
to sit at the feet
of the master, the sage
– perhaps for the last time …
Looking around the great arena
Veteratoris,
(the experienced practitioner)
saw many of his pupils
from across the years
– some now masters themselves.
Veteratoris smiled to himself,
remembering their hunger for learning.
Over to one side he spied
a particular group
that he remembered fondly
for their many questions
and debates.

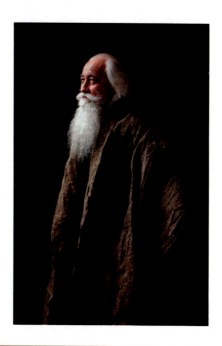

Notas Memoriae 1: Ancient Twitter
Each day at the symposium – highlights of the discussion were passed around as mementos and memory aids of the discussion on mini scrolls.

Veteratoris remembered telling this group
about Aristotle's[2] three intellectual virtues
who spent their time pursuing
teaching, learning, and practice.

Epistêmê:
was a youth of some stature
who portrayed the virtue of independent knowledge.
He loved science with a passion
and applauded truths that were universal,
invariable, and independent of context.

Tékhnê:
found virtue in practice and being practical.
Her desire was to create practical tools and strategies,
to learn how things worked and how to make things
to suit the current task and goal.
Her favourite answer was "it depends".

Phrónêsis:
reflected virtue in quiet achievements.
She often pondered over whether
her planned actions would be wise and proper
as well as practical.
She was fascinated by two ideas
praxis – a tantalising blend
of reflective right, and transformative practice
and *poiesis* – developing technique
through artistry and creativity.

Veteratoris concluded that
each of these three virtues demonstrated excellence of mind.
He challenged his pupils to think about what they wanted for their future
and what sort of person, teacher, or practitioner they wanted to be.
He now reflected on how his pupils had shaped their lives.

Notas Memoriae 2: Pursuing Interests and Reflection
Having an understanding of our technical, practical and emancipatory interests (see Habermas, 1972) and actively pursuing these and continually reflecting on our progress is a path towards wise practice.

Summus Tironis
(once called Tironis, or "the apprentice")
he was now called Summus Tironis
("leader of the apprentices").
As a young scholar, he had replied
in that long ago class,
"If I am to become a great teacher
then science must be my guide.
I will spend my time searching for The Truth
I will teach from strength not 'maybes'."
Now a learned scientist
His many scientific works and writings
were legendary.
Tironis was sitting here today with his own coterie
of hegemonic leaders and students.

Peritus
(the "skilled one")
had worked extensively with practitioners
over the years leading them in upholding
the primacy of practice
and seeking to derive knowledge
from practice experience
and value reflexive practice.
On many occasions
it was to her that people turned
when the world posed practical challenges
and people needed new ways
to face complex challenges
or new problems unimagined, yesterday.

Notas Memoriae 3: Professional Craft Knowledge
Professional craft knowledge is derived from practice experience through critical appraisal, reflection and testing of knowledge claims in practice. It stands in credibility alongside propositional knowledge derived from research and theorisation (Higgs & Titchen, 1995). Experiential knowledge is gained by personal experience. Some crucially important human knowledge exists which is distinct from and not reducible to either scientific or deductive knowledge (Vico, in Berlin 1979). Kolb (1984) describes experience-based knowledge generated through four different and combined processes: concrete experience, reflective observation, abstract conceptualisation and active experimentation.

***Semper* Novitius**
had added Semper to her name over the years
to reflect her need to be always learning.
In her youth she had told Veteratoris
"I want to be a good practitioner
so I need to learn the craft and virtue of *Tékhnê*.
I want to critique my practice
so I need the virtue of *Epistêmê*
to learn new ideas and strategies
that science can offer.
And, more than everything else,
I want someday to be wise like you
to make what I do
make a positive difference to people's lives
so I need to accept the challenge of *Phrónêsis*
to bring reflection, ethics, and practicality
to my journey of becoming
a good and wise practitioner".

She led her students and colleagues
in using and developing practical strategies and practices
and constantly inspired them to pursue *praxis* and *poiesis*.
She immersed herself in pursuit of wise and proper practice
that served the needs of other
and sought to attain and foster *eudaimonia*
or human flourishing.

Notas Memoriae 4: Phrónêsis

"Without this missing ingredient [practical wisdom] ... neither rules (no matter how detailed and well monitored) nor incentives (no matter how clever) will be enough to solve the problems we face" (Schwartz & Sharpe, 2010, p. 5).

Notas Memoriae 5: Eudaimonia

Eudaimonia is about human flourishing and living well. Aristotle used the term for the highest human good. Eudaimonia is central to developing wisdom and encompasses personal values and human virtues in relation to the ethical drive for decency and a good life. Professionalism could be considered as the pursuit of a "higher calling" characterised by eudaimonic values that motivate a commitment to excellence when helping others. Both professions and public institutions advocate and follow ethical, moral and just behaviours as expected by society.

PRACTICE WISDOM DEVELOPMENT

HISTORIES

Over the three days
of the symposium
Veteratoris invited members of the symposium
to reflect on their histories and experiences
in the pursuit and use
of practice wisdom.

A TEACHER'S TALE

Early on Day 1
An esteemed teacher came down from her seat
to address the audience.
Watching her was as stimulating
as listening to what she had to say
– she held the audience in the palm of her hand.
She began with this observation:
I wonder if my task is harder
than anyone else's to come.
As a teacher,
talking to you all about teaching
and the practice wisdom of teaching
I am role modelling what I'm talking about
so I have to think at the same time
about the words I'm saying
the actions I'm demonstrating
and how they fit together.

175

As she spoke she moved
around the stage
sometimes standing,
sometimes sitting on the edge of the stage
talking earnestly with a particular group
sometimes standing quite still
and holding her hands in front of her
while she created a particular
shape that evoked
the unique point of her story.

At the end she said –
over the years
I've learned much
from many of my own role models
both excellent teachers
and some that I wanted not to emulate.

The greatest question I could ask them was
"could you please explain
how and why
you just taught like that?"
I wanted them to bring
their invisible wisdom
out into the open
so I could appreciate it.

And, I learned to ask myself the same question,
drawing my practice into my mind,
seeking to name the tacit
and understand the wordless –
learning as much from my answers
when I had not liked my teaching
as when it had gone well.

Notas Memoriae 6: Zone of Proximal Development

Vygotsky's notion of the Zone of Proximal Development (ZPD) offers a model for the acquisition of practical wisdom. "The ZPD occurs in a cultural and emotive context as it is implied by Vygotsky that such advancements in learning imply a set of values shared by the learner and the more competent peer or teacher. Through these means, practical wisdom can be both developed and refined" (see Rothwell Chapter 21).

A MEDICO'S MUSING

The medico,
when it was his turn,
said this …
I often think
my greatest ability is making sense
– at the same time –
of multiple stories and puzzles
that are being told
often in different languages
by different people
all wanting me to hear their story
loudest and clearest.
There is the story of my patient
sometimes wrapped up
in their immediate pain or problem
and looking to me for a solution *right now*
or perhaps someone who has lived
with a failing mind and body
for a long time and wanting me to
listen to their wisdom of self knowing.
The next story is from the signs I see before me
as a result of tests and records –
what are these patterns telling me?

Other stories come from carers
in the clinic and home
who might see the patient's ways of coping
and their ease or dis-ease,
their abilities and their dis-abilities
what can I learn from these? – and
there are the "foreign language" stories of my peers
whose eyes notice different things than I do.

I have had to develop fluencies for each of these
various conversations
and mindfulness in these different cultures
in order to relate my sense making
and construe unique offerings for this person
at this time and place
and then to abide as patiently as them
while we see the outcomes
of our agreed health pathways.

Notas Memoriae 7: Expertise and Practice Wisdom

Have you considered the relationship between expertise and practice wisdom? Does either include the other? Should they? Often expertise in professional practice emphasises technical skill and people seek out practitioners who are highly skilled and achieve excellent technical outcomes. Others want humanity and people-centred practices alongside technical expertise. Others seek the skilled decision making of expertise and want these decisions imbued with deep people knowledge and wisdom. Boshuizen and Schmidt (2019) present a model of expertise in medical practice where the highest levels of decision making are informed by knowledge and understanding of people as well as their medical conditions. Such stories provide instantiated scripts to inform person-centred and situation-centred decision making.

"Clinical reasoning is a sophisticated set of reflexive, encultured capabilities that are deeply contextualised in the reasoner's discipline, their ways of knowing, their owned practice model and in their work setting, typically across multiple communities of practice. Somewhere on the journey from learning clinical reasoning as a systematic, conscious, risk-managed, novice-oriented process to the highly attuned wise practice of professional experts, practitioners should come to appreciate clinical reasoning as the most critical, integrative dimension and capability of professional practice" (Higgs, 2019, p. 29).

Notas Memoriae 8: Encultured Decision Making and Epistemic Fluency

"Linking this (epistemic) fluency to knowledge construction and co-construction and the derivation of knowledge from practice, we can recognise the way that clinical reasoning and decision making rely on epistemic fluency. Both reasoning and decision making involve understanding knowledge, appreciating different ways of knowing, using different sources and forms of knowledge in reasoning and placing different knowledge (including client's knowledge) as the influences and benchmarks that drive and determine decisions. We can think of epistemic fluency within clinical reasoning as a capability that is most clearly demonstrated by experienced and expert practitioners. Overall practice capability requires clinical reasoning fluency" (Higgs, 2019, p. 24).

THE EVIDENCE DEBATE

Around noon on the second day
four colleagues took their seats
for a group debate.
The topic was evidence in practice.
One debater had the clear stance of that person
whose role is to hold others to account.
For these resources and time –
what is the best you can achieve?
What mattered was the bottom line.
The second expected evidence to be sound,
grounded in measurement and logic,
well articulated and in common agreement.
The third argued strongly
for different forms of knowledge
practice-based as well as research and theory-based
to be equally valid as evidence to inform practice decision making.
The fourth questioned the nature of evidence
saying – who says this is true?
what if there are more than one truths?
How do we compare different forms of evidence?

> *Notas Memoriae 9: Evidence and Professional Decision Making*
> Many current practices in the professions serve to diminish the role of practical wisdom and encourage a positivistic oriented techno-scientific approach. Rothwell (see Chapter 21) argues that the evidence-based practice movement which has expanded into most professions and many non-professional areas has served with its "means ends" philosophy to reduce the role of professional decision making. See also Higgs and Turpin (2019).

WISDOM, ACCOUNTABILITY AND AUTONOMY

On the third morning
a distinguished-looking man took the stage.
He was a well-known judge.
Today, he said, I'd like to reflect on the place
of choice and wisdom
in the context of rules and accountability.
In my earlier career I was a lawyer
and so I was a professional person
and faced both the privileges of that role
such as autonomy as well as its responsibilities,
particularly duty of care to my clients and society.
I also worked in a world
where rules and laws mattered.
As a judge I see the tensions
of these competing influences even more strongly.
There are times when dutiful law enforcers
standing before me
report on the choices they had to make
in stressful and urgent situations
between following strict rules
and making moral choices
around leniency and humanity.
Wisdom, for me, has built over the years
in layers of understanding
of a balance between
things that remain more steadfast
and things that are particular.
I have learned a great deal
about humility – my own and others
and about the depths of ethics and morality
and the purpose and process
of my working world of the law.

> ### *Notas Memoriae 10: Cultural Humility*
> "In our attempts at working towards cultural humility we must not stop as simply being 'sensitive' and 'aware' but must remain diligent in seeking to remediate those injustices that we have come to understand around us" (Gallardo & Ivey, 2014, p. 246).

PRACTICE WISDOM DEVELOPMENT

OUTRO

On the last day the hushed crowd
enjoyed the rare delight
of listening to Veteratoris himself
reflecting on his life and learning.
With humility he recalled
many points of learning
across his life and answered
his audience's questions.
As a privileged listener
here are the words
I will remember most
when he spoke
about the three things that most informed
his *Practice Wisdom*.

Bringing a Heightened Level of Attention to My Being in the World

First, I have found that
the greatest contribution to my own practice wisdom
is to learn from others and from the world around me.
This requires me to bring
a heightened sense of awareness
and mindfulness to my perceptions and understandings.
This is mindfulness of myself, of the situation I am in
and of others – their interests, their actions and their contexts.
I need to listen with a mind open to hearing and to learning
but also a mind that is self-critical and reflective
indeed, actively metacognitive.

Notas Memoriae 11: Attentiveness

Increased consciousness is the key to learning that is liberating. Such attention involves "a higher quality of attention than we ordinarily bring to bear on our affairs" (Torbert, 1978, p. 109), and it is necessary for the search for shared purpose, self-direction and quality work which "create the possibility for adult relatedness, integrity, and generativity" (Torbert, 1978, p. 110). According to Mezirow (1985) the promotion of "critical awareness" should be aimed at helping learners to direct their own learning, and learn how to make meaning out of their experience and identify values in their lives.

Being in a Space of Dissonance and Creativity

My second awakening to practice wisdom
said Veteratoris
is something that I learned one day
when I went swimming.
I was in a lagoon
it was a warm summer's day.
At one stage I swam into a place of shadows
where little light penetrated
and my vision was limited.
In an attempt to find my way
I stirred up the floor silt
and caused even more disorder.
I had created a space of dissonance –
but amid the partial obscurity
I saw shapes and images
that were not there before.
Moving into another part of the pool
I was engulfed in warm eddies
and colours that fired my creative soul.

Over the years I have often remembered
the different ways these confusions
and creativity
are both vital to my sense making,
and my being and my becoming wise.
They have taken my mind, my soul and my pen
on many journeys to many realms
that my logical mind
could never have discovered.
Wisdom involves being open
to unknowing, appreciation
and creative imagining.

Notas Memoriae 12: Realm of Unknowing

The Realm of Unknowing is that primal domain of personhood forever beyond conscious reach, where thought, feeling and intent are one – or more accurately, where such distinctions are unthinkable (McKenzie, 1999).

"The Realm of Unknowing" and "muddy waters" may have roles in enabling our lifework of becoming. Poetry can be an art of poignant enigma; poets and poetry lovers are able to brave such lack of clarity; sometimes they luxuriate in it. For poets, lingering in muddy waters is core business (McKenzie, 2014).

Sense Making

Finally, Veteratoris concluded:
my final interpretation of practice wisdom
is interpretation itself.
When we are being and doing in the world
we are seeking to make sense of it,
of who we are and who we are becoming.
So learning to understand,
reflect, appraise and appreciate this world
involves meaning making.
And, this interpretation makes sense to us if
it integrates our awareness of context,
builds on our prior understandings,
is particular to ourselves, our goals and interests
while embracing of others' ideas and cultures.
And so I thank all of you
for sharing your wisdom
and wish you rich lives
in pursuit of your life contributions
and life's wise appreciation.

Notas Memoriae 13: Hermeneutics and Sense Making

"People make meaning and make sense of their worlds in relation to their contexts (including traditions, culture, language, interests, values, current circumstances). They make changes to their knowledge, practices and circumstances through critical appraisal, interpretations and actions to modify the status quo" (Higgs, 2010, p. 321).

"Hermeneutics is as an overarching means of meaning making in practice. ... Meaning making is a fundamental way of making sense of the world across many endeavours ... Hermeneutics emphasises the social, cultural and historical nature of inquiry and rests on the assumption that understanding cannot be separated from the social interests and the standpoints assumed by individuals, within a particular culture (Thompson, 1990)" (cited in Higgs, 2010, p. 309).

NOTES

[1] Higgs, J. (2011). Realising practical wisdom from the pursuit of wise practice. In E. A. Kinsella & A. Pitman (Eds.), *Phronesis as professional knowledge: Practical wisdom in the professions* (pp. 73-85). Rotterdam, The Netherlands: Sense.

[2] Aristotle (c. 400 BCE/1999).

REFERENCES

Berlin, I. (Ed.). (1979). *Against the current: Essays in the history of ideas*. London, England: The Hogarth Press.

Boshuizen, H. P. A., & Schmidt, H. G. (2019). The development of clinical reasoning expertise. In J. Higgs, G. Jensen, S. Loftus, & N. Christensen (Eds.), *Clinical reasoning in the health professions* (4th ed., pp. 57-65). Edinburgh: Elsevier.

Gallardo, M. E., & Ivey, A. (2014). What I see, could be me. In M. E. Gallardo (Ed.), *Developing cultural humility: Embracing race, privilege and power* (pp. 239-264). Los Angeles, CA: SAGE.

Habermas, J. (1972). *Knowledge and human interest* (J. J. Shapiro, Trans.). London, England: Heinemann.

Higgs, J. (2010). Hermeneutics as meta-strategy. In J. Higgs, N. Cherry, R. Macklin, & R. Ajjawi (Eds.), *Researching practice: A discourse on qualitative methodologies* (pp. 309-322). Rotterdam, The Netherlands: Sense.

Higgs, J. (2019). Re-interpreting clinical reasoning: A model of encultured decision making practice capabilities. In J. Higgs, G. Jensen, S. Loftus, & N. Christensen (Eds.), *Clinical reasoning in the health professions* (4th ed., pp. 13-31). Edinburgh: Elsevier.

Higgs, J., & Titchen, A. (1995). The nature, generation and verification of knowledge. *Physiotherapy, 81*, 521-530.

Higgs, J., & Turpin, M. (2019). Learning to use evidence to support decision making. In J. Higgs, G. Jensen, S. Loftus, & N. Christensen (Eds.), *Clinical reasoning in the health professions* (4th ed., pp. 465-473). Edinburgh: Elsevier.

Kolb, D.A. (1984). *Experiential learning: Experience as the source of learning and development*. Englewood Cliffs, NJ: Prentice-Hall.

McKenzie, A. (1999). A ferret tail-chase – the perpetual closed loop of open system reflecting-theorising. *Paper presented at the Issues of Rigour in Qualitative Research Conference, Association for Qualitative Research*. Bundoora, Australia: Association for Qualitative Research.

McKenzie, A. (2014). *Meaning making: A university curriculum framework for the twenty-first century* (Unpublished doctoral dissertation). Charles Sturt University, Australia.

Mezirow, J. (1985). A critical theory of self-directed learning. In S. Brookfield (Ed.), *Self-directed learning: From theory to practice* (pp. 17-30). San Francisco, CA: Jossey-Bass.

Schwartz, B., & Sharpe, K. (2010). *Practical wisdom: The right way to do the right thing*. New York, NY: Riverhead Books.

Thompson, J. L. (1990). Hermeneutic inquiry. In L. E. Moody (Ed.), *Advancing nursing science through research* (Vol. 2, pp. 223-286). Newbury Park, CA: SAGE.

Torbert, W. R. (1978). Educating toward shared purpose, self-direction and quality work – the theory and practice of liberating structure. *Journal of Higher Education, 49*, 109-135.

Joy Higgs AM, PhD (ORCID: https://orcid.org/0000-0002-8545-1016)
Emeritus Professor, Charles Sturt University, Australia
Director, Education, Practice and Employability Network, Australia

BRADLEY ROBERTS AND JOY HIGGS

16. MASTER MARINERS AND PRACTICE WISDOM

There is a sea within, where currents thrum
with silvered fish sensations –
where scrimshawed emotion and sinew
engage and enact my craft –
where this sea's whispered swash barely
crests my knowledge of my journey.
And yet this sea touches far shores –
where nations ringed about
with traditions and conventions –
myths and marbled heroes – all subsumed
like the sound of distant surf –
yet compelling me on my voyage.

In this chapter we enter the fascinating and challenging world of master mariners. Through their narratives we set out to examine what this space is like and how its exploration can shed light on what practice wisdom means and how it is realised in the varied lifeworlds of master mariners. We present the following key arguments:

– Being a master mariner is a complex role that blends professional practice and experience-based practice;
– While many professionals work in organisations and corporations, master mariners work in unique venues where they are both master and employee;
– Today's master mariners face many challenges that relate to being individual professional practitioners, team leaders, organisational managers and chief executive officers reporting to company directors – at each of these levels, decision making has different and potentially conflicting challenges and human/economic/ethical/practice accountabilities;
– There is considerable pressure on these master mariners being both ship "ruler" and senior responsible officer – present in the midst of both calm seas and crises and part of a corporate command tethered to distant overseers;
– Master mariners today are equipped with advanced technology and face the imperative of scientific-based evidence in this age of global and multinational corporate accountability; and
– Practice wisdom is an often-overlooked centrality in all of these spaces.

Practice wisdom can be defined as "the capacity to understand and practice in a common-sense manner that is scientifically based, sensitive to … [client] needs, ethically grounded and professionally satisfying" (Higgs, 2016a, p. 69).

Practice wisdom involves knowing in a way that involves insight, discernment of moral outcomes and the ability to choose between options with sound judgement, wisdom and foresight, drawing upon experience, learning, reflecting, critical dialogue, and making and testing hypotheses (Higgs, 2012; Klein & Bloom, 1995).

MASTER MARINERS AS PROFESSIONALS: THEIR LIFEWORLD

Historically, a master mariner was the captain of a commercial vessel, with the word "master" indicating mastery of this occupational role. Today the term refers to the highest level of qualification among mariners. An advanced diploma qualification is awarded to those senior ships officers whose competence has been assessed under the international STCW A-II/2 syllabus (International Maritime Organization [IMO], 2017). University degrees also exist such as a bachelor degree for master mariners at the Svendborg International Maritime Academy[1] and the Master of Marine Science and Management degree at the University of Sydney.[2]

Master mariners have experienced unprecedented change in their roles in recent decades. The lifeworld of master mariners (captains of seagoing ships) is highly paradoxical. It is anchored in archaic traditions, yet in the current age it is also technologically sophisticated. It is a solitary role, as well as a role that is increasingly enmeshed with global stakeholders, decreasing the master's autonomy on his/her ship. It draws upon archetypes of authority and infallibility, while contending with human limitations (of self, crew and corporate owners) and contested power bases (both on board and on land). These insights demonstrate that the occupation of master mariner is in transition, growing in complexity and ambiguity as stakeholders become interdependently, and intimately, connected while traditional power and authority becomes challengeable.

This complexity and evolution is further complicated by the impact of "liquid modernity". This term, introduced by Polish philosopher and sociologist Zygmunt Bauman (2000), emphasises the chaotic continuation of modernity with increased privatisation of services across global capitalist economies and an increasing chaos and the pressure of responsibility on individuals through their fluid careers. In such a world, Cherry (2005, 2014) argues that individuals need to engage in constructive learning to achieve mastery in the face of complex practice dilemmas and to be prepared for complex practice demands. Further, she contends that managerial authority and professional discretion are matters that require negotiation (Cherry, 2016). Lippi (2013) also confronts the requirements of leadership in the face of liquid modernity, calling for "liquid learning" that draws upon insights from liquid modernity to navigate its fluid leadership conditions.

If the various interested parties or stakeholders (company owners and managers, senior staff onboard, other crew, passengers, shareholders) in this liquid modern world rely solely, or even predominantly on scientific knowledge and evidence-based practice to manage, or indeed triumph, over these paradoxes then, we contend, this reliance is built upon an over-simplistic interpretation of the complexity of this role, a limited understanding of professional practice and a failure to appreciate the significance and worth of practice wisdom and wise practice. Our chapter proceeds to reveal the foundations of this argument.

Master mariners face the responsibilities of professional practice. Professionals have been identified as serving the interests of society, applying to their practice a unique body of knowledge, and being held to higher standards of conduct and performance by society (Higgs, 2016b). Master mariners fit these criteria by providing global access to manufactured goods and commodities that make possible our 21st century world, by performing their roles according to international seafaring training standards (IMO, 2017), with their contribution acknowledged each year on 25 June, the International Day of the Seafarer (IMO, 2018).

It is an interesting question as to where knowledge fits in the practice of master mariners, and what practices, roles, capabilities and responsibilities encompass their professional practice. In many of the established professions a unique body of academic knowledge grounded in the behavioural and physical sciences as well as discipline-specific knowledge and technical skills underpin professional educational curricula. In the case of guild-based learning a long history of practice-based knowledge and competencies underpin training. Professions typically have codes of ethical practice and professional organisations that regulate the standards of their members and monitor codes of conduct. In the case of master mariners such expectations are addressed by the International Maritime Organization's conventions of Safety of Life at Sea (SOLAS), Maritime Labour Convention (MLC), Standards of Training, Certification and Watchkeeping (STCW) and Maritime Pollution (MARPOL) (Freeth, 2015). These standards are supported by professional maritime associations such as The Nautical Institute, whose aim is to provide "the strongest possible professional focus" for the occupation and its practice (Freeth, 2015, p. 1). Practice wisdom builds on education, work-based training and learning, peer learning, mentoring and reflexivity. Such development can generate practice wisdom that exceeds knowledge, and can promote capabilities within wise practice that extends technical expertise. This will be illustrated below through the findings of doctoral research conducted by our first author, Brad Roberts.

RESEARCHING MASTER MARINERS

In his doctoral research on master mariners Brad Roberts (see Roberts, 2018) interviewed master mariners who commanded medium-sized ships (see Figure 16.1) with crews of around 22 seafarers. Such ships attend to the needs of oil and gas platforms: both resupplying them and towing them to new locations. The masters and their crews conduct intensive, round-the-clock operations for periods of five weeks at a time in some of the most remote regions on earth, such as Australia's North-West Shelf. This section of the chapter presents findings arising from this research; quotes identified with a hash mark (#) refer to the anonymised interview transcripts from which the quotes were taken.

Figure 16.1. Offshore vessel and oil rig.

The Roles of Master Mariners

From this research the vast diversity among master mariners was a notable finding; it was evident that the participants had each built their own uniquely personal practice wisdom. This finding supports the argument that there is no generic profile of a master mariner. The research participants demonstrated a complexity in their roles and the potential for encountering wicked problems. Wicked problems cannot be solved in a traditional linear fashion, because the problem definition evolves as new possible solutions are considered and/or implemented. The term was originally coined by Horst Rittel (see Rittel & Webber, 1973). Wicked problems typically occur within challenging, hazardous and isolated environments (Lurås, Lützhöft, & Sevaldson, 2015; Misangyi, 2016). Such professional practice challenges call for practice wisdom, to address complex, paradoxical elements and achieve positive outcomes arising from these challenges.

Master mariners' professional practice is a composite of many roles. In the case of the work of Brad's participants, their practice involves the logistical planning and scheduling associated with supply chain operations. Towing of oil platforms at sea requires significant planning associated with major engineering and construction projects, due to the relocation of oil platforms weighing up to 22,000 tonnes. Other roles involve business leadership, with many master mariners describing their role as being like a CEO. The work also incorporates the traditional skills of navigating and steering the ship, including manoeuvring within metres of oil and gas platforms.

Additionally, master mariners are people managers, who contend with the people issues that arise from leading a group of people in high pressure situations within tight environmental confines for weeks at a time. For example, one master mariner described his actions upon being challenged by a belligerent crew member during a safety meeting, "*I stopped the meeting, and I said 'You do not run the deck'. I about-turned, walked up to the bridge console and said 'Meeting closed'. That was it*" (Interview #0361).[3] In contrast to this highly directive managerial focus, master mariners also attend to the human needs of the crew with a surprising degree of compassion – "*You are a mother*" (one participant advised) (#0897). Indeed, the wise attention to such paradoxical leadership dimensions (Lewis & Smith, 2014) can be particularly challenging within the environment of a ship at sea. As one master described this, "*When you're at sea, after a period of time the whole world shrinks basically. These things [human issues] sort of grow, because, like I said, the world shrinks*" (#0190). Learning to manage both the task/functional and relationship/people dimensions of leadership (see Hersey & Blanchard, 1969) and helping crew members maintain perspective in this paradoxical dynamic of a "*shrinking*" world where issues appear to be "*magnified*", calls for wisdom in action.

Knowledge, Wisdom and Meaning Making

Work and life at sea is inherently hazardous, often resulting in catastrophic incidents: including the *Piper Alpha* oil platform explosion in 1988 (killing 167 crew) (O'Byrne, 2011), the *Deepwater Horizon* platform explosion of 2010 (killing 11 people and causing the worst environmental disaster in United States history) (Lekka & Sugden, 2011), and the capsizing of the *Bourbon Dolphin* while towing an oil platform, killing eight crew (Lyng et al., 2008). Each catastrophe has triggered the development of an additional layer of maritime regulation. As remarked by the Norwegian Government Commission investigating the capsizing of the *Bourbon Dolphin*, "There is no shortage of written material of both the obligatory and advisory kind" (Lyng et al., 2008 p. 134). Regulatory elements and actions can be seen as part of the "hegemonic rationality" (see Higgs, 2012, p. 75) of the professions. As one master described the regulation of practice in Brad's research, "*Everything is black and white in our industry. You either do it right or wrong*" (#0768).

However, the master mariners' narratives in Brad's research suggest a broader perspective; it was evident that they attend to many nuanced aspects of their roles that are less codified and "black and white" than these technical aspects alone account for. Master mariners must address paradoxical challenges such as tightly coordinating the activities of their crew during round-the-clock operations while maintaining harmony, engagement and a balanced perspective among the crew. As such, successful master mariners have made sense of these paradoxical tensions (Lewis & Smith, 2014) and have developed wise ways to contend with these challenges (see also Cherry, 2014; Higgs, 2016a).

There were many examples reported by participants in their narratives during this study of practice wisdom. The following vignette illustrates practice wisdom and sensemaking. The example involves a master mariner contending with the demands of towing an oil platform during extremely challenging weather and sea state. In his initial comments, he describes the felt pressure to meet charterer demands in these volatile operating conditions:

> *And it's those charterer demands – push, push, push, push – that really impact upon our abilities to make maybe the correct decisions. We are fully aware that it costs money to run that rig, and every time we delay it means that someone in the office is going to make a judgement upon us. We love it when we see [names several competitor companies]. ... We love it when they're out there, and they can't do it and we can.* (#0353)

This account reveals that, paradoxically, while the Master can say "No" when it is not safe to operate, there is a strong pressure to meet customer demands. Indeed, several narratives from Brad's research suggested that going against customer requirements can have long-term outcomes if the customer's needs are not met: "*And they might say to [the company] 'Your Captain doesn't know what he's doing. We want him off'*" (#0361). This pressure to perform is not solely coercive, as the Master states they "*love it*" when they can perform when other vessels are not able to. That is, sometimes the master and crew want to demonstrate their expertise which may prompt them to take undue risks. These dynamic tensions between authority and relationships, and between safety and commercial imperative, are (using the words of Lewis & Smith, 2014) "highly paradoxical" and "dripping with perplexities" (see Macklin & Whiteford, 2012, p. 94), particularly in urgent situations where decisions must be made in the moment. The master quoted above went on to describe the way in which he balances these competing pressures between operational safety and meeting charterer demands, as *"finding the line"*:

> *Well, to find out where that line is, to establish that line, you'll look at 'Why am I doing it? Why do I do this?' The ship is operational so I draw the line. My experience, my confidence in the systems and the training of the crew, the knowledge that the rig is ready and the crane is ready for me, and that the operation can go as quickly and as safely as possible, I know where that line is. ... As soon as there's a change, such as [a] crane driver's no longer available, I'll move away just far enough to be able to come back and continue the job. So, I redraw the line; no crane driver, therefore the line's moved, I'll move away – I'm now back in an equilibrium that I'm happy with. You're continually reassessing where you need to draw that line.* (#0353)

This approach shows an attentiveness to emerging conditions to harmonise tensions via a "dynamic equilibrium" point (see Smith & Lewis, 2011) ("the line") between maintaining safety and preserving the customer relationship. Therefore, the master avoids the contingency approach described by Johnson (2014) and Lewis and Smith (2014) as an "either/or" framing by utilising a more nuanced "both/and" conceptualisation. The narratives of master mariners, such as the above vignette, suggest they apply practice wisdom (as a type of knowing/being/enacting) in their roles. Additionally, they make meaning of their situation for their crew regarding the customer's requirements, as well as for their customers regarding the vessel's operating state: "*It's like an hourglass in both directions*" (#0535).

The hourglass analogy was very compelling. See Brad's sketch in Figure 16.2. This sketch shows a master mariner at the nexus of the hourglass, making meaning at the local level for the crew, as well as making meaning on a global level for the customer. This meaning making is a two-way exchange in such situations. The master's hands are open and outstretched, signifying tactile perception and bodily engagement. Meaning coming from all sources allow the master mariner to "find the line" and share this position both locally and globally.

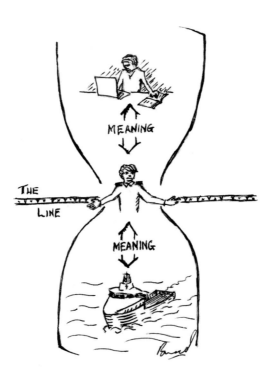

Figure 16.2. The hourglass analogy for practice wisdom.

Making meaning for diverse groups, rather than merely stating technical facts, requires a high degree of wisdom to be sensitive to the various stakeholder concerns as well as being effective in creating understanding that allows optimal performance (safety and commercial outcomes) on a broader yet integrated scale (Cunliffe & Coupland, 2012; Weick, 2001). This hourglass approach, as a wise and necessary practice adaptation, contrasts starkly with traditional, unilateral, command-and-control autocracy that was prevalent in the pre-21C maritime world.

Embodied Wisdom

This section explores the embodied elements of practice wisdom, as revealed in master mariner narratives, but also as explained by practice theory. It highlights the hidden nature of embodied practice wisdom, how this intertwines with professional practice traditions, and causes difficulty in reflecting on and developing wise practice. According to Patton and Fish (2016), professional practice "is embedded in practice traditions ... and embodied in [an] individual practitioner's performance" (p. 55). Master mariners incorporate bodily elements into their practice wisdom through their tactile, visceral connection with the vessel. For example, one master described his bodily engagement with his ship while avoiding a potential collision with another ship:

> *You know that that ship is about to plough into you. I mean it was close, we got close. So, four engines, flat out, and then you're just hoping. And it just happened that quick. But, it was a very frightening, yeah, very frightening position. I then turned the ship to face the stern so that if [the other ship] did hit, well, I was a bit further up. You know, your engines are ramped up and you can see the massive thrust coming out of the stern, and you are doing this type of thing [hands to head, moans in a worried manner]. You know, there's nothing more you can do. You've taken your action, the engines are doing their job, and all you are doing now is just seeing how effective that was. You're hanging onto those sticks, putting as much power down as you can without blacking that engine out, and you're just thinking 'Gee, come on, come on, come on, come on!'.* (#0768)

In Brad's fieldwork on such vessels, he observed embodied wisdom was present in the everyday, routine engagements with the vessel, such as finely adjusting its position in relation to the sea state and weather to marginally ease the load on its engines and thrusters. He noticed master mariners integrating multiple streams of digital information from sophisticated sensors with tactile stimulus such as the vibrations of the ship's engines through the soles of their feet, in order to form a nuanced and dynamic awareness. They incorporated practice wisdom into their decision making and responses by attending to envelopes of information and situation observation/experience to enable optimal performance on a moment-by-moment basis, largely through feel and subtle adjustment to controls, and without conscious awareness of their practice. Such wisdom is enacted via a "lived body" (Dall'alba, Sandberg, & Sidhu, 2018, p. 275), or as described by Sheets-Johnstone (2015), "the body I have" (p. 26).

Master mariners enact their practice wisdom through their bodily actions, and the bodies of their crew, sometimes employing them, as King (2007) describes in her study of fishing boat captains, as bodily "prostheses" in the service of the captain's will. One master described his orders to the crew when he noticed a crane was incorrectly positioned when the ship was about to come alongside the wharf:

> *And I'm going 'Get the crane up! Get the crane up!' I said to the Mate 'Stop the ship! Right now!' I said 'Get the f%@*ing crane up! Get it up!' So, I could*

see a potential, we could damage a crane, damage the wharf, damage the company's reputation ... That's the vision I had of what was going to happen. (#0361)

This example shows that practice wisdom can also be extended through engagement with the ship and with the crew as bodily extensions of master mariners (Clark & Chalmers, 2016).

Embodied practice wisdom is also revealed in the language these master mariners use: in phrases such as *"finding the line"*, achieving *"equilibrium"*, being *"comfortable"* (#0353), and *"being on firm footing"* (#0068). Embodied metaphors reflect an ongoing, experience-based "feeling out" of sensory patterns in the master mariners' lifeworlds as it is experienced. There is a tactile, almost grasping, quality in the way they make sense of, and express, their situations.

Considerable research has identified neural linkages between embodied metaphors and bodily associated neural responses within the brain (see also Gibbs, 2011; Stickles et al., 2016). For example, when a master mariner uses the words *"I just ran"* (#0768) to describe avoiding a collision between his ship and another vessel, his words would also activate those areas of the brain associated with running. As such, there is a neural connection between the body and the language used that is "alive in the minds of speakers" (Lakoff, 2012), contributing meaning to their lived experience. This meaning is reinforced in powerful "two-way cascades" of neural activity (i.e. language-to-body and body-to-language).

This bodily reinforcement and connection with language and meaning is carried out unconsciously (Lakoff, 2012). Therefore, not only do embodied metaphors enmesh the language of practice with the "body-I-have" (Sheets-Johnstone, 2015), but this process is powerfully reinforcing and unconscious. This scientifically validated process explains how practice wisdom becomes bodily inscribed via invisible means beyond the practitioner's awareness. It is important to view embodied practice wisdom not as the fortuitous intersection of separate domains of mind and body (McGilchrist, 2011; Tucker, 2007), but as the product of an integrated, enmeshed system (Claxton, 2015; Gordon, 2013) that encompasses thinking, feeling, action, sensing, experiencing, knowing, remembering, creating, reflecting, narrating, extending, being and becoming (Cunliffe & Coupland, 2012; Froese & Fuchs, 2012; Kinsella, 2015).

Practice Wisdom and Habitus

Practice wisdom is not developed in isolation. It is enmeshed in a broader, socially constructed domain identified by Mauss, and systematised by Bourdieu, as the *habitus* (Silva, 2016). Bourdieu (2013) defined the habitus as "a system of lasting, transposable dispositions ... integrating past experiences, functions at every moment as a matrix of perceptions, appreciations, and actions" (pp. 82-83). As such, the habitus produces both individual and collective practices via history and the engagement of "durably installed generative principles" that guide perception, sensemaking and action (Bourdieu, 2013, p. 78).

Habitus is also largely unconscious, in that those who participate within their habitus forget its history through becoming part of it (Bourdieu, 2013). In terms of master mariners, the seafaring habitus involves a "deep immersion" and "carnal entanglement" (Wacquant, 2011) with enduring and pervasive concepts of what it means to be a master mariner. Master mariners gave voice to their habitus in comments such as *"I'm the guy with the ticket. You should be listening to me. You shouldn't tell me how to do my job"* (#0068). *"As long as I've got those stripes on my shoulder, nobody comes onto my bridge and talks to me like that"* (#0520).

According to Silva (2016), the habitus is "a mode of being embodied with an orientation to the world which is lived in everyday life and practices" (p. 75). As such, the habitus appears to be reinforced via the same neural processes as the embodied metaphors described above and therefore has the potential to influence wise practice in ways that are hidden to the professional. Indeed, the habitus may be where the "body-I-have" becomes the "body-I-am", as it shapes the identity of the master mariner along traditional, historic terms (Sheets-Johnstone, 2015). The master mariners' habitus has thousands of years of history coiled within its constructs, tapping into ancient archetypes of unchallengeable autocracy and infallibility (Hershey, 1988; King, 2011; Roberts, 2018).

Therefore, the master mariner habitus may be a hidden yet pervasive aspect of *professional hegemony* (see Higgs, 2012), that shapes, and potentially limits, the capacity for wise practice in favour of historically preferred ways of being, perceiving and acting. Its historic and durable nature makes the habitus biased towards the past, and slow to evolve (Lizardo, 2013) in the face of rapid change, as found in today's maritime sector and the broader world of work. This helps to explain many of the paradoxical tensions and wicked problems that have been described by the master mariners in their narratives. However, as Patton (2016) notes, it takes courage, particularly courage in the appropriateness of their actions, for professional practitioners to challenge the taken-for-granted practices enshrined within their professional habitus.

BRAD'S LETTER TO MASTER MARINERS

Some of you have told me your accounts of critical events; your stories of moments that challenge your professional practice. I listened to the sort of words you used to describe what you do in those moments. Now, respectfully, I would like to share my interpretations of those moments; to translate those words to provide further meaning of what you are doing and saying.

You point to the volumes of regulation that control your industry and set standards and expectations for your knowledge and skill. Many of these regulations were built on the back of a catastrophic event where the procedures at that time fell short. Despite their benefit, this fact shows that eventually, the procedures you follow will fall short also, and you will find yourself facing complex, ambiguous and unprecedented events, where it will fall on your shoulders to act wisely in the moment for the good of all.

Typically, the industry expects black and white outcomes – "you either do it right or wrong". This was easier to achieve, in simpler and earlier times, when you would receive a telegram now and then, and your authority would be sufficient and unquestioned for all else in between. However, the world, and your world at sea, has become increasingly complex in its accountabilities and more interconnected with stakeholders who can access you in real time, at any time, at any place.

These stakeholders want to collaborate in (or at times, take over) your decisions, to receive frequent updates and to change plans to fit just-in-time commercial imperatives. They are no longer across the globe. They are in your ears, and "in your face". They bring complexity, they challenge your authority, and they bring problems that are difficult to solve through black-and-white, either-or responses.

You do not talk of practice wisdom, as I do. Instead, you use terms such as "intuition", "just knowing what to do", or "just experience", and yet what you are doing, and the knowledge you are using is more than these things. Practice wisdom taps into your expertise, your pragmatic sense of what is ethically right and what is wrong and what is the best thing to do at the time. It is underpinned by your perceptions, your feelings, your thoughts and your every-day actions, all distilled into pragmatic and sound solutions for complex and exceptional as well as more regular circumstances.

Practice wisdom taps into your creativity, and your motivation to come through and deliver results in the most challenging of contexts. Wise practice lies both within and beyond the routine procedures and regulations that are appropriate for 99 percent of what you do. It is also in that one percent, in the toughest of times, that your practice wisdom will be particularly called upon and when the rules and standards aren't enough – there's no rule for this current situation yet. Practice wisdom is not unknowable or the preserve of the exceptional, extremely wise master. If it seems elusive, it is because it is often hidden in levels deeper than your rational thinking, etched in actions that are outside of your words, embedded in your values, your feelings and your knowing built through your experiences.

Wise practice also needs to be sought out and not taken-for-granted as embedded truth and certainty in the ingrained, traditional ways of seeing and doing your role, and the role of seafaring, that have been passed on to you. I have called this "habitus" in the pages above, but you can also think of this as "traditions" and "the way we do things".

You learn these ways from your mentors, your colleagues, and even the way you perform your role. These ingrained ways shape your practice in ways that are often unconscious or hidden. They seep into your perceptions and actions automatically.

However, these ingrained ways are not unquestionably wise. Sometimes, due to their long traditions, they may be out of step with the dynamics of modern shipping, giving rise to new problems and tensions. As such, relying solely on these ingrained, traditional ways without careful thought can be quite unhelpful. What is important to you and those you work with and for, is that you question your own practices and the inherited ways of doing things, particularly if you lay claim to the title of professional.

I hope this enables you to see your practice wisdom with fresh eyes, and to find its thread in what you do and how you think about your role. This type of wisdom is invaluable, legitimate and hard won. It serves you well, and you have told me of it in your triumphs and in your trials, but also in your everyday practice. Learn to look for your practice wisdom, nurture it, and treasure it – but above all, share it.

BRAD'S LETTER TO MASTER MARINERS' MANAGERS

Today's technology provides you with unprecedented capacity and power to interact with and influence others. Additionally, commercial and operational systems increasingly provide the opportunity to optimise and adapt operational practice in real time. Both of these factors provide the potential for impacting upon the leadership and performance of Master Mariners at sea.

By taking up these means of engaging and influencing maritime operations in real time, you make yourself part of their operation and their world. You are no longer shore-based spectators in this process, distanced from the activities at sea. You have a responsibility for co-managing the difficult to resolve problems and challenges that master mariners face, such as the need to maintain exceptional levels of operational safety in high-stakes work contexts, while meeting the challenges of commercial imperatives.

This requires you to be mindful of the impacts, both direct and indirect, that your interactions may have on the practice of seafaring leaders. It also requires you to work with master mariners in assisting them in developing beneficial concepts of their contemporary role, modifying some traditional notions of seafaring practice to better integrate with a rapidly changing maritime sector.

The accounts of these master mariners in my recent research emphasise that many interactions with shore-based stakeholders (senior managers and customers) leave master mariners compromised, both operationally and in leadership terms. Their hands are (somewhat/or very) tied. It places them in difficult predicaments between meeting commercial needs and maintaining operational safety at all costs. Likewise, the fluid and collaborative engagement made possible by real-time, rich communication with the vessel at sea is often in conflict with traditional concepts of master mariner authority and autonomy. That is not to say that such collaboration is inappropriate or unwise. However, I am proposing that it is up to both you and your master mariners to find ways to harmonise issues of power and relationship, autonomy and real-time engagement, safety and commercial outcomes. This requires a degree of reflective practice wisdom by both of you.

By and large, master mariners have a deeper knowledge than the technical aspects of their role. Their practice wisdom involves personally held professional values, along with finely tuned ways of perceiving and making sense of their environments that have been shaped by their experience over the course of their careers. As such, their practice wisdom has typically been hard won and honed over decades of practice.

It has been integrated with their perceptions, actions and their identities, through daily physical engagement in their jobs, in subtle ways that may make it difficult for them to identify. However, there will come times when prescribed safety regulations and standard operating procedures fall short in their coverage of unexpected and unprecedented critical events. In these extreme circumstances, master mariners' practice wisdom (deep practice-based practical and ethical knowledge and judgement) can find an optimal path between complex alternatives in the most trying of circumstances. This makes the development of professional practice wisdom essential for organisations within the maritime sector.

CONCLUSION

The lifeworld of master mariners has shifted significantly due to increased information and communication technology, and a shift in global business forces typified by volatility, uncertainty, complexity and ambiguity. These forces apply "tectonic" tensions against the current seafaring habitus, with its archetype of unchallengeable autocracy, autonomy and infallibility. As such, master mariners contend with paradoxical tensions between authority and work relationships, and between operational safety and commercial imperatives.

However, the master mariners interviewed in the study reported in this chapter provided rich narrative examples of practice wisdom they use in resolving critical events at sea. Their practice wisdom was personalised and diverse, yet had common features of being deeply embodied, embedded in their seafaring context, enacted during their everyday practice but being particularly prominent and vital in extreme moments of decision making and situational challenges. Practice wisdom is experience-based and draws heavily on personal values to provide an ethical grounding to master mariners' actions.

Being closely enmeshed in their daily, embodied practices, their practice wisdom is often tacit and therefore hidden from their explicit awareness. One of the key challenges of practice wisdom is to bring this understanding to the surface, to critically appraise it and be able to articulate and justify this wisdom as a sound and defensible basis for decision making.

During Brad's research the master mariners' practice wisdom consistently came to the fore in their narratives as the decisive factor in optimally managing critical events – taking its place alongside their technical knowledge and the requirements of standard procedures. Practice wisdom enables master mariners to "find the line" between paradoxical tensions that are impossible to solve when people take the side of one pole (alternate decision) in lieu of the other. As such, practice wisdom is a valuable component of professional practice that is not particularly realised by these professionals, yet it plays a critical role in the challenges they increasingly face.

Practice wisdom is sometimes expressed in bodily terms and, via embodied metaphors, this language is presented in recent research as having a powerful neural capacity to bodily inscribe practice wisdom in ways that are hidden to the professional. This bodily inscription is heavily shaped by the socially constructed habitus of the master mariner. This habitus provides a durable and embodied matrix of perceptions and actions that taps into traditional seafaring archetypes of (apparently) unchallengeable autocracy and infallibility. Therefore, habitus both shapes and constrains the capacity for wise practice, which becomes problematic when this habitus is at odds with contemporary changes within the maritime industry.

There are deep implications from both conscious/owned and embodied/felt notions of practice wisdom. The reinforcing and unconscious nature of habits make them elusive and resistant to superficial change efforts. The challenge, then, is to equip master mariners with the ability to bring these hidden aspects of embodied practice wisdom and habitus into their awareness, to understand how they influence each other. This will enable greater reflection on and ownership of wise ways of practising that are less encumbered by historical archetypes of unchallengeable autocracy and infallibility. These monolithic archetypes, as habitus, are increasingly in paradoxical tension with the emerging nature of maritime operations, as typified by the volatility, uncertainty, complexity and ambiguity of liquid modernity. Professionals today cannot defend adopting a position of unquestioning acceptance of hegemonic practices and habitual understandings or rules.

NOTES

[1] http://studyindenmark.dk/study-options/danish-higher-education-institutions/schools-of-maritime-education-training/svendborg-international-maritime-academy-simac
[2] https://sydney.edu.au/courses/courses/pc/master-of-marine-science-and-management.html
[3] Italicised quotes are data quotes.

REFERENCES

Bauman, Z. (2000). *Liquid modernity.* Cambridge, England: Polity Press.
Bourdieu, P. (2013). *Outline of a theory of practice.* Cambridge, England: Cambridge University Press.
Cherry, N. (2005). Preparing for practice in the age of complexity. *Higher Education Research & Development, 24*(4), 309-320.
Cherry, N. (2016). Organising, managing and changing practice: Negotiating managerial authority and professional discretion. In J. Higgs & F. Trede (Eds.), *Professional practice discourse marginalia* (pp. 197-204). Rotterdam, The Netherlands: Sense.
Cherry, N. L. (2014). New stories of mastery: Constructive learning in the face of complex dilemmas of practice. *Studies in Continuing Education, 36*(3), 241-256.
Clark, A., & Chalmers, D. (2016). The extended mind. *InterAction, 8*(1), 48-64.
Claxton, G. (2015). Corporal thinking: Recent research in cognition gives new meaning to the term 'carnal knowledge'. *The Chronicle of Higher Education, 62*(4), B4(2).
Cunliffe, A., & Coupland, C. (2012). From hero to villain to hero: Making experience sensible through embodied narrative sensemaking. *Human Relations, 65*(1), 63-88.
Dall'Alba, G., Sandberg, J., & Sidhu, R. K. (2018). Embodying skilful performance: Co-constituting body and world in biotechnology. *Educational Philosophy and Theory, 50*(3), 270-286.

Freeth, M. (2015). *On command* (3rd ed.). London, England: The Nautical Institute.
Froese, T., & Fuchs, T. (2012). The extended body: A case study in the neurophenomenology of social interaction. *Phenomenology and the Cognitive Sciences, 11*(2), 205-235.
Gibbs, R. W. (2011). Evaluating conceptual metaphor theory. *Discourse Processes, 48*(8), 529-562.
Gordon, S. (2013). *Neurophenomenology and its applications to psychology*. New York, NY: Springer.
Hersey, P., & Blanchard, K. H. (1969). *Management of organizational behaviour: Utilizing human resources*. Englewood Cliffs, NJ: Prentice Hall.
Hershey, R. (1988). The primacy of the Master and its consequences. *Maritime Policy & Management, 15*(2), 141-146.
Higgs, J. (2012). Realising practical wisdom from the pursuit of wise practice. In E. A. Kinsella & A. Pitman (Eds.), *Phronesis as professional knowledge: Practical wisdom in the professions* (pp. 73-85). Rotterdam, The Netherlands: Sense.
Higgs, J. (2016a). Practice wisdom and wise practice: Dancing between the core and the margins of practice discourse and lived practice. In J. Higgs & F. Trede (Eds.), *Professional practice discourse marginalia* (pp. 65-72). Rotterdam, The Netherlands: Sense.
Higgs, J. (2016b). Professional practice and discourse. In J. Higgs & F. Trede (Eds.), *Professional practice discourse marginalia* (pp. 3-10). Rotterdam, The Netherlands: Sense.
International Maritime Organization (IMO). (2017). *STCW: International Convention for Standards of Training, Certification and Watchkeeping for Seafarers* (2017 ed.). London, England: Author.
International Maritime Organization (IMO). (2018). *International Year of the Seafarer*. Retrieved from http://www.imo.org/en/about/events/dayoftheseafarer/pages/day-of-the-seafarer-2018.aspx
Johnson, B. (2014). Reflections: A perspective on paradox and its application to modern management. *The Journal of Applied Behavioral Science, 50*(2), 206-212.
King, T. (2007). Bad habits and prosthetic performances: Negotiation of individuality and embodiment of social status in Australian shark fishing. *Journal of Anthropological Research, 63*(4), 537-560.
King, T. (2011). The 'skipper effect': Riddles of luck and rhetorics of individualism. *Human Organization, 70*(4), 387-396.
Kinsella, E. A. (2015). Embodied knowledge: Toward a corporeal turn in professional practice, research and education. In B. Green & N. Hopwood (Eds.), *The body in professional practice, learning and education* (pp. 245-260). London, England: Springer.
Klein, W. C., & Bloom, M. (1995). Practice wisdom. *Social Work, 40*(6), 799-807.
Lakoff, G. (2012). Explaining embodied cognition results. *Topics in Cognitive Science., 4*(4), 773-785.
Lekka, C., & Sugden, C. (2011). The successes and challenges of implementing high reliability principles: A case study of a UK oil refinery. *Process Safety and Environmental Protection, 89*(6), 443-451.
Lewis, M. W., & Smith, W. K. (2014). Paradox as a metatheoretical perspective. *The Journal of Applied Behavioral Science, 50*(2), 127-149.
Lippi, J. (2013). Leadership in liquid modernity. *The Journal of Contemporary Issues in Business and Government, 19*(1), 35-45.
Lizardo, O. (2013). Habitus. In B. Kaldis (Ed.), *Encyclopedia of philosophy and the social sciences* (pp. 405-407). Thousand Oaks, CA: Sage.
Lurås, S., Lützhöft, M., & Sevaldson, B. (2015). Meeting the complex and unfamiliar: Lessons from design in the offshore industry. *International Journal of Design, 9*(2), 141-154.
Lyng, I., Andreassen, D., Fiksdal, G., Loken, G., Skolvy, Y., & Petternsen, T. (2008). *The loss of the 'Bourbon Dolphin' on 12 April 2007: Report from a Commission appointed by Royal Decree of 27 April 2007* (Official Norwegian Reports 2008:8). Oslo, Norway: Government Administration Services.
Macklin, R., & Whiteford, G. (2012). Phronesis, aporia and qualitative research. In E. A. Kinsella & A. Pitman (Eds.), *Phronesis as professional knowledge: Practical wisdom in the professions* (pp. 87-100). Rotterdam, The Netherlands: Sense.
McGilchrist, I. (2011). Paying attention to the bipartite brain. *The Lancet, 377*(9771), 1068-1069.
Misangyi, V. F. (2016). Institutional complexity and the meaning of loose coupling: Connecting institutional sayings and (not) doings. *Strategic Organization, 14*(4), 407-440.

O'Byrne, C. (2011). Remembering the *Piper Alpha* disaster. *Historical Reflections, 37*(2), 90-104.

Patton, N. (2016). A praxis perspective. In J. Higgs & F. Trede (Eds.), *Professional practice discourse marginalia* (pp. 37-46). Rotterdam, The Netherlands: Sense.

Patton, N., & Fish, D. (2016). Appreciating practice. In J. Higgs & F. Trede (Eds.), *Professional practice discourse marginalia* (pp. 55-64). Rotterdam, The Netherlands: Sense.

Rittel, H. W. J., & Webber, M. M. (1973). Dilemmas in a general theory of planning. *Policy Sciences, 4*(2), 155-169.

Roberts, B. (2018). Recasting Odysseus: Embodied sensemaking among seafaring leaders. *Australian Journal of Maritime & Ocean Affairs, 10*(1) p. 19-34.

Sheets-Johnstone, M. (2015). Embodiment on trial: A phenomenological investigation. *Continental Philosophy Review, 48*(1), 23-39.

Silva, E. B. (2016). Habitus: Beyond sociology. *Sociological Review, 64*(1), 73-92.

Smith, W. K., & Lewis, M. W. (2011). Toward a theory of paradox: A dynamic equilibrium model of organizing. *Academy of Management Review, 36*(2), 381-403.

Stickles, E., Oana, D., Dodge, E., & Hong, J. (2016). Formalizing contemporary conceptual metaphor theory. *Constructions and Frames, 8*(2), 166-213.

Tucker, D. M. (2007). *Mind from body: Experience from neural structure*. New York, NY: Oxford University Press.

Wacquant, L. (2011). Habitus as topic and tool: Reflections on becoming a prizefighter. *Qualitative Research in Psychology, 8*(1), 81-92.

Weick, K. E. (2001). *Making sense of the organization*. Malden, MA: Blackwell Business.

Bradley Roberts (ORCID: https://orcid.org/0000-0003-0654-8010)
Faculty of Business and Law
Swinburne University of Technology, Australia

Joy Higgs AM, PhD (ORCID: https://orcid.org/0000-0002-8545-1016)
Emeritus Professor, Charles Sturt University, Australia
Director, Education, Practice and Employability Network, Australia

ANGIE TITCHEN AND NIAMH KINSELLA

17. LEARNING EMBODIED PRACTICE WISDOM

The Young Sapling Learning from the Old Tree

Angie: For many years, I have "walked" (physically and metaphorically) alongside co-inquirers, doctoral students, practitioners, educators and practice developers, as their critical-creative companion. My intention has been to help them to meld, blend and embody the *underground* dimensions of practice wisdom, i.e. multiple knowledges, ways of knowing and intelligences, through professional artistry. In recent years, the focus has been on embodying ways of knowing, doing, being and becoming within the epistemological and ontological frameworks of critical creativity (e.g. McCormack & Titchen, 2006; Titchen & McCormack, 2010, forthcoming) and critical-creative companionship (e.g. Titchen & Hammond, 2017).

My cumulative research (e.g. McCormack & Titchen, 2014; Titchen, 2004, 2009; Titchen & Higgs, 2001; Titchen & Horsfall, 2011) shows me that over time, practice wisdom can be grown *above ground* through extensive, re-iterative cycles of "walking in Nature" (a metaphor for connecting with Nature and the body in some way), dialogue between "Elders/mature trees" and "young trees", critical-creative introspection, reflection and reflexivity, eventually taking invigorated practice wisdom back into practice for testing and evaluating. Some cycles later, refined wisdom goes back *underground*. Yes, I will ask Niamh (a "young tree") to inquire with me (a "mature tree" and critical-creative companion), about if and how *background* professional artistry lights up practice wisdom. I will show her how *underground* networks and flowing rivers of practice wisdom and professional artistry can be brought into the *foreground/above ground* through particularised care of, or practice with, service users, clients, patients, colleagues and students, as well as through therapeutic love in the form of loving-kindness.

The chapter will be set within the critical creativity landscape (a paradigmatic synthesis developed by Brendan McCormack and myself) in which the purpose of practice, learning and inquiry is growth, searching for meaning, transformation and, ultimately, human flourishing. Within this landscape, people bring to consciousness, not only what they already know through their minds and what they know unconsciously within their bodies and practices, but also the metaphysical (soulful, spiritual, archetypal) and aesthetic (Titchen, Cardiff, & Biong, 2017). So critical creativity is concerned with use of the whole self (mind, body, heart, imagination and soul/spirit) in connection with Nature,[1] ecosystems, ancient wisdom, creative imagination and expression, and spirituality (searching for meaning at the edge of the known).

The chapter could be useful as an introduction to health/social care practitioners, as well as practice developers, educators and researchers, in terms of learning and helping others to learn, how to embody wisdom and become an authentic embodiment (role model) of it with colleagues and students. Relevant concepts and strategies from my research are emphasised throughout in italics and expanded upon in Chapter 5.

FROM DARKNESS TO LIGHT: BRINGING TO CONSCIOUSNESS ONE'S OWN AND OTHERS' EMBODIED WISDOM

> Loving-kindness means universal,
> non-judgmental love
> that sits alongside compassion,
> equanimity,
> and benevolence
> in Buddhist meditative practice.

Niamh: I am an occupational therapist who has recently submitted my doctoral study. I contacted Angie about 18 months ago and asked if she would help me to clarify my thinking about critical creativity. We connected occasionally and electronically for about a year. Nonetheless, these connections enabled us to get to know each other (this is – *particularity* – getting to know and work with the particulars of the other as a whole person in his/her situation and contexts [Titchen, 2004]). Thus, Angie was able to particularise her critical-creative companionship practice with me.

Our Initial Skype Meeting

Angie: At our first Skype meeting, I observed that Niamh was very nervous and imagined that this might be because she had read my work with Brendan McCormack (her supervisor) and might feel a little in awe. When she shared her paintings with me, I got a much deeper sense of where she was coming from – she exhibited a blackness of fear as she faced the unknown in her research practice (as in Kinsella, 2017). *Loving-kindness* (as in Salzberg, 2002) played a strong role in that first meeting.

Our First Walk

Last April, Niamh and Angie walked together in the university grounds. Angie took the opportunity to work with Niamh using meditative strategies and with the concept of *intentionality* (Titchen, 2004 – being deliberate and purposeful, cognitively and intuitively). Angie deliberately *role modelled* and *articulated* her professional craft knowledge developed from her experience (Titchen, 2004) to show Niamh how *to learn through the body* by connecting with Nature in silence and creating the conditions for human flourishing as follows.

Like the grasses and fuchsias that dance with the wind, persons can flourish when the right conditions are created and when the right energies are in place. (McCormack & Titchen, 2014, p. 10)

Stillness in the landscape – Being still, open and empty in the place and space, suspending habitual ways of seeing, letting go and opening up to our senses and observing what is happening within and outside us.

Becoming the rock – Being a living example of particularised practice and loving-kindness within a critical creativity landscape.

Nurturing, flowing, connecting – The hidden being of the practitioner, leader, manager, practice developer, researcher, educator as they enable stillness in the landscape and support for becoming the rock – both for themselves and others) (Titchen & McCormack, 2010).

As they left the building, Niamh told Angie that this was the first time she had taken a walk around the lake in the grounds during her several years at the university. Angie suggested they walk in silence and open up all their senses. Angie intentionally role modelled, by touching leaves and grasses, listening to and running her fingers through water and smelling the earth, to help Niamh know what she could do. This also helped Angie to become more in harmony with Nature and with herself and gave her space to let go of ego and noise and distraction of the office. She became more fully in her body, more connected to the earth and attuned to Niamh's needs and could help Niamh through her presence.

Our Skype Inquiry Conversation

Spool forward eight months to the morning of their Skype inquiry conversation. Niamh says that she has just walked this way to prepare for their critical-creative dialogue and has expressed her insights in photographs and words (that she later used to craft her story for this chapter). During the dialogue, Angie took notes, asked a few questions for clarification and sent them to Niamh later for checking that they were accurate. Niamh offered further reflections and insights on these notes. The quality of her theoretical, reflexive and introspective reflections seemed to indicate that Angie's *observing, listening and questioning* strategy during the Skype meeting, helped Niamh considerably in surfacing and articulating her practice wisdom.

With Niamh's permission, Angie analysed these two documents using concepts unearthed from her research that were relevant to particularised practice: loving-kindness, the dimensions and processes of professional artistry, and the critical creativity conditions for enabling human flourishing. She sent the analysis to Niamh and they agreed that Angie's analysis and discussion (underground rivers and backlight) would interlace and illuminate Niamh's story (shaded boxes).

AT THE EDGE OF THE DARK AND LIGHT:
MEANING-MAKING THROUGH A WALK IN THE RAIN

I decided to go for a walk to explore Angie's questions about learning and embodying *therapeutic love* and *particularised care* in professional practice. I had not been feeling a lot of energy for my work but one of the things that I had managed, and been happy about and proud of, was my development of wisdom in dealing with uncertain, unique situations in kind, loving and intuitive ways. So when I started to walk I really had no answers or ideas except the knowledge that "I can do this". I also knew that particularised care and loving-kindness towards self was the only way I would be able to engage with these questions.

> First, I am interested to see that Niamh decided to go for an *intentional* walk in natural surroundings, just as we did together last April. This suggests to me that my *role modelling* and *articulation of my professional craft knowledge* (from Titchen, 2001) of how to connect with Nature, first with the body, heart and soul and then with the mind, has been effective! This combination is much more powerful than role modelling alone. However, Elders/mature trees often find it difficult to articulate their expertise, let alone their *professional artistry*. Paradoxically, it is young saplings and young trees who help them to unearth their practice wisdom, using the simple, but immensely effective strategy of *observing, listening and questioning* (see Chapter 5, Figure 5.2, at entry to learning cycle).

> For example, I encourage junior staff nurses to ask wise practitioners if they could observe, listen and record their everyday practice. Then, as soon as possible afterwards, ask them what they were trying to do, why and how. These questions should be specific to detail, for example, "Today, the ward is really busy, but when you were with Mrs Jones you seemed to be totally focused on her, whereas the rest of the team looked like headless chickens". And keep drilling down to get deeper than their book knowledge. "How did you do that with so much going on? How did you feel when …? What alerted you? What was in your mind? What was your intention? What were you imagining/ hypothesising?"

It was a cold, wintery day but I was walking slowly and intentionally trying to empty my mind. As I walked I picked up pieces of nature that mean something to me in relation to therapeutic love and particularised care. The first things I saw and picked up were dead oak leaves. These dead leaves challenged me – they represent the falling away of this kind of care and wisdom. However, I also thought, "Oak trees represent wisdom. A 'falling away' of the leaves is necessary for us to notice our surroundings/practice background, and for rebirth and growth to happen".

> Niamh is beginning to create for herself the condition, *Stillness in a Landscape* – which refers to clearing the mind, being creative and bringing the unconscious to consciousness and the invisible to visible. Maybe she is not quite there yet as she seems to be looking consciously for things that have meaning, rather than allowing herself just to be drawn to things for no apparent reason. Many people

are unfamiliar with this way of being and companions can help them *open up to all ways of being*. Walking in nature is a non-threatening and simple way of doing this. Niamh is using the professional artistry dimension of *creative imagination and expression* to embrace her *known and yet to be known*, thus she is using both sides of her brain, as well as drawing on the professional artistry dimension of *different ways of knowing*, like myth and ancient wisdom.

It is beautiful to see her acknowledging the wisdom of Nature and seeing the same natural process occurring in practice settings (where the conditions may not be in place to enable the learning and embodiment of practice wisdom) and recognising the need *to let go* in order for the new to grow. The professional artistry process of *synchronicity* (where two unconnected events seem to the individual concerned, to have meaning that is pertinent to the particular situation) is at play here too.

When I read Niamh's thought about the wisdom of oak trees, a burst of energy went through me because my preparation for our co-inquiry was so very similar. There are oak leaves in front of me now that I picked up on my walk. I feel underground rivers and tendrils of *energy*, connecting us and I feel excited and close to her.

As I began to walk I closed my eyes, took a breath, and suddenly noticed that I was walking in the rain. I usually don't like going outside when it's raining – it's cold, it takes me a long time to warm up from it, and I have so much work to do to clean my clothes and get myself together afterwards. However, as I walked I realised how refreshing, grounding and freeing walking in the rain is. I thought walking in the rain is a good metaphor for the wisdom of *particularised care* and *loving-kindness*. It is often uncomfortable, hard work, unusual and exposing. But it feels great when you embrace these characteristics and embody it.

Niamh is now becoming aware of her body and therefore is more *present in this moment*. It is good to see her allowing herself to feel the joy of "getting her paws muddy", i.e. being her natural self. She is also using metaphor and symbols from Nature to express the tacit nature of practice wisdom and its embodiment.

As I continued to walk I noticed a boundary fence that I was following. It was blocking me from walking away from the path that I was expected to follow but it also meant that I could not explore the whole of the area I was walking in.

Particularised practice means stepping over or knocking down boundaries to explore and truly understand who a student/person/service user/patient/colleague is. These might be strong and well-established boundaries that are in place everywhere you turn. It is a form of therapeutic love to understand and work with these boundaries if it is safe and necessary to do so. I noticed as I was walking along the boundary that I could choose to jump over it if I wanted. I wondered what would happen if I did. For me, I understood in that moment of questioning, that the ability to understand, change or overcome these boundaries to particularised care means that I must make myself vulnerable also. I must take a risk to stand "alone on the edge" and explore what I needed to take a step forward over the boundary. This meant that I needed to understand what was stopping me from stepping forward and why I was continuing to follow the path. I needed to understand myself first. This realisation reminded me about something I already knew about person-centred practice (McCormack & McCance, 2017); that we must understand ourselves, our feelings/emotions about practice and our boundaries as facilitators, healthcare practitioners and researchers in order to develop practice wisdom.

> Notice that Niamh is noticing! Noticing is vital when we take a loving-kindness or meditative inquiry walk, because it helps us to access our unconscious and knowing what matters/what is significant/what needs to be paid attention to. This is what I call *saliency* (Titchen, 2004). Niamh immediately saw the meaning of the boundary for her, but even if what we notice may have no meaning at the time, it will probably surface when expressing the experience of the walk, perhaps through painting or writing a poem, or in a dream or dialogue with a critical-creative companion. Niamh is showing insight here into the need to step over or knock down boundaries to *particularity* and she recognises that it requires therapeutic love or loving-kindness to do so as well as making oneself vulnerable (*graceful care*). Graceful care (Titchen, 2004) means authentically engaging the other or oneself as a whole person (mind, body, heart and soul) and being kind/present/emotionally engaged but balanced. Acts of defiance are necessary sometimes to step out of conventional ways of knowing, doing, being and becoming in our workplaces. This requires the professional artistry dimension of *artistic qualities* of courage, audacity and disposition to do good. In coping with the difficult emotion of vulnerability, these acts need the professional artistry dimension of *emotional intelligence* (Titchen, 2009 – gives people an awareness of, or attunement to, their own and others' feelings, appropriate responses to pain or pleasure, facilitating social adeptness, empathy, compassion, motivation and caring).

The walk continued and I started to smell something familiar – grass when it rains. This smell reminded me of my childhood and where I come from. With the questions about practice wisdom in mind, it also reminded me of the importance of awareness, gentleness, graceful care and loving-kindness towards self. I thought, "This is the essence of embodiment of practice wisdom". I remembered reading about practice from the heart (Wood, 2004). It was about intuitive practice and intentional self-engagement, which enables overcoming boundaries that get in the way of knowing a person's particulars and creating space for them to develop their potential.

Niamh is learning how to embody this knowing through the intentional use of emotion within *graceful care*.

I noticed a semi-circle of benches and trees beside the boundary that reminded me of the kind of space that is needed for practice wisdom to be facilitated and particularised care to emerge. The space was large enough to walk around, natural and full of potential but it was surrounded by benches that created and unobtrusively supported it.

I imagined that if the support had not been there, and a person did not take time to sit and be still, the space would never be used to develop practice wisdom. The other side of the semi-circle was empty for growth to happen and it offered freedom for a person/patient/student/service user to make a choice about their direction, growth and care. I had read two books called *Presence* (Senge et al., 2005) and *Theory U* (Scharmer, 2016) before I took this walk. I thought about how Senge and Scharmer believe that having spaces like this to be still and present with our self and the persons we are working with are necessary if we are to overcome boundaries, work with our emotions, and to consequently develop and engage practice wisdom. Scharmer actually believes that ignoring or not creating spaces like this leads to a process of "absencing" or disconnection from our whole self, so practising from the ego and not overcoming the boundary to practice wisdom. I did not sit down. On I walked.

If organisations do not have physical and metaphorical space, it will be difficult to create the conditions for learning to embody practice wisdom for oneself and others. There is *stillness in the landscape* here, held by gentleness. The benches are expecting/inviting people to take time to be present, but they are not pushy. Thus space for growth and choice (*mutuality*) enables critical-creative companions to *become the rock*, the embodiment of particularised practice and loving-kindness. The professional artistry process of *synthesis* (Titchen, 2009) is visible in Niamh's blending and melding of propositional (book) knowledge with her professional craft knowledge. She is also conducting an artistic and cognitive critique in learning how to be authentically present, as well as letting go of ego. This might require us to access our Greater Self and our struggle to get anywhere near that Self can be painful emotionally, as Niamh has shown. I am thinking about how being in a very beautiful landscape and feeling awe and wonder lifts me up so that I can transcend my baser self and move towards my Greater Self. I think this transcendence links not only to beauty, but also to the professional artistry dimension of *spiritual intelligence* (Titchen 2009) that enables us to address and solve problems of meaning and value and place our actions, lives and pathways in wider, richer, meaning-giving contexts. It gives us our moral sense and allows us to aspire, dream and uplift ourselves.

I continued to walk the path, now in heightened awareness of the path and boundary I was following, the bench space forgotten. I moved away from the boundary but five swans soon blocked my path. Usually I would have turned back or changed my course because I am afraid of the swans. On this walk I intentionally continued the way I was going but respected their space. This meant that I actually walked off the path that I was following, over a boundary, but also faced my fear. I did this by being flexible and respectful, by taking a risk and making myself vulnerable to them. I was aware that I would not make it to where I needed to go if I did not face this fear and develop flexibility. I challenged myself and offered myself and the swans kindness in the space we shared. I think I was using my emotional intelligence here. For me this means being able to recognise my emotions but also to understand them, change them and work with them.

Niamh is using what is happening unexpectedly in the *here and now* to embody intentionality and to make meaning of it through *resonance and symbolism*.

Making it safely to the end of my walk, I saw a young tree that was growing in the arms of an external, natural material support made of wood and leather. The support around the young tree prompted me to consider how I had come to understand and begin to embody practice wisdom and particularised care. I had been offered a space that was natural yet supportive by critical-creative companions. These supportive companions created conditions that gave me the opportunity to learn how to balance engagement with my own roots and hidden gems, as well as engagement in intentional relationships.

Just as the tree grows and the natural support becomes less necessary, as loving-kindness is expressed, practice wisdom embodied and particularised care realised, the critical-creative companionship changes.

Niamh acknowledges the professional artistry processes of *balance* here and perhaps between the lines, *interplay* and *flowing* through deep introspection into self, influences (roots and rivers) and hidden gems alongside intentional critical, creative relationships that flow and sensitively change as the young tree progresses towards maturity.

CODA

All this reminds us of the *synchronicity, balance* and *energy* exchange of the forest ecosystem and the relationship between Elders, saplings and young trees and between trees and fungi. This journey shows that motivation to clarify, develop and embody this kind of wisdom arises existentially from our own beliefs and values about who we want to become and in terms of what we think we are here for. We can each develop a vision of what this looks like for ourselves as practitioners, educators and researchers and people living on this planet. This vision acts as a monitor for us, helping us to evaluate our daily practice and life. Having critical-creative companions like Niamh and Angie is essential and enriching. They can offer loving-kindness and an accepting space, which is required for a person to come to know themselves, to create a vision for their future and to have the courage to realise their greater purpose.

ACKNOWLEDGEMENTS

Warm thanks to Donna Frost and Doro Bechinger-English for their helpful comments on chapter drafts.

NOTE

[1] People make their own connections with nature and with learning spaces in different ways. If you are interested in engaging with the natural world in a metaphysical, archetypal way, you might be interested in *Reclaiming the Wild Soul: How Earth's Landscapes Restore us to Wholeness* (Reynolds Thompson, 2014) and *Women who Run with the Wolves* (Estés, 1994).

REFERENCES

Estés, C. P. (1994). *Women who run with the wolves: Contacting the power of the wild woman.* London, England: Rider.
Kinsella, N. (2017, February 3). *A journey in paintings by Niamh Kinsella* [Blog post]. Retrieved from https://criticalcreativity.org/2017/02/03/a-journey-in-paintings/
McCormack, B., & McCance T., (2017). *Person-centred practice in nursing and health care: Theory and practice.* Oxford, England: Wiley-Blackwell.
McCormack, B., & Titchen, A. (2006). Critical creativity: Melding, exploding, blending. *Educational Action Research: An International Journal, 14*(2), 239-266.

McCormack, B., & Titchen, A. (2014). No beginning, no end: An ecology of human flourishing. *International Practice Development Journal, 4*(2).

Reynolds Thompson, M. (2014). *Reclaiming the wild Soul: How earth's landscapes restore us to wholeness.* Ashland, OR: White Cloud Press.

Salzberg, S. (2002). *Loving-kindness: The revolutionary art of happiness.* London, England: Shambala Classics.

Scharmer, C. O. (2016). *Theory U: Leading from the future as it emerges.* Oakland, CA: Berrett-Koehler.

Senge, P., Scharmer, C. O., Jaworski, J., & Flowers, B. (2005). *Presence: Exploring profound change in people, organisations and society.* London, England: Nicholas Brealey Publishing.

Titchen, A. (2001). Critical companionship: A conceptual framework for developing expertise. In J. Higgs & A. Titchen (Eds.), *Practice knowledge and expertise in the health professions* (pp. 80-90). Oxford, England: Butterworth Heinemann.

Titchen, A. (2004). Helping relationships for practice development: Critical companionship. In B. McCormack, K. Manley, & R. Garbett (Eds.), *Practice development in nursing* (pp. 148-174). Oxford, England: Blackwell.

Titchen, A. (2009). Developing expertise through nurturing professional artistry in the workplace. In S. Hardy, A. Titchen, B. McCormack, & K. Manley (Eds.), *Revealing nursing expertise through practitioner inquiry* (pp. 219-243). Oxford, England: Wiley-Blackwell.

Titchen, A., Cardiff, S., & Biong, S. (2017). The knowing and being of person-centred research practice across worldviews: An epistemological and ontological framework. In B. McCormack, S. van Dulmen, H. Eide, K. Skovdahl, & T. Eide (Eds.), *Person-centred healthcare research* (pp. 31-50). Oxford, England: Wiley-Blackwell.

Titchen, A., & Hammond, K. (2017). Helping health-care practitioners to flourish: Critical companionship at work. In B. McCormack & T. McCance (Eds.), *Person-centred nursing – theory and practice* (pp. 162-171). Oxford, England: Wiley-Blackwell.

Titchen, A., & Higgs, J. (2001). Towards professional artistry and creativity in practice. In J. Higgs & A. Titchen (Eds.), *Professional practice in health, education and the creative arts* (pp. 273-290). Oxford, England: Blackwell Science.

Titchen, A., & Horsfall, D. (2011). Embodying creative imagination and expression in qualitative research. In J. Higgs, A. Titchen, D. Horsfall, & D. Bridges (Eds.), *Creative spaces for qualitative researching: Living research* (pp. 179-190). Rotterdam, The Netherlands: Sense.

Titchen, A., & McCormack B. (2010). Dancing with stones: Critical creativity as methodology for human flourishing. *Educational Action Research: An International Journal, 18*(4), 531-554.

Titchen, A., & McCormack, B. (in press). *Dancing the mandalas of critical creativity in nursing and health care: A collection of new work, published papers, book chapters, creative media and blog entries with weaving commentary.* Edinburgh, Scotland: Queen Margaret University.

Wood, W. (2004). The heart, mind and soul of professionalism in occupational therapy. *The American Journal of Occupational Therapy, 58*(3), 249-257.

Angie Titchen DPhil (Oxon)
Independent Practice Development & Research Consultant

Niamh Kinsella MSc Occupational Therapy (ORCID: https://orcid.org/0000-0001-8160-3812)
School of Health Sciences, Queen Margaret University, Edinburgh, Scotland

PHILLIP DYBICZ

18. PRACTICE WISDOM OF EXPERT INQUIRERS

Primum non nocerum (First do no harm). (Hippocrates the physician)

As opposed to academic disciplines (e.g. biology, history, philosophy) which simply represent fields of specialised knowledge in academia, the very essence of defining a profession (e.g. social work, nursing, law) is not the body of specialised knowledge itself, but rather, the application of this knowledge in society in the form of an occupation (e.g. social worker). Thus for professionals, practical experience in applying the specialised knowledge of one's field represents a form of learning in and of itself; professionals seek to hone their craft via continuous self-reflection on their performance. This knowledge gained from practical experience is valued to such a degree among service professions that most if not all professional schools – such as elementary and secondary education (e.g. Goldhaber, Krieg, & Theobald, 2017), law (e.g. Marchbanks, 2015), nursing (e.g. Mollica & Hyman, 2016) and social work (e.g. Petrila et al., 2015) – include an extended internship as part of their educational training and value it as an important education tool. For the case of social work, this field education is commonly recognised as the signature pedagogy of social work education (Council on Social Work Education [CSWE], 2008).

Interestingly, while the various professional fields all highlight the importance of practice experience to hone their craft, there are only two main service professions – social work and nursing – which use the term *practice wisdom* in their professional literature to capture an additional component contributing to good practice. Approximately fifteen years ago, I pursued an inquiry into the nature of practice wisdom (Dybicz, 2004). This work will serve as the starting point to revisit the topic of practice wisdom and begin a new inquiry that seeks to delineate various nuances to further explore pedagogical approaches for nurturing students' practice wisdom.

In my previous inquiry, a distinction was made between intelligence and wisdom. Intelligence was linked to learning – both in terms of the acquisition of knowledge and the competent application of this knowledge. As such, intelligence was the quality linked to practice experience that promotes knowledge acquisition and application during field experience. Concerning wisdom, Socrates was turned to as a model for defining its features and was famously declared the wisest man in Ancient Greece by the oracle at Delphi. This was based upon Socrates' position that what made him wise was his recognition that "I know that I don't know." As such, wisdom is seen as the adoption of wilful ignorance set in opposition to one's acquired knowledge (defined philosophically as an *aporia*), as the following quote by McAvoy (1999) so adequately captured in his book on Socrates:

[t]his condition of aporia is one Socrates regularly creates and exists in, referring to it as a situation where he cannot agree with himself. He can divide himself up into two Socrates who are continually at loggerheads, one a violent questioner who seems to know and not know, the other a gentler creature who seems to be forever in perplexity, but who is prepared to endure it and the attendant abuse, in the reasonable belief that he might be benefited by it. (p. 21)

This adoption of ignorance is a concerted attempt to hold one's biases in check while seeking to apply one's professional knowledge to a helping situation. Consequently, while intelligence is drawn upon in the application of professional knowledge, wisdom is drawn upon in the application of values and integrity to the knowledge gathering and application process comprising the helping situation. Thus, wisdom in this sense represents much more than simply ethical decision making to solve ethical dilemmas. It undergirds a broad value-infused practice that seeks to honour the client's contribution to the collaborative effort at truth-seeking when sincerely attempting to confront the client's life struggles.

Arising from the above premises, the following contrasts can thus be drawn. Practice experience promotes competence, whereas practice wisdom attacks hubris. Thus, practice experience engenders expert knowing, whereas practice wisdom engenders expert inquiring. As the means to aid in advancing the helping process, expert knowers seek the continuous refinement of their knowledge, whereas expert inquirers seek to maintain a condition of *aporia* – a heightened awareness of the abuse of power in the creation and application of knowledge guiding practice.

PRACTICE EXPERIENCE AND EXPERT KNOWERS

In the early part of the 20th century, social work began the process of transitioning from its status as charity work to a status of being recognised as a profession. Toward this end, in the United States a well-known American educator, Abraham Flexner, was invited to speak upon the topic of professionalisation in 1915 at the National Conference of Charities and Correction. To the dismay of many present, Flexner (1915) concluded that social work fell short in meeting the criteria determining status as a profession. While social work met some criteria defining a profession (that it is "essentially intellectual in character"; and, that it involved the practical application of knowledge), he noted that the field of social work fell short in that it did not possess its own distinct body of knowledge, and thus did not possess its own unique area of competence in the application of this knowledge. This led to a key social work project during the 20th century to develop such a distinct body of knowledge grounded in the social sciences and a defined area of applied competence.

The intellectual nature of social work remains a prominent feature today. And as noted earlier with field education being recognised as the signature pedagogy, the ability to practically apply social work knowledge holds prominence as well. Thus Flexner's (1915) understanding of the role of intelligence within a profession aligns with the definition I am offering here: that intelligence is responsible for the acquisition and competent application of knowledge. Practice experience involves the application of academic knowledge and reflection upon one's application forms a localised acquisition of knowledge. Such reflection can be taken a step further by formalising this reflection as a research study seeking evidence-based practice; an endeavour that is not unique to social work but rather represents a recent movement in academic literature spanning the professions (e.g. Trowler, 2015).

Drawing upon the Ancient Greek philosophical definition of *tékhnê* as applied knowledge (Plato, 380 BC/2004), reflection on practice experience yields technical knowledge. A research endeavour seeking evidence-based practice adds to the academic professional body of knowledge. However, more commonly, reflection on practice experience contributes to our working body of knowledge. To declare ourselves as professionals, we must offer some type of professional expertise. Hence, continuous reflection upon our practice experience contributes towards refining the role of social workers as expert knowers.

PRACTICE WISDOM: ATTACKING HUBRIS

As noted earlier, the professions of social work and nursing contain the term *practice wisdom* in their literature, whereas many other professions such as education and law do not. What accounts for this difference? All four are service professions, yet social workers and nurses embrace a prominent role for this idea of practice wisdom in the delivery of their service whereas others do not, at least they do not in any formalised way in their professional literature. All four professions have a prominent role for values in guiding their service delivery in the form of a professional code of ethics. I am taking the position that wisdom involves the application of values concerning service delivery. Consequently, all four professions rely upon wisdom to some extent to ethically guide their actions when providing service to people.

So what makes social work and nursing distinct in this regard? In my opinion there exists the real possibility that nurses and social workers may end up causing more harm than good to the people they serve. In terms of teachers and lawyers, for example, it may be possible to imagine some scenarios in which serious harm is visited upon the person being served if the teacher or lawyer is corrupt, or highly incompetent. But given a situation in which teachers or lawyers possesses minimum competence and serve with good intentions, it is difficult to imagine any scenarios which would lead to the conclusion that "The person being served would have been better off on their own, having received no education or legal counsel whatsoever". The same cannot be said for nursing and social work. The prescription "First do no harm" can be traced back to Hippocrates in the field of medicine. And while social work has only been recognised and practised as a profession for a little over a century, its short history already unfortunately contains many examples in which clients were harmed by appropriately competent social workers, despite their good intentions. Thus, as opposed to lawyers and teachers, for social work (and nursing) the practice of wisdom entails more than simply ethical decision making.

Throughout the 20th century, and still today, social work embraced a medical model to guide practice (as reflected in various social work practice textbooks such as Miley, O'Melia, & DuBois, 2017). I am using the term *medical model* broadly here to denote an approach that is based prominently in science; one in which the basic steps of the scientific method are followed to guide a helping effort geared towards enhancing functioning: data gathering, hypothesis generation and hypothesis testing to produce a diagnosis/assessment and pursue an intervention /treatment designed to reduce or eliminate the identified symptoms and restore/enhance proper functioning. It is interesting to note that when the Council on Social Work Education (CSWE) was formed in the US during the 1950s, its first major task was an attempt to define a commonality of social work that cut across its many subfields (ranging from community organising to psychiatric social work) that could provide a shared educational foundation. CSWE concluded that this commonality in social work lay in a three-step intervention process followed by all; using the terms "study, diagnose and treatment" for these three steps, they succinctly mimicked the basic steps of the scientific method (Strean, 1978).

Thus, the common thread connecting social work to nursing now becomes clearer: they both follow a scientific, medical model designed to restore and/or enhance human functioning. There is a bit to unpack with this seemingly innocuous statement. First, with the rise of science in the modern era, great faith has been placed in the scientific method as a vehicle for establishing truth. In the eyes of many (both professionals and clients being served), truth is primarily equated with scientific fact. And with both nursing and social work being primarily anchored in science (nursing in the natural sciences and social work in the social sciences), it is easy for professionals to adopt a stance that they "know" – that they have a firm grasp of the reality comprising the helping situation based upon their education.

While part of declaring oneself as a professional involves embracing the role of expert knower, basing one's expertise in science can easily lead to hubris. This hubris arises from an inordinate faith being placed in science due to an inadequate understanding of the limitations of science. There are very few scientific truths that achieve the level of certainty of a scientific law; and there are assuredly no scientific laws guiding social work interventions. Consequently, the science guiding social work practice traffics in probabilities not certainties. Compounding the problematic nature of social workers being "expert knowers" is that by being anchored in the social sciences, social work is more susceptible to fall prey to pseudoscience masquerading as science (Thyer & Pignotti, 2015). When this hubris guides attempts to "correct" or "enhance" the biological, psychological or social functioning of an individual, the "enhancement" sought may degrade into simply that of a realignment of the individual to cultural mores or elite interests of society. In other words, the social work intervention becomes an exercise in social control rather than one of truly enhancing the functioning of the individual. And this is how social workers with good intentions who are competent in the technical knowledge of the profession, through their hubris, may visit harm upon those they are seeking to serve.

In the US, examples of such hubris in action began with the birth of the profession in the late 1800s and early 1900s. There is the example of "scientific" charity being employed by the various Charity Organization Societies through their adoption of the slogan "not alms but a friend". The science of their day guided them to the conclusion that the best way to help those who were suffering from economic hardship was to primarily provide moral counselling, with material aid as a "carrot" to motivate clients to conform to moral standards such as thrift and temperance (Lowell, 1884). By locating the cause for economic suffering predominantly within the individual rather than oppressive structural factors, social workers of this time were duped into promoting the interests of the economic elite over those of the oppressed and downtrodden: the opposite of what our professional mission calls for us to do. This happened because of imprudence not incompetence. The knowledge that values such as thrift and temperance contribute positively towards establishing economic self-sufficiency is technically sound; however, it was the hubris that this knowledge represented a fairly complete picture of the clients' situation which stifled curiosity to explore further.

We can also examine prominent examples from the field of mental health illustrating how pseudoscience masquerading as science can lead social workers and other mental health professionals through their hubris to visit harm upon clients. This is because while pseudoscience can be viewed as better than simply pure conjecture, it still has a proclivity for producing erroneous conclusions. *The Diagnostic and Statistical Manual* (DSM) put out by the American Psychiatric Association (APA) is a prominent example of Karl Popper's (1959) definition of pseudoscience: the scientific "truths" of the various diagnostic categories are not derived from falsification, but rather, through confirmatory evidence. Since its inception, social workers have prominently embraced and utilised the DSM to guide their practice. The most infamous example of an erroneous conclusion resulting in harm was how in the first two editions of the DSM, homosexuality was classified as a mental illness (APA, 1968).

By relying solely upon confirmatory evidence in making truth claims, recent authors have noted how inclusion of categories occurs more as a result of a political process rather than through scientific merit (Kutchins & Kirk, 2003) and how this feeds a "diagnostic inflation" which results in the continuous growth in the number of categories. Overpathologisation that can occur through a hubristic application of the DSM has been a critique offered by numerous authors in recent times (e.g. Kutchins & Kirk, 2003). The recognition that a diagnostic label can easily assume the role of a master status defining the individual, let alone the possible harm arising from medication being prescribed for a condition of questionable scientific merit, should give social workers pause. Despite their best intentions, competent but unwise social workers face a real danger in visiting oppression on clients (by falling prey to being recruited into the role of social police) and in visiting harm upon clients (by brashly employing pseudoscientific technical knowledge). This points to the important role that practice wisdom has to play in guiding social work practice, and hence the necessity for the expert inquirer to be constantly questioning the expert knower.

PRACTICE WISDOM AND EXPERT INQUIRERS

I have turned to Socrates as a role model for wisdom as the inquiry he epitomises serves as a premier example of how to attack the hubris that one knows; this is accomplished by dividing himself into the expert knower and the expert inquirer. The expert inquirer recognises the fallibility of one's knowledge, embracing this recognition of one's ignorance to operate in a condition of *aporia*. The expert inquirer values the important role that wisdom plays when applying scientific technical knowledge, especially in situations wherein applying such technical knowledge may inadvertently cause harm. Complacency in one's expertise breeds hubris. The condition of *aporia* offered by the expert inquirer disturbs our complacency and frees us from unrecognised shackles.

The wisdom arising from an *aporia* is seen as the application of values to epistemology: i.e. to the knowledge gathering and application process. Thus, while the social work profession has always maintained a strong base of social work values, the wisdom arising from an *aporia* demands more than our typical understanding of these values being employed as a code of ethics to guide behaviour. The application of these values to epistemology spurs a more generative form of inquiry in contrast to the normative form offered by the expert knower. Hence, while the expert knower is informed by evidence-based practice, the expert inquirer is informed by value-based practice.

Postmodern Theory

Postmodern social work scholars and practitioners have turned to a number of theorists to guide this value-based, generative form of inquiry (Heiddeger, Berger and Luckmann, Wittgenstein, Foucault, and Ricœur, to name a few). Two particular theories of merit are chosen to advance this discussion: social constructionism as articulated by Berger and Luckmann (1966) and Foucault's (1980) notion of power/knowledge.

Social Constructionism Theories

These theories contend that there are multiple possible realities that exist for every phenomenon (Berger & Luckmann, 1966). This is because in addition to observing its physical properties, as human beings we imbue meaning to phenomena in the process of interacting with them. Thus, for example, the US $20 bill could be, at the same time, recognised as currency of a determinate worth, a constructed essence arising from the social discourse, and (for people living in a different reality such a tribe in the Amazon jungle) it could be seen as tinder material.

This insight that multiple realities are possible attacks the very heart of the hubris that one knows. Our understanding of any phenomenon can no longer breed a complacency arising from the stance that this understanding represents a definitive reality or truth. We are constantly spurred to inquire into and consider other possible realities, always on the lookout for a different reality that may better serve the interests of clients. The field of mental health serves as one example of how this plays out in social work. When clients describe symptoms and life struggles, common practice is to assign these symptoms a name as a means to guide helping efforts in addressing them. However, it also has been noted by social work scholars that these labels can begin to infuse the client's identity, serving to disempower them (Saleebey, 2002). The following question may be asked: At what point does the naming of client symptomology move from being a signpost to guide the social worker's and client's efforts in the helping process to that of being an albatross around the client's neck serving to disempower him/her? The answer to this question is reached through employing practice wisdom as an expert inquirer, not practice experience as an expert knower.

Power/knowledge. As human beings, we face the daily challenge of navigating the world in which we live. While social constructionism informs us that multiple realities exist for any phenomenon, when interacting with phenomena in the process of navigating our world we do not operate within multiple realities simultaneously. Our understanding and the resulting actions we take are based upon a single reality we choose to embrace. Thus, a particular socially constructed reality will assert itself over others, establishing its legitimacy in guiding our actions. Foucault (1980) offers the insight that power circulating within the social discourse will cause some socially constructed realities and truths to rise to prominence and legitimacy while subjugating others. Embracing Foucault's insight into the nature of power reminds us that the truths arising from one's knowing are not only a result of scientific merit, but also contain the political operation of power.

Harm can be visited upon clients when the hubris of social workers blunts their ability to question the legitimacy of pseudoscientific knowledge that is disempowering or pathologising to clients. Harm can also be visited upon clients by systems and classifications, and also when social workers' construction of reality differs from that of their clients and is imposed rather than negotiated. The need for such negotiation is facilitated by postmodern practitioners who are prompted to conclude that client resistance, as it is typically understood, is a misnomer (e.g. De Jong & Berg; 2008). Within this understanding, clients are resisting the imposition of a reality or label constructed by social workers. To expert knowers, client resistance represents an uncooperative stance of clients that must be broken down and overcome so that the expert's assessment of the situation is accepted by clients. To expert inquirers, client resistance is a wake-up call to collaboratively engage in dialogue with clients to explore possible realities and find one that is mutually acceptable to both social workers and clients.

An important item to note is that the *aporia* being maintained by the expert inquirer does not involve the wholesale jettisoning of expert knowledge in favour of simply blindly accepting the socially constructed and imposed reality under which clients are operating. Practice wisdom spurs social workers to open up a dialogue with clients, a dialogue in which the expert knowledge of social workers plays a part. Hence, practice wisdom incorporates knowledge gathered by the expert knower; however, it privileges the perplexity of expert inquirer arising from one's recognition of the limitations of that knowledge.

Postmodern Practice

A "not knowing" approach to therapy is a term first coined by Anderson and Goolishian (1992) to describe a collaborative, dialogical effort to co-construct with a client the meaning of the client's life struggles and the reality of the helping situation; their notion of "not-knowing" draws upon a Socratic method of inquiry:

> Therapeutic questions ... are not rhetorical or pedagogical questions. Rhetorical questions give their own answers; pedagogical questions imply the direction of the answer. Questions in traditional therapy are often of this nature; that is, they imply direction (correct reality), and leave the client a hint in order to reach the 'correct' answer. In contrast, not-knowing questions bring into the open something unknown and unforeseen to the realm of possibility. (p. 34)

By further stating that "not-knowing means the therapist is humble about what she or he knows" (Anderson, 2005, p. 502), Anderson describes it as an approach which seeks to attack hubris. In turn, maintaining such an open, collaborative dialogue with clients requires drawing upon the practice wisdom of the expert inquirer, not the practice experience of the expert knower.

Similar to Socrates, with this type of inquiry there are two types of dialogues occurring simultaneously: a public dialogue one engages in with the other person(s) and an inner dialogue that takes place among multiple aspects of oneself. The public dialogue relies upon what Rober (2005) describes as a *receptive self*; this receptive self is similar to McAvoy's (1999) earlier description of Socrates in the mode of being "a gentler creature who seems to be forever in perplexity" (p. 21) and thus receptive to the possibilities offered by others. This receptive self embodies a condition of *aporia* fostered by one's inner dialogue, resulting in a genuine curiosity (Anderson & Goolishian, 1992) that opens conversation space for the co-constructing of a mutually satisfying reality of the helping situation. Drawing upon the work of Gadamer (trans. 1999), Anderson (2005) describes the action of this genuine curiosity as a hermeneutic endeavour in which one immerses oneself in the other's horizon of understanding, further stating "It is in this act of immersion – this quest for meaning – that we try to comprehend and make sense of the familiar and unfamiliar" (p. 499). However, as Rober (2005) is quick to point out, the goal of this inquiry is not simply that of a passive understanding duplicating the speaker's meaning. Drawing upon the work of Bahktin, Rober (2005) describes this public dialogue as an effort in which "understanding becomes an active, creative process in which the meanings of clients make contact with the meanings of therapists. In this process, new meanings emerge that are different from the original" (p. 482).

The meanings of the therapist contributing to the public dialogue arise from an inner dialogue taking place within the therapist. Rober (2005) describes this mode of a therapist's use of self as being a *reflexive self*. Drawing upon the philosophy of both Volosinov (1973) and Bakhtin (1986), Rober describes this reflexive self as consisting of an inner dialogue between a polyphony of inner voices. Once again, we can see the similarity of this reflexive self to McAvoy's (1999) earlier description of Socrates, this time as "a violent questioner who seems to both know and not know" (p. 21). Rober (2005) uses the term *professional self* to capture the aspect of the reflexive self acting as the violent questioner who knows, and the term *experiencing self* to capture the aspect of the reflexive self acting as the violent questioner who does not know. The experiencing self represents "a not-knowing receptivity toward the stories of the clients and toward what is evoked by these stories in the therapist" (p. 487); whereas the professional self entails the therapist bringing to bear her/his knowledge as the expert knower. An inner monologue consisting solely of the expert knower, or professional self, results in the seeking of patterns in which to explain client behaviour. This reflects the pedagogical form of inquiry described above by Anderson and Goolishian (1992); an inquiry designed to move clients into accepting the reality of these identified patterns. Conversely, the inner dialogical clash between the experiencing self and the professional self results in seeking a uniqueness that prioritises clients' individuality (Morson & Emerson, 1990).

Cultural humility. Due to the birth of the civil rights movement in the 1960s and the feminist movement of the 1970s in the US, there came a growing awareness in social work education of the importance of including curriculum content on respecting diversity (Jani et al., 2011). Soon after, the term *cultural competence* was coined to capture this goal of ably accounting for cultural difference in practice. This competence reflected a notion that culture is static and reflects knowledge that can be acquired and applied to adapt normative models so that they account for cultural difference (Minahan, 1987). Hence, cultural competence entails the acquisition of cultural knowledge and its application by expert knowers.

At the turn of the 21st century, due to the inroads made by postmodern thought into the helping professions, a different goal was envisioned concerning respecting diversity in one's practice: that of adopting a stance of *cultural humility* (Tervalon & Murray-Garcia, 1998). Such a stance attacks the hubris that one can truly know another's culture and life experiences and thus be competent in them (Laird, 1998). Cultural humility relies upon the wisdom of expert inquirers rather than the intelligence of expert knowers. Rather than a product to be acquired, cultural understanding is viewed as a process in which to recognise our limitations in fully knowing another's cultural experiences and where we need to pursue a continuous dialogue with clients in order to continue seeking to learn and inquire. Laird (1998) describes this process as requiring one to be an "informed not-knower".

There are a few ways in which cultural humility may be nurtured among social work students. Most directly, this would involve the prominent inclusion of literature on cultural humility when addressing diversity content in the curriculum.

Case studies can provide a means for students to practise this stance of being an informed not knower. In addition, students can use the disorientation and experiences of their internship placements and overseas travel programs to critically reflect upon their own biases and assumptions. (e.g. Gilin & Young, 2009; Wehbi, 2009).

THE *NICOMACHEAN ETHICS*: OFFERING A FURTHER DISTINCTION

In the *Nicomachean Ethics*, Aristotle (349 BC/2016) defines three categories of knowledge: *epistêmê, tékhnê* and *phrónêsis*. *Epistêmic* knowledge is driven simply by the goal of understanding reality. As such, scientific facts and theory are considered epistemic knowledge, representing what Plato (Plato, 380 BC/2004) describes as "justified true belief". *Epistêmê* can act as a partner to *tékhnê* (Plato, 380 BC/2004), with *tékhnê* representing applied knowledge driven by the goal of producing some result or product: for social work, this being the intervention. The application of *epistêmic* knowledge creates a knowledge of its own (*tékhnê*) in both the form of a technique or approach as well as the local knowledge relating to the specific application. For example, attachment theory (*epistêmê*) may inform social workers as to the importance of examining the bond between client and primary caregiver. The method of a bio-psycho-social assessment (*tékhnê*) is used in order to gather specific information (*tékhnê* as local knowledge) of the client's attachment to primary caregiver(s). This partnership between *epistêmê* and *tékhnê* leads to *gnôsis*, which Plato (Plato, 380 BC/2004) defines as aptitude or competence. And it is *gnôsis* that defines social work practice of the 20th century and its quest to demonstrate competence in order to distinguish itself as a profession. It is also reflective of the recent movement of evidence-based practice. Thus, applying one's intelligence to reflect upon one's practice experience promotes *gnôsis*.

In social work practice derived from *gnôsis*, *epistêmic* knowledge places social workers in the role of expert knowers. And, technical knowledge directs expert knowers in pursuing a pedagogical inquiry as described earlier by Anderson and Goolishian (1992) in which the intervention entails providing hints to clients on how to reach the "correct" answer determined by the expert knower. Additionally, values take the form of a code of a professional ethics; thus, values do not contribute to the *epistêmê-tékhnê* knowledge generating process captured by the notion of evidence-based practice. Rather social work values are employed simply to circumscribe the boundaries within which *gnôsis* operates. For example, while the expert knower may provide the hint to clients that anger management classes are needed, if a client strongly takes a position against doing so, the ethical application of self-determination does not allow social workers to "force" the issue.

It is interesting to note that when *gnôsis* operates within the field of religion, it leads to *gnôsticism* (Gnosticism, 2018): professional practitioners of religion (i.e. *gnôstics*) who possess a secret knowledge of transcendence and thus assume the mantle of "the Knowing Ones" in order to guide those individuals deprived of *gnôsis* yet possessing *pistis* (i.e. belief). When science achieves a cult-like status in the mind of social work practitioners, despite good intentions and a vigorous code of ethics to guide practice, the resulting hubris arising from assuming the mantle of "the Knowing One" can easily lead down a path of visiting oppression and harm upon clients. This was illustrated earlier by the historical examples of social workers adopting the slogan "not alms but a friend," and the treating of a diagnostic label as a master status.

Phrónêsis is the third category of knowledge identified by Aristotle (349 BC/2016). *Phrónêsis* is roughly translated into English as *prudence*. Merriam-Webster's offers four definitions of prudence:

1: the ability to govern and discipline oneself by the use of reason.
2: sagacity or shrewdness in the management of affairs.
3: skill and good judgment in the use of resources.
4: caution or circumspection as to danger or risk. (Prudence, n.d.)

Each of the above definitions capture an aspect of *phrónêsis* highlighted by Aristotle (349 BC/2016). The ability to employ reason to govern oneself speaks to ethics and involves not only an understanding of values but also reasoned deliberation when seeking to apply them to guide one's actions. Sagacity and good judgement speak to reason being employed as practical wisdom concerning values; while their employment in the management of affairs or use of resources speak of political calculation comprising part of this practical wisdom. Thus, Aristotle proposed that both thinking abilities as well as political abilities were required for *phrónêsis*. Lastly, caution as to danger reflects the notion of "do no harm" that was offered earlier as a defining feature of practice wisdom.

Tékhnê also serves as a partner to *phrónêsis*; the application of *phrónêtic* knowledge creates a knowledge of its own (*tékhnê*) in both the form of a technique or approach as well as the local knowledge relating to the specific application. For example, the value of self-determination (*phrónêsis*) informs social workers as to the importance of respecting clients' free will when attempting to facilitate client change. Social workers employ the method of a strengths assessment (*tékhnê*) in order to gather specific information (*tékhnê* as local knowledge) of clients' goals and dreams – which will then serve as the main understanding guiding the type of intervention and its direction. This partnership between *phrónêsis* and *tékhnê* leads to *praxis*, which Aristotle (349 BC/2016) defines as principled action.

Thus, Aristotle makes a distinction between principled action (*praxis*) and competence (*gnôsis*); similarly, this chapter has laid out an argument on how practice wisdom is distinct from practice experience. When employed in the social work helping situation, this partnership between *phrónêsis* and *tékhnê* represents the operation of practice wisdom which seeks to promote praxis. This notion of principled action fits with the idea of a value-based practice – as stated earlier, a term embraced by postmodern practitioners to contrast their approach to that of evidence-based practice. Hence, in social work practice derived from *praxis*, *phrónêtic* knowledge places the social worker in the role of expert inquirer, and technical knowledge directs this expert inquirer in pursuing a Socratic inquiry as described earlier by Anderson and Goolishian (1992), an inquiry seeking to "bring into the open something unknown and unforeseen to the realm of possibility" (p. 34).

Consequently, the local knowledge (*tékhnê*) generated (i.e. brought into the open) by the partnership representing practice wisdom arises from the application of values to the treatment *planning* process. The social worker acting as expert inquirer, through applying the value of self-determination, brings into the open the specific dreams and goals of clients, which then are employed to direct the treatment process. Within this type of inquiry, scientific knowledge (*epistêmê*) takes on the supporting role of circumscribing the boundaries within which *praxis* operates. For example, if a client's goal is to reduce or eliminate the need for anti-psychotic medication, bio-chemical scientific knowledge informs social workers as to the best means to accomplish this goal. Hence in this example, bio-chemical scientific knowledge does not generate knowledge concerning the creation of the treatment plan (i.e. the goal feely chosen by clients, which arises from the application of self-determination); it merely directs the expert inquirer as to the most efficient means for achieving this goal. Thus, when employing praxis, scientific knowledge plays an important role, but does not play a role in the knowledge/wisdom generating process used to plan the intervention.

CONCLUSION

Having pursued this inquiry up until this point, a clear distinction has been offered between practice experience and practice wisdom, between the expertise comprising expert knowing and expert inquiring, and between competence and principled action as the means to generate knowledge used to plan the intervention. The conclusion of such an inquiry leads to a new question to consider: As the profession of social work moves into the 21st century, what prominence and role should be given to practice experience and practice wisdom? The main objective of the 20th century was to establish the competence of the profession; to this end, a medical model employing scientific knowledge in a problem-solving approach was embraced as the means to establish competence. In this evidence-based practice, scientific knowledge is prioritised and practice experience is relied upon in the treatment planning process. Values play the complementary role of helping guide implementation of plans.

Postmodern practitioners have laid out a different path for the social work profession to take as we progress through the 21st century; one which seeks to prioritise principled action over competence. This path embraces value-based practice wherein practice wisdom is relied upon in the treatment planning process. Scientific knowledge is thus relegated to the complementary role of helping to guide how values-based plans are implemented. In such a complementary role, there is no danger of scientific knowledge leading to hubris, as the expert knower is constantly being questioned by the expert inquirer. Practice wisdom engenders cultural humility and promotes a stance of informed not-knowing to guard against unintentional harm and oppression. Social workers of this century face two paths from which to choose. Their choices will determine the future identity of the profession. Many (myself included) have cast their lot on the path of value-based practice leading to principled action. This chapter serves as an invitation to join us on this path.

REFERENCES

American Psychiatric Association (APA). (1968). *DSM-II: Diagnostic and statistical manual of mental disorders.* Washington, DC: Author.

Anderson, H. (2005). Myths about "not-knowing". *Family Practice, 44,* 497-504.

Anderson, H., & Goolishian, H. (1992). The client is the expert: A not-knowing approach to therapy. In S. McNamee & K. Gergen (Eds.), *Social construction and the therapeutic process* (pp. 25-39). Newbury Park, CA: Sage.

Aristotle. (2016). *Nicomachean ethics.* (W. D. Ross, Trans.). Overland Park, KS: Digireads. (Original work published 349 BC)

Bakhtin, M. (1986). *Speech genres & other late essays.* Austin, TX: University of Texas Press.

Berger, P. L., & Luckmann, T. (1966), *The social construction of reality: A treatise in the sociology of knowledge.* Garden City, NY: Anchor Books.

Council on Social Work Education (CSWE). (2008). *Strengthening the profession of social work: Leadership in research, career advancement, and education.* Retrieved from http:/www.cswe.org/File.aspx?id=14136

De Jong, P., & Berg, I. K. (2008). *Interviewing for solutions* (3rd ed.). Belmont, CA: Thomson Brooks/Cole.

Dybicz, P. (2004). An inquiry into practice wisdom. *Families in Society, 85*(2), 197-204.

Flexner, A. (1915). *Is social work a profession? Social Welfare History Project.* Retrieved from http://socialwelfare.library.vcu.edu/social-work/is-social-work-a-profession-1915/

Foucault, M. (1980). *Power-knowledge: Selected interviews & other writings 1972–1977* (C. Gordon, ed.). New York, NY: Pantheon Books.

Gadamer, H. G. (1999). *Truth and method* (2nd ed.). (J. Weinsheimer & D. G. Marshall, Trans.) New York, NY: The Continuum Publishing Company. (Original work published 1960)

Gilin, B., & Young, T. (2009). Educational benefits of international experiential learning in an MSW program. *International Social Work, 52*(1), 36-47.

Gnosticism. (2018, January 21). In *Wikipedia: The free encyclopedia.* Retrieved from https://en.wikipedia.org/w/index.php?title=Gnosticism&oldid=821600487

Goldhaber, D., Krieg, J., & Theobald, R. (2017). Does the match matter? Exploring whether student teaching experiences affect teacher effectiveness. *American Educational Research Journal, 54,* 325-359.

Jani, J., Ortiz, L, Pierce, D., & Sowbel, L. (2011). Access to intersectionality, content to competence: Deconstructing social work education diversity standards. *Journal of Social Work Education, 47,* 283-301.

Kutchins, H., & Kirk, S. (2003). *Making us crazy; DSM: The psychiatric bible and the creation of mental disorders.* New York, NY: Free Press.

Laird, J. (1998). Theorizing culture: Narrative ideas and practice principles, In M. McGoldrick (Ed.), *Re-visioning family therapy* (pp. 20–36). New York, NY: The Guilford Press.

Lowell, J. (1884). *Relief and private charity.* New York, NY: GP Putnam's Sons.

Marchbanks, E. (2015). Law school dilemmas: Paid internships vs. for-credit externships. *Affiliate, 40,* 1-2.

McAvoy, M. (1999). *The profession of ignorance: With constant reference to Socrates.* Lanham, NY: University Press of America.

Miley, K. K., O'Melia, M., & DuBois, B. (2017). *Generalist social work practice: An empowering approach.* Boston, MA: Prentice Hall.

Minahan, A. (1987). Cultural competence. In *Encyclopedia of social work*. Washington, DC: National Association of Social Workers.
Mollica, M., & Hyman, Z. (2016). Learning and teaching in clinical practice: Professional development utilizing an oncology summer nursing internship. *Nurse Education in Practice, 16*, 188-192.
Morson, G., & Emerson, C. (1990). *Mikhail Bakhtin: Creation of a prosaics*. Stanford, CA: Stanford University Press.
Petrila, A., Fireman, O., Fitzpatrick, L., Hodas, R., & Taussig, H. (2015). Student satisfaction with an innovative internship. *Journal of Social Work Education, 51*, 121-135.
Plato. (2004). *Republic.* (C. D. C. Reeve, Trans.). Indianapolis, IN: Hackett. (Original work published 380 BC)
Popper, K. (1959). *The logic of scientific discovery*. New York, NY: Basic Books.
Prudence. (n.d.). In *Merriam-Websters online dictionary*. Retrieved from https://www.merriam-webster.com/dictionary/prudence
Rober, P. (2005). The therapist's self in dialogical family therapy: Some ideas about not-knowing and the therapist's inner conversation. *Family Process*, 44, 477-495.
Saleebey, D. (2002). Introduction: Power in the people. In D. Saleebey (Ed.), *The strengths perspective in social work practice* (3rd ed., pp.1-22). Boston, MA: Allyn and Bacon.
Saleebey, D. (Ed.). (2006). *The strengths perspective in social work practice* (4th ed.). Boston, MA: Pearson/Allyn and Bacon.
Strean, H. (1978). *Clinical social work: Theory and practice*. New York, NY: Free Press.
Tervalon, M., & Murray-Garcia, J. (1998). Cultural humility versus cultural competence: A critical distinction in defining physician training outcomes in multicultural education. *Journal of Health Care to the Poor and Underserved, 9*(2), 117-125.
Thyer, B. A., & Pignotti, M. (2015). *Science and pseudoscience in social work practice.* New York, NY: Springer Publishing Company.
Trowler, P. (2015, July). Editorial. *Higher Education Quarterly.* doi:10.1111/hequ.12073
Volosinov, V. N. (1973). *Marxism and the philosophy of language*. New York, NY: Seminar Press.
Wehbi, S. (2009). Deconstructing motivations: Challenging international social work placements. *International Social Work, 52*(1), 48-59.

Phillip Dybicz PhD (ORCID: https://orcid.org/0000-0001-6190-0457)
Dewar College of Education and Human Services
Department of Social Work
Valdosta State University, United States of America

PATRICIA BENNER

19. SKILL ACQUISITION AND CLINICAL JUDGEMENT IN NURSING PRACTICE

Towards Expertise and Practical Wisdom

This chapter explores expertise and practical wisdom in nursing through an exploration of skill acquisition and clinical judgement in nursing practice. Three studies using the Dreyfus model of skill acquisition were conducted over a period of 21 years. Nurses with a range of experience and reported skilfulness were interviewed. Each study used nurses' narrative accounts of actual clinical situations. These studies extend the understanding of the Dreyfus model to complex, underdetermined and fast-paced practices. The skill of involvement and the development of moral agency are linked with the development of expertise and practical wisdom, as the practitioner becomes more skilful. Taken together, these studies demonstrate the usefulness of the Dreyfus model for understanding the learning needs and styles of learning at different levels of skill acquisition.

Stuart E. Dreyfus, an applied mathematician, and Hubert L. Dreyfus, a philosopher, developed a model of skill acquisition based on the study of chess players, air force pilots, and army tank drivers and commanders (Dreyfus, 1982; Dreyfus & Dreyfus, 1977, 1979, 1980, 1986). The Dreyfus model of skill acquisition has illuminated ongoing research on skill acquisition and articulation of knowledge embedded in expert nursing practice. This model is developmental, based on situated performance and experiential learning. The three studies of skill acquisition in nursing were guided by the Dreyfus model (Benner, 1982, 1984; Benner, Hooper-Kyriakidis, & Stannard, 2011; Benner, Tanner, & Chesla, 2009). Hubert and Stuart Dreyfus served as consultants for the three studies.

The first study,[1] conducted between 1978 and 1981 (Benner, 1982, 1984), was based on 21 paired interviews with newly graduated nurses and their preceptors. Interviews and/or participant observations were conducted with 51 additional experienced nurse clinicians, 11 newly graduated nurses, and 5 senior nursing students to further delineate and describe characteristics of nurse performance at different levels of education and experience. The interviews (small group and individual) were conducted in six hospitals: two private community hospitals, two community teaching hospitals, one university medical centre, and one inner-city general hospital. A second study of skill acquisition and clinical knowledge of critical care nurses was conducted between 1988 and 1994 (Benner et al., 1992, 2009, 2011). One-hundred and thirty nurses practising in intensive care units and general floor units from eight hospitals, seven of which are located in the far western and one in the eastern region of the country, comprised the study population. Small group narrative interviews, individual interviews and participant

© PATRICIA BENNER, 2005 | DOI: 9789004410497_019

observation were used as data collection strategies. The two aims of the study were: (a) to describe the nature of skill acquisition in critical care nursing practice; and (b) to delineate the practical knowledge embedded in expert practice. The third study was an extension of this study, conducted between 1996 and 1997 to include other critical care areas (including emergency departments, flight nursing, home health, the operating room, and post-anaesthesia care units [$N = 75$ nurses]) and to enlarge our sample of advanced practice nurses. This chapter presents key findings of these three studies using data from each of the studies.

Nursing, like other practice disciplines, is not merely an applied field in the sense that the practice is complex, varied and underdetermined. Good practice requires that the nurse develop skilful ethical comportment as a practitioner and that the nurse use good clinical judgement informed by scientific evidence and technological development. The sciences of medicine and nursing are broad and multidisciplinary and require translation into the particular practice situation. Basic sciences of biochemical, physical and biological processes; physiological processes; research and development of specific therapies and technologies; and finally, clinical trials, make up a broad range of science used in nursing practice.

A recent development in nursing and medical practice has been to aggregate clinical trial research outcomes to summarise and recommend the best evidence for treatment of specific clinical conditions. However, the logic of scientific decision making and the logic of the practitioner working with single cases or unique populations are necessarily different. The practitioner must reason across time about the particular, through changes in the patient's condition and changes in the clinician's understanding of the patient's condition. Because practice in the individual case is underdetermined (i.e. open to variations not accounted for by science), the practitioner must use good clinical reasoning to intelligently select and use the relevant science. Perceptual acuity in recognising salient signs, symptoms and responses to therapies are required for the clinician to use good clinical judgements in particular clinical cases.

Recognising and keeping track of clinical changes in the patient over time requires the logic of reasoning in transition (Benner, 1994; Taylor, 1993). This is a form of argument about the outcomes of successive changes. Patient changes must be evaluated as improved, stable or deteriorating over time. Clinicians call this "recognising trends" in the patient. Some aspects of practice can be subjected to more standardisation and to what Aristotle described as *tékhnê*. For example, standard measurement of vital signs and laboratory metrics are clinical assessments that can be reduced to *tékhnê*. Skilfulness and craft based on experience may still be essential to successful performance of *tékhnê*. In situations where the patient's particular response must be considered and perceptual acuity is required to recognise salient changes in the patient, and situations where attuned relationships and judgement require skilful comportment, both *tékhnê* and *phrónêsis* (situated actions based on skill, judgement, character and wisdom) are essential.

At the heart of good clinical judgement and clinical wisdom lies experiential learning from particular cases. Bad judgements must be refined and corrected in particular cases; anomalies and distinctions must be noticed. The Dreyfus model of skill acquisition addresses this kind of experiential learning in a complex, under-determined field over time. The model is situational rather than being a trait or talent model because the focus is on actual performance and outcomes in particular situations. The model is developmental in that performance changes in particular situations can be compared across time. However, the model does not focus or identify particular traits or talents of the person generating the skilful performance.

Nursing, as a practice, requires both *tékhnê* and *phrónêsis* as described by Aristotle. *Tékhnê* can be captured by procedural and scientific knowledge that can be made formal, explicit and certain, except for the necessary timing and adjustments made for particular patients. *Phrónêsis*, in contrast to *tékhnê*, is the kind of practical reasoning engaged in by an excellent practitioner lodged in a community of practitioners, a practitioner who, through experiential learning and for the sake of good practice, continually lives out and improves practice (Benner et al., 2011; Dunne, 1997; Gadamer, 1960/1975; MacIntyre, 1981; Shulman, 1993). *Tékhnê*, or the activity of producing outcomes, is governed by a means-ends rationality where the maker or producer governs the thing produced or made by gaining mastery over the means of producing the outcomes. By contrast, *phrónêsis* is lodged in a practice and so cannot rely solely on a means-ends rationality because one's acts are governed by concern for doing good in particular circumstances, where being in relationship and discerning particular human concerns are at stake must guide action. For example, nurses describe the excessive use of power over a patient that subjects the patient to unwanted, futile therapies to prolong his or her life at any cost as *flogging* the patient, violating both good nursing and good doctoring (Benner et al., 2011). In such bad practice, means and ends are violently separated so that both are distorted.

Nursing particular patients requires relational and communication skills and art. The relationship between the patient and nurse, for example, determines what will be disclosed, what can be thought about and talked about together, and what level of acceptance and endorsement of the therapies will be acceptable to patients and clinicians alike. Patients often rehearse their most fearful concerns with nurses who they expect to be more approachable and effective in helping them communicate with physicians. Technique alone cannot address interpersonal and relational responsibilities, discernment and situated possibilities required by caring for persons made vulnerable by illness and injury. *Phrónêsis* is required. Means and ends are inextricably related in caring for the ill. Clinician and patient bend and respond to the other so that horizons and world are opened and reconstituted so that new possibilities can emerge.

As the Dreyfus model suggests, experiential learning requires the stance of an engaged learner rather than a stance of one expert in *tékhnê* who skilfully applies well-established knowledge in pre-specified, clear circumstances. Experiential learning requires learner openness and responsiveness to improve practice over time. The learner who develops an attuned, response-based practice learns to recognise whole situations in terms of past concrete experiences, as in the Dreyfus model. We found that responding to the situation as an instance of particular concern, is central to the logic of excellent practice. An example is a situation of heart-pump failure or fluid depletion. Interventions depend on clarifying and confirming the nature of the clinical situation at hand. The skilful practitioner learns to hold his or her background understandings in a fluid or semi-permeable way so that he or she can recognise when these tacit expectations are not met. For example, a nurse with expertise in detecting heart arrhythmias on a unit where all patients' cardiac functioning is monitored, will only notice aberrations in sound patterns rather than attending to the familiar sounds in the foreground of attention. These expert nurses would need to make a case that includes articulating their perspective and evidence to get the appropriate physician intervention. In emergencies, when there is no physician available, the nurse must be able to articulate clearly the reason for using a standing order or protocol or going beyond the usual boundaries of nursing practice. This is expected and defensible when it is critical for the patient's survival. Recognising the unexpected (when tacit global expectations of patients' recovery are not met) is also a hallmark of expert practice.

MAJOR SHIFTS IN PRACTICE STYLE WITH THE DEVELOPMENT OF EXPERTISE

As noted above, the nurse's capacity for effective moral agency changes with developing practice skills and insights from experience. Also, the skills of problem and person engagement grow more attuned. The development of agency and skills of involvement can be seen at each stage of skill acquisition. The nurse increasingly is able to recognise when he or she does not have a good grasp of clinical situations. This lack of a sense of understanding guides questioning and problem solving. As the skill model predicts, with more experience comes an increased grasp of the nature of particular clinical situations, including opportunities and constraints, which then guides the nurse's actions and interactions. Consequently, responses to patients become more contextualised and attuned. This is practical wisdom in action. Across our research practical wisdom is synonymous with expertise. Recognition of clinical situations moves from abstract textbook accounts of general features to an experience-based response to the situation. Grasp of the situation, with its possibilities and constraints, enables the competent nurse to move from rule-governed thinking to an intuitive grasp of the situation (Dreyfus & Dreyfus, 1986). This intuitive grasp is based on experience and not based on extrasensory powers or wild hunches. It is situated in the clinician's grasp of the situation. Improved skills of involvement create disclosive spaces in which pressing concerns or the most plausible actions can be discovered. Relational skills are schooled by learning to be at home in a highly differentiated clinical world where some actions are plausible and effective and others are experienced as ill-timed or implausible. A sense of salience develops over time so that some things stand out as more plausible and appropriate than others. The proficient practitioner develops a richer sense of the ends and possibilities of practice based on shared notions of good practice within the profession (Rubin, 2009). Because the Dreyfus model of skill acquisition is a situated and descriptive phenomenological account of the development of skill over time, it does not point to isolated competencies nor enabling traits or talent. Consequently, it allows that a practitioner may be at different levels of skill in different areas of practice based on the particular practitioner's background experience and knowledge. For example, a practitioner skilled in caring for adults at an expert level will not be at that level of skill when caring for young children or premature infants. The continuities in one's patient populations determine the opportunities for experiential learning.

Novice: First Year of Education

The novice stage of skill acquisition occurs in areas in which the student has no experiential background to base understanding of the clinical situation. For example, the art and skill of a range of medical and nursing interventions on particular patients will be new. The educator must offer good descriptions of features and attributes of the situation that the novice can recognise. For example, to determine fluid balance, students are given clear parameters and guidelines.

> To determine fluid balance, check the patient's morning weights and daily intake and output for the past three days. Weight gain and an intake that is consistently greater than 500 cc. could indicate water retention, in which case fluid restriction should be started until the cause of the imbalance can be found. (Benner, 1984 p. 21)

An experienced clinician will immediately think of all the situations where this evaluation would be inappropriate or too stringent. But the novice is given clear directions of safe ways to proceed until the significance of fluid balance for different clinical conditions can be learned. The rules and guidelines must not require prior experience for their recognition. They must provide a safe beginning point for specific, situated learning in the clinical situation. Fluid balance is salient, but what the novice must learn is the particular salience of fluid balance for particular patients. The rule-governed behaviour of the novice is extremely limited and inflexible. The student is coached in comparing and matching textbook examples with actual clinical cases. Skills that are performed easily on a mannequin in a skills lab require adaptation and communication and reassurance when performed on a range of patients who may be calm or highly anxious. The nursing instructor must carefully select patient care situations that are relatively stable and that provide coaching about possible changes in the patient's condition. The instructor forecasts for the student what he or she should expect, and students typically rely on standard nursing care plans to guide their planned care activities. Exceptions and contraindications must be identified for the student by the nursing instructor or staff nurse caring for the patient. The meanings of vital signs in the particular situation must be reviewed with the instructor or practising nurse and the range of relevant signs and symptoms are reviewed in terms of relevance and are assessed in the particular patient. A large number of signs and symptoms (e.g. lethargy, skin turgor, mental status) can only be recognised and assessed after they have been seen in a range of patients.

The best clinical educators are good ethnographers who can give students access to the culture and expectations of the clinical units where they are gaining clinical experience. The clinical educator offers broad guidelines and timelines to guide the student's understanding of the task world and of the subculture of expectations of a particular unit. Good informants are identified as resources for new students in the unit, and the clinical supervisor is on call to deal with questions or emergencies encountered by the students. Novices have only a very limited ability to forecast futures because of their lack of experience with other patients. Usually, the student must rely on textbook forecasts.

Advanced Beginner, New Graduate

The newly graduated nurse has usually functioned very close to the level of a beginning staff nurse in his or her final year of nursing education. Typically, newly graduated nurses will not have functioned in any administrative or managerial functions, though they will have studied principles and practices related to these roles. The striking change for the newly graduated nurse is that he or she now has full legal and professional responsibility for patients. This new level of responsibility and entitlement brings with it changes in the way nurses experience themselves and the practice environment. They no longer feel that *they can* always look to other nurses to tell them what to do or to bear their responsibility. This level of individual and team professional responsibility heightens the new nurse's sense of engagement with the patient and with clinical problems. This new level of felt responsibility increases the beginning nurse's attentiveness to his or her recognition of features and relevant aspects of the situation; however, the style of evaluation remains detached and typically lacks integration with other objectively evaluated signs and symptoms. Beginning nurses look to patients and family members to fill in expectations of them in their newly forming role. This heightened and qualitatively different kind of engagement heightens experiential learning and spurs the development of a sense of moral agency in the professional role.

> The quality of learning is quite different for new as opposed to more experienced nurses. Beginners have a level of trust in the environment and in the legitimacy of co-workers' knowledge, which allows them to absorb information as fact. This trust sets up qualities of freedom and exhilaration in learning that are probably only available to those who do not yet comprehend the contingent nature of both the situation and what is known about it. This freedom in learning is furthered because advanced beginners do not yet feel responsible for managing clinical situations with which they are unfamiliar. (Benner et al., 2009, p. 100)

In what follows, an advanced beginner evidences this "lightness of being" about learning as he describes with excitement and enthusiasm a post-operative patient who had undergone complex gastrointestinal (GI) surgery.

> I had learned so much. There are two clinical nurse specialists involved right now. There are people on the unit who are CNII's and CNIII's who are just really knowledgeable on major GI surgery on infants. I talked to all these

people and paediatric surgery were really helpful, and our Attendings and fellows were ... I mean, I just learned so much in the last three days, I couldn't even tell you. (Benner et al., 2009, p. 52)

Advanced beginners have a heightened awareness of any feedback on performance and pay close attention to the practice of colleagues. They actively search for credible sources of good and useful information. The nurses now attend to their ability to recognise these aspects of the situation as they are pointed out by colleagues and as they come to notice them on their own. In the situation above, clinical nurse specialists assisted with the care of the infant but also engaged in intensive teaching of the new nurse. The advanced beginner can experience each situation as a myriad of competing tasks, all of which may feel of equal priority to the new nurse. Anxiety and excessive fatigue are frequent experiences for new nurses. Worry and anxiety tend to be more global because advanced beginners do not yet have a sense of salience with a range of situations, and the anxiety of learning to perform new tasks is ever present.

> And I just talked to myself and I had a great night because this was the first time I did it ... I was (saying to myself) "Okay. Just take it one step at a time. You're only human, do one thing then go onto the next thing. It will all get done, it will get done easier if you're calm and because you think better that way" ... And the shift went great. (Benner et al. 2009, p. 27)

In coaching an advanced beginner, strategies for keeping anxiety at bay and staying calm enhance performance capacity. The sense of foreboding and anxiousness over particular clinical situations is not yet very attuned to the demands, possibilities and constraints of the situation simply because of a lack of similar past experiences. Anxiety is ameliorated by this very lack of attunement and sense of salience. Therefore, much of the experiential learning required of an advanced beginner has to do with recognising more subtle aspects of the situation. Advanced beginners rely on textbook accounts of patient signs and symptoms related to diseases, injuries and therapies, but they may have difficulty recognising subtle variations and cannot gauge the level of severity in comparison with other cases simply because of their lack of experienced past and future trajectories with similar patients. For example, advanced beginners collect their assessment data carefully and then consult about the meanings of the numbers and signs and symptoms in a particular case. They will need to ask questions such as the following: Is this the usual amount of bleeding? Such presentations may vary with specific procedures, patient conditions and characteristics. The range and variegations cannot be captured fully in textbooks, a problem known in philosophy as "the limits of formalism". Also, the perceptual skills associated with recognising fuzzy or family resemblances, qualitative distinctions and real-life presentations with their range of manifestations cannot be captured in two-dimensional textbooks or single case presentations. This relationship to clinical mentors is vividly illustrated as follows.

> This man is a very pleasant fellow, very bright, very alert and awake, and was unfortunately requiring tracheal suctioning approximately every hour to two

> hours for moderate amounts of tracheal secretions which were relatively tenacious in character, relatively white tannish in colour. He unfortunately did not tolerate the suctioning extremely well. It was relatively uncomfortable for him, caused a moderate amount of cough and gag reflex, which in turn caused a transient increase in blood pressure. Following suctioning on one occasion, as I was replacing his tracheal mist mask, he began coughing up very copious amounts of bright red blood per mouth. I mildly panicked, called for help from the nurse next door, placed him in a moderate Trendelenberg position, opened his I.V. to a rapid rate, and continued to experience mild panic. Perhaps more like moderate panic. (Benner, 1984, p. 19)

This advanced beginner nurse performed well considering the enormity of the situation. The student wonders tacitly whether his suctioning technique was too traumatic and therefore whether it caused the bleed. But notice that the advanced graduate cannot know this because he has had little experience with patients with similar compromised situations and with the skill of suctioning itself. There are extraneous details of the story, and the language is couched in textbook terms. His account responds to the immediate situation, with little or no forecasting of the future. He gives a full account of his own anxiety in the situation that results, in part, from his lack of experiential knowledge about what can be done in the situation. Like the novice, the advanced beginner is dependent on others for filling in his or her experience-based comparisons, interpretations and qualitative distinctions.

Competent Stage: 1 to 2 Years in Practice

Developing skill and clinical grasp in particular cases is dependent on experiential learning. Consequently, how fast someone can gain competence depends on how varied and complex his or her patient population is. Obviously, nurses working in a high-volume heart surgery centre will gain more experience sooner. But even in the high-volume centre, it is usually a while before the newer nurse is assigned complete responsibility for complicated postoperative patients. Competence with particular patient populations will develop unevenly depending on experience with that population and with the quality of clinical teaching available in the institution.

The competent stage of skill acquisition is typically a time of heightened planning for what are now more predictable immediate futures. The competent nurse now decides what is more or less important based on informal yardsticks learned from past experiences with other patients. The nurse tries to limit the unexpected through planning and analysis and by forecasting the needs and contingencies of the immediate future, but he or she realises that there are no rules to help him or her do it. Anxiety is now more attuned to the situation, as illustrated in the following example where the nurse describes her discovery (experiential learning) that a post heart transplant surgery patient could not maintain good oxygenation when placed on the nonoperative side, a physiological principle that the new graduate would probably recognise in a formal, written test but that is more ambiguous to her in the actual situation.

Nurse: It kind of humbles you. [She realizes that the physiological explanation for this occurrence was straightforward, but that she had not been able to recognize the problem as manifested in the particular patient.] At one point, I'm feeling like I have things straight now, and I can handle the situations, and when something like this happens, I think, well, I still have a lot of learning to do. I can handle the situations that are status quo; it's the unexpected that I have to learn to deal with now. But then I think back to situations when I was brand new. Things that are status quo now weren't back then. Things I can trouble-shoot and solve now were much different back then. I usually needed help. (Benner et al., 2009, p. 95)

Anxiety is now more tailored to the situation than it was at the novice or advanced beginner stage when a general anxiety exists over learning and performing well without making mistakes. Coaching at this point should encourage competent-level nurses to follow through on a sense that things are not as usual, or even on vague feelings of foreboding or anxiety, because they have to learn to decide what is relevant with no rules to guide them. There is now enough of an experiential base to have these emotional responses to act like fuzzy recognition of similar and/or past clinical dissimilar situations. Nurses at this stage feel exhilarated when they perform well and feel remorse when they recognise that their performance could have been more effective or more prescient because they had paid attention to the wrong things or had missed relevant, subtle signs and symptoms. These emotional responses are the formative stages of aesthetic appreciation of good practice. These feelings of satisfaction and uneasiness with performance act as a moral compass that guides experiential ethical and clinical learning. There is a built-in tension between the deliberate rule- and maxim-based strategies of organising, planning, prediction and developing a more response-based practice (See critical-care study.)

... not needing help, ordering the task world, and planning based on goals and predictions structure what the nurse notices, and what are considered issues. It is not accidental that this vision of performance and agency is institutionally rewarded and encouraged as "standard". Structuring the day by goals and plans, however, interferes with perceiving the demands of the situation and with timing interventions in response to the patient's responses and readiness. The competent nurse seldom sees that signs and symptoms *have* taken on a new relevance in a clinical situation due to changes in the patient's condition. Their skill of seeing is hampered by the need to organise data collection and to achieve goals. Inevitably the clinical situation intrudes by not matching the goals and plans and the nurse must adapt ... conceptual descriptions do not automatically lead to recognition of actual signs, and varied responses require time to assimilate and interpret. Slavishly following one's plans and holding on to pre-set expectations can limit perceptual grasp ... Holding on to this deliberative form of agency (sense of personal influence in the situation) prevents the nurse from having expert clinical and ethical comportment because response-based organisation is not yet achieved. (Benner et al., 2009, pp. 88-89)

Experiential learning with past patient care enables the nurse to develop a greater sense of salience. As illustrated in the nurse's statement above, there is an increasing sense of when the nurse has or does not have a good clinical grasp of the situation. He or she can use his or her sense of confusion or questioning to propel his or her understanding of the clinical situation. Because nurses have now lived through more clinical futures, they can now better predict immediate likely events and needs of patients and can plan for them.

Toward the upper limits of competent performance, the nurse may begin to apprehend the limits of formal and practical knowledge. Nurses can now recognise that not everyone is a proficient or expert clinician, just at the point that they realise that they must develop a perspective on the situation to perform well in the situation. They typically buy more comprehensive reference works and medical and nursing textbooks at this point because loss in confidence in the advice of specific others may be overgeneralised, and consequently, the nurse may feel hyper-responsible. This inability to trust colleagues can be aggravated by encountering incompetence and a lack of social integration and informal coaching in the particular clinical unit.

Proficiency: A Transitional Stage on the Way to Expertise

It is the felt crisis in the limits of formalism and the limits of planning and prediction along with an enhanced ability to read the situation that may propel the nurse into the proficient stage of performance. Whereas skill development up until this point has been incremental, now the learner must make a qualitative leap in the way he or she engages and performs in the situation. The nurse must learn to situate himself or herself differently in relation to work. At this stage, first-person, experience-near narratives (Geertz, 1987) often take the form of describing situation changes. The narrative structure is often as follows: "I went into the situation thinking that I knew what was going on, or that this particular thing was going on, only to have it disconfirmed by the patient's responses to my assessment". This is evidence for developing the ability to let the situation guide nurses' responses.

The nurse is now synthesising the meaning of patients' responses through time. She imagines that a computer could capture all her readings, but she fails to recognise that her understanding of the patient is now situated, and based upon a practical understanding of the patient's responses (and qualitative changes) made over time rather than a collection of data points. The clinician struggles with articulating this practical grasp. Though difficult to articulate, this practical grasp is not mystical. It reflects the skill of seeing practical manifestations of changed physiological states, patient responses and noticing these transitions.

A practical grasp and engaged reasoning is perceptually grounded and response-based and requires being open to correction and disconfirmation as the situation unfolds. The clinician is always in the situation with some practical understanding, and this practical understanding is revised or confirmed. When the practitioner's grasp of the patient's clinical situation is jarred by changes or unexpected patient responses, the practitioner searches for a new grasp and deliberation becomes necessary and if all goes well, experiential clinical learning occurs. They describe the frustrating situation of "chasing a problem" and never being quite "in sync" with the situation when they do not have a good perceptual grasp of the situation at hand (Benner et al., 2009, 2011). The ethos of openness, rather than prediction and control, and fidelity to what one sees and hears, rather than excessive suggestibility and confusion, are embodied and linked to emotional responses to the situation. Thus, one's skilled emotional responsiveness guides perceptual acuity *and* responsiveness to changes in situations that are similar or dissimilar to past situations, but when novelty or surprise occurs, the nurse tries to identify why and how this situation is different (Benner et al., 2009).

The nurse gains a much more differentiated world of practice at the proficient level. The nurse feels increasingly at home in the situation and can now recognise when she or he has a good sense of the situation. In the following excerpt the nurse demonstrates this new comfort level by describing open-heart surgery trajectories.

> Nurse: I feel pretty comfortable, and you learn when they're warming to start giving the volume and when to stop because now maybe they need a little bit of Levophed to keep their blood pressure up, when to shut off the Levophed because they're waking up and you know their catecholamines have kicked in and that kind of thing. It's almost routine, whereas before it took a lot of trial and asking questions. This change is based on procedural knowledge and protocols, but the transition being described is the flexible recognition of patient changes in particular situations. This recognition occurs in the context of the predictable changes over time in a recovering heart surgery patient. These decisions cannot be based on quantitative physiological measures alone, but must be based on understanding the relationship between the numbers and the way the patient looks and responds. This form of response-based action is crucial for performing well in a rapidly changing emergency. (Benner et al., 2009, p. 112)

Because the proficient level nurse is learning to adjust his or her responses to the situation, the skill of both problem and person engagement becomes more differentiated and attuned. Observing nurses across situations reveals that they vary their relationships with patients and families based upon their understanding of what the situation requires. Timing becomes much more refined, and recognising opportunities in the situation for patient learning or for supporting a patient is now more attuned to the needs and concerns of the patient. Once begun, the proficient nurse usually continues to refine his or her reading of particular situations. Refining discriminations through deliberate comparisons with past experiences and other patients improves the nurse's grasp of the situation.

Expertise: Phrónêsis (Practical Wisdom)

Once a nurse has progressed to proficiency, the style of being a situated, response-based performer propels experiential learning and the ability to switch from taken-for-granted tacit expectations to switching to focusing on aspects of the situation that are changing and creating an altered sense of the situation. The expert nurse is response-based in using *tékhnê* and *phrónêsis*. The expert can now integrate his or her grasp of the situation with his or her responses. The expert is able to take up theories and ends of practice in multiple ways, often creating new possibilities in the situation (Taylor, 1991). These situated practical innovations or sensible variations in practice seem intuitively obvious to the practitioner and might not be captured easily in a narrative description of the situation. This is why observation and informal interviewing in actual situations are required to discover and describe all levels of practice, but particularly proficient and expert levels of practice. The innovations or sensible variations in practice typically make sense to others as the most effective response in the situation. They are not breaks with the understanding of good practice; rather, they extend good practice in challenging underdetermined situations. Ways of seeing the situation increasingly call for appropriate actions.

Intuitive links develop between seeing and responding to the situation. This was revealed in our research by observing nurses in practice. In extreme circumstances, possible responses are often fewer, and experienced nurses developed the capacity to see and respond, a performance shift from less experienced times. The amount of recognition and assessment language were minimal, in part, because the number of actions per problem were limited, but also because recognition and assessment language became so linked with actions and outcomes that they became self-evident or "obvious" for the expert practitioner. This is the kind of "maximum grasp" of the expert that is not available to the proficient performer. Immediate futures obvious to the expert order the situation. In this case the nurse becomes the situational leader because of this maximum grasp of this particular patient, and the sequence of events. The integrated rapid response is the hallmark of expertise (Benner et al., 2009).

Based on enriched experiential learning spawned by increasing ability to read the current situation in terms of their deep familiarity with similar and dissimilar situations, nurses develop a sense of whether they have a good (better or poorer) grasp of the situation. Skilled know-how now allows for more fluid and rapid performance of procedures. Narratives often focus on new clinical learning or troubling moral dilemmas or conflicts in the situation. Qualitative distinctions associated with nuanced responses make the nurse able to know and do more than he or she can tell or think to describe (Polanyi, 1958/1962). [This is expertise. Notice there is no talk here of innovation.]

Attunement allows for flexible fusion of thought, feeling and action. Seeing the unexpected based on having a rich set of expectations as well as a rich sense of the particular situation requires engagement with the patient and openness to notice when things do not go as implicitly expected, and evidence that disconfirm one's assumptions can be encountered (Benner et al., 2011). The relational skills of attunement to the patient's concerns and to the clinical situation create the possibility for patients and family members to disclose or reveal their concerns and fears to the nurse and for the nurse to notice changes in the patient or family across time (transitions). The quality of attentiveness and of the relationship literally creates different disclosive spaces and moods for the patient and family so that different clinical issues are noticed based on qualitatively different disclosive possibilities.

[This is as innovative as expertise gets.] Now it is possible to compare the expert's narrative below of the situation involving the patient who developed a carotid haemorrhage with the advanced beginner's account given earlier:

> I had worked late and was just about ready to go home, when a nurse preceptor said to me, "Jolene, come here." Her voice had urgency in it, but not Code Blue. I walked in and I looked at the patient and his heart rate was about 120, and he was on the respirator and breathing. And I asked her: "What's wrong?" There was a new graduate taking care of him. And he just pointed down to the patient who was lying in a pool of blood. There was a big stream of blood drooling out of his mouth. This man's diagnosis was mandibular cancer, which had been resected, and about a week previous to that he had had a carotid bleed from external carotid, which had been, ligated secondary to radiation erosion. That wound had become septic and he had developed respiratory failure and he was in ICU for that. So I looked at the dressing and it was dry, the blood was coming out of his mouth. The man had a tracheostomy because of the type of surgery that had been done. He also had an N.G. [Nasogastric] tube in for feedings, and I got to thinking that it might be the innominate or the carotid artery that had eroded. So we took him off the ventilator to see if anything was going to pump out of his trach. There was a little blood, but it looked mostly like it had come down from the pharynx into the lungs. So we began ventilating him, trying to figure what was inside his mouth that was pumping out this tremendous amount of blood. (Benner, 1984, p. 17)

This nurse went on to describe her quick actions to draw blood for a cross-match and typing and preparing the man for an immediate transfer to the operating room after marshalling all the resources for the surgical team. She gives us an immediate, direct grasp of the nature of the situation. Action, thought and feeling are fused. She evaluates the resistance in the lungs by hand ventilating the patient. Fortunately, because of her rapid responses, the patient survived the haemorrhage.

Expert practice, by its very nature, is of local, specific knowledge; know-how; and technical and scientific knowledge that is more transferable to other practice contexts. Because practice is a way of knowing through experiential learning and embodied know-how, it is highly valuable to study and articulate the knowledge embedded in highly complex practices such as nursing and medicine. Articulation of the knowledge embedded in proficient and expert practice, plus articulation of the range of practical knowledge learned by beginning practitioners in local settings, creates the possibility of self-improving practice based on making experiential learning public and therefore open to development so that experiential learning and practical wisdom becomes cumulative and shared.

REFLECTIONS ON THE DREYFUS MODEL

Each of the studies reported above was based on extensive first-person, experience-near narrative accounts of clinical situations that stood out in the participants' minds. In addition, a subsample of participants was observed and informally interviewed in their practice. We deliberately sampled nurses with a range of experience and reported skilfulness and interviewed nurses with like backgrounds in small group narrative interviews. We created an open dialogue with the tenets of the Dreyfus model of skill acquisition and the philosophical basis for this model. We found that the model was predictive and descriptive of distinct stages of skill acquisition in nursing practice. The most qualitatively distinct difference lies between the competent and proficient level, where the practitioner begins to read the situation. The proficient performer begins to increasingly change his or her perception of the nature of the situation and then deliberates about changing plans or strategies in response to the new understanding of the situation. The expert develops yet another qualitatively distinct way of being in the situation by developing the capacity to fluidly respond to the situation, even as the situation changes and the relevance of the actions taken change.

The study of nursing practice, because it is an underdetermined, complex practice that requires skilful comportment, articulation and highly developed relational skills, allowed us to identify qualitatively distinct forms of moral agency and skills of involvement at different levels of skill acquisition. The development of moral agency and the influence of emotional engagement with the person and the problem, as well as emotional climate, on skill acquisition vary distinctly at each stage of skill acquisition. For example, the advanced beginner focuses on getting everything done adequately. The competent nurse increases his or her ability to advocate for the patient, getting what the patient needs or requests. At the expert level, the moral agency and skills of involvement create disclosive spaces that would not have even been imagined at the earlier stages. New possibilities and notions of good practice are instantiated in more skilful, ethical comportment and relational capacities. Expert nurses are extremely pleased when they are able to comfort or assist patients in coping with the demands of their illnesses.

We found that nurses who had some difficulty with understanding the ends of practice and difficulty with their skills of interpersonal and problem engagement did not go on to become expert nurses (see Rubin, 2009). They literally thought of rational calculation as the scientific and objective way of practising, and thus, they failed to see significant moral concerns and failed to recognise qualitative distinctions between situations because they attempted to apply the same metric of rationally calculating odds, prevalence and evidence in each situation. This computational and calculative approach to practice, coupled with a disciplined stance of detachment, blocked experiential learning. The model was also useful in helping us articulate knowledge and skill embedded in the practice of nursing. The rational-technical vision of performance is that of a practitioner or technical expert developing mastery of a body of knowledge and applying that knowledge in prespecified ways for prespecified outcomes.

The rational-technical model does not account for development of relational, perceptual or skilful comportment over time. It also does not account for the role of experiential learning in learning to practice in a dynamic, underdetermined and complex practice such as nursing and medicine. A strict technical application of knowledge does not take into account the skills required for discerning the nature of the situation and its possibilities and constraints. Even the expert in the Dreyfus model of skill acquisition must stay attuned to the situation and must remain open to the unexpected. Practitioners must remain open to experiential learning and reading changes in transitions in fast-paced, open-ended environments. In the Dreyfus model, the practitioner is assumed to dwell with increasing skill and finesse in a meaningful, intelligible, but changing, world.

CONCLUSION

This research on the Dreyfus model of skill acquisition explored the transition of nurses from novices to experts. Through the deep exploration of this evolution this research has contributed significantly to understanding the way development expertise (wisdom) occurs through the actual experiences and narratives of nurses. In all of these research studies on development of expertise, expertise and practical wisdom are considered synonymous. In the Dreyfus model of skill acquisition research, "wisdom in action" is further delineated in terms of characteristics of human expert and masterful performance (Benner et al., 2009, 2011; Dreyfus & Dreyfus, 2005). Through the deep exploration of this evolution this research has contributed significantly to understanding the way development of expertise (wisdom) occurs through the actual experiences and narratives of nurses.

ACKNOWLEDGEMENTS

This chapter is derived from the following publication. The author holds copyright. Benner, P. (2005). Using the Dreyfus model of skill acquisition to describe and interpret skill acquisition and clinical judgment in nursing practice and education. *The Bulletin of Science, Technology and Society Special Issue: Human Expertise in the Age of the Computer, 24*(3) 188-199.

NOTE

[1] The first study was sponsored by a grant from the Department of Health and Human Services, Public Health Service, Division of Nursing, Bureau of Health Professions (Grant No. 7 D10 NU 29104-03). The Helene Fuld Health Trust funded the second and third studies.

REFERENCES

Benner, P. (1982). From novice to expert. *American Journal of Nursing, 82*, 402-407.
Benner, P. (1984). *From novice to expert: Excellence and power in clinical nursing practice*. Reading, NIA: Addison-Wesley.
Benner, P. (1994). The role of articulation in understanding practice and experience as sources of knowledge in clinical nursing. In J. Tully (Ed.), *Philosophy in an age of pluralism: The philosophy of Charles Taylor in question* (pp. 136-155). New York, NY: Cambridge University Press.
Benner, P., Hooper-Kyriakidis, P., & Stannard, D. (2011). *Clinical wisdom and interventions in acute and critical care: A thinking-in-action approach* (2nd ed.). Philadelphia, PA: W.B. Saunders.
Benner, P., Tanner, C. A., & Chesla, C. A. (1992). From beginner to expert: Gaining a differentiated clinical world in critical care nursing. *Advances in Nursing Science, 14*(3), 13-28.

Benner, P., Tanner, C. A., & Chesla, C. A. (2009). *Expertise in nursing practice: Caring, clinical judgment, and ethics* (2nd ed.). New York, NY: Springer.

Dreyfus, H. L., & Dreyfus, S. E. (1977). *Uses and abuses of multi-attribute and multi-aspect model of decision making* (Unpublished manuscript). Berkeley, CA: University of California.

Dreyfus, H. L., & Dreyfus, S. E. (1986). *Mind over machine: The power of human intuition and expertise in the era of the computer.* New York, NY: Free Press.

Dreyfus, H. L. & Dreyfus, S. E. (2005). Peripheral vision: Expertise in real world contexts. *Organization Studies, 26*(5), 779-792.

Dreyfus, S. E. (1982). Formal models vs. human situational understanding: Inherent limitations on the modeling of business expertise. *Office: Technology and People, 1,* 133-155.

Dreyfus, S. E., & Dreyfus, H. L. (1979). *The scope, limits, and training implications of three models of aircraft pilot emergency response behaviour* (Unpublished report). Berkeley, CA: University of California.

Dreyfus, S. E., & Dreyfus, H. L. (1980). *A five-stage model of the mental activities involved in directed skill acquisition* (Unpublished report). Berkeley, CA: University of California.

Dunne, J. (1997). *Back to the rough ground: Practical judgment and the lure of technique.* Notre Dame, IN: Notre Dame Press.

Gadamer, H. (1975). *Truth and method* (G. Barden & J. Cumming, Trans.). New York, NY: Seabury. (Original work published 1960)

Geertz, C. (1987). Deep play: Notes on the Balinese cockfight. In P. Rabinow & W. Sullivan (Eds.), *Interpretive social science: A second look* (pp. 195-240). Berkeley, CA: University of California Press.

MacIntyre, A. (1981). *After virtue: A study in moral theory.* Notre Dame, IN: University of Notre Dame Press.

Polanyi, M. (1962). *Personal knowledge: Towards a post-critical philosophy.* Chicago, IL: University of Chicago Press. (Original wok published 1958)

Rubin, J. (2009). *Impediments to the development of clinical knowledge and ethical judgment in critical care nursing* (2nd ed., pp. 171-198). New York, NY: Springer.

Shulman, L. S. (1993). Teaching as community property. *Change, 25,* 6-7.

Taylor, C. (1991). *Ethics of authenticity.* Cambridge, MA: Harvard University Press.

Taylor, C. (1993). Explanation and practical reason. In M. Nussbaum & A. Sen (Ed.), *The quality of life* (pp. 208-231). Oxford, England: Clarendon.

Patricia Benner PhD
Professor Emerita
Department of Social and Behavioral Sciences
University of California, San Francisco, United States of America

LESTER J. THOMPSON

20. HEALTH AND HUMAN SERVICE PROFESSIONALS AND PRACTICE WISDOM

Developing Rich Learning Environments

> Managerialism has seen a marked paradigm shift away from traditional professional values to embrace instead … expanded policy directives, decreased professional autonomy, increased accountability, altered ethical values, creeping proceduralism … and greater emphasis on social compliance and social control. (Lonne, 2003, p. 279)

> Unfortunately, as a result of [such][1] changes and resulting added pressures, many HCPs are burned out, a syndrome characterized by a high degree of emotional exhaustion and high depersonalization …, and a low sense of personal accomplishment. (Dyrbye et al., 2017, n.p.)

Healthcare professionals (HCPs) experience de-professionalisation, lethargy and burn-out when organisational pressures demand repetitive use of procedural skills (van Mol et al., 2015). The application of "mindfulness" processes can commonly be used when such pressures impact (van Mol et al., 2015) and enhanced personal characteristics like resilience and positive self-esteem are seen to help (Collins, 2007). This chapter uses social science knowledge to explain how motivated and highly accomplished helping-professionals maintain enthusiasm and functionality. Through recognising human needs for integrity and personal-efficacy, the self-affirmative processes of reflective mindfulness can be understood as value-based tools for enhancing performance and growth (Cohen & Sherman, 2014; Siegel, 2007). This provides insight into how the professional values of effective practitioners are maintained and how they encourage motivational processes which invigorate them over de-professionalised workers.

The discussion considers the development of undervalued forms of understanding as "practice wisdom" or *phrónêsis*, which is considered value-based because of its dependence upon an affective personal commitment to the pursuit of excellence (Lepper & Woolverton, 2002). Thus, critical exploration of professional mastery and wise practice requires some broad deliberation on the:

1. constitution of wisdom as a process being engaged in, rather than possessed
2. values and the ethical dedication which motivate its commitment
3. critical insights and the personal confidence required when innovating.

Throughout this early discussion, the underpinnings of wise, effective professionalism are examined. This enquiry provides insight into the development of deeply personal values (commitments) and virtues (self-efficacies) which promote wise practice in dynamic social contexts.

THE CONSTITUTION OF WISDOM: OWNED CONTENT OR PROCESS?

McPherson's (2005) exploration of knowledge applies sophisticated analyses to the learning of practical wisdom. It commences by critiquing mechanical metaphors about upskilling drivers and expert technicians. Its explanation of *phrónêtic* learning (achieving wisdom) builds on a model of expertise which transitions through:

- unconscious incompetence (unawareness of deficits)
- conscious incompetence (awareness of naïveté)
- conscious competence (deliberative but non-spontaneous)
- unconscious competence (see Figure 20.1).

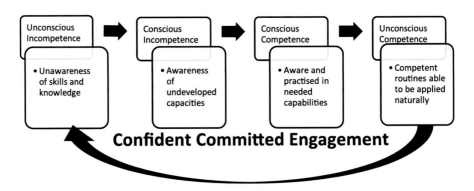

Figure 20.1. *Critical learning for mastery.*

Unconscious competence highlights internal (automatised) processes which allow ongoing aptitude when carrying out complex but mechanical activities. Professionals faced with routine client cases might also achieve this unconscious competence about consistently applying familiar empirical, theoretical and even procedural knowledge (Thompson & West, 2013), yet the complexity of human needs might then require committed engagement with intuitive and creative steps towards new challenges – "the unexplored". This analysis thus progresses towards accepting that spirited engagement in competent interpersonal activity requires self-esteem when professionals self-confidently meet new and unfamiliar challenging contexts.

It is evident, then, that this application of multiple knowledges requires self-motivation about challenges, appreciation of flawed analyses, positive self-value and some discernment recognising unknowns. It thus expects a tacit capacity for critically examining and valuing self-efficacy or accepting incompetence (Cohen & Sherman, 2014; Collins, 2007) (see Figure 20.1).

Though "explicit knowledge" about facts or theory might be easily identified and transmitted, the "tacit" (including value-based) knowledge required when meeting new challenges is intangible, highly personal and too informal to communicate. Because this knowledge is specific to the individual, it is built within the worldview and understanding of the person concerned. The challenge of learning to be tacitly knowledgeable is that it commences when existing analyses and intuitions are used in reviewing personal identity, judging weaknesses and predicting what is to be learned from experiences. Whitaker and Reimer (2017) explore this process as a contextual matter requiring a personal commitment to critical reflection on identity in complex social situations. Thus, learning to be wise is not about being taught, but about reflective examination of personal use of knowledge, personal effectiveness and how revisions and reconsiderations enlighten practices in context.

McPherson's (2005) critique of mechanical metaphors provides a base understanding of routine practice upon which interpersonal knowledge and value-based reflective practice can be considered. For example, health and human service practices might parallel craft-based mastery, when interpersonal communication modes and human relationship skills are routinely applied like tools of trade. Yet, if wisdom is about helping clients, rather than just applying tools, then reflection on success and failure is needed for new communication modes which encourage satisfaction. Innovation in uncovering these unknowns then requires a reflectively developed openness and interactive sensitivity. Those motivated by the drive to care for others could proceed furthest in these two areas of openness and sensitivity, but only by exploring "self" as a relationship-building tool. Such ethically-driven "use of self" deemphasises technical/rational assessment skills and theory to emphasise more nuanced activities in the creation of sociality, relationships and shared-understanding (Rossiter, 2011). Thus, in human relations, mastery is driven, not by unconsciously applied knowledge-based competencies, but by unconscious ethical, relational and reflective processes. It is a value-based commitment to people.

If, in summary, wise practice is about sustained commitment to care through ethics, relationality and reflection, then its development pertains to the nature of the person involved. The subsequent development of a wiser "self" must be a structured process regarding the systematic identification of interpersonal skills for trust-building, engagement, relationships and information transfer, but it must also involve character building or personal growth. Such (reflective) development is normally considered to be a process that acknowledges the reflexive nature of identity formation and involves post-order re-examination of key events for their contextualised importance and human impact. By interpreting the actual, theoretical and emotional content of interactions, individuals determine not just what has happened, but who they are becoming as engaged, relational beings. These theoretical and emotional examinations of interactive events help to define both ontological reality and the identity of the participants. This dynamic reflection influences personal values, ethics, insights and self-concept, thereby encouraging commitment to the pursuit of wisdom. Though the components of wisdom cannot be captured and possessed, the development of wisdom can be examined as a personal growth project involving a strategic devotion to ethics and personal growth which emphasises the motivating effect of certain values.

IDENTITY: VALUES AND ETHICS IN PHRÓNÊTIC COMMITMENT

Consistent with the discussed reflective, value-based constitution of wisdom, Aristotle (349 BC/2004) defined *phrónêsis* as socially practical but not technical prudence. He saw it as ethical by nature, as contextually appropriate and as a general value-based rationality. It was not about wisely applying universal truths and routines (i.e. *sophia*) but about innovative rational thinking about how to act well in varying contexts (Aquileana, n.d.). Thus, personal values and virtues define the core commitments of developing wisdom, and as such there should be consideration of Aristotle's (*eudaimonic*) concerns regarding the ethical drive for decency and a good life. Professionalism could be examined as the pursuit of a "higher calling" characterised by those *eudaimonic* values which motivate a commitment to excellence when helping others.

Recent understanding about the close links between values, emotions and motives allows *phrónêtic* development (a professional personal growth project) to be partially understood as a value-driven motivational matter. Personal *phrónêtic* development can be seen to require some individual commitment to higher mastery, focused by the pursuit of personal understanding (growth) which provides *eudaimonic* fulfilment (high-level satisfactions). Logically, the values that encourage intrinsic personal growth drives are important. They provide direction for personal commitment through confident action and a commitment to wise practice. This requires an examination of personal motives personal motives that promote this commitment, what Maslow (1943) called the self-actualisation motive. Analysis involves the *eudaimonic* drives that encourage each professional to effectively help their clients so as to achieve personal satisfaction and the desire to continue.

Wisdom demands some pursuit of insight, which itself requires committed integration and critical examination of knowledge that is empirical, theoretical and procedural (see Figure 20.2).

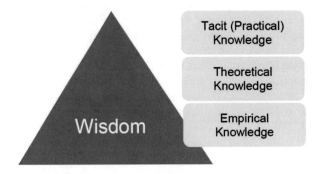

Figure 20.2. The reflective precursors to wisdom.

IDENTITY: INSIGHT AND CONFIDENCE AS PHRÓNÊTIC COMMITMENT

Socratic ideas of wisdom centre on the understanding that it is not what we know that constitutes wisdom, but our confident willingness to recognise what we don't (Dybicz, 2004). In a highly personal account about her mental health, the academic, Joanna Fox (2017) substantiated this idea, highlighting the rewards of "experiential" wisdom derived from "service users and carers" (p. 481). It seems that when professional discourse fixes upon "user expert" awareness, rather than specialist proficiency, personal experiences can be acknowledged, professional alienation overcome and welfare improved (Fox, 2017). In this case, professional wisdom involves engagement in "dialogue and partnership in a participatory process within a paradigm of constructivism" (Samson, 2015, p. 123). This case study unlocks for consideration the idea that there are several ways that masterful practitioners prepare themselves to "wisely" open their minds and approach new insights when theoretical expertise (content) is inadequate. Wisdom is here understood as a relational social-construction process involving reflection upon human engagements (Fox, 2017), affective identity development and new meaning. A personal drive to care (ethics), and a confident pursuit of new insight opened professional knowledge up to valorised client knowledge and new understanding (Rossiter, 2011).

DEFINING PRACTICE WISDOM AS ACHIEVABLE PHRÓNÊTIC PRACTICE

> Discussing practice wisdom, including common sense, practice-based knowledge, tacit knowledge and process knowledge, is not a new agenda ... Nevertheless, it remains debatable whether it is possible to be cognitively aware of the non-cognitive facets of one's thoughts. (Cheung, 2017, p. 25)

The paradox presented by Cheung requires that the first aim of this discussion is to define the Socratic conceptualisation of practice wisdom as a concept that can be understood, examined and then practically worked upon to engage *phrónêsis*. Such deliberation demands an openness to change (Seligson, 2004) and wisdom thereafter appears, not as something owned, but as something that is virtuously engaged with and committed to. After combining these themes, logic then portrays the pursuit of wisdom in terms of the following themes for examination:

1. critical methods using evidence, theory and tacit understanding of complexity in human needs
2. a critical but self-assured dedication to discovery
3. a dynamic capacity for employing existing understanding in innovative, creative explorations and new methods of enquiry (Kline & Bloom, 1995).

Dybicz (2004) developed a concept of practice wisdom that acknowledged these factors and was "more ... a process than a product" (p. 199). In heeding the Socratic view of wisdom as technique, applied to exposing ignorance, he elevated the active search for missing knowledge and emphasised (subsequent) mindful awareness of learning needs (Dybicz, 2004).

Goldstein's (1990) "competent action" model of practice wisdom permitted more recent interpretations to conceptualise it as, commitment to "processes" rather than skills or knowledge. These processes might then expose a strategy for overcoming Cheung's paradox (above) about identifying and observing the unknown. If "commitment to competent practice and a willingness to maintain that practice are hallmarks of a professional" (Rigney & Cooper, 2004, p. 51), then the achievement of dynamic wise-practice requires that a professional be motivated to actively judge both the needs of situations and the facets of their own knowledge. The active processes of wisdom can be seen as dynamic interplays of "insights, skill and values" routinely applied when judging a complex world (Dybicz, 2004, p. 200). Judging complex situations may be knowledge-based, in regard to applying relevant facts, theory and tacit knowledge; yet when assessing the limitations of existing knowledge (reflecting), there is a need for critical skills, intuition (Halverson, 2004) and value-based judgement (Dybicz, 2004). The judgement process requires the development of an affective preparedness for investigation and an openness to cooperative enquiry and knowledge generation. Thus, it is challenging to judge what knowledge "should" be in place, and this process must be seen as an affective dedication to critical, intuitive and creatively exploratory processes, as described in Figure 20.3.

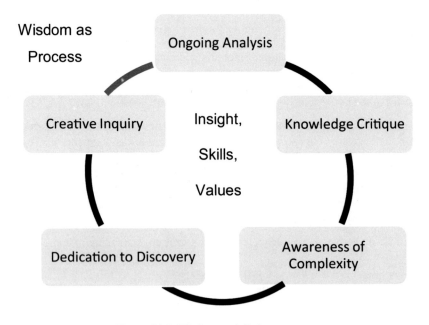

Figure 20.3. Wisdom modelled as a process.

Just as wisdom is a process involving a commitment to new understanding, this requires reflective practice which is a preparedness to critique the use of self, "use of self" training, involving critical examination of past practice (reflection) and modelling and practice that is developed using "purposeful" dynamic-reflective techniques. Ericsson and Pool's (2016) exposition of "expertise" systematically considers developmental techniques for complex professional capabilities including the "use of self" but, unlike skill-development in sport or trade work, dedicated critical discovery requires fundamental changes in the psycho-social identity of the professional. This deliberation demands "a nondefensive attitude ... understanding that one is never above improvement" (Seligson, 2004, p. 533).

In clarifying a philosophical picture of practice wisdom as *phrónêsis*, McPherson (2005) built upon Dreyfus and Dreyfus' (1988) staged learning model. By supplementing this wisdom-unaware model, he apprehended two later stages recognising "mastery" and "practice wisdom" (Dreyfus, 2001; McPherson, 2005). In contrast with earlier mechanistic learning ideas, which focused upon repetition, habituation and "automatisation of schemas", the last two stages, when combined, demand reflexive self-examination and insight into personal coherence, integrity, judgement, prioritisation and values. A committed focus must valourise the continuous examination of processes. These values motivate the search to discover what is unknown, until this creative agenda ceases to be unusual. Preconceptions and predispositions are reflected upon in wise decision making, so that professionals value self-responsibility for better decision making, planned investigation and personal transformation.

Good practice requires more than fluid competence formed around the ownership of appropriate content knowledge. It requires that professionals are value and affectively driven to continually: apprehend reality; audit activity; humbly criticise their knowledge base; consider alternate knowing; reflect upon life skills; and apply intuition to challenge existing applications of knowledge and skills. This is obviously a commitment beyond the expectations of common "rational-actor" predictions of managerial behaviour, especially regarding maximising personal outcomes for effort and efficiently achieving performance indicators. In spite of managerial elevations of objectivity and evidence (Thompson & Wadley, 2016), "reflective practice is preferable to evidence-based practice [as] ... the process of decision-making in the real world is, in fact, context-dependent" and complex (Cheung, 2017, p. 30). The *phrónêtic* exploration of new knowledge comes about as a result of an institutionalised personal (professional) commitment to directed but relationally-engaged (interactive) reflective practices.

VALUES AND REAL-WORLD MOTIVATIONAL MATTERS: WHY BE WISE?

Though, in the "short to medium" term, managerial administrative systems are unlikely to extrinsically reward any professional commitment to knowledge auditing and *phrónêsis*, in the longer term the drive to achieve wise practice might raise professional status, the "esteem" of others and the employability of wise practitioners. Thus, there can be personal rewards involved in a longer-term commitment to the pursuit of wisdom. Deferring gratification and committing (intrinsically) to better practice is required in the search for what might be called "*eudaimonic* wellbeing" or the pursuit of a better life (McIntyre, 1999). This benefit means that personal values can drive the pursuit of wisdom and that professional learning should acknowledge the centrality of value-based development for good practice (Rigney & Cooper, 2004).

McPherson (2005) saw in *phrónêtic* development a deliberate integration of insight and a commitment to the understanding of diversity in worldviews. This awareness tends to highlight the feelings of reward gained through insight itself. McPherson (2005), like many others, perceived wisdom as based upon both a dedication to reflexive engagement with other views, and an active interpretation of the self in relation to others.

Samson (2015) extended this reflexive (rather than reflective) interpretation, recognising that "the helping process encompasses creativity, intuition and inductive reasoning in combination with values, morals and beliefs" (p. 122). He argued that it was not just about critically applying theories, procedures and auditing processes; rather, wisdom required a dynamic self-reflexive value-driven and ethical analysis in "connection with the world". In accord with Aristotelian philosophy, the rewards of reflection lie in a better understanding of self, personal motives and how to be *eudaimonically* happy. Beyond creativity and insight, self-reflexive engagement with values is important to personal insight when melding art and theory in practice such that professionals feel self-actualised.

Summarising the *phrónêtic* learning model from these outlines, it is logical to view good practice as dependent upon professional commitment to, and confident engagement with, the application of critical reflection and engaged reflexive development. Knowledge-based competence is needed as a baseline, but wisdom builds upon this as commitment to processes that confidently engage with: a recognition of the limits of personal knowledge bases; personal strength in exploring the unknown; and a motivation which subverts pressures regarding managerial performance indicators. Though this logic highlights the importance of values and personal virtue, it still underplays Aristotle's perspective regarding the importance of ethical values. Rossiter (2011) sees professional virtue not as achieved by "intelligibility, but by sociality—the moment at which we are receptive to the revelation from the Other" (p. 988). In this view, relations are central to human satisfaction and professional wisdom holds its own rewards in bringing individuals closer together so that they can take pleasure in their relationships. Reflection and practice excellence provide their own rewards and are self-motivating.

BUILDING VALUE-BASED COMMITMENT AND AFFECTIVE CONFIDENCE

If, at its most basic, practice wisdom lies in recognising the limitations of our knowledge then wise practitioners must be committed to reflective (and reflexive) development, must be self-assured about doing so and must be effective in this dynamic aim (Dybicz, 2004). As professionals are characterised by both tertiary educational achievement (qualifications) and the expectation of wisdom (*phrónêtic* growth), this discussion argues that normal professional value-based training should be used in learning environments. Such motivation might be encouraged, first by reinforcing confident achievement and, second, by rewarding *phrónêtic* commitment to reflection (Seligson, 2004). Halverson (2004) argued that "the only way to learn about practice wisdom is to turn to mentoring or apprenticeship and to participate in the lifeworld of the phronimos" (p. 119).

Though the traditions of Socratic and Aristotelian teachings supported the idea that mentoring is paramount in the pursuit of wisdom, it has been possible to alternately encourage professional values and commitment, (Fisher & Somerton, 2000) and to support confident reflection on better practice (Fook, 2016). By examining the social construction of good practice, insight can be gained into how to promote the values which exploit innate motivation and support growing confidence and commitment.

Though the need to care arguably represents an innate driver of behaviour, its enactment is determined by culturally defined professional values (Thompson & Wadley, 2016; Thompson & West, 2013). In his *Archaeology of Knowledge*, Foucault (1969) explained how all knowledge is socially determined. Thus, as each parameter of wisdom is collectively constructed, it varies across ethnicities and boarders. Though caring is considered an innate drive, caring ethics will vary such that enquiry is required if personal motivations are to be understood and if initial encouragement is to be effective. The pursuit of socially (professionally) approved theory and the creative review of practices (recently, "client expertise") are similar critical cultural challenges. In the view of Gilligan (1982), both the perception of being cared for, and of caring for others, are satisfying rewards after ethical activity. Thus caring-ethics are a potential motivator of professional reflective action which promotes caring assistance for clients and feelings of relational closeness and contentment (see Figure 20.4). Professional acculturation processes might initially apply encouragement as a reward to those learning about wise, reflective practices. The encouragement of learners might promote those feelings of care which are experienced as satisfactions after the human need for care. The achievement of satisfaction is a reward that will promote associated behaviours, such as reflection.

As commitment and confidence are personal virtues rather than capabilities, they demand some personal passion. If interactive "knowledge generation" is a central imperative of practice wisdom, then this passion must be drawn out and encouraged in its pursuit. Such passions are driven by strongly held values about what is important and pursuable. Especially in the human-service professions, the desire to assist others for better health, welfare and satisfaction aligns with the desire to live a rewarding life (*eudaimonia*). Such reflective dynamism can become an effective driver of intrinsic-motivation for practice wisdom when personal values esteem success through wise practice.

Practice wisdom can be encouraged by directly reinforcing those learners who reflect on events, who judge their meaning and then who consider how to reapply their meaning (or cast more broadly) in future events. Encouragement and guidance should be given until successes result in enough self-esteem that affective confidence becomes a basis for motivation (Baumeister, 1993). Goleman (1996) implies that professionals can achieve such self-motivating reflection. The reflective goals which individuals set for themselves are influenced by needs for affiliation and achievement and thus confidence about such successes provides a source of motivation (Butler, 2007; Lewthwaite & Piparo, 2002; (Elliot et al., 1999).

Figure 20.4. Motivation and virtue: Phrónêtic processes.

The goals of affiliation may be partially met by a mentor who assists learners to observe events, connect these with patterns and meaning, and reapply learning in somewhat similar circumstances. This process assists motivation, yet Westberg and Hilliard (2001) additionally emphasise the role of achievement, stating that:

> there are two key ways to help others learn from experience, ... First, we must help them to become reflective practitioners who regularly think about and assess their work and invite the reflections and feedback of others ... Second, we must give them timely, constructive feedback on their work and self-assessments. (p. vii)

Amy Rossiter's (2011) work reconceptualises human service practice using client rather than professional expertise as fundamental knowledge (feedback). By placing ethics, rather than expert-knowledge, as the driving influence on practice, she emphasises affiliation motives and learned values about caring achievements. Such a pursuit of ethical virtue rather than informed action highlights the eudaimonic desire to live a good life through engagement and care. This important acknowledgement of ethics as the impetus for collaborative client service highlights the motivational significance of caring and opens for consideration the role that innate drives might play in informing the development of professional wisdom. If learning strategy is seeking to prompt and routinise reflective practice, and to motivate *phrónêtic* processes, then the affective drive-to-care might be a foundation, or core drive, for nurturing within the educative process. Learning to engage with client knowledge might substitute for a mentor's assistance when recognising the quality of newly found knowledge. Reflection on achievements might come to positively reinforce the process (as in Figure 20.5).

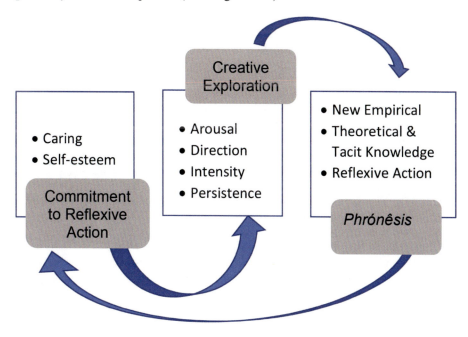

Figure 20.5. Eudaimonic motivation, reflection, innovation and wisdom.

Phrónêtic development can be encouraged when a personal commitment to critical exploration of knowledge (Rigney & Cooper, 2004; Cheung, 2017) is esteemed and rewarded to promote a higher personal value for knowledge integration and reflection. Thus, value-based, process and affective changes create a *eudaimonic* identity within which intrinsic motivation continually drives reflexive practice in the pursuit of *phrónêtic* habits or wisdom. Reflection has long been considered an essential component of professionalism (see Schön, 1983) and, though it has been encouraged within social work education, the dynamics of its longer-term encouragement received less consideration until recently (Thompson & West, 2013). This work has contradicted expectations about the centrality of mentoring. Arguments about the motivational nature of *eudaimonic* (*phrónêtic*) commitment seem to provide useful analyses and strategies for *phrónêtic* learning throughout a professional life rather than just during the educational phase. Commitment to reflection seems central.

CONCLUSION

As professionalism is founded upon professional ethics, professional education has assumed that professional values can be encouraged in practice. It is known that values underpin motives and that these value-based commitments can drive profession energy. This discussion has assumed that values can be learned through educative processes such as mentoring and also encouragement towards reflective practices. The implication is that value-based learning can drive professionals towards an affective determination to seek wisdom and become wise practitioners. The nature of wisdom has been shown to be less about possessed knowledge (content) and more about an affective "preparedness" regarding the desire to engage in learning processes. As such, wisdom is a virtue regarding openness to new ideas and a demonstrated intuition regarding how to develop new content and process knowledge. The pursuit of new knowledge is difficult to define when a learner does not know what is needed. It is, however, argued that engaging with others is the key to dealing with a paradoxical need to find direction when seeking to explore the unknown. It is thus suggested that value-based learning builds upon caring desires and personal confidence to promote value-driven commitment to relationships and competent reflective practices.

Educational strategy in healthcare should address professional values regarding lifelong learning and commitment to *phrónêtic* reflection in demanding work contexts. Experiential learning and motivation in the workplace are therefore important areas for consideration if the affective, process and value-based precursors of wisdom are to inoculate professionals against toxic managerialism. Arguments have already established constructive feedback as a reinforcement regime and reflective mindfulness as a response to burnout. This implies an intuitive rather than theoretical consensus about interrelations between motivation, reflective practice and self-esteem (see Collins, 2007; Fisher & Somerton, 2000). Goleman (1996) provides reason to consider "helping" and "constructive feedback" as motivating factors in a shared narrative of good practice.

If individuals perceive their particular desires for development as important to professional success and if they see that increased effort in the workplace leads to success, then their need for affiliation and achievement will promote on-the-job arousal, direction, intensity and persistence (Robbins et al., 2003) in respect to reflective practice. The self-efficacious (confident) setting of valued goals about wise practice will thus influence the persistence, focus, intensity and therefore motivation (commitment) to achieve these perceived needs. Learned affective, process-based and value-driven aspects of professional identity become the virtues of wise practitioners whose self-esteem and resilience promote professional success.

NOTE

[1] Such changes pertain particularly to administration and reporting related managerial pressures in high pressure medical contexts. The influences are parallel.

REFERENCES

Aquileana. (n.d.). *La audacia de Aquiles: El mundo visible es sólo un pretexto* [The audacity of Achilles: The visible world is just a pretext]. Retrieved from https://aquileana.wordpress.com/2014/02/01/aristotles-three-types-of-knowledge-in-the-nichomachean-ethics-techne-episteme-and-phronesis/

Aristotle. (2004). *The Nicomachean ethics* (J. A. K. Thomson, Trans., revised by H. Tredennick). London, England: Penguin Classics. (Original work published 349 BC)

Butler, R. (2007) Teachers' achievement goal orientations and associations with teachers' help seeking: Examination of a novel approach to teacher motivation. *Journal of Educational Psychology*, 99(2), 241-252

Chan, K. L., & Chan C. L. W. (2004). 'Social workers' conceptions of the relationship between theory and practice in an organizational context. *International Social Work*, 47(4), 553-557.

Cheung, J. C.-S. (2017). Practice wisdom in social work: An uncommon sense in the intersubjective encounter. *European Journal of Social Work*, 20(5), 619-629.

Cohen, G. L., & Sherman, D. K. (2014). The psychology of change: Self-affirmation and social psychological intervention. *Annual Review of Psychology, 65*(1), 333-371.

Collins, S. (2007). Statutory social workers: Stress, job satisfaction, coping, social support and individual differences. *British Journal of Social Work, 38,* 1173-1193.

Dreyfus, H. (2001). *On the internet*. London, England: Routledge.

Dreyfus, H. L., & Dreyfus, S. E. (1988). *Mind over machine: The power of human intuition and expertise in the era of the computer*. New York, NY: Free Press.

Dybicz, P. (2004). An inquiry into practice wisdom. *Families in Society: The Journal of Contemporary Social Services, 85*(2), 197-204.

Dyrbye, L. N., Shanafelt, T. D., Sinsky, C. A., Cipriano, P. F., Bhatt, J., Ommaya, A., West, C. P., & Meyers, D. (2017). *Burnout among health care professionals: A call to explore and address this under recognized threat to safe, high-quality care* (Discussion Paper). Washington, DC: National Academy of Medicine. Retrieved from https://nam.edu/burnout-among-health-care-professionals-a-call-to-explore-and-address-this-underrecognized-threat-to-safe-high-quality-care

Elliot, A. J., McGregor, H. A. & Gable, S. (1999) Achievement Goals, Study Strategies and Exam Performance: A Meditational Analysis. *Journal of Educational Psychology*, 91(3), 549-563.

Ericsson, A., & Pool R., (2016). *Peak: Secrets from the new science of expertise*. Boston, MA: Houghton Mifflin Harcourt.

Fisher, T., & Somerton, J. (2000). Reflection on action: The process of helping social work students to develop their use of theory in practice. *Social Work Education, 19*(4), 387-401.

Fook, J. (2016). *Social work: A critical approach to practice.* London, England: Sage.

Fox, J. (2017). The contribution of experiential wisdom to the development of the mental health professional discourse. *Schizophrenia Bulletin, 43*(3), 481-485.

Foucault, M. (1969). *The archaeology of knowledge*. New York, NY: Pantheon Books.

Gilligan, C. (1982). *In a different voice: Psychological theory and women's development*. London, England: Harvard University Press.

Goldstein, H. (1990). The knowledge base of social work practice: Theory, wisdom, analogue, or art? *Families in Society, 71*(1), 32-43.

Goleman, D. (1996). *Emotional intelligence: Why it can matter more than IQ*. London, England: Bloomsbury.

Halverson, R. (2004). Accessing, documenting, and communicating practical wisdom: The phronesis of school leadership practice. *American Journal of Education, 111*(1), 90-122.

Klein, W. C., & Bloom, M. (1995). Practice wisdom. *Social Work, 40*(6), 799-807.

Lepper, M., & Woolverton, M. (2002). The wisdom of practice: Lessons learned from the study of highly effective tutors. In J. Aronson (Ed.), *Improving academic achievement: Impact of psychological factors on education* (pp. 135-158). Orlando, FL: Academic Press.

Lewthwaite, R. & Piparo, A. J. (2002) Goal Orientations in Young Competitive Athletes: Physical Achievement, Social–Relational, and Experiential Concerns. *Journal of Research in Personality*, 27(2), 103-117.

Lonne, R. L. (2003). Social workers and human service practitioners. In M. F. Dollard, A. H. Winefield, & H. R. Winefield (Eds.), *Occupational stress in the service professions* (pp. 281-310). London, England: Taylor & Francis.

Maslow, A. H. (1943). A theory of human motivation. *Psychological Review, 50*(4), 370-396.

McIntyre, A. (1999). *Dependent rational animals: Why human beings need the virtues*. London, England: Duckworth.

McPherson, I. (2005). Reflexive learning: Stages towards wisdom with Dreyfus. *Educational Philosophy and Theory, 37*(5), 705-718.

Rigney, D., & Cooper, L. (2004). Preparing for practice. In J. Maidment & R. Egan (Eds.), *Practice skills in social work and welfare* (pp. 51-68). Crows Nest, Australia: Allen & Unwin.

Robbins, S., Bergman, R., Stagg, I., & Coulter, M. (2003) *Management* (3rd ed.). Frenchs Forest, Australia: Prentice Hall.

Rossiter, A. (2011). Unsettled social work: The challenge of Levinas's ethics. *British Journal of Social Work, 41*(5), 980-995.

Samson, P. L. (2015). Practice wisdom: The art and science of social work. *Journal of Social Work Practice, 29*(2), 119-131.

Schön, D. A. (1983). *The reflective practitioner: How professionals think in action*. New York, NY: Basic Books.

Seligson, L. V. (2004). Beyond technique: Performance and the art of social work practice. *Families in Society: The Journal of Contemporary Social Services, 85*(4), 531-538.

Siegel, D. J. (2007). *The mindful brain: Reflection and attunement in the cultivation of wellbeing*. New York, NY: W.W. Norton & Co.

Thompson, L. J., & Wadley, D. A. (2016). Countering globalisation and managerialism: Relationist pedagogy and ethics in social work. *International Social Work*. doi:10.1177/0020872816655867

Thompson, L. J., & West, D. (2013). Professional development in the contemporary educational context: Encouraging practice wisdom. *Social Work Education: The International Journal, 32*(1), 118-133.

van Mol M. M. C., Kompanje, E. J. O. Benoit, D. D., Bakker J., & Nijkamp M. D. (2015). The prevalence of compassion fatigue and burnout among healthcare professionals in intensive care units: A systematic review. *PLOS One, 10*(8), e0136955.

Westberg, J., & Hilliard, J. (2001). *Fostering reflection and providing feedback: Helping others learn from experience*. New York, NY: Springer.

Whitaker, L., & Reimer, E. (2017). Students' conceptualisations of critical reflection. *Social Work Education, 36*(8), 946-958.

Lester J. Thompson PhD (ORCID: https://orcid.org/0000-0002-6534-4184)
School of Health
University of New England, Australia

RODD ROTHWELL

21. THE PLACE OF WISDOM IN CLINICAL PRACTICE

Taking a Vygotskyian Approach

This chapter explores the notion of wisdom and its importance in clinical practice. The question of the place of wisdom in effective professional practice and how it is acquired has been the subject of recent interest among professional educators as well as health professionals. This interest has been motivated by what has been seen by a number of writers as a gap or inadequacy in the conceptualisation and articulation of professional skills and decision making; of what it means to be a good practitioner. Among others, Kemmis (2012), and Kinsella and Pitman (2012b), have expressed concern about the domination in professional training of an instrumentalist positivistic value system. Kinsella and Pitman (2012a) express this concern thus:

> We were grappling with a sense that something of fundamental importance – of moral significance – was missing in the vision of what it means to be a professional, and in the ensuing educational aims in professional schools and continuing professional education. (p. 1)

The question I wish to explore in this chapter is what is "missing" or what is the "gap" in professional practice, how is it acquired (can it be taught and learned) and how does it differ from what we may refer to as instrumentalist knowledge or "practical know-how", that some academics argue dominates profession practice and professional decision making? To address this goal I will firstly overview some current work that seeks to address this gap in practice by drawing on Aristotle's notion of practical wisdom (*phrónêsis*) as a model for professional judgement and decision making. Following this I will explore how certain current practices in the professions serve to diminish the role of practical wisdom and encourage a positivistic oriented techno-scientific approach. I will argue that the Evidence–Based Practice movement which has expanded into most professions and many non-professional areas has served with its "means ends" philosophy to reduce the role of professional decision making. Thirdly, I will offer some suggestions of how practical wisdom may be restored to practice – how it may be acquired – by an exploration of the work of the Russian psychologist/philosopher Vygotsky. I will suggest that Vygotsky's notion of the Zone of Proximal Development (ZPD) may offer a model for the acquisition of practical wisdom.

Much of the work on characterising this missing quality of practical wisdom has been in the field of education which has highlighted aspects of teaching and judgements that require more than abstract knowledge and a set of (or a list of) abstract skills or competencies. Some academics in the professional practice field refer to this additional requirement as "practical wisdom". Cooke and Carr (2014) refer to this in the context of teaching as:

> A practical enterprise (that) seems to require flexible and adaptable context-sensitive judgement in complex and ever-changing circumstances, it would also appear to defy reduction to any simple or unexceptionable set of rules or prescriptions, or to the mastery of a pre-specifiable repertoire of technical competencies. (p. 96)

Cooke and Carr and many others draw on Aristotle's notion of *phrónêsis* or practical wisdom as a model for effective teaching practice. *Phrónêsis* is considered a particularly apt concept as it suggests something more than cognitive meaning and practical "know-how" knowledge, referring to the achievement of a form of wisdom or a moral judgement where practice decisions take into account both facts and know-how, although these facts and know-how do not serve and cannot serve to determine the action or decision taken.

Aristotle distinguishes *phrónêsis* from two forms of knowledge he refers to as *epistêmê* and *tékhnê*. *Epistêmê* refers to what we today would call scientific knowledge; abstract, objective, context independent knowledge and empirical research can provide us with such knowledge. *Tékhnê* is practical knowledge, or craft knowledge that is practical and driven by conscious goals. In contrast, *phrónêsis* comprises a form of knowledge that involves value judgements based on reflection and on experience. It does not exclude knowledge of any sort but seeks to ensure that knowledge should be applied for the "good". Referring to "the good" (or "the virtuous") implies such decisions are value based and incorporate the emotions or (in Aristotelean terms) "the Passions". The terms "emotions" and "values" are often seen by practitioners to be avoided as they are said to lead one away from objective research-based judgements. But *phrónêsis* does not exclude either *epistêmê* or *tékhnê* or theoretical and practical knowledge though they are distinct.

To act with practical wisdom (*phrónêsis*) in a specific clinical and professional practice context implies that the competent practitioner will be aware of and sensitive to the specific morals and needs of the situation and will act in accordance with what is good, decent and fair for the client or patient for their "wellbeing". Such judgement cannot be constrained by any set of abstract principles or codified rules, or even guidelines, because such rules/laws/guidelines cannot determine their own application to specific situations. "You cannot remove the agency of the professional to a passive application of universal (abstract) principles to particular circumstances … judgement is required" (Abizadeh, 2002, p. 270). Judgement or professional decision making in specific circumstances however will require the guidance of the research evidence (evidence-based practice), although this information (or data) cannot determine or provide all the information for decisions that have to be made in that specific situation. Scientific findings, laws or guidelines do not provide sufficient information for decisions in relation to how they are to be applied.

It is not the intention of this chapter to go into the details and debates around Aristotle's notion of *phrónêsis*. My goal is to suggest that it is crucial to professional practice. The important features of *phrónêsis* for the purposes of this chapter are:

- It is a form of practical knowledge that includes both theoretical and practical skills and knowledge but is not reducible to any of these.
- Essentially it is a form of knowledge that is achieved by individuals through experience with others, not through formal teaching.
- *Phrónêsis* for Aristotle was a moral virtue involving value judgements that include a "passionate element" or the emotions. Abizadeh (2002) argues that Aristotle's answer to "What is the written law lacking that renders it insensitive to the particular circumstances?" is that, It is lacking "the passionate element" which "is not present in law but every human soul necessarily has it" (p. 271).
- *Phrónêsis* involves real life context-dependent decisions in circumstances where guidelines or a set of principles are insufficient to guide such decisions.
- This chapter will argue that accounts of *phrónêsis* as "individualistic" or presented as personal achievements are limited and that to understand the process of the acquisition of wisdom it must be placed in a broader social perspective or context. This point will be addressed later in the chapter.

If, as I argue, a set of guidelines or rules cannot replace the value considerations of practical wisdom, what is it in professional practice that has in fact historically led, at best, to the downgrading, and at worst, to the ignoring of the role of wisdom in decision making? I propose that what has replaced, or at least downgraded, the role of practical wisdom is a newly emerging practice that assumes that such judgements are subjective and thus invalid or unscientific. I refer here to Evidence-Based Practice that prioritises the role of empirical research in professional practice. There has been an almost universal call from many professionals to become evidence based. What this means for practice and clinical decisions is explored next.

EVIDENCE-BASED PRACTICE AS THE BASIS FOR PROFESSIONAL ACTION AND DECISION MAKING

The notion of practical wisdom has not been a major focus of practice in healthcare or clinical education and in recent decades a movement has emerged towards objective empirically-based research driving decisions under the name of evidence-based practice (EBP). Tyreman (2000) argues that, in the case of modern medical teaching and practice, the main focus has been on technical instrumental practice rather than practical wisdom; "issues of uncertainty and under-determination as facts of life in clinical decision-making remain major challenges for the novice practitioner and medical teacher" (p. 119).

EBP had its origins in medicine (known as evidence-based medicine [EBM]) where it rapidly became the major paradigm for clinical practice and clinical decision making. It has rapidly spread among many other health professions such as physiotherapy, dentistry, nursing, occupational therapy and social work and, more recently, to many other non-health areas such as management. Biesta (2007) argues that EBP is a notion of professional action as intervention, and looks, "to research for evidence about the effectiveness of interventions. Research needs to find out, in other words, 'what works,' and the main if not the only way of doing this, so it is often argued, is through experimental research, most notably in the form of randomized controlled trials (RCT) seen by many EBP advocates as the 'Gold Standard' of research" (Biesta, 2007, p. 7).

Thus, EBP is an interventionist model that is basically concerned with the effectiveness of certain actions and procedures. In medical practice one can understand the relevance of this since the concern is whether certain practices work. An RCT can show in broad or macro terms, for example, what drug or procedure may "work" and what may not for certain medically diagnosed issues. In the health sciences EBP is seen as providing incontrovertible objective data on effective practice. In this view it is a more effective way of informing clinical action and decision making replacing entrenched practices based on outmoded traditions and unsupported subjective "unscientific" opinion. There is an implicit view within EBP that clinical decision making and action should be clearly supported and backed by research evidence (of a certain kind at that) and that personal experience or subjective judgement should play no major part in the action taken.

> At one extreme, there are those who think that research will be able to give us 'the truth,' that 'the truth' can be translated into rules for action, and that the only thing practitioners need to do is to follow these rules without any further reflection on or consideration of the concrete situation they are in. (Biesta, 2007, p. 12)

According to Clegg (2005) the practice of giving priority to RCTs is as follows:

> The epistemological argument at the centre of the evidence-based practice debate relates to the practice in systematic review of giving precedence to data from experimenter-manipulated controlled (preferably with random assignment) trials. While there are systematic reviews that include other sorts of data, as Davies (2000) points out, the idea of meta-ethnography sits uneasily with the form of the cumulative generalisation assumed by the argument for 'evidence' in systematic reviews. The power of (intervention) as opposed to natural variation, is both compelling and simple. By assigning control conditions to an intervention, and focusing on clear outcome measures, it is possible to make the argument that it is the intervention, not other causal factors, that is producing the desired effect. (p. 419)

There are, of course, more nuanced notions of EBP where practitioner experience is not relegated to mere opinion but is said to be a factor to take into account along with EBP in professional decision making. The question that arises is the nature of that interaction. The research evidence will provide information on what has worked in a specific experimental situation or (if qualitative research is providing the information) in specific contexts but cannot provide solutions to, or rules for, the specific situation in which the professional is actually working. The practitioner has to make decisions for the client or patient they are currently working with and the question is what is the basis for that decision? Even in medical practice, for example, best practice may not always mean simply adopting the drug or practice that is shown to be the most effective but using what is best for a specific client, taking into account their wishes.

The technical instrumental evidence-based focus of professional practice has been questioned by a number of writers in the arena of education. In Australian higher education, an academic and practice field known as ALL (Academic Language and Learning), also known as Academic Skills Advising, Language and Learning Development and Student Support, are areas of research that are "...basically concerned with assisting students with language and learning required at university" (Chahal, 2017, p. 2). The ALL Association journal *Academic Language and Learning* contains numerous papers on teaching, learning, evaluation and teaching methods among other diverse topics. EBP is the underlying discourse of the ALL journal with emphasis on EBP for all learning and teaching practices and outcomes. The ALL emphasis on EBP is an example of a now universally accepted approach in education and also health science professions that emphasises that professional decisions and practices should be based only on "scientific research". The emphasis is on "… scientific research, evaluation and statistics [that] along with performance data constitute the empirical evidence used to inform decisions" (The US Institute of Educational Sciences, in Chahal, 2017, p. 5).

This assertion seems to ignore the practical or experiential knowledge of the practitioner who has to make decisions in specific situations. What it particularly ignores is that even though the experimental data provides information on "what works" or the most effective action to achieve a particular end this may not be the best solution to the particular client's situation and a professional practitioner may consider another course of action more appropriate. As Biesta (2007) argues, the most effective practice (to achieve a specified end goal) may not be either a moral or a wise way of acting. Thus the argument here is that evidence, such as that from systematic reviews, can serve as a useful tool for professional practice. However, it is a tool and has to be recognised and used as a tool and does not in itself provide the information necessary for its translation into professional practice. Professional work is holistic and involves interactions with others and the situation or environment in which the work is taking place.

As pointed out by Biesta (2007), much of the work on EBP is implicitly dualistic in that it makes a distinction between the knower and the known with the knower seen as a passive onlooker in relation to the external world. However, a non-dualistic view (Biesta refers to John Dewey's work) conceives of individuals as always in an organic relation to the external world that is altered by an individual's actions and those changes feed back to the individual. This is a continuous circle of action reaction. The professional worker interacts with clients/students/patients and other professional workers and is changed by those interactions. The experienced practitioner is aware of the impact of these changes on their own actions, which include the actions and interactions with involved others. This includes tacit "know-how" based on their experience including the input from other professionals and also an understanding of the client's wishes and needs. In short, the professional worker gains practical wisdom as a result of their interactions with others and the external world. This raises questions about the education of professional practitioners. It has already been noted that an essential aspect of such practice is practical wisdom that can't be taught as a set of skills. In the section that follows I want to discuss an interactive notion of professional wisdom and how it may be gained. In doing this I will draw on the work of the Russian philosopher/psychologist Vygotsky with particular reference to his notion of the Zone of Proximal Development (referred to in the literature as the ZPD). But first some details on Vygotsky.

VYGOTSKY

Lev Semovich Vygotsky (1896–1934) was a Russian psychologist whose work within a short life left an impressive body of work that has to this day had a significant influence on psychology, education, linguistics, philosophy and many other areas. Vygotsky entered the field of psychology without any formal training in psychology; he graduated in law from Moscow University in 1917 with a background in the humanities in literature, art and philosophy. That year (1917) marked the beginning of the Russian Marxist revolution and the beginning of a period of revolutionary change in all areas of Soviet culture with a motivation to overthrow all those approaches that were based on non-materialist ideals. The task they set themselves was enormous, covering all areas of society including, particularly, education. The situation at that time was that of mass illiteracy with millions of people without any basic education at all. Thus, the reform of the educational system, the development of learning in schools and science in higher learning were critical priorities.

It was not until the early 1920s that Vygotsky entered the field of psychology with a doctorate in the Psychology of Art, an area not at that time seen as a standard psychology thesis. His formal entry into psychology began in 1924 after giving what was regarded as an impressive paper at the All Russian Psychoneurological Congress. As a result he was invited by the Director of the Moscow Psychological Institute K. N. Kornilov to become a member of that institute, thus launching his career in psychology (see Kozulin et al., 2003).

The institute where Vygotsky began his work in psychology was committed to creating a new approach in psychology based on Marxism or Dialectical Materialism. The institute's program was to develop new and fresh approaches to psychology in a period of immense change in Soviet society. A significant goal in this was the application of psychology to educational processes relating to the goal of the education of millions of hitherto totally illiterate masses of people, many of them serfs under the old Czarist regime. It was an immense challenge though resources were made available and new forms of studying psychological processes were encouraged (see Cole & Scribner, 1978).

Vygotsky, though knowledgeable in all areas of Marxist thought, especially the work of Engels and Marx himself, became familiar with the work of many Western thinkers including Freud, Piaget, the American pragmatists G. H. Mead, John Dewey and William James, and the early behaviourists J. B. Watson and E. L. Thorndike. He was also familiar with the work of well-known Soviet psychologists such as I. P. Pavlov and V. N. Bekhterev whose work on classical conditioning and reflexology respectively had dominated psychology in Russia. His theoretical work shows the influence of all these important figures and through a critique of their work he was able to formulate his own unique sociocultural position.

Though Vygotsky's work was broad and covered many areas, it was in the study of the development of consciousness or the higher mental processes in children that was unique and for which he was to be best known. His goal was to show the role of language (or signs) and tools as mediators in the development of the higher mental processes by which he meant the development of skills, of thinking and of external action. Vygotsky's approach to this development was influenced by Piaget's (and Freud's) developmental or genetic method and Marx's and Engel's notion of the mediating function of tool use as a means of enhancing the performing of physical tasks not able to be carried out without that tool. There is an interaction between tool and sign in adults: a tool is a physical object used to make changes in the external environment, a sign serves an internal means of using that tool. The process of the development of a child's cognitive ability and physical skills involves initial interactions with others, more competent others, who assist the child to perform tasks they are not able to undertake without such assistance. Eventually the child becomes able to perform that task without such assistance and, in Vygotsky's terms, the task is internalised as a sort of locus of internal control of one's actions. "The mastering of nature and the mastering of behaviour are mutually linked, just as man's alteration of nature alters man's own nature" (Vygotsky, 1978a, p. 55, see also pp. 52–57).

To further explain Vygotsky's notion of the mediated development of higher mental functions I will take a small diversion here and refer to an everyday example of such mediation that Vygotsky himself used. The example is of the development of pointing in a young child. Initially the child may begin with an action of seeking to unsuccessfully grasp some object in her environment that is out of her reach. Her hand remains, fingers grasping, poised in the air. Her mother comes to the rescue realising that the child wants something and gives it to her. For the mother, the child is pointing that she wants some object and she is given that object. This fundamentally changes the situation for the child as she has achieved her goal by the action of another person. Vygotsky says "The child's unsuccessful attempt engenders a reaction not from the object ... but from another person" (Vygotsky, 1978b, p. 26). The meaning of the action is established by others and it is only later that the child understands that her action is one of pointing. The child's action only becomes a meaningful gesture when others understand that the child is pointing. Vygotsky refers to this series of transformations as "internalisation"; "the interpersonal process is transformed into an intrapersonal one" (Vygotsky, 1978a, p. 57).

This seemingly quite simple description of the acquisition of a social gesture is more complicated than it appears. Eun, Knotek, and Heining-Boyn (2008) make the point that "a major characteristic of Vygotsky's writings stems from the fact that Vygotsky was rooted in the traditions of high-context cultures. Writers within this tradition often omit or do not elaborate on concepts that are self-evident to them" (p. 134). His contemporary readers would understand that this was not a one-sided interaction between mother, or more competent other, with the child who is a passive recipient of input from a more powerful other. The child even at a young age is not a passive recipient of his mother's input but is actively engaging her. For Vygotsky, the child is reality oriented and seeks to continually adjust herself to the surrounding environment; this is understood as making adaptations to the social or cultural environment. Pointing is not simply a natural action but a cultural one since the child learns to use a symbolic gesture to achieve a goal by means of another individual.

The example from Vygotsky illustrates his notion of the social (and we may add the cultural) origins of thought (and values and language). This principle of development, initially by means of cooperation with other more competent individuals, was incorporated into Vygotsky's notion of the Zone of Proximal Development. Vygotsky proposed that children in working with others on tasks can perform at a higher level than if they were undertaking that task on their own. In a social interaction, the more competent others compensate for the lack of biological or neurological development and extend the child's performance beyond this natural level: "They extend the child's memory beyond the biological dimensions of the human nervous system and permit it to incorporate artificial, or self-generated stimuli, which we call signs" (Vygotsky, 1978a, p. 39). The "internalisation" of those signs changes the psychological structure of memory eventually enabling the child to direct its own behaviour without assistance.

Vygotsky's ZPD, in its original form as indicated with the example of mother and child, was seen by him as a natural process of enculturation. The mother and the child would not have been fully cognisant of the impact of their actions though the outcome was a fundamental change in the cognitive structure of the child (and the mother). However, this natural process has provided a valuable tool or method for teaching and learning and it has been extensively adopted and adapted by educators and psychologists in many countries and different cultures up to the present time.

The ZPD has been extended to cover moral education (Balakrishnan & Narvaez, 2016), language learning (Maftoon & Sabah, 2012), second language learning (Shabani, 2016), primary healthcare (Hopwood, 2015) and creativity and the arts (Connery, John-Steiner, & Marjanovic-Shane, 2018) in adults and children. Some writers have also emphasised the role of the emotions (which they argue is implicitly held by Vygotsky himself) as a crucial aspect of the ZPD; "Thus, the dynamic process of establishing and maintaining the ZPD is successful only when emotionally laden reciprocal relations between the learner and the instructor allow for participants' comfort and trust, which are manifested in constant negotiation of the subject of inquiry and the way it is presented and acquired" (Levykh, 2008, p. 97).

It thus is now accepted by many Vygotskian experts that the ZPD need not be limited to child learning practice nor to the acquisition of practical or conceptual skills. It has been shown to be a useful tool for understanding the process of learning in adults and in the internalisation of values (Franklin, 2014). The ZPD occurs in a cultural and emotive context as it is implied by Vygotsky that such advancements in learning imply a set of values shared by the learner and the more competent peer or teacher: "The very process of internalization from social speech (speech for others) to ego-centric speech, and then to inner speech (speech for oneself), is not merely emotionally laden, but originates in human emotions and desires" (Levykh, 2008,

p. 96). A more recent interpretation of Vygotsky's ZPD by Roth and Radford (2010) argues that:

> conceptualizing the zone of proximal development in the manner we suggest here rests on a non-transmissive form of knowing and on a non-individualistic conception of the participants. As to the former, knowing is not theorized as the reception of already-made pieces of cultural-historical knowledge. Knowing refers rather to the possibilities that become available to the participants for thinking, reflecting, arguing, and acting in a certain historically contingent cultural practice. (p. 10)

In an analysis of a teacher/student-based interaction in a second grade mathematics classroom based on the ZPD approach, Roth and Radford (2010) developed an interpretation of the nature of the interaction that supports a non-individualistic interaction: "Our analysis shows that far from exhibiting an asymmetry, the zone of proximal development is an interactional achievement that allows all participants to become teachers and learners" (p. 303). In the ZPD situation they argue that teacher and student are already in a context where they share a common cultural/language background that enables that interaction. The teacher may be the competent participant and the students the learners, but the teacher can learn also from the interaction. She may realise that certain strategies she uses do not work so she adjusts her approach to that of the student who also positions herself to become receptive to the teacher. In the ZPD it is not a matter of a competent other simply correcting a less competent other who serves as some sort of sponge who absorbs already preconceived knowledge, but an interaction occurs that achieves a common conceptual ground; this is how learning occurs in the ZPD. The knowledge or skills achieved by the interaction constitutes new learning for all participants.

This "new learning" is not to be conceived as the acquisition by just one party of what may be referred to only as the learning of already established objective knowledge or as a learned skill but as a new understanding of the task at hand. As Roth and Radford (2010) put it, "Within this context, we need to better understand how participants draw from those resources to position themselves in zones of proximal development and to tune to others in conceptual and affective layers to collectively reach interactional achievement" (p. 306). Through these means practical wisdom can be both developed and refined.

REFERENCES

Abizadeh, A. (2002). The passions of the wise: Phronesis, rhetoric, and Aristotle's passionate practical deliberation. *The Review of Metaphysics, 56*(2), 267-296.

Balakrishnan, V., & Narvaez, D. (2016). A reconceptualisation of Vygotsky's ZPD into ZCD in teaching moral education in secondary schools using real-life dilemmas. *Cogent Education, 3*(1), 2-15.

Biesta, G. (2007). Why 'what works' won't work: Evidence-based practice and the democratic deficit in educational research. *Educational Theory, 57*(1), 1-121.

Chahal, D. (2017). Evidence-based practice and its discontents in academic language and learning. *Pedagogy, Culture & Society, 25*(4), 601-607.

Clegg, S. (2005). Evidence-based practice in educational research: A critical realist critique of systematic review. *British Journal of Sociology of Education, 26*(3), 415-428.
Cole, M., & Scribner, S. (1978). Biographical note on L. S. Vygotsky. In M. Cole, V. John-Steiner, S. Scribner, & E. Superman (Eds.), *L. S. Vygotsky: Mind in society: The development of higher psychological processes* (pp. 15-16). Cambridge, MA: Harvard University Press.
Cooke, S., & Carr, D. (2014). Virtue, practical wisdom and character in teaching. *British Journal of Educational Studies, 62*(2), 91-110.
Connery, C., John-Steiner, V., & Marjanovic-Shane, A (Eds.). (2018). *Vygotsky and creativity: A cultural-historical approach to play, meaning making, and the arts*. New York, NY: Peter Lang.
Eun, B. E., Knotek, S., & Heining-Boyn, A. (2008). Reconceptualising the Zone of Proximal Development: The importance of the third voice. *Educational Psychology Review, 20*(2), 133-147.
Franklin, S. (2014). Vygotsky: Revolutionary psychology for contemporary social work. *Critical and Radical Social Work, 2*(3), 285-386.
Hopwood, N. (2015). Understanding partnership practice in primary health as pedagogic work: What can Vygotsky's theory of learning offer? *Australian Journal of Public Health, 21*(1), 9-13.
Kemmis, S. (2012). Phronesis, experience, and the primacy of practice. In E. A. Kinsella & A. Pitman (Eds.), *Phronesis as professional knowledge: Practical wisdom in the professions* (pp. 147-161). Rotterdam, The Netherlands: Sense.
Kinsella, E. A., & Pitman, A. (2012a). Engaging phronesis in professional practice and education. In E. A. Kinsella & A. Pitman (Eds.), *Phronesis as professional knowledge: Practical wisdom in the professions* (pp. 1-11). Rotterdam, The Netherlands: Sense.
Kinsella, E. A., & Pitman, A. (Eds.). (2012b). *Phronesis as professional knowledge: Practical wisdom in the professions*. Rotterdam, The Netherlands: Sense.
Kozulin, A., Gindis, B., Ageyev, G. S., & Miller, S. M. (2003). *Vygotsky's educational theory in cultural content*. New York, NY: Cambridge University Press.
Levykh, M. (2008). The affective establishment and maintenance of Vygotsky's Zone of Proximal Development. *Educational Theory, 58*(1), 83-101.
Maftoon, P., & Sabah, S. (2012). A critical look at the status of affect in second language acquisition research: Lessons from Vygotsky's legacy. *Brain: Broad Research in Artificial Intelligence and Neuroscience, 3*(2), 36-42.
Roth, W.-M., & Radford, L. (2010). Re/thinking the Zone of Proximal Development (symmetrically). *Mind, Culture, and Activity, 17*(4), 299-307.
Shabani, K. (2016). Implications of Vygotsky's sociocultural theory for second language (L2) assessment. *Cogent Education, 3*(1). doi:10.1080/2331186X.2016.1242459
Tyreman, S. (2000). Promoting critical thinking in health care: Phronesis and criticality. *Medicine, Health Care and Philosophy, 4*(2), 117-124.
Vygotsky, L. S. (1978a). Mastery of memory and thinking. In M. Cole, V. John-Steiner, S. Scribner, & E. Superman (Eds.), *L. S. Vygotsky: Mind in society: The development of higher psychological processes* (pp. 38-51). Cambridge, MA: Harvard University Press.
Vygotsky, L. S. (1978b). Tool and symbol in child development. In M. Cole, V. John-Steiner, S. Scribner, & E. Superman (Eds.), *L. S. Vygotsky: Mind in society: The development of higher psychological processes* (pp. 19-30). Cambridge, MA: Harvard University Press.

Rodd Rothwell PhD
Faculty of Health Sciences
University of Sydney, Australia

DEBORAH BOWMAN

22. WISDOM AND ETHICO-LEGAL PRACTICE

Ways of Seeing and Ways of Being

ON WISDOM: WHY "WAYS OF SEEING, KNOWING AND BEING"?

This chapter considers how different ways of seeing, knowing and being might inform how clinicians and practitioners make judgements, particularly in relation to the ethico-legal questions and considerations that arise in their work. What is meant by "ways of seeing, knowing and being" and why are these useful when thinking about the nature of wisdom? Since Foucault (1976) conceptualised the medical "gaze" that characterised work in the clinic, the lens of healthcare work has been a preoccupation of philosophers, anthropologists and sociologists. The way in which a healthcare professional is trained to see is detached, expert and powerful, yet there are other ways of seeing that, it is argued, inform wise practice. Ways of knowing describes the different types of knowledge and discernment that are required when practising medicine and engaging with its ethico-legal dimensions. Ways of being refers to the characteristics, behaviours and qualities that inform how someone responds when managing different types of knowledge in a context where uncertainty, emotion, complexity and pressure are common. Both ways of knowing and ways of being in practice are often implicit and under-considered yet are fundamental to practice, choice and, specifically, the nature of wisdom.

This chapter discusses that relationship between wisdom, ways of seeing, knowing and being, and the ethico-legal questions, considerations and challenges of medical practice. I argue, drawing on Havi Carel's (Carel, 2013, 2016; Carel & Kidd, 2014, 2016) work on epistemic justice in healthcare, that wisdom, when understood as shaped by ways of seeing, knowing and being, serves as a valuable force in healthcare: as a counter to inherent imbalances of power, as a guide for education and development, as protection against burnout and compassion fatigue and as a reminder of the essence of what it is to be an individual clinician and an individual patient in a demanding, resource-constrained system.

WHAT IS WISDOM?

Wisdom has been a feature of virtue ethics since Ancient times; from the scepticism of Socrates about the possibility and limits of knowledge (Miller & Platter, 2010; Plato, c. 400 BC/2010) to Aristotle's distinction between theoretical and practical wisdom (Aristotle, 349 BC/2004; Dowie, 2000). The nature of wisdom has preoccupied philosophers for centuries with the focus being predominantly, although not exclusively, on the personal rather than the systemic.

It speaks to how an individual perceives and responds to that which he or she encounters. For the purposes of this chapter, wisdom intersects with other character traits and depends on an integration of character, mind and virtue. Ethics and ethical practice are informed by wisdom in different ways, for instance, it may be a normative ideal or virtue but it also reflects a way, even a method, of responding to moral questions and conflict.

Contemporary ethicists too have prioritised wisdom, often conceptualised as *phrónêsis* in recognition of the practical and applied expression of wisdom in clinical practice (Chiavaroli & Trumble, 2018; Dowie, 2000; Kaldjian 2010). For the purposes of this chapter, wisdom is considered to be a constellation of traits, dispositions and behaviours that commonly encompass the features shown in Figure 22.1. These features, it is argued, are essential to the recognition of, and response to, the ethico-legal aspects of clinical practice which are often experienced as discomforting.

- Awareness of personal values and capacity to act, for the most part, in accordance with those values
- Openness to experience and to others
- Capacity for forgiveness (of others and self)
- Reflectiveness about experiences and willingness to continue learning
- Interest in, and not being threatened by, diverse perspectives
- Empathy and kindness
- Curiosity and inquiry
- Flexibility and openness
- Humility and reflexivity
- Sensitivity to context, time and circumstance when considering response
- Capacity for recognising and addressing conflict
- Acceptance and management of uncertainty
- Awareness of personal strengths and limitations
- Commitment to the wellbeing of others, whilst taking care of self (with ego in check)
- Tendency to seek a balanced life

Figure 22.1. Features of wisdom.

THE RELATIONSHIP BETWEEN CLINICAL PRACTICE, ETHICS AND LAW

Clinical practice prompts a myriad of moral questions and takes place within a legal framework. It is impossible for any healthcare professional to avoid the ethico-legal dimensions of their work. Yet, ethics and law as subjects are often misunderstood. Law may be seen as the "trump" card: ethics being "nice to have" but the most important thing is often regarded as ensuring that one is practising "legally". Such a view often reflects misconceptions about the nature of law itself.

There is often the implication that the law will provide a structure and guidance that is more valuable than ethical analysis. Yet, there are swathes of clinical practice on which the law offers only high-level direction: a section of a statute may set out a standard or requirement, but its extent, meaning and application remains a matter for interpretation. That interpretation may be advanced by codes of practice, such as those that supplement the Mental Health and Mental Capacity Acts, or delegated legislation such as statutory instruments in which terms are defined. Further attention to interpretation will, in common law systems such as England and Wales, be found in case law which may, depending on the level at which a decision is made, create precedent. Yet, the essence of cases is that they are particular and are decided on their own facts and merits. The principles of law derived from cases, such as those relating to consent in the case of Montgomery,[1] are still subject to interpretation for clinicians negotiating what it is that individual patients wish to know. The law therefore depends on an integrative and interpretative approach in which knowledge of legal standards provides a starting point, but this must be considered alongside the nature of the law itself, the situation at hand and the needs, preferences and priorities of the individual patient.

In contrast to overstating the law as definitive and therefore determinative, ethics and ethical analysis may be perceived as elusive and even "woolly". As such, for some, ethics as a subject has limited value. The notion that multiple arguments and competing demands may exist is frustrating for some. Often too, ethics is represented with reference to "the dilemma" which, by definition, concerns choice between two options when, in practice, the challenge may be to see, name, frame and respond to multiple ethical questions or considerations presenting in a single consultation or encounter. Inherent in such misunderstandings of the law and ethics may be discomfort with uncertainty and judgement. Such discomfort is an understandable response: to have to proceed and make decisions in the face of ambiguity and unresolved, and perhaps unresolvable, questions is unsettling and anxiety provoking. It is a characteristic of clinical practice, whatever the specialty, and yet it is rarely discussed explicitly, still less with reference to the emotions that interpretation in the context of uncertainty engenders. Consider the relationship of the law and ethics in the case of Maddie in Figure 22.2.

The law provides the ways in which Maddie's capacity and preferences should be considered. It will be useful in articulating the criteria by which the team evaluates whether Maddie has the capacity to make her own decisions and what should happen if, as seems likely from the brief description, she lacks that capacity. The Mental Capacity Act (UK) also sets out principles on which care should be predicated and capacity considered. The common law or case law is also informative in offering further insights into the ways in which concepts such as best interests have been determined in specific situations. Nonetheless, the law only provides a framework within which interpretation and judgement will have to be exercised to determine what is the best way for to care for Maddie.

Wisdom is part of the mitigation that renders interpretative work possible and perhaps even bearable. Yet, wisdom itself can seem amorphous: What does it look like? Where is it found? Can it be learned? Are there conditions which make wisdom more or less likely to flourish? How might we nurture wisdom in ourselves and in others? These are the questions that inform this chapter's exploration of types of wisdom and its relationship to ethico-legal questions in clinical practice.

> Maddie is 57 and she has learning disabilities. She lives in a specialist home and she communicates in a limited, non-verbal way with her carers. Maddie develops symptoms suggestive of cancer. She is referred to the oncology team for investigations. Maddie finds the investigations distressing and it is difficult for everyone to see her so upset. Unfortunately, Maddie is found to have a high-grade, Stage 3 cancer and chemotherapy is indicated. Maddie's carer who accompanies her to appointments expresses the view that Maddie will "never cope" with chemotherapy.

Figure 22.2. Introducing Maddie.

DISCERNMENT AND WISDOM

When someone identifies and frames an ethical question or problem, they are engaged in a moral act (Bowman, 2015). To identify, name and frame a question or concern reflects context and preferences, conscious and unconscious. Sensitivity and attention to the ethico-legal dimensions of practice and awareness of the influences on the same requires wisdom even before one grapples with the substance of the ethical question. The insight to recognise how power, perspective and privilege may inform the identification and representation of ethical problems and to consider whose voices, priorities and experiences may be being overlooked, is a manifestation of wisdom. Beauchamp and Childress (2001) refer to the virtue of "discernment". It is characterised by the capacity to recognise context and to demonstrate sensitivity in considering principles and norms in diverse situations. For Wisnewski (2015), the concept is moral perception which demands that practitioners develop a nuanced and sensitive approach that extends beyond codes of practice or ethical guidelines.

To return to the experience of Maddie, the framing and discernment of the ethical dimensions of her care, matter. To assume that she lacks capacity because she has a learning disability would be a legal error but it would also be an error of discernment. The Mental Capacity Act is clear that capacity is a functional and dynamic concept rather than something determined by a specific diagnosis or impairment. Not to consider whether and how to capture Maddie's preferences, perceptions and experiences – irrespective of capacity – is to disregard her humanity. It would be possible to proceed simply by following an agreed treatment pathway or evidence-based protocol for her type, grade and stage of cancer. Yet, without attention to Maddie and her responses to the investigations that she has undergone, along with consideration of the concerns raised by the carer who knows Maddie best and reflection on what is not yet being heard or perceived and how that may change, the response will be partial and ethically constrained. The wisdom to identify the absent as well as the present and to recognise the context as carefully as the foreground are crucial aspects of ethical practice.

WAYS OF SEEING, KNOWING AND BEING

An essential element of training as a clinician is the development of a unique way of seeing. It may be literal perception – the ability to identify, describe and categorise a sign or the capacity to begin to navigate the human body and its landmarks in early dissection and clinical skills sessions. It will also be a metaphorical way of seeing which reflects a disposition that is dispassionate, clinical, boundaried and carefully neutral. To see or even to consider beauty (or its opposite) is not the focus, literally, of the medical way of seeing. It is observation rather than imagination that is emphasised. Yet, there are other ways of seeing that will infuse an encounter with a patient and/or carers. Their perceptions will be about noticing change in self and embodiment that may be redolent with fear, regret, sadness or despair.

For a surgeon, a scar may be reviewed for neatness, pressure or infection. For a patient, the scar may represent a fracturing of self, an affront to identity, a loss for which to grieve and a marker of determination or resolve. It may be something they cannot bear to behold and yet also be something of which they are constantly aware. For a physician, a sign may be interrogated for clinical meaning as a marker of new or progressive disease or a manifestation of a biological mechanism that requires specific investigations and management. For a patient, the sign may represent the loss of hope, fear for the future and anxiety about work and security. The facility to recognise these different ways of seeing, their meaning and the implications relies on openness, curiosity, humility and, above all, wisdom.

Discernment and wisdom depend on appreciating that there are multiple ways of knowing and that those collide in medicine and healthcare. In a single consultation or encounter, the objective and the subjective, the rational and the emotional, the inductive and the deductive, the specific and the general, theory and practice, the individual and the population, the quantitative and the qualitative, the physical and the ephemeral, the certain and the ambiguous, the present and the absent, will jostle for attention, priority and recognition (Bowman & Bowman, 2018). Knowledge, in all its permutations, is rarely discrete, complete and neatly presented. Rather it is partial, complex and contradictory. To act wisely and ethically is to attend to ways of knowing and understanding (Kumagai, 2014). It is to recognise and even to relish the multiplicity of ways in which knowledge exists and meaning is sought in clinical work. It is to engage with, rather than deny, the ambiguity, the variance, the challenge, the fallibility, the interpretation and the messiness that imbue healthcare practice. It is to acknowledge that knowledge of care, including self-care, may be distinct from the forms of knowledge that dominate in biomedicine, yielding new ways to think about ethical practice (Chambon & Irving, 2003).

Wisdom demands more than merely just recognising epistemological difference or categorising ways of knowing. It is suggested that a manifestation of wisdom is to understand and to acknowledge that some ways of knowing are commonly privileged over others. This privileging of knowledge is fundamental to the concept of epistemic injustice in healthcare (Carel & Kidd, 2014) where systemic power imbalances and engrained preferences for expression risk marginalising the vulnerable. To recognise the existence and prevalence of epistemic injustice is to act ethically. To take steps to mitigate against epistemic injustice in practice is to act with wisdom.

Maddie's voice is, literally, silent because she is non-verbal. Yet, there are many ways in which she may communicate, and to seek out her perspective and those of the people who know her best is to mitigate the risk of epistemic injustice and act wisely. Wisdom will appreciate both the general and the specific and how each informs the care of Maddie. A wise practitioner will recognise the differential and often poor experiences of healthcare for, and by, people with learning disabilities. He or she will reflect on the concepts of discrimination, best interests and quality of life whilst understanding that to do so without the perspective of Maddie and her carers would be constraining and unacceptable. It is a conscious approach that is focused on ethical reasoning and the goals of care (Kaldjian 2010). Each consultation and interaction with Maddie will seek meaning that is contextual, specific and derived from multiple sources. A wise practitioner will attend to the scientific and clinical evidence-base, a patient's and/or carer's experience, individual preferences and perceptions and consideration of the past, present and future (Widdershoven et al., 2017).

Clinical work is, by definition, a practical endeavour. However skilled one may be at ethical discernment and analysis, decisions must be made and plans have to be negotiated. Enactment that is underpinned by wisdom is likely to have greater impact and/or effectiveness. Revisiting the case of Maddie, it would be possible to spend a lot of time discussing and debating the different ethical questions and discerning the potential for epistemic injustice. That may be time well-spent and if the process were inclusive and engaged diverse perspectives that were open to interrogation and challenge, the outcome would likely be rich learning. Yet, choices and care must follow. It may be necessary to foster wise discussion and reflection, but it is not sufficient. Enactment is unavoidable and it is in enactment that practical wisdom finds expression. *Phrónêsis* guides action where knowledge, or as this chapter argues, ways of knowing, depend on appreciating context or circumstances (Chaivaroli & Trumble, 2018).

That is not to say that action is required. Indeed, one of the more memorable interactions with a mentor that this author experienced was when she was advised "don't just do something, stand there". Taking time, creating space and deciding that the best choice is not to intervene may well be wise, particularly in complex situations such as Maddie's. Of course, in some circumstances, swift action is required and can be life-saving. Wisdom encompasses the ability to discern when and how temporality informs care. An emergency doctor who reflects at length rather than responding to the haemorrhaging patient may be negligent rather than wise. Yet, if that haemorrhaging patient is a 17-year-old Jehovah's Witness, whose wishes are unknown and who is accompanied by her mother urging the doctor not to give blood products, wisdom is likely to mean that unreflective adherence to the protocol for the treatment of haemorrhage may not be a wise response. Of course, the devil is in the phrase "may not be" and it is that ambiguity which renders wisdom both so valuable and so elusive in an ethico-legal context.

Yet, if one conceptualises wisdom as attention to ways of knowing and ways of being, there will be multiple possible approaches and conclusions to the same clinical scenario or facts. That is unavoidable. However, by considering different perspectives, context and variables, types of knowledge, the potential for epistemic injustice and what it means to be respectful, to attend to dignity and to show humility in any given situation, wise enactment is more likely to ensue.

The facility to recognise that whilst wisdom is always valuable, it may be more needed in situations of uncertainty both to guide decision making but also to liberate from the futile quest for definitive "answers". Where practice becomes difficult, as it has potentially in Maddie's case, wisdom allows for a conscious response that notices the difficulty but is not overwhelmed by it. Wisdom can accommodate and complement the limits and constraints of contemporary medicine, including those of evidence and bioscience (De Freitas et al., 2012). Wisdom allows the practitioner to continue to be in consultations where, inevitably, facts, emotion, knowledge, experience and judgement swirl. Wisdom-as-practice develops confidence, judgement and the ability to balance the competing demands on an individual practitioner (Banks, 2013), although the inherent wisdom of the novice practitioner should not be underestimated (Chandler, 2012). Wisdom acknowledges that it is possible for anyone to be wise and that no one will be wise all the time (Grossmann, 2017). It is a fluid, responsive and engaged way of being that endures throughout a career. It is not predicated on credentials, role or hierarchy; it is based on a virtuous approach to clinical interactions that prioritises respect, integrity, fairness, kindness, inclusivity and dignity.

ANALYSIS AND WISDOM

When learning about ethico-legal practice, students may be introduced to many different theories and analytic models. There is no shortage of options for those who seek structure and consistency in their approach to ethico-legal analysis. Different people will favour some models over others and the literature is full of papers advocating particular theoretical approaches or tools. Whatever an individual's preference or disposition, analysis informed by wisdom is likely to be more effective.

Wisdom is what unlocks analytic choices. It recognises that each situation is unique and may not be fully captured by universal laws or principles, however well established. Without attending to that specificity, without attention to the same, moral analysis will be partial and inadequate. Wisdom acknowledges that analytic models are useful, but inevitably, limited. Yet, it is wisdom that will enhance and enrich one's analytic response to an ethico-legal question, from its discernment in the first instance to arriving at a reasoned response. Wisdom enables a practitioner to select the right analytic tool or approach for different ethico-legal questions. Wisdom recognises that there is a temporal element to ethico-legal practice and that the point at which analysis occurs will inform the ways in which it is possible. Wisdom will ensure that, rather than being defensive or afraid of disagreement, the practitioner will seek out and engage with those who have different or contradictory opinions and views. Analysis that is grounded in wisdom recognises that it may not always be possible to reach consensus but recognises that there is value in dialogue, sharing norms and exploring values and tensions (Widdershoven, Abma, & Molewijk, 2009; Zucker, 2006). Wisdom recognises the value of testing a response with others. Wisdom allows individuals to recognise emotion and intuition in analysis (van Thiel & van Delden, 2009) without necessarily privileging either response. A wise approach to ethico-legal analysis acknowledges that a perfect, definitive answer may be illusory.

What might such an approach mean in Maddie's case? It would be possible, of course, simply to draw on a preferred theoretical approach or model and engage in rigorous analysis. Wisdom, however, will elevate that analysis. It does so by recognising that choices are made in a context of uncertainty, by engaging with those who have different perspectives on Maddie's situation, by considering and testing the ways in which contrasting conclusions may be reached on identical facts, by attending to the interpretative nature of the task and by acknowledging the discomforting and maybe even painful emotions (Leget, 2004) and the strength of intuitions whilst seeking a balance (Widdershoven et al., 2017). A wise analytic response is an iterative process whereby those who seek meaning recognise that it may need to be revisited and are sufficiently flexible, humble and open to adapt to new or changing circumstances. Above all, the content and outcomes of any analysis will be accountable and explicable to Maddie, her carers, the multidisciplinary team and those who have a stake in the case.

INTEGRATION AND REFLECTION

Wisdom in response to ethico-legal questions or problems is essentially interpretative and integrative. It depends on the recognition of, and response to, multiple ways of knowing and understanding, including facts, evidence, skills, experience, perceptions, emotions and intuition. The enactment of wisdom draws on common ways of being, whereby virtues are its antecedents and a commitment to kindness, integrity, dignity, inclusivity and fairness are prioritised. It is not enough merely to be able to recognise and cite each of these elements in isolation or list form. To act and to continue to act with wisdom requires the integration of different ways of knowing and being. It is moving beyond articulation of discrete elements to a complete and holistic response which may prioritise some aspects of a case over others, but is always aware of the whole as well as the constituent parts.

The relationship between wisdom and learning is key. There are two senses in which the relationship matters. First, learning may be part of a specific response to a situation: for example, discovering previously unknown information, reflecting on the doctor-patient relationship, better understanding the limits of specialist services, identifying systemic vulnerabilities or developing insight into personal factors affecting performance. Secondly, a disposition to learning, in general, may be a feature of a wise practitioner. Learning may be thought to have moral virtue. It can make difficult and regrettable events, incidents or experiences, purposeful. Learning may allow meaning to emerge from the chaotic emotions a person may feel after encountering a difficult or testing case. Learning can inform the future and make sense of the past. Although, it may be that some individuals are better placed to learn effectively and to facilitate the evolution of wisdom from experience. Glück and Bluck (2013) suggest that individuals must have four traits, namely: mastery, openness, reflectiveness and emotional regulation/empathy. It is these characteristics, they argue, that enable an individual to integrate experience or challenges into his or her life span and allow the emergence of wisdom.

It is possible to idealise "learning" in ways that are understandable, but may suggest denial rather than wisdom, particularly when things have gone wrong or errors have occurred. If one accepts the inherent uncertainty and inevitable risks of healthcare, emphatic claims that future mistakes or harm can be definitively prevented may suggest an urgent desire to believe in the redemptive power of "learning". It isn't surprising. The notion that future errors can be avoided has seduced policy makers, academics, professional organisations and patients. How much more attractive the idea must be to a doctor who feels bruised and is struggling to live with the consequences of his or her mistake or misjudgement. The wise response therefore may be to take a cool, realistic appraisal of learning. If one can accept medicine as an uncertain discipline practised by fallible human beings, how comforting to believe that those same human beings "learn" so effectively from missteps that they are eliminated in future. No wonder it is sometimes idealised and unrealistically embraced. Learning then, can be a limited panacea that both promises and disregards too much in well-intentioned efforts to contain the discomforting realities of clinical work. The trick is to develop a wise approach to learning that values its place in becoming and being a wise practitioner whilst not idealising it to the extent that it obfuscates what it is to be human, fallible and constantly changing.

Wisdom and its development are central to clinical education and training (Edmonson & Pearce, 2007). It has been argued that attention to wisdom in clinical education improves care (Marcum, 2013). Yet, its presence in curricula and training varies, with the term "judgement" more commonly used than wisdom (Kaldjian, 2010; Kotzee, Ignatowicz, & Thomas, 2017). Sometimes, wisdom is carefully and deliberately included with opportunities for learners to reflect on their experiences, discuss concepts and develop strategies for the workplace that are supportive and effective. Unfortunately, sometimes, wisdom is developed in spite of, rather than because of, the learning that trainees experience. Silence and perceived conflict about the challenging, contextual and uncertain nature of clinical practice (Zucker, 2006), coupled with negative interactions with what might better be described as cautionary tales rather than role or behaviour models are damaging, but they can throw into sharp relief the need for wisdom to be embedded into medical education and clinical training.

It can be difficult to find space in the crowded curriculum or busy clinical services. It may even be that the competency-based model of medical education and training is at odds with the development of wisdom (Kumagai, 2014). To foster wisdom is a more demanding task than scheduling "medical ethics" sessions. Indeed, Cowley (2012) suggests that increasing knowledge of moral philosophy may impede rather than facilitate wisdom. The opportunity and time to reflect, both in writing and verbally, with the support of skilled facilitators and mentors, is crucial to creating the circumstances in which wisdom and the traits on which it depends can flourish (de Cossart, Fish, & Hillman, 2012).

In Maddie's case, whatever the team or an individual may decide to do (and there are likely to be multiple decision points and choices to be considered), wisdom demands that there is space to reflect on, discuss, assimilate and evaluate diverse perspectives, experiences and ideas. The scientific and clinical (which in the scenario description have been left deliberately open) will be interrogated alongside the philosophical, social and psychological. Maddie's interests will be contextualised and attention afforded both to that which is said and unsaid by those who know and love her. Even if, and when, matters appear "resolved", wisdom will prompt ongoing reflection on what has happened and what might have been done differently. Facts and emotions will be equally explored with a sense of shared purpose: to ensure that the humanity of both Maddie and those who cared for her remains respected and endures, long after the final words have been entered into the medical record. When a new patient arrives, that approach will enable the team to meet the future because of what they did and how they did it, in the past. For wise practice begets wisdom and individual patients and doctors transform the collective clinical endeavour.

CONCLUSION

Wisdom is central to clinical practice. It is especially valuable in discerning and engaging with the ethico-legal dimensions of healthcare work with its inherent uncertainty, ambiguity and significance. Wisdom may assist both with the specific response to a particular question or problem, whilst simultaneously indicating a way of interacting with others in relation to ethico-legal questions that applies irrespective of the content of a case, story or scenario. Wisdom elucidates and facilitates the interpretative and complex nature of ethico-legal questions and problems. It is a deep and ongoing pursuit that attends to the individual's ways of seeing, knowing and being. In so doing, it acknowledges both the privilege and burden of medicine. Compassion fatigue, burnout and ethical erosion are constant threats for even the most committed of clinicians; wisdom is sustenance. It protects both doctors and patients against the impact of under-resourced and pressurised systems because it is inextricably linked to the essential humanity of healthcare.

Attention to, and support for, wisdom, enables that humanity to flourish irrespective of context. Wisdom is essential and its impact offers the greatest gift to patient and professional alike.

NOTE

[1] Montgomery v Lanarkshire Health Board [2015] SC 11.

REFERENCES

Aristotle. (2004). *The Nicomachean ethics* (J. A. K. Thomson, Trans., revised by H. Tredennick). London, England: Penguin Classics. (Original work published 349 BC)

Banks, S. (2013. Negotiating personal engagement and professional accountability: Professional wisdom and ethics work. *European Journal of Social Work, 6*(5), 587-604.

Beauchamp, T, L., & Childress, J. F. (2001). *Principles of biomedical ethics* (5th ed.). Oxford, England: Oxford University Press.

Bowman, D. (2015). What is it to do 'good medical ethics'? Minding the gap(s). *Journal of Medical Ethics, 41*(1), 60-63.

Bowman, D., & Bowman, J. (2018). The seeing place: On medicine and theatre. *Arts and Humanities in Higher Education, 17*(1), 166-181.

Carel, H. (2013, June). *It's hard to think without your pants on: Patient testimonies and epistemic injustice.* Keynote 3 presented at *A Narrative Future for Healthcare Conference*, London, England.

Carel, H. (2016). *The phenomenology of illness*. Oxford, England: Oxford University Press.

Carel, H., & Kidd, I. J. (2014). Epistemic injustice in healthcare: A philosophical analysis. *Medicine, Healthcare and Philosophy, 17*(4), 529-540.

Carel, H., & Kidd, I. J. (2016). Epistemic injustice and illness. *Journal of Applied Philosophy*, doi:10.1111/japp.12172

Chambon, A. S., & Irving, A. (2003). They give reason a responsibility which it simply can't bear: Ethics, care of the self and caring knowledge. *Journal of Medical Humanities, 24*(3-4), 265-278.

Chandler, G. E. (2012). Succeeding in the first year of practice: Heed the wisdom of novice nurses. *Journal for Nurses in Professional Development, 28*(3), 103-107.

Chiavaroli, N., & Trumble, S. (2018). When I say ... phronesis. *Medical Education.* Retrieved from https://doi.org/10.1111/medu.13611

Cowley, C. (2012). Expertise, wisdom and moral philosophers: A response to Gesang. *Bioethics, 26*(6), 337-342.

de Cossart, L., Fish, D., & Hillman, K. (2012). Clinical reflection: A vital process for supporting the development of wisdom in doctors. *Current Opinion in Critical Care, 18*(6), 712-717.

De Freitas, J., Haque, O. S., Gopal, A. A., & Bursztajn, H. J. (2012). Response: Clinical wisdom and evidence-based medicine are complementary. *Clinical Ethics, 23*(1), 28-36.

Dowie, A. I. (2000). Phronesis or 'practical wisdom' in medical education. *Medical Teacher, 22*(3), 240-241.

Edmonson, R., & Pearce J. (2007). The practice of health care: Wisdom as a model. *Medicine, Health Care and Philosophy, 10*(3), 233-244.

Foucault, M. (1976). *The birth of the clinic*. London, England: Routledge.

Glück, J., & Bluck, S. (2013). The MORE life experience model: A theory of the development of personal wisdom. In M. Ferrari & N. M. Weststrate (Eds.), *The scientific study of personal wisdom: From contemplative traditions to neuroscience* (pp. 75-97). Dordrecht, The Netherlands: Springer.

Grossmann, I. (2017). Wisdom in context. *Perspectives on Psychological Science 2017, 12*(2), 233-257.

Kaldjian, L. C. (2010). Teaching practical wisdom in medicine through clinical judgement: Goals of care and ethical reasoning. *Journal of Medical Ethics, 36*, 558-562.

Kotzee, B., Ignatowicz, A., & Thomas, H. (2017). Virtue in medical practice: An exploratory study. *Journal of Medical Humanities, 29*(1), 1-19.

Kumagai, A. K. (2014). From competencies to human interests: Ways of knowing and understanding in medical education. *Academic Medicine, 89*(7), 978-983.

Leget, C. (2004). Avoiding evasion: Medical ethics education and emotions theory. *Journal of Medical Ethics, 30*(5), 490-493.

Marcum, J. A. (2013). The role of empathy and wisdom in medical practice and pedagogy: Confronting the hidden curriculum. *Journal of Biomedical Education.* Retrieved from http://dx.doi.org/10.1155/2013/923810

Miller, P. A, & Platter, C. (2010). *Plato's apology of Socrates: A commentary*. Norman, OK: University of Oklahoma Press.

Pellegrino, E. D, & Thomasma, D. C. (1993). *The virtues in medical practice*. Oxford, England: Oxford University Press.

Plato. (2010). *The last days of Socrates* (C. Rowe & H. Tarrant, Trans.). London, England: Penguin Classics. (Original work published c. 400 BC)

van Thiel, G. J. M. W., & van Delden, J. J. M. (2009). The justificatory power of moral experience. *Journal of Medical Ethics, 35*, 234-237.

Widdershoven, G., Abma, T., & Molewijk, B. (2009). Empirical ethics as dialogue. *Bioethics, 23*(4), 236-248.

Widdershoven, G. A. M., Ruissen, A., van Blakom, A. J. L. M., & Meynen, G. (2017). Competence in chronic mental illness: The relevance of practical wisdom. *Journal of Medical Ethics, 43*, 374-378.

Wisnewski, J. J. (2015). Perceiving sympathetically: Moral perception, embodiment and medical ethics. *Journal of Medical Humanities, 36*(4), 309-319.

Zucker, A. (2006). Medical ethics as therapy. *Medical Humanities, 32*, 48-52.

Deborah Bowman PhD (ORCID: https://orcid.org/0000-0002-1020-2058)
St George's, University of London, United Kingdom

LAURA BÉRES

23. VALUING CRITICAL REFLECTION AND NARRATIVES IN PROFESSIONAL PRACTICE WISDOM

I was recently talking with a graduate student who was in the final weeks of a Critical Reflection and Appraisal of her Social Work course that I facilitate in a Canadian university context. As we chatted about her learning process, we realised that while beginning social workers and counsellors might believe they can talk about their intuitions or "gut feelings", they probably do not feel quite as comfortable describing themselves as having "practice wisdom". We realised the term "wisdom" connotes age and experience.

In this chapter, with a sense of humility, I will describe how critical reflection and a commitment to narrative ways of working have contributed to what could be described as the development of my professional "practice wisdom". I am old enough now to try using this term. I begin by describing a little of my background to provide the context from which I am writing and then present an incident from my practice which I have examined through the theoretical frameworks which are part of Fook's model of critical reflection (Fook, 2002; Fook & Gardner, 2007). I will focus on an incident from my teaching practice, which has contributed to the ongoing development of not only my teaching but also my counselling practices. I am interested in exploring the process of critically reflecting upon professional practices and I suggest this process provides the possibility to reimagine what it means to be "experienced"; I offer the opinion that someone who reflects upon their practice will become "radically undogmatic" (Gadamer, 1960/2000, p. 355), always committed to being prepared to learn afresh, and thereby also continually developing practice wisdom.

BACKGROUND

Narrative Therapy and Critical Reflection

I have been a clinical social worker for almost 30 years and have been integrating narrative ways of working into my practice for at least the last 20 of those years. This commitment to narrative practices was first inspired by attending one of Michael White's (1995b) narrative therapy training workshops regarding therapeutic conversations as collaborative inquiry and I was later able to train with him at the Dulwich Centre in Australia (White, 2006, 2007a). In a similar vein, I was first inspired by Jan Fook's work on critical reflection and critical social work (1993, 1999) while pursuing doctoral studies but it was not until later that I had the opportunity to meet her and participate in a critical reasoning workshop. These two areas of my practice have come together as I am interested in the manner in which narrative therapy and critical reflection share many common underlying philosophies and principles (Béres, Bowles, & Fook, 2011), and also in how they might each support further development of the other.

For the past 15 years I have been an academic within the School of Social Work in a small Catholic liberal arts university. I primarily teach direct practice courses, facilitating a *Narrative Therapy; Theory and Practice* elective as well as a *Critical Reflection and Appraisal of Practice* required course in the Master of Social Work program. Finally, in addition to this academic position, I work one night each week at a local counselling agency, where I offer individual psychotherapy appointments.

I am happy to be engaged in a counselling practice as well as an educational practice. Not only is it rewarding to be meeting with people each week, it also provides opportunity for me to continue developing my clinical practice skills. In addition, being involved in a clinical practice ensures I am teaching the related practice skills more effectively. It keeps me grounded in the real world, alert to my strengths and challenges, and more aware of the changing demands in the field.

The above interests are perhaps what well position me to write in this chapter about valuing critical reflection and narratives of professional practice. However, I also have a keen interest in the area of spirituality, which I will describe further.

Spirituality

In pursuing the study of spirituality over the last several years, I have found two definitions of spirituality to be the most helpful when attempting to describe what I mean by this term. Canda, who has written extensively on the topic of spirituality within the field of social work, defines it as "the human quest for personal meaning and mutually fulfilling relationships among people, the non-human environment, and, for some, God" (Canda, 1988, p. 243). Cook, Powell, and Sims (2009) of the Royal College of Psychiatrists in the United Kingdom define it as follows:

> Spirituality is a distinctive, potentially creative and universal dimension of human experience arising from both within the inner subjective awareness of individuals and within communities, social groups and traditions. It may be experienced as relationship with that which is intimately 'inner', immanent and personal, within the self and others, and/or as relationship with that which is wholly 'other', transcendent and beyond the self. It is experienced as being of fundamental or ultimate importance and is thus concerned with matters of meaning and purpose in life, truth and values. (p. 4)

Keeping these broad definitions of spirituality in mind, thinking of it as being what provides meaning and purpose to people, and also considering Ghaye's (2010) contention that it can support "human flourishing" it appears to me that it could be unethical *not* to integrate conversations about spirituality into psychotherapeutic practices and the teaching of those practices. Holloway and Moss (2010) and Pargament (2011) suggest professional practitioners are unprepared to deal with the area of spirituality, indicating that while 58% of service *users* in the United States of

America describe themselves as being religious or spiritual, only 24% of service *providers* describe themselves that way. I have observed that some of my Canadian social work students, having identified the damage caused, and abuses perpetrated, by organised religion (which are, admittedly, many), can become almost dogmatically opposed to anything religious or spiritual. Therefore, in teaching students to conduct bio-psycho-social-spiritual assessments, I encourage them to explore with people both the problems and strengths inherent in each of these areas of their lives. This involves finding a way to hold onto their own positions less dogmatically so that they can be curious and respectful about how others engage with spirituality in their lives. For instance, Canda and Furman (1999) and Crisp (2010) suggest that people's spiritual activities can range from attending late night clubs and raves, walking in nature, practising yoga and mindfulness, participating in sweat lodges, to attending more formal services offered by organised religions. All these activities provide people with opportunities for feeling connected to something other than themselves.

I offer two short examples here to indicate how people might discuss their spirituality in a counselling setting. The first involves meeting with a middle-aged woman who had been referred to me due to recently disclosing having been sexually assaulted by a priest when she was a child. I expected to hear from her that she was angry at the Church and had given up on religion altogether. However, she reported that she held the individual priest responsible for the abuse, and she continued to find peace in attending her local church services regularly. The second example is of meeting with a young woman who requested counselling regarding the grief associated with having given birth to a stillborn baby two years earlier. When first asked about whether she had any spiritual practices that assisted her, she described her love of using rocks as a method of grounding herself. She was able to engage in mindfulness practices, holding on to a smooth rock in each hand, focusing on the weight and texture of each as a method for staying present and slowing her otherwise racing thoughts. She went on to describe the comfort she received from keeping her baby's memory alive through various means, like journaling and speaking of her baby often. I did not suggest these practices to these two women. Rather, I merely assisted them in reflecting upon and identifying what was meaningful to them and might, therefore, continue to be useful. I offer these examples as a way of highlighting the point that integrating spirituality into practice is not about creating an avenue for proselytising or imposing our own beliefs, or lack of beliefs. It is about being curious regarding what the people who consult us value, which is consistent with a narrative therapist's stance and approach to working with people.

NARRATIVE THERAPY'S CONTRIBUTIONS TO VALUING PRACTICE WISDOM

The philosophical and political underpinnings of narrative therapy are the primary reasons why I continue to be committed to this way of working with people. White (1995a, 2007b) suggests narrative therapists take a de-centered but influential posture within therapeutic conversations. This stance encourages a privileging of "insider knowledge" (what the people requesting counselling know about their lived experiences). I encourage students, as a result of this approach, to celebrate that we may become experts in asking good therapeutic questions, but we cannot be experts of another person's life. We should not be attempting to interpret what people say to us but rather we should be maintaining curiosity about how people make meaning of the events in their lives, what their hopes and preferred storylines for their lives are, and what is "absent but implicit" (White, 2007a) in what they are saying. White developed this idea of the "absent but implicit" in therapeutic conversations within the theoretical framework of postmodernism, and particularly through considering Derrida's theorising regarding elements of language and the role of deconstruction.

> For Derrida ... each element acquires meaning only through a play of differences, the intersignificative relationship to one another of elements which themselves lack self-present meaning. Each element is so interwoven with every other that it is constituted only by the traces within it of the other bits in the chain or system. There are no independent meanings but only traces of traces. (Wyschogrod, 1989, p. 192)

Using these insights and integrating them within a therapeutic conversation, allows narrative therapists to become curious about what is "absent" and unarticulated in a person's story, but which is implied. Using a framework of the "absent but implicit" conversational map provides a structure which suggests how a therapist can ask the types of questions which facilitate the reflection process for people so that they can uncover and then articulate what was implicit in what was said; the therapist does not interpret or suggest what they think might be implied. The therapist only asks questions to support the other person becoming clearer about these underlying assumptions. These taken-for-granted assumptions often have to do with what the person particularly values, based upon what they have learned, and the skills they have developed over the course of their lives (Béres, 2014; Carey, Walther, & Russell, 2009; White, 2007a).

Listening to peoples' stories with a narrative therapist's curiosity, privileging others' insider knowledge, and assisting them in articulating how they make meaning of events in their lives, has been a humbling experience. I have found that meeting with people and assisting them in moving towards preferred ways of being in their lives brings great joy also. There has been much written over the years regarding the risks of burnout and vicarious trauma, and I have certainly heard many heart-breaking stories of abuse and sorrow. Yet, walking alongside people as they explore and develop their stories of resilience can result in "vicarious resilience" (Hernández, Gansei & Engstrom, 2007) and a sense of wonder regarding people's ability to resist pathologising accounts and step into new choices regarding the directions of their lives. People become more comfortable celebrating their wisdom, and I wonder whether we, as narrative therapists, can begin to experience some of that wisdom vicariously. Certainly, the narrative therapist's stance of honouring insider knowledge, and demonstrating curiosity about the person's meaning-making and personal values, operationalises a radically undogmatic position, whereby counsellors do not interpret from their own knowledge base. Rather, narrative therapists constantly learn from the people with whom they engage in therapeutic conversations. This stance shares something of the flexibility and improvisation which Payne (2007) suggests are required for social workers to "embody or incorporate knowledge and understanding to become a 'wise person'" (p. 94). He argues that while discourses surrounding evidence-based practice and many social work theories attempt to promote the impression of certainty and order, interpersonal interactions between social workers and the people who consult us cannot help but be inherently uncertain. He describes the process of developing comfort with the uncertainty as involving a willingness to improvise, drawing upon not only theoretical knowledge, but also upon knowledge about organisations, situations, those people who consult us, and self. He concludes:

> My conceptualisation of practice is to say that it is always provisional. We improvise a performance with and alongside the people we serve and our colleagues. We incorporate and embody knowledge and understanding that we have achieved as our persona as a wise person. We restructure and incorporate knowledge and evidence, in accordance with the needs of the situation and the people in it; that is our wisdom. (Payne, 2007, p. 95)

This description of the development of practice wisdom and the persona of the social worker as a wise person shares much in common with the underlying attitudes of White and Epston's (1990) narrative practices as well as Fook's (2002) critical reflection.

CRITICAL REFLECTION'S CONTRIBUTIONS TO PRACTICE WISDOM

Social work is often described as both an art and a science. It involves academic study, learning theory and skills, but then in the moment of working with people, the social worker may need also to draw upon creativity, to consider their intuitions, and sometimes just "fly by the seat of their pants", or improvise, as Payne describes it. We respond to what people raise in counselling sessions, and we cannot and should not expect to be fully prepared for every situation. People will surprise us. Samson (2015), in fact, suggests that practice wisdom is about bridging this gap between theory and practice, or creatively filling this gap between "art" and "science". This is one of the key elements of critical reflection.

I have taught Fook's model of critical reasoning by using Fook and Gardner's (2007) *Practising Critical Reflection: A Resource Handbook* to provide a straightforward overview of the model's theory and practice. In this handbook the critical reasoning model is described as being made up of four theoretical frameworks, or lenses, through which an incident from practice can be examined to learn about and further develop our practice. These four lenses are: the Reflective Approach; Reflexivity; Postmodernism and Deconstruction; and Critical Social Theory. Using the Reflective Approach lens, drawing upon Schön's (1983) work in particular, allows for an examination of the differences between our espoused theories and how we actually have practised, and what this implies about our implicit but previously unarticulated theories which have perhaps filled that "gap" in our practice. Reflexivity suggests it is important to consider how we as observers of our practice colour what we see due to our own personality, and social location. Postmodernism and Deconstruction encourage an examination of the language and discourses we have used in the description of our practice, encouraging an openness to including multiple perspectives, and the "unpacking" of any discourses which might have subtly influenced our point of view. Critical Social Theory ensures the inclusion of an examination of power and the broader social structures which might be maintaining certain relationships of power within our practice. Brookfield (2016) suggests it is the inclusion of Critical Social Theory that makes critical reflection *critical*. However, Fook (2017) has more recently also been adding to these four theoretical frameworks a fifth: Spirituality. For this reason, I have also added the topics of spirituality (Hunt, 2016) and human flourishing (Ghaye, 2010) to the four theoretical frameworks presented in Fook and Gardner's (2007) handbook when I teach critical reasoning.

Fook's Critical Reasoning Model is made up of two stages. The aim of the first is to support people in uncovering their underlying fundamental assumptions, which, in addition to their espoused theories and commitments, are influencing their practices and their reactions to situations. This is somewhat similar to the notion of the "absent but implicit" as described in relation to narrative therapy. The second assists people in then articulating and labelling their newly identified knowledge. Recognising the connection between language, knowledge and power, this step of naming the new insights takes on significance. The person who has moved through the two stages of the critical reasoning process is then better positioned to consider how to integrate this "practice-based evidence" into their work, generalise learning to other contexts and share this new knowledge with others.

With these above ideas as a backdrop, I will present an incident from my teaching of a critical reasoning course. This will demonstrate the process of taking a radically undogmatic stance in my teaching practice and the resulting dialogue that developed between a graduate student and myself, which has supported both of us in our learning and development of practice wisdom.

A CRITICAL INCIDENT AND RESULTING LEARNING

As I write this chapter, I am in the final weeks of teaching the *Critical Reflection and Appraisal of Practice* course for the second time. The first year I taught the course, Jan Fook and I received research ethics approval to examine the process of teaching and learning critical reflection within this academic setting. As one part of the research process I incorporated the use of Stephen Brookfield's Critical Incident Questionnaires (CIQs).[1] These questionnaires are designed to be given to students at the end of each week's class, asking them anonymously to respond to a series of questions like "At what moment in class this week did you feel most engaged with what was happening?" and "What about the class this week surprised you the most?" I decided as I began to teach the course for a second time that I would continue to use these CIQs each week. My intention in using them this second time was to facilitate students' reflection on their learning process. Incorporating the use of CIQs also offers me the opportunity to consider if I need to adjust anything in my teaching style and the chance to respond to any concerns. During this second year of teaching critical reasoning, in the second week I talked about the power of discourses and the social construction of ideas we begin to hold as truth. Within this context I discussed the role of hegemony, and then went on to talk about how power can be both personal and social, and how critical social theory encourages us to examine this interplay of the social structures of power, and how people individually are able to access or respond to that power. A student asked how powerful I thought religion is within this context. I found this an interesting question, and at that moment my mind went to arguments about how much more secular a society we have become and how little influence the Christian church thinks it has in a Western context. I felt I had been open and non-defensive to this question although I may not have articulated all my thoughts that had been triggered by this question. Having also already described my commitment to a stance of vulnerability, as an element of transformative learning, I then shared an anonymised incident from my counselling practice and in small groups students began generating questions to ask of me, informed by the four theoretical frameworks of critical reasoning. Later, when I reviewed the CIQs for that class, one of the comments unsettled me. The comment was made in response to the question about what had surprised them that week: "I guess I was surprised by what I felt was discomfort speaking about the impact of religion on hegemony. I suppose it should be expected – this is a Christian school. But I do feel *a lot* of damage has been done to people because of religion, especially in terms of hegemonic practices. We could have explored this more" (Anonymous CIQ comment, September 18, 2018). My mind kept going back to this comment during the week and I fretted about it. These were good signs that it could be useful to examine this feedback as a critical incident, and I decided to use the critical reasoning framework to journal about it. I realised that there was clearly a "gap" between how I had wanted to come across – as open and willing to discuss any related topics in class – and how I had come across at least to this one student. I acknowledged that it is important to me always to examine the effects of my actions rather than only considering my intentions, and in regards to critical social theory and relations of power, I wrote:

> I have power as the professor and we are in a powerful educational structure. I can feel vulnerable and insecure and frustrated but I am the one with tenure and I will be the one grading. The students have power to resist and power to complain but I still have more power. How do I share power, since that is one of my values? The students have the ability to use the CIQs to point out things like this anonymously. I have a love hate relationship with these CIQs. (Journal entry, September 24, 2018)

Since I was attempting to teach in a non-dogmatic fashion and had expressed a willingness to be vulnerable and accept my own fallibility (following Brookfield, 2016), I attempted to model these commitments in my response to this comment the following week. I explained how I had worried about the comment all week and said that the university was first and foremost an institution committed to academic freedom and intellectual exploration and it was not because it was a "Christian" setting that I responded poorly to the question. I explained that it was due to the fact I had been thinking about how religious studies scholars are more apt to consider us living in a secular society that I was thinking religion does not currently have very much power. However, I went on to share my experiences of working with Indigenous communities and acknowledged the damage done by religion in the past. I explained my understanding of the difference between domination (which the churches exerted in the past in relation to the residential schools for Indigenous children in Canada, for example) and hegemony, where power is used in a more subtle and "sneaky" way, resulting often in winning consent from us to conditions which are not to our benefit. I also admitted that during the week I had come to realise that religion probably does continue to have hegemonic influences, offering the example of how Alcoholics Anonymous incorporates an understanding of a higher power. As we stopped to take a coffee break, a student came to speak to me, apologising for having caused me stress during the week because of his comment. He indicated being surprised by how carefully I had read the CIQs and how seriously I took them, but also said he thought his reaction and the comment he had made the week before had more to do with his own past experiences with religion than they did with me and my behaviours. However, he also thanked me for clarifying the differences between domination and hegemony. This set the stage for further discussions between the two of us, over the term, about both spirituality and the paradigm shift he has experienced as he has immersed himself in the critical reasoning process. I will describe how this incident and my response to it provides an example of the ongoing process of developing practice wisdom. It clearly demonstrates the role of critical reasoning in practice wisdom, since the incident came about while teaching critical reasoning, and I also used a critical reasoning framework to begin to deconstruct it. It also provides a narrative of how my practice wisdom continues evolving. However, what I want to do more fully is highlight how my narrative therapy stance, with its commitment to holding onto professional knowledge undogmatically and maintaining curiosity about the other's insider knowledge, also provides the conditions necessary for becoming an "experienced person", as Gadamer (1960/2000) uses this term: someone wise enough to know there is always more to learn.

PRACTICE WISDOM AND THE "EXPERIENCED PERSON"

A common-sense understanding of an experienced person might suggest such a person has merely gathered more experiences than someone else. In this scenario each experience might merely reinforce or deepen previous experience. Gadamer (1960/2000), however, suggests experience can stand in opposition to what a person previously believed themselves to know and understand, opening up the possibility for a kind of learning that unsettles previously held beliefs. Chambon (1999) poetically suggests that "transformative knowledge is disturbing by nature. It disturbs commonly acceptable ways of doing and disturbs the person implementing it. It ruffles the smoothness of our habits, rattles our certainties, disorganizes and reorganizes our understandings" (p. 53). If critical reasoning can assist us in realising that how we have been understanding and making sense of the world is just one perspective, influenced by taken-for-granted assumptions, then it will disturb and ruffle. These are good consequences, keeping us humble and open to developing wisdom. A person is experienced, therefore, not due to having gone through a certain number of experiences but rather due to being open to new experience. Gadamer describes "being experienced" as not consisting of knowing everything or knowing more than anyone else. He says, "the experienced person proves to be, on the contrary, someone who is radically undogmatic" (Gadamer, 1960/2000, p. 355). Being undogmatic suggests holding knowledge tentatively and being willing to be surprised by new ways of thinking and being.

By going through the critical reasoning process in relation to two incidents I experienced while teaching the critical reasoning course the first time, I realised that while I might have been unsettled by how vulnerable I felt while teaching this course I was also committed to this as being a necessary element of transformative teaching. Oyler and Becker (1997), moving beyond the dichotomy of traditional versus progressive forms of teaching, argue that a "different place" is found between these opposite points of the teaching continuum, which involves sharing both authority and vulnerability. They say teachers should open up their own imperfections so as to make room in the classroom for students also to show their imperfections. "To share authority with our students requires that we become vulnerable. To do otherwise puts us back in one of the old places: the rock of unquestionable authority or the soft place of acquiesced authority" (Oyler & Becker, 1997, p. 463).

Meyer, Le Fevre, and Robinson (2017) also hold a positive view of vulnerability. They argue, "[t]o be honest and open means to accept responsibility and expose one's own mistakes or weakness, in other words, to show vulnerability" (p. 222). They say showing vulnerability can actually be seen as a strength, signalling a genuine desire to reflect on and inquire into one's own position. Their research provided me with encouragement to continue showing my vulnerability and thus contribute to a sense of trust and willingness in students to also show vulnerability, which is often required for engaging in the critical reasoning process. However, what has been interesting for me to consider, despite what I consider a positive outcome in the incident I described above, is how unsettled I felt about the CIQs. In fact, I discontinued using them halfway through the course this year. I realised that without asking students to put their names on the CIQs they were less careful about how they wrote about one another and their reactions to the class process.

Liechty (2018) has provided me with one way of making sense of my reactions, reporting on her research in which she explored the definitional challenges of the term "use of self". She facilitated three focus groups with 10 Bachelor of Social Work educators with a mean of 16 years of teaching experience.

> The participants described use of self as an essential factor in the social worker-client relationship that they strive to inculcate in their students and manifest in their own practice. The findings depict use of self as the ultimate integration of theory and practice embodied in the social worker and enacted in the social worker-client relationship. (Liechty, 2018, p. 151)

She goes on to present the themes that emerged from her analysis of the focus groups' discussions within two different frameworks: the personal qualities, and the professional capabilities, required for appropriate use of self. The personal qualities that influence use of self are described as openness, self-reflectiveness, attunement to others, commitment to social work, and emotional maturity. Openness is described as including elements of trust, curiosity and wonder, authenticity, willingness to share uncertainty, and courage. Attunement to others is described as including elements of caring and empathy, intuition, awareness of how others experience us, and emotional boundaries (Liechty, 2018). Her comments resonated with my own commitments to authenticity, vulnerability and curiosity, contributing to considerations of how I am also engaging in the use of self as I teach. I have often suggested to students that I am interested in ensuring congruence between various elements of life, so that I do not "take off and put on different hats" as I move from one role to another in my life. Obviously, the consistent element across these various areas of my life is my sense of self. However, what was new and most helpful for me was her description of the need to balance the awareness of how others experience us with the need for emotional boundaries. She says:

> Participant 9 responded, 'It includes an awareness and sensitivity to how others experience us.' This sensitivity is desirable but can be overwhelming. Participant 10 noted, ... 'At the same time we're trying to become empathetic, we become blind in the process, to tune out some of that, because it's too much stimulation.' He noted, 'There are really two processes – perceiving and protecting yourself simultaneously'. (Liechty, 2018, p. 154)

She describes emotional boundaries as requiring adequate personal boundaries "to develop and maintain empathy while balancing perception and self-protection" (p. 154). This idea of needing to balance self-protection with an openness to others and willingness to be vulnerable provided me with an "aha" moment.

This particular academic term in which this described incident occurred was a particularly busy and emotionally draining four months for a variety of reasons. My past experiences and practice wisdom suggested continuing to model vulnerability and authenticity and also to continue using the CIQs to assist with attunement to students' experiences. However, at a certain point I trusted my intuition and discontinued the use of the CIQs, and I have realised this has contributed to my practice wisdom by helping me realise that I also need to engage in self-protection through the use of emotional boundaries at times. Using the critical reasoning lens of Reflexivity, I recognise there are elements of my personal life that have positioned me to be hyper-aware of other's emotions and the dynamics between people, so what I require for self-protection might be quite different from what someone else might need. As Liechty (2018) points out, the use of self, when incorporating the personal qualities reviewed above, results in practice wisdom along with other professional capabilities, such as the embodiment of the integration of theory and practice in the social worker and the enactment of a nurturing therapeutic relationship.

CONCLUSION

I have explored how the critical reflection process and particular commitments of narrative practices have contributed to how I have been able to conceive of, and develop, practice wisdom. I have presented these explorations by describing a recent incident in my teaching practice and the resulting learning. This learning has contributed to my practice wisdom which remains undogmatic, provisional and always open to further adjustment. As Payne (2007) suggests, practice wisdom can be considered as being embodied in the practitioner in their persona as a wise person. That wise person then improvises and performs their wisdom in their therapeutic and educational relationships. I believe it is useful to consider practice wisdom in this way as an ongoing process and enactment, rather than as a commodity or skill that we have, or do not have. It is through its integration into relationship and dialogue that this wisdom may contribute to the human flourishing of others as well as the improvement of our own practices.

ACKNOWLEDGEMENTS

Thanks to all the students in the Critical Reflection and Appraisal of Practice Course for taking the chance to jump into the critical reasoning process and allowing me to learn alongside them.

NOTE

[1] http://www.stephenbrookfield.com/ciq

REFERENCES

Béres, L. (2014). *The narrative practitioner.* Basingstoke, England: Palgrave Macmillan.
Béres, L., Bowles, K., & Fook, J. (2011). Narrative therapy and critical reflection on practice: A conversation with Jan Fook. *Journal of Systemic Therapies, 30*(2), 81-97.
Brookfield, S. (2016). So what exactly is critical about critical reflection? In J. Fook, V. Collington, F. Ross, G. Ruch, & L. West (Eds.), *Researching critical reflection: Multidisciplinary perspectives* (pp. 11-22). London, England: Routledge.
Canda, E. R. (1988). Spirituality, diversity, and social work practice. *Social Casework, 69*(4), 238-247.
Canda, E. R., & E. D. Furman. (1999). *Spiritual diversity in social work practice: The heart of helping.* New York, NY: Free Press.
Carey, M., Walther, S., & Russell, S. (2009). The absent but implicit: A map to support therapeutic enquiry. *Family Process, 48*(3), 319-331.
Chambon, A. S. (1999). Foucault's approach: Making the familiar visible. In A. S. Chambon, A. Irving, & L. Epstein (Eds.), *Reading Foucault for social work* (pp. 51-82). New York, NY: Columbia University Press.
Cook, C., Powell, A., & Sims, A. (Eds). (2009). *Spirituality and psychiatry.* Glasgow, Scotland: RCPsych.
Crisp, B. (2010). *Spirituality and social work.* Farnham, England: Ashgate.
Fook, J. (1993). *Radical casework: A theory of practice.* St. Leonards, Australia: Allen & Unwin.
Fook, J. (1999). Critical reflectivity in education and practice. In B. Pease & J. Fook (Eds.), *Transforming social work practice: Postmodern critical perspectives* (pp. 195-210). St. Leonards, Australia: Allen & Unwin.
Fook, J. (2002). *Social work: Critical theory and practice.* London, England: Sage.

Fook, J. (2017). Critical reflection and spirituality. In Béres, L. (Ed.), *Practising spirituality: Reflections on meaning-making in personal and professional contexts* (pp. 17-29). London, England: Palgrave Macmillan.

Fook, J., & Gardner, F. (2007). *Practising critical reflection: A resource handbook.* Maidenhead, England: Open University Press.

Gadamer, H.-G. (2000). *Truth and method* (2nd rev. ed., J. Weinsheimer & D. G. Marshall, trans. rev. ed. 1989). New York, NY: Continuum. (Original work published 1960)

Ghaye, T. (2010). Editorial: In what ways can reflective practices enhance human flourishing? *Reflective Practice, 11*(1), 1-7.

Hernández, P., Gansei, D., & Engstrom, D. (2007). Vicarious reliance: A new concept in work with those who survive trauma. *Family Process, 26*(2), 229-241.

Holloway, M., & Moss, B. (2010). *Spirituality and social work.* Basingstoke, England: Palgrave Macmillan.

Hunt, C. (2016). Spiritual creatures? Exploring an interface between critical reflective practice and spirituality. In J. Fook, V. Collington, F. Ross, G. Ruch, & L. West (Eds.), *Researching critical reflection: Multidisciplinary perspectives* (pp. 34-47). London, England: Routledge.

Liechty, J. (2018). Exploring use of self: Moving beyond definitional challenges. *Journal of Social Work Education, 54*(1), 148-162.

Meyer, F., Le Fevre, D. M., & Robinson, V. M. J. (2017). How leaders communicate their vulnerability: Implications for trust building. *International Journal of Educational Management, 3*(2), 221-235.

Oyler, C., & Becker, J. (1997). Teaching beyond the progressive-traditional dichotomy: Sharing authority and sharing vulnerability. *Curriculum Inquiry, 27*(4), 453-467.

Pargament, K. I. (2011). *Spiritually integrated psychotherapy: Understanding and addressing the sacred.* New York, NY: The Guilford Press.

Payne, M. (2007). Performing as a 'wise person' in social work practice. *Practice, 19*(2), 85-96.

Samson, P. L. (2015). Practice wisdom: The art and science of social work. *Journal of Social Work Practice, 29*(2), 119-131.

Schön, D. A. (1983). *The reflective practitioner: How professionals think in action.* New York, NY: Basic Books.

White, M. (1995a). *Re-authoring lives: Interviews and essays.* Adelaide, Australia: Dulwich Centre Publications.

White, M. (1995b, March 22 & 23). *Therapeutic conversations as collaborative inquiry.* Two-day training sponsored by the Brief Therapy Training Centres International (a division of Hincks-Dellcrest, Gail Appel Institute), Toronto, Canada.

White, M. (2006). *Seven-month narrative therapy extern training program.* Program sponsored by the Dulwich Centre, Adelaide, Australia.

White, M. (2007a, December 10-15). *Level 2 narrative therapy training.* Training sponsored by the Dulwich Centre, Adelaide, Australia.

White, M. (2007b). *Maps of narrative practice.* New York, NY: W.W. Norton.

White, M., & Epston, D. (1990). *Narrative means to therapeutic ends.* New York, NY: W.W. Norton.

Wyschogrod, E. (1989). Derrida, Levinas, and violence. In H. J. Silverman (Ed.), *Continental philosophy II: Derrida and deconstruction* (pp. 177-194). New York, NY: Routledge.

Laura Béres PhD (ORCID: https://orcid.org/0000-0001-6926-0562)
School of Social Work
King's University College at Western University, Canada

JOY PATON AND SHERIDAN LINNELL

24. EMBODIED WISDOM IN THE CREATIVE ARTS THERAPIES

Learning from Contemporary Art

Practice wisdom in any field can be learned. However, it is not the kind of knowledge that can be codified for instruction manuals under some notion of "best practice" (Cheung, 2017). As Jean-Paul Sartre once stated, "[s/he] who begins with facts will never arrive at essences" (in Becker, 2009, p. 59). This sense of journeying to the "essence" or embodied heart and mind of knowledge is practice wisdom's locale. It is unsurprising therefore that it may feel elusive to those in the early years of their profession and most certainly an enigma for those in training. Practice wisdom is a form of "moral practical reasoning" (Tsang, 2008, p. 131); a "personal and value-driven system of knowledge" (Klein & Bloom, 1995, p. 799). It is the "knowing-in-action" evident in "the artistic, intuitive processes" skilled and experienced practitioners bring to difficult or uncertain situations (Schön, 1983, p. 49).

Practice wisdom provides a bridge between thinking and doing. It goes beyond the theory/practice binary, to embrace how one's initial training and guiding theories are tested, modified and refined through lived professional experience. Learning in this embodied sense is about the kind of "knowing" equated with "changes in understanding" derived from experience rather than fact acquisition (Ramsden, 2003, p. 37). Those who engage deeply with their subject matter, "with the heart ... the mind, and the spirit of play ... will more likely come to grasp it at its core than those who rely on information, quantification, or objectification" (Becker, 2009, p. 59). The reference to play here is crucial: "to play is to [be] free ... from arbitrary restrictions [which] fosters richness of response and adaptive flexibility" (Nachmanovitch, 1990, pp. 42-43). These are hallmarks of practice wisdom.

Embodied learning is transformative, not only of knowledge but of the practitioner him or herself. This "knowing" becomes part of the learner's "way of interpreting the universe" (Ramsden, 2003, p. 60), and engaging with it. However, there is also engagement with the idea that all knowledge is fallible and uncertain: "truth" remains provisional (Perry, in Ramsden, 2003). The starting place for such learning is, according to Eisner (2003), "the activation of our senses" (p. 341). This suggests the tactile and experiential nature of artmaking is pivotal for learning in the creative arts therapies. Central here, we argue, is an engagement with the insights and practices of contemporary art alongside an ongoing relationship to one's personal artmaking. In considering the significance of contemporary art for the theory and practice of art therapy, a space is opened up to explore the particular form of embodied, practice wisdom – the *artistry* – that stems from developing and maintaining a visual arts practice.

THERE IS NOTHING IN THE HEAD THAT IS NOT FIRST IN THE HAND[1]

In the psychotherapies and counselling, practice wisdom is most often thought to derive from years of reflexive *clinical* practice (Rabu & McLeod, 2018). While this is also true of creative arts therapies, there is another, equally important area of practice through which creative arts therapists develop embodied knowledge. For these therapists, the development and maintenance of a personal arts practice can be an ongoing source of wisdom that deepens insight into the therapeutic possibilities of the arts. For visual art therapists, artmaking is key to the making of a specific professional identity and the development of an approach in which creativity is to the fore. This is so for trainees, beginning therapists, experienced practitioners and educators in the field.

The education and training of art therapists is about preparing practitioners to develop *artistry* in doing their work (Rubin, 2011). Such practitioners are able to use their imagination and skills of improvisation in conjunction with their accumulated knowledge of art and therapy. They can "think artistically about what they do … experience their work as it unfolds … exploit the unexpected, and … make judgements about its direction on the basis of feeling as well as rule" (Eisner, 2003, p. 343). These trademark skills of wise practice are also skills and processes cultivated in and by "the artist". Having some kind of training and experience in the arts is a prerequisite for the professional art therapist. This seems obvious enough. However, developing the kind of "sense/ability" that constitutes embodied practice wisdom in the creative arts therapies requires something more.

An ongoing engagement with art media is a fundamental aspect of the profession and is the "soil" within which practice wisdom can be cultivated. A committed arts practice and being active as a practising artist are central to being an "attuned" art therapist (Kramer, 1979). And here, it is the processes and materials of art *making* that come to the fore, even while the product of these combined "forces" – the artwork – is, seemingly, the *raison d'être* of such activity. This is true of client work in the therapeutic space as much as it is in the art therapist's personal artmaking space. Through the direct hands-on experience of materials and media, the art therapist learns about the therapeutic potential of art. Indeed, making art "in a sustained, mindful and self-invested way", the art therapist creates the conditions for not just understanding, but also for *embodying* such potential (Allen, 1992, p. 23).

The interaction between artmaking and art media is a self-reinforcing learning experience stemming from and feeding back into the development of a material sensibility. Crucial though, to this virtuous cycle of "cumulative causation" (see Myrdal, 1944), is the giving of oneself over to the "play": allowing space for the art media to lead and then "following the possibilities assiduously" (Kentridge, 2014a, p. 107). For this, the studio space (and the therapeutic space) need to be "safe places for stupidity", by which Kentridge (2014a) means making space for uncertainty, for "following impulses … without a destination … [without premature evaluation] … allowing the work to take [its] time" (p. 128).

Inferring from Maclagan's work (2001), sustaining and accumulating artistic experiences in this way is as important for the art therapist as working with one's own dreams might be for a psychoanalyst. Regular art practice can sustain art therapy practitioners over time as they face the difficulties and vicarious pain of working closely with clients who are experiencing distress, and it can provide a safe space in which to explore what may be provoked for the therapists themselves. Practitioners can embrace the contingency and uncertainty of artmaking and thereby expand their possibilities for "knowing" and "being":

> Although the process of making is uncertain, I felt excited within that, as [the work] came together. Knowledge gained from art making is different to that of science and speaks without words, a form or style of knowing something. Art making expands my sense of self. (Robert Hulland, in Paton & Linnell, 2018, p. 103)

Just as practice wisdom from lived professional experience needs to develop across time, so the embodied wisdom that comes from arts practice needs to be sustained through a reflexive process of "seeing" and "doing" across time. One dimension of this is by "taking a long look at art", as Andrea Gilroy (2004) recommends. Doing so gives us the opportunity to reflect on what we see and to be changed by that encounter (Paton, Horsfall, & Carrington, 2017). The conditions for such transformation stem from what Dewey (1934) describes as the capacity of a work of art to hold "story" and to generate empathy in its communication of suffering and injustice. In this, art bridges different worlds through its capacity to open up "new fields of experience" or to reveal something new within the already familiar aspects of life (ibid, p. 144).

Secondly though, in the dimension of "doing", it is through a long immersion in arts practice and the cultivation of work or bodies of work across time, that practice wisdom becomes embodied in the "artist self" (Hyland Moon, 2002) of the art therapist. Practice wisdom in the creative arts therapies is a "bodily knowing"; a sensitivity that stems from "work with oneself – to make art [and] to feel the connection between oneself and the materials" (Levine, 1995, p. 183). For reflexive practitioners, "art as a way of life" generates knowing/s and ways of being beyond the clinical setting that can then be transposed back into the therapeutic context where art can serve as a "container for pain and suffering" (ibid, p. 15).

Meaning cannot be forced and will reveal itself at the right time. Artists similarly sit, literally or metaphorically, with a blank canvas, with the tentative beginning of mark-making, the emergence of an idea, of processes. The art process can be therapeutic, even play the part of the therapist:

> I wait half dressed, frozen by the fear of judgement and rejection. Through the lens I pause time and witness the different emotions ... the camera becomes my therapist, she reflects, she focuses, and I see myself from another point of view. (Nicola Slack in Paton & Linnell, 2018, p. 105)

The materiality of art practice offers a specific opportunity to explore and reflect in ways that are simultaneously imaginary and real, embodied and conceptual. Literally and metaphorically, the practice of art "gives us pause". It cultivates the embodied knowledge of waiting for and recognising *Kairos* – "the right time" (Tsang, 2008) –

which according to Murri art therapist Carmen Lawson also resonates with Indigenous ways of knowing (Lawson, Woods, & McKenna, 2019).

As knowledge becomes embodied, practice becomes more responsive, reflexive and nuanced. Practitioners develop *artistry,* a concept that both incorporates and exceeds the concept of skill (Paterson, Wilcox, & Higgs, 2006). Artistry in this sense is possible in any profession and brings together the dimensions of creativity and criticality. Such artistry is not limited to but is particularly resonant for art therapists. Artmaking is itself a partner in this process of developing artistry as an art therapist. As Georgia Freebody writes: "…art threads its way, effortlessly, into and out of the stone vaults we construct, or inherit ... its continuum descriptive of pathways, threads we may follow to freedom" (in Paton & Linnell, 2018, p. 103).

BUILDING BRIDGES AND CROSSING BOUNDARIES

However, "freedom" is a social as well as an individual possibility. Sensitivity to the importance of "activism" and social justice (Newton, 2011) is necessary to being an effective art therapist. Art therapy can actively involve both personal and social transformation, placing social justice at the centre of practice. Karcher (2017), for example, has argued that art therapists have a responsibility to address social and political sources of oppression and trauma experienced by those living with marginalised identities. Yet this is not the main emphasis in most psychotherapy training, including art therapy, where culture and the social are often reduced to a notion of "context" and ideas of individual pathology tend to dominate.

In contrast, much contemporary art engages directly with social and cultural issues: crossing boundaries between the intrapersonal, interpersonal and the collective dimensions of experience. An engagement with contemporary art facilitates a social justice perspective, encouraging art therapists to expand their practice beyond a psychological view centred in and on the individual. Furthermore, contemporary art sensitises people to diversity and challenges the binary of "normal" and "abnormal", an important ethic for any therapist seeking social justice as the inspiration for and, ideally, outcome of therapy. Responding to and practising contemporary art is a means to develop practice wisdom in which the practitioner comes to embody and practise a socially just approach to art therapy. Moreover, the diversity of media, materials and processes characteristic of contemporary art significantly expands the possibilities for therapeutic communication (Hyland Moon, 2010) and therefore the capacity to dialogue with difference.

Furthermore, there is much we can learn from contemporary artists about the wisdom of sitting with uncertainty. Working across multiple contemporary and traditional art forms – visual arts, film, theatre and opera – William Kentridge (2014b) describes his multidimensional arts practice as being about "the provisionality of the moment". Well known for his gestural charcoal drawings that form the basis of animations referencing apartheid, these embody the marks of erasure and addition that speak to the provisionality and uncertainty at the core of his art and philosophy. Kentridge (ibid) suggests that uncertainty, ambiguity and contradiction are the central lifeblood not only of art, but also of life: they are not just mistakes at the edge of understanding, but are the way that understanding is constructed. This is a pivotal lesson on the journey to practice wisdom.

For Kentridge (2014b), there is a self-awareness built into the process of art that helps us "make sense of the world", rather than provide instruction on what the world means. Meaning is always provisional; art therefore has an important polemical and political role in "defending the uncertain" (ibid). In this sense, art is the provocateur, the trickster (Hyde, 1998), standing between humility and authoritarian certainty. There is a need, therefore, to maintain a critique of all forms of certainty. Not just of authoritarian politics (of which Kentridge has lived experience), but also the certainty of any "knowledge". That knowledge is fallible and contingent is not always a welcome message for trainee therapists seeking the comfort of formulaic approaches to their craft. However, in surrendering to this kind of "uncertain" thinking about knowledge, about art and about life, art therapists give themselves permission to develop and grow practice wisdom.

EMBEDDED AND EMBODIED CURRICULUM EXPERIENCES

The critical postmodern *sensibility* (sense-ability) that informs Kentridge's work and contemporary art generally, is more than a theoretical framework. It can also inform, and even form, learning and teaching practices that draw attention to and challenge the broader forces of socialisation and acculturation that shape people's identity and values. Postmodern thinking problematises dualisms and the "truths" built on binaries so that the rich variety of human potentiality can be brought to the fore. In the process of deconstructing "dominant discourses", critical postmodernism gives a central position to diversity, and questions the idea of a singular "truth" of who we are and what we can be:

> Due to my Asian appearance, many treated me like a foreigner ... I felt confused and unable to see myself ... In this work, I created self-portraits ... which emulate an oriental Asian ink drawing and the finger-painting symbolises 'self-recognition' ... the process became one akin to mindful meditation, which allowed me to be aware of myself. (Nadia Lee in Paton & Linnell, 2018, p. 103)

In Lee's work the personal redress of injustice through art is both ethical and aesthetic. The embodied effects/affects from racism experienced earlier in the life of an art therapy trainee begin to be undone through an embodied repetition of the process of creating self-portraits. Lee reclaims aspects of cultural heritage (Asian ink drawing, meditation practices), bringing these together with a hands-on practice of finger painting often used by children and with the appropriation of mindfulness, both of which feature in Western culture. She counters the effects of how she was seen as problematically "different" and became invisible to herself: creating a hybrid form and practice through which she can recognise herself, be more aware and generate more awareness in her audience.

Also working in ink on paper in ways that are culturally informed, Yi Cao maps an arts-based, embodied process of self-discovery into a three-dimensional installation of the therapeutic encounter. Engaging the viewer through both sight and sound, she directly invokes and evokes the quality of *presence* that a therapist is required to embody and practise in a therapeutic relationship. She demonstrates that practice wisdom is not only the province of experienced practitioners – it can be cultivated through aesthetic as well as clinical practice. Cao notes that

> The whole process was painstaking, frustrating, at the same time meditative … Therapeutic presence requires letting go of self-concerns and requires an attitude of openness, acceptance, interest and immersion. The process of art-making reflected my experience of therapeutic encounter and helped me further understand its importance. (Cao, in Paton & Linnell, 2018, p. 109)

Embodied learning through art is also crucial to decolonising art therapy. Carrie Fraser, an artist/student whose mother is a member of a stolen generation of Indigenous people, explored art as a means to document and challenge the ongoing legacies of colonisation. An experienced exhibiting artist, as are many art therapists in training, Fraser had developed an aesthetic practice and language that appropriated colonial practices. This came together with an exploration of her heritage and family of origin in a powerful and beautifully realised diptych that can be understood as both personal and social history:

> These drawings were made to honour my late mother who was a member of a stolen generation … The drawings are tallies; that is, they document increments of time in my mother's life … The socio-cultural-historical significance of pen and paper are as tools for privilege and power. I appropriate [these] colonial tools and create a visual language that produces a counter-document. (Fraser, in Paton & Linnell, 2018, p. 107)

As is evident in the examples above, a sustained and sustaining visual art practice has become increasingly central to the pedagogy of the Master of Art Therapy at Western Sydney University, a program that is strongly influenced by both the principles of social justice and the insights and practices of contemporary art. As the authors have written elsewhere, "art therapy trainees at Western are … inducted into the profession as art makers, art therapists and agents of social transition" (Paton & Linnell, 2018, p. 102). Reconceptualising this pedagogy and practice as the development of practice wisdom enables a further level of understanding of the central importance of artmaking in the making of art therapists.

The training engages students in a collaborative and arts-based enquiry into the interaction of theory and practice, within and across the domains of art therapy and contemporary art. It offers trainee art therapists an opportunity to extend their art practice as a form of ongoing research into key troubling questions about art therapy as a practice of individual, family and community healing embedded in the principles of social justice. Students are supported and inspired to investigate the parallels and differences between artistic and clinical practice, hone their abilities to respond empathically to vulnerable others, and consolidate the "artist identity" in the art therapist and the wider professional community.

Arts-based pedagogies and practices foreground relationality and generate potential for social, subjective and cultural transformations. In this spirit, the public statements of our student artists in their capstone exhibition underscore how an openness to uncertainty and the discipline of staying with an unfolding process are cultivated through arts-based enquiry. This ethos is central to the habitus of the contemporary artist and art therapist alike. However, embodied learning through art is not inherently either easy or benign. It requires rigour; reflexivity; and a carefully calibrated orientation towards a partnership between students and staff that encourages collaboration and openness without eliding considerations of responsibility and power. The importance of locating and enacting this pedagogy within a social justice framework cannot be underestimated. With many of the students in the Master of Art Therapy coming from a first degree in visual art wherein the tradition of the public "art crit" is potentially undermining (Belluigi, 2009) and even shaming, justice extends to and is modelled in a collegial approach to the exhibition, viewing and assessment of artwork. One artist/student even made shame the subject of her final work:

'You don't matter. You don't deserve attention. No one will love you if they find out who you REALLY are.' On top of these familiar messages is a cube ... my way of meeting shame & organising it: reframing it ... The drawings on the floor are not yet organised shame, creating a barrier from intimacy with the cube. I invite the viewer to trespass this barrier, to interact with the piece and get a closer view ... Shame loses power when it is spoken, what happens when it is made visible? (Laura Kent in Paton & Linnell, 2018, p. 107)

Kent's interactive artwork drew the audience of students and staff into an embodied consideration of shame, deepening our understanding of how shame is embedded and embodied in social institutions and practices – including in postgraduate education. The work enabled an embodied understanding of how shame may shape the responses of our "clients" and ourselves. By "placing value explicitly on the reflexivity between creativity and critical thinking" (Belluigi, 2009, p. 715) and, crucially, requiring this reflexivity of ourselves and other staff as well as students, we foster and sustain not just a process, but a *transformational culture* of embodied learning. This collaborative and iterative process of enquiry is folded into each student artist's statement of intent, and into the community of artists (students and staff) who co-curate and audience the final student exhibition. Practice wisdom is thus engendered and recognised as a form of community rather than individual professional practice. The importance of a community of art practice was reinforced in a recent staff exhibition at Western Sydney University which had its genesis in the acknowledgement that while an ongoing arts practice is central for those training and practising in the field of art therapy, this is not always easily achieved.

Indeed, it is not uncommon for art therapists to struggle in maintaining their personal commitment to artmaking (Gilroy, 2004). It can be challenging to cultivate and maintain one's creative expression within the matrix of work, family and community commitments. Tending to this important part of the art therapist's ongoing professional development, *Mind the Gap* (Paton & Lever, 2018) provided a creative platform for generating important conversations for staff and students about the "interface" where art and therapy overlap and co-exist. This builds on an emergent tradition of staff collaborating and exhibiting together that can "cross knowing with not knowing ... making ourselves visible ... in ways not normally accessible to our students, our clients and our peers" (Linnell et al., 2019, p. 259).

Sheridan Linnell's (2018) work for the exhibition was a response to being given an old music roll of the song *Moonlight Bay* by another exhibitor. Working back into the delicate paper scroll, a material reminiscent of aging skin, evoked "the void" and gestured toward what may endure beyond the individual self:

> A gift from a friend. Traces of moonlight on water. Memories of sound perforate a long scroll. Silence cracks open. It ... I ... am tattooed with memories. Reach after faded words. I mind the gap. Step carefully across a void in time where a pianola plays ... *Agap*e, the love that transcends self, brushes my skin, thinning like paper... (Linnell in Paton & Lever, 2018, p. 23)

Linnell "found" poems among the words of the song and the words of the other artists' statements, transcribed these onto tracing paper and incorporated them, blurring the distinction between creation and appropriation, self and other, image and word. The muted palette, candle wax traces and crossings in Linnell's piece resonated with and literally sat alongside the work of Anita Lever and Joy Paton, who radically extended the exploration of intersubjectivity, relationality and materiality in the contemporary art of art therapists.

In their collaborative encaustic work comprising eight panels, Lever and Paton (2018) worked "together apart". Some basic parameters were agreed upon – colour palette, ground, size, quantity – and they shared notes, encouragement and support. However, they did not to show their images to each other during the process, allowing the materiality to have its own agency. What emerged was a process reflective of the qualities embedded within arts psychotherapy:

> Parallel experiences revealed themselves in the making: creating a solid ground; stepping into unpredictability and relinquishing control; outcomes unknown and discovered through the process itself ... the alchemy of wax, paint, salt and gold is one of surrender, contemplation and witness to both absence and presence, elements inherent within the agency of the materials. (Lever & Paton in Paton & Lever, 2018, p. 21)

CONCLUSION

Art and aesthetics provide "a different way of knowing and understanding human existence and experience" (Carr & Hancock, 2003, p. 3). A practice wisdom discourse informed by contemporary art and aesthetics paves the way to an epistemological framework within which art therapy training can embed and promote an embodied, therapeutic practice of social justice. In the training of art therapists, an extended engagement with the theory and practice of *contemporary* art, including the opportunity to develop a work/body of work, has a "multiplier effect", expanding and deepening the potentiating opportunities for learning and laying the basis for development of practice wisdom in the maintenance of an ongoing arts practice as professional practitioners.

Perhaps most importantly of all, the experience of embodied learning through contemporary art practice provides a template for art therapists to work with the people who come to them for therapy. Located within a realm of practice wisdom, far from the codified and disembodied forms of expertise critiqued at the beginning of this chapter, what is offered here is a template for how to embrace uncertainty and practise with artistry. It is a signpost into the territory of lived professional experience that also orients art therapists to how to be with others. Practised and embodied over time, this enables art therapists to increasingly work in ways that uncover and enhance the practice wisdom of those who come to therapy, which is already present, albeit often hidden, within people's own accounts and images of lived experience and expressed through their artmaking. When the tightly interwoven nets of dominant discourse begin to unravel, the practice wisdom inherent in both art and life reveals itself. We, and those whose journeys we accompany, find "threads we may follow to freedom" (Freebody in Paton & Linnell, 2018, p. 103).

NOTE

[1] This phrase, attributed to Susanne K. Langer in Eisner (2003), paraphrases Thomas Aquinas: "Nothing is in the intellect that was not first in the senses".

REFERENCES

Allen, P. (1992). Artist-in-residence: an alternative to 'clinification' for art therapists. *Art Therapy, 9*(1), 22-29.
Becker, C. (2009). *Thinking in place: Art, action and cultural production*. Boulder, CO: Paradigm.
Belluigi, D. Z. (2009). Exploring the discourses around 'creativity' and 'critical thinking' in a South African creative arts curriculum. *Studies in Higher Education, 34*(6), 699-717.
Carr, A., & Hancock, P. (Eds.). (2003). *Art and aesthetics at work*. New York, NY: Palgrave Macmillan.
Cheung, J. C.-S. (2017). Practice wisdom in social work: An uncommon sense in the intersubjective encounter. *European Journal of Social Work, 20*(5), 619-629.
Dewey, J. (1934). *Art as experience*. New York, NY: The Berkley Publishing Group.
Eisner, E. W. (2003) The arts and the creation of mind. *Language Arts, 80*(5), 340-344.
Gilroy, A. (2004). On occasionally being able to paint. *International Journal of Art therapy, 9*(2), 72-78.
Hyde, L. (1998). *Trickster makes this world: Mischief, myth and art*. New York, NY: Farrar, Straus and Giroux.
Hyland Moon, C. (2002). *Studio art therapy: Cultivating the artist identity in the art therapist*. London, England: Jessica Kingsley.
Hyland Moon, C. (Ed.). (2010). *Materials and media in art therapy: Critical understanding of diverse artistic vocabularies*. New York, NY: Routledge.
Karcher, O. P. (2017). Sociopolitical oppression, trauma, and healing: Moving toward a social justice art therapy framework. *Art Therapy, 34*(3), 123-128.
Kentridge, W. (2014a). *Six drawing lessons*. Cambridge, MA: Harvard University Press.
Kentridge, W. (2014b). *How we make sense of the world*. Interview. Louisiana Channel, Louisiana Museum of Modern Art. Retrieved from https://www.youtube.com/watch?v=G11wOmxoJ6U
Klein, W. C., & Bloom, M. (1995). Practice wisdom. *Social Work, 40*(6), 799-807.
Kramer, E. (1979). *Childhood and art therapy*. New York, NY: Schocken Books.

Langer, S. K. (1937*). Problems of art*. New York, NY: Scribners.
Lawson, C., Woods, D., & McKenna, T. (2019). Towards Indigenous Australian knowing. In A. Gilroy, S. Linnell, T. McKenna, & J. Westwood (Eds.), *Art therapy in Australia: Taking a postcolonial, aesthetic turn* (pp. 77-105). Leiden, Boston: Brill Sense.
Lever, A., & Paton, J. (2018). *(IN-Fuse) salt for gold*. In J. Paton & A. Lever (Eds.), *Mind the gap: Tending the interface of art and therapy* (Exhibition Catalogue). Sydney, Australia: Western Sydney University.
Levine, E. (1995). *Tending the fire: Studies in art, therapy and creativity*. Toronto, Canada: Palmerston Press.
Linnell, S. (2018). *Moonlight Bay*. In J. Paton & A. Lever (Eds.), *Mind the gap: Tending the interface of art and therapy* (Exhibition Catalogue). Sydney, Australia: Western Sydney University.
Linnell, S., Perry, S., Pretorius, J., & Westwood, J. (2019). Where knowing and not knowing touch. In A. Gilroy, S. Linnell, T. McKenna, & J. Westwood (Eds.), *Art therapy in Australia: Taking a postcolonial, aesthetic turn* (pp. 253-281). Leiden, Boston: Brill Sense.
Maclagan, D. (2001). *Psychological aesthetics: Painting, feeling and making sense*. London, England: Jessica Kingsley.
Myrdal, G. (1944). *An American dilemma*. New York, NY: Harper & Row.
Nachmanovitch, S. (1990). *Free play: Improvisation in life and art*. New York, NY: Penguin Putnam.
Newton, K. F. (2011). Arts activism: Praxis in social justice, critical discourse, and radical modes of engagement. *Art Therapy: Journal of the American Art Therapy Association, 28*(2), 50-56.
Paterson, M., Wilcox, S., & Higgs, J. (2006). Exploring dimensions of artistry in reflective practice. *Reflective Practice, 7*(4), 455-468.
Paton, J., Horsfall, D., & Carrington, A. (2017). *Picturing recovery: Stories about living well with mental illness* (Exhibition Catalogue). Sydney, Australia: Western Sydney University. doi:10.4225/35/59dd8b66f6e1f
Paton, J., & Lever, A. (2018). *Mind the gap: Tending the interface of art and therapy* (Exhibition Catalogue). Sydney, Australia: Western Sydney University.
Paton, J., & Linnell, S. (2018). 'The art therapist is present': Embedding arts therapy practice and education in the praxis of contemporary art. *Australian and New Zealand Journal of Arts Therapy, 13*(1&2), 101-111.
Rabu, M., & McLeod, J. (2018). Wisdom in professional knowledge: Why it can be valuable to listen to the voices of senior psychotherapists. *Psychotherapy Research, 28*(5), 776-792.
Ramsden, P. (2003). *Learning to teach in higher education* (2nd ed.). New York, NY: RoutledgeFalmer.
Rubin, J. (2011). *The art of art therapy: What every art therapist needs to know*. New York, NY: Routledge.
Schön, D. A. (1983). *The reflective practitioner: How professionals think in action*. New York, NY: Basic Books.
Tsang, N. M. (2008). Kairos and practice wisdom in social work practice. *European Journal of Social Work, 11*(2), 131-143.

Joy Paton PhD (ORCID: http://orcid.org/0000-0003-2492-9431)
School of Social Sciences and Psychology, Western Sydney University, Australia

Sheridan Linnell PhD (ORCID: http://orcid.org/0000-0002-0190-7283)
School of Social Sciences and Psychology, Western Sydney University, Australia

JANICE ORRELL

25. WISE PRACTICE FOR TEACHING

Messages for Future Generations of Teachers

This chapter examines the nature and generation of practice wisdom in use by teachers in education plus the value and limitations of practice wisdom and its interplay with formal educational theory. Next, the chapter draws upon what I have learned from my own experiences in education as a teacher and a teacher educator; I put into words some key values and universal principles I have drawn upon to design educational programs and experiences for those who are about to become teachers. My motivation in this chapter is to underscore the importance of recognising teachers as builders of wise practice and practice wisdom in education and to make a case for the value of creating spaces and processes that elucidate and scrutinise the wisdom of teachers gained from practice. Creating opportunity to make wisdom of practice public and shared has the potential to support and enrich newly appointed academics.

WHY IS PRACTICE WISDOM IMPORTANT?

This chapter is intended to speak to those whose role it is to lead, educate and prepare the next generation of teachers. The content of this chapter is informed largely by my own 52 years of experience and scholarship as a teacher, most of it in higher education, but it is also influenced from time as a teacher in schools. The ideas presented are also informed by sustained engagement in scholarship of teaching and learning. Mostly, however, my thinking about teaching and learning has been informed by dialogue with university colleagues from many settings who have placed a high value on their responsibility to ensure that they provide educational experiences that are innovative, contemporary, engaging and relevant to their students' immediate needs and future career aspirations. To write this chapter I have reflected on these diverse experiences and conversations to identify some key values and convictions I hold about effective teaching and learning in higher education, especially in education for practice such as teaching. I have attempted to formulate this reflection as a set of guiding principles. I also refer to key scholarly ideas that have prompted me to make significant changes in the way I teach and have stayed the distance of time and that have subsequently helped to validate my core beliefs. I find it impossible to discuss the principles that shape what I consider to be wise educational practice without also engaging with key theories and theorists that have influenced me over the years. I regard theory and practice as symbiotic knowledge domains. It is hard to perceive how one domain could be advanced without the other.

© KONINKLIJKE BRILL NV, LEIDEN, 2019 | DOI: 9789004410497_025

I have always loved teaching and recognise this passion for good teaching in most teachers I meet, as well as the commitment it takes to teach well. No one sets out to teach poorly. I hope to be a champion for the wisdom found in teachers' practice expertise that is so rarely publicly acknowledged. Politicians, journalists and parents who have had no formal knowledge of education and pedagogy perceive themselves as experts in teaching and teacher education because they have all been taught! As a result, many all too readily lay the blame for failures in education on teachers and teacher educators, citing poor pedagogical knowledge and practices. I want this chapter to be a catalyst for educational leaders in schools and universities taking up the cause of validation and respect for teachers' expertise and wisdom.

BECOMING A UNIVERSITY TEACHER

To establish the context for this exploration of practice wisdom that has relevance for teacher education, I reflected on the condition of becoming a teacher of new teachers. Many academics are appointed based on their experience and success in developing expert practice teaching in schools and possibly as mentors for new teachers and supervisors of preservice teachers undertaking practicum. Thus, new academics to teacher education will already have robust personal practical theories about teaching, learning and learning to teach. But where and how are these tacit but influential theories elucidated or challenged? Teaching in higher education is significantly different to teaching in schools, particularly in relation to the relationship between learners and teachers. Some teacher education academics will possibly draw upon their own experiences from their time as a university student. Others will emulate their colleagues' practices or be presented with a ready-made curriculum that they are expected follow. Those more fortunate are provided with opportunities to attend orientation programs that induct them into their particular university's expectations regarding higher education teaching.

Merely copying the practices of others, whether it is those of one's own teachers or one's peers, can be problematic if it is not accompanied by insight into the underlying rationale. Britzman (2003) has argued cogently that relying on practice alone to generate further practice runs the risk of embedding erroneous, taken for granted assumptions that become commonly accepted and expected in practice. In contrast, formal academic teacher development programs, whether they are face-to-face or online, are useful as they provide theoretical frames to guide teaching academics to consider challenges and to deliver high-quality learning experiences. At the same time considerable innovation and imagination has been exercised to provide education that is engaging, exciting and liberating, but often tacit and rarely shared. It is important that this wisdom is made explicit and shared.

TEACHERS AS CREATORS OF PEDAGOGICAL KNOWLEDGE

A basic premise of this chapter is that teachers are creators of practice knowledge in relation to both teaching and learning that they use to teach and explain their practice. There has already been considerable scholarship about the nature of the knowledge that teachers generate about teaching and learning, which is variously called teachers' wisdom of practice, teacher know-how and teachers' personal practical theories of teaching and learning. Shulman (1987) identified four possible sources of teachers' knowledge base: scholarship in the content discipline and pedagogy, institutional policies and procedures, curriculum documents and wisdom from experience. He argued that the art of teaching is grounded in the professional knowledge of teachers which is distinctively practical and a major source of which is "wisdom of practice". According to Shulman (ibid), this knowledge gained from practice is the least codified of all knowledge sources and represents predominantly implicit maxims that guide practice and this practice-based knowledge is:

> of special interest because it identifies the distinctive knowledge of teaching. It represents the blending of content and pedagogy into an understanding of how particular topics, problems, or issues are organised, represented and adapted to the diverse interests and abilities of learners and presented for instruction. Pedagogical content knowledge is the category most likely to distinguish the understanding of the content specialist from that of the pedagogue. (p. 11)

Shulman claimed that personally held pedagogical knowledge was not readily available even to the teachers themselves because it was largely tacit, having developed incrementally through classroom learning and teaching experiences. It is also notable that, unlike many other professions, students entering teacher education will have well developed rich, tacit, personal theories of learning and the work of teachers is based on their own experiences of being taught. Shulman (2004) compared the complexity of practice wisdom required by physicians and teachers and claimed that the demands of making context-based judgements employing practice wisdom was far greater for classroom teachers than medical practitioners.

TEACHERS' PRACTICAL KNOWLEDGE: WISDOM OR ADAPTATION?

Before all teachers' practice-based knowledge becomes indiscriminately valourised, however, the question must be asked: is "wisdom of practice", so named by Shulman (1987), "wisdom" in the true sense, or merely practical strategic adaptations and knowledge derived from accommodating situational demands? Importantly, Britzman (2003) warns against relying solely on practice-generated knowledge because much of this commonly accepted practice knowledge requires considerable critical, informed scrutiny because, while valuable, it may be grounded in erroneous, taken for granted assumptions. Wisdom, change and improvement in teaching is best achieved through deliberate, informed, collaborative critical reflection on teachers' practical experiences of teaching. Csikszentmihalyi and Rathunde (1990) described wisdom as a way of knowing universal truths rather than specific or specialised knowledge. They argue that this universality is an important quality for comprehending how various aspects of reality are related to each other and they claim that the worth of wisdom lies in its holistic, integrating view and its capacity to perceive fundamental and integral relationships between diverse tenets, ideas and conditions and that it (universality) is the central contribution of practice wisdom. Csikszentmihalyi and Rathunde also claim that wisdom is not value free, but acknowledge the limitations of the human capacity to reason objectively and consider the distorting effects of past experiences, fortuitous association, others' opinions, cultural patterning and self-interest.

Following on from these conceptions that help to explain the nature of wisdom itself, it could be suggested that a number of qualities are required for teachers' personally held knowledge, practice and decision making to be considered "wise". Wisdom can be confused with the accumulation and quantity of knowledge particularities, at the cost of knowledge of the whole. Furthermore, while specialised knowledge shows immediate effects, wisdom's benefits are, by definition, slower to appear and less obvious. While knowledge might be expressed in declarative certitude, wisdom must compare, raise questions and suggest restraint. Wisdom of practice engages with a concern for the long-term social, moral and cognitive consequences of teaching and learning actions. A wise teacher has a holistic, long-term view of the act of teaching and its role in student learning and of the role of education as a social, moral enterprise. Wise practice is critically self-reflective and actively seeking of feedback, and it entails strategies that would assist in learning from past mistakes in both teaching and learning. As a desirable condition, teachers' wisdom embodies a disposition towards ongoing, collaborative review, leading to outcomes of student emancipation, learning autonomy and self-regulation.

PROPOSITIONS FROM PRACTICE WISDOM

The discourse of this chapter will now progress from the theoretical considerations of teachers as creators of pedagogical knowledge and practice wisdom to an exposition of my personal reflections on my 52 years of experience as a teacher and a scholar of teaching. The outcome of this deliberate reflective process has culminated in a number of propositions that would be my core guiding tenets if I were to begin my career again and were to assume the responsibilities of a leader in a teacher education program. My reflective process was aided by deliberate conversations with three teacher educators. One conversation was with an experienced, retired academic who was the coordinator for a degree program for nurse educators. In addition, we had worked together more than a decade ago in a program that inducted new academics of every disciplinary persuasion for their role as university teachers. The other conversation took place with two newly appointed teacher education academics appointed to leadership roles in an early childhood degree program, having been sessional tutors for some time in the same program. The following propositions will be supported by exemplars and theoretical concepts that have captured my attention over decades and provided me with frameworks that have withstood scrutiny and challenges from practical experience.

Proposition 1: Learning to Teach is a Developmental Process

Time as both a mentor teacher and university supervisor of preservice teachers in their professional experience, plus reflections from my own growth as a teacher have taught me that teaching is a developmental, staged process. Drawing upon the ideas of Kugel (1993), Boice (2000), Evans (2002) and others, I suggest the following as a reasonable illustration of stages of development through which a teacher might proceed. The following outline of these stages has also resonated with audiences from professional education programs other than teacher education.

- Stage 1: The focus is self, survival and teacher activities. In this stage the guiding question is "What will I do, what do I know, and is it enough to answer any questions?". This stage is often characterised by excessive preparation time largely spent on content preparation.
- Stage 2: The focus is on student activities. After some time the question arises "What will they (the students) do?". Preparation is characterised by the development of activities to occupy students' attention.
- Stage 3: The focus is on learning. This stage represents a paradigm shift. Here the guiding question is "What is important for the students to learn?".
- Stage 4: The focus is teaching strategies to foster learning. This stage is guided by the question "How might my teaching make student learning possible?". This is where theoretical pedagogical concepts of motivation, instruction and learning begin to have traction and are applied (hopefully) to shape the teaching, learning and assessment processes.
- Stage 5: The focus is holistic and on education as a social, moral enterprise. This stage once again represents a significant paradigm shift towards a holistic, curriculum focus. It is at this stage that the practitioners draw upon core values and universal principles, and consider the fundamental social and moral purposes of education. Teachers and educational leaders who reach this stage (and perhaps not all teachers do) are more likely to be those who can articulate core propositions of wise practice. It is at this stage where teaching is recognised as an Art rather than a science and attends to the integration and arbitration of tensions between public intentions and localised possibilities.

It is not to be expected that new teachers would attain Stage 5. Some teachers never will. Learning to teach is a lifetime process that is influenced by personal dispositions and the contextual conditions of practice. What does matter is that those who mentor and teach them recognise that becoming a teacher is a developmental process. As such, supportive strategies need to be employed that will promote early career teachers' capacity to become agents of their own progression from one stage to another.

Proposition 2: It Is Important to Know What You Don't Know

Students' capacity for critical self-reflection and noticing the limitations in their planning is an important part of asking the right questions in order to help change and enhance their practice. To do this they need to know what they don't know. This is really important. I recall my own teacher education in the 1960s when, as students, we were *forced* to identify and record our assumptions about the class and their learning needs for every lesson plan. It was so irritating, as I just wanted to get in there and "teach". I would grumble to myself, "After all isn't that what I am here for, to be a teacher?". Now 50 years later I applaud that the strategy was required because it has been a catalyst to a lifetime habit that I have never lost of questioning my assumptions before I plan any teaching or presentation. In hindsight I suspect it may have been more effective at the time if I had been made aware of its significance.

The significance of being able to question one's own practice in order to further develop as a practitioner was reinforced by Ann Kerwin whom I met as a visiting scholar in the 1990s and who, with her colleagues, had developed a course in medical education in *Medical Ignorance* (Witte et al., 1989). The premise for the course was that the most important thing doctors needed to know was *what they didn't know*! This later became known as an *Ignorance Curriculum*.

Ignorance is such a powerful word that it immediately attracts attention and an emotional response. This proposition applies to all professions, including nurses and teachers. Since becoming acquainted with the ignorance curriculum my first act on entering a classroom, no matter the level of students, is to say to my class *"Ignorance! This is what we will discuss in this class, what do we feel most ignorant about? Once we know this, we will know what we have to learn, me included"*. This has particularly captured the attention of mature students as they say it has given them the confidence to raise questions, speak of their doubts and understand that it is reasonable to be a learner, rather than a knower of practice. I suggested to my Deputy Vice-Chancellor that I thought that ignorance was the business of universities in both teaching and research! The idea was not appreciated!

Proposition 3: Teachers Should Possess Dispositions and Capabilities of Care

A curriculum for the development of competent, confident practitioners requires attention to acquisition of the elements of practice knowledge, capabilities and skills that are sufficiently evident in curriculum documentation and attract the attention of teacher education course accreditors. Teachers' professional dispositions are an important aspect of any educational experience; however, they are often invisible in curricular, instruction and assessment. This absence of explicit attention to the development of teacher dispositions is regrettable because these values impact on and shape teachers' observations and decision making.

According to Tronto (2005), Noddings (2005) and Zembylas, Bozalek, and Shefer (2014) (my favourite and recently discovered theorists), caring is a challenge that schools face and is an important need amongst students since care occurs within relationships. The capacity to care is a fundamental professional disposition and capability for teachers to possess. Importantly, Tronto argues that caring isn't merely an individual capability, it is also an organisational competence that must be fostered by leaders. Tronto outlines a theory of the *integrity of caring* as having five elements, all of which are equally essential in the exercise and practice of care. These elements are: (1) having awareness of needs, (2) taking responsibility to act, (3) possessing and exercising competence when providing care, (4) evaluating the impact of care and (5) fostering trust and solidarity with those needing care.

Tronto's theory of *integrity of care* emphasised that care is more than a disposition, it includes *responsibility* and willingness to respond in some way. Caring also requires the *capability and skills* to exercise care in ways that make a difference. Tronto also argued that it was important to be *mindful and reflective* about the impact of the caring on the recipient. All too often caring might produce positive emotions for the carer, but not the individual who is cared for. Finally, Tronto believed that the integrity of care needed to be conducted with respect, trust, reciprocity and solidarity between the receivers and providers of care. This conceptual notion of care has provided me with an increased critical insight into what might be features and practices of teachers and schools and the qualities of student-centred education. Care between teachers and students and within student peer relationships is an important element of positive education. What might a teacher education curriculum look like if it was framed by Tronto's integrity of care concept? What would the interaction between student teachers and academics be like if it were to be pursued as an organisational competence?

Proposition 4: Students Need to Learn How to Notice What is Important

Noticing and perceiving people's needs requires a knowledge of the potential impacts of social, economic and cultural factors that produce poverty, neglect, isolation, loneliness, stress and anxiety. Experienced, wise practitioners in human services have a well-developed capacity to notice what cues are important in their field of practice that indicate the need for caring and attention. An important challenge in education is how this capacity might be fostered in teachers. The capacity to notice is often overlooked in curriculum and instructional design. I became aware of the importance of developing students' capacity to notice when working with academic colleagues in social work. At the time I was teaching human development to nursing students. To refine my students' ability to notice they went to social venues such as parks, cafés such as McDonalds or other places where children, teenagers and adults gathered, to observe and record their perceptions of what was happening. They were encouraged to notice and interpret nonverbal cues that might give them more information and to consider what made those cues significant. We reviewed each student's observations in class to identify differences in interpretations and consider what might have influenced those differences.

Proposition 5: Teachers Should Not be Afraid to be Authentic

Being authentic is another important disposition for teachers to develop. Engaging with and relating to students is best when teachers are authentic and do not use their role or positional power as a defensive barrier. Teachers who are authentic know themselves and their strengths and are comfortable to admit to their personal limitations. They are sensitive in exercising their formal power in the contexts of learning and teaching and as a result are able to be more honest and open with their students. They are able to take risks and attempt innovations because they share their vulnerabilities with students when they are trialling new methods. Authentic teachers perceive the interplay of teaching and learning, and perceive themselves to be lifelong learners and, as such, invite their students to engage in the process of evaluation and critique of teaching and learning processes and the effectiveness of newly introduced strategies. Thus, tensions between formal educational systems and students' learning needs can be negotiated and students feel empowered to be active agents in the educational process. I recall a time as a graduate student when my supervisor shared a draft of an article he was writing with our graduate group and asked us for feedback. I can still recapture that feeling of empowerment and self-worth that his request generated amongst us as nascent researchers. As a result, we felt committed to apply effort in our responses to honour the respect, trust and responsibility that had been given to us. We also learnt that it is not necessary to have everything perfect before sharing ideas.

Principle 6: The Main Purpose of Teaching and Assessment is to Make Learning Possible

The importance of teaching making learning possible, I gained from Paul Ramsden (1992). It is one of those simple but provocative statements that had a prevailing impact for me, particularly focusing on discerning "what is most important". I have combined the notion of making learning possible with Carol Dweck's (2007) idea of "not yet", and applied it to the assessment of student learning. All too often in assessment of learning the focus is on proving that learning is accurate and has occurred within time constraints. Increasingly I have come to recognise that education pays far too much attention to proving learning has occurred and far too little attention to improving learning and making it possible. Making learning possible must be an overriding principle.

There have been interesting developments in medical education research that produced a shift to Programmatic Assessment for Learning (PAL) curriculum that I have long felt has a place in teacher education. Introducing PAL requires a system-wide cultural shift towards assessment as learning at both a program and an institutional level. Assessment outcomes are considered information that can be used to guide future learning and teaching efforts. Students have learning coaches who guide them at regular intervals to determine what the assessment results and feedback suggest about on what and how a student should best focus their learning efforts. PAL utilised fewer decision-making points regarding passing and failing, and more opportunities for identifying what has "not yet" been mastered and what has yet to be done to enhance learning and skill development. Through this process of dialogues and interpretive analysis of assessment outcomes between learning coach and learner, students are encouraged and expected to become agents of their own learning within an infinite curriculum. This agentic disposition will contribute to students' preparation for a career that will require them to be learners for the longer term (Boud & Falchikov, 2007). Shifts in government understanding of education, institutional leadership understanding and student expectations are needed for this transition to assessment as making learning possible to occur. Within such a paradigm shift, students can no longer be passive receivers of knowledge. They must become active builders of their own knowledge. This approach aligns with John Biggs' (1999) claim that it is important that teachers know how to design engaged learning environments, because design shapes students' approaches to learning, and determines "what the student does".

It has for some time been my belief that the adoption of a PAL approach to teacher education curriculum would constitute a powerful cultural shift that would reverberate across all systems of education. The experience of a PAL driven curriculum would provide a model for teacher education students to transfer into their own practices as teachers who would challenge teaching and assessment rituals and test the outdated educational ideology that drives compulsory education's assessment practices today.

Proposition 7: Teacher Education Programs Should Make the Whole Course Count

Many individual teacher educators and teachers in schools have actually developed similar strategies. However, it is not good enough for students to experience one or two teachers who take an innovative and more learning enabling approach. The whole system of policies and professional learning for academics and teachers needs to embrace a combined and sustained approach to making learning possible. Profession-based courses such as education, medicine, nursing, health sciences and engineering are required to include opportunities for students to have learning experiences within professional work places. Unlike the placements students have in more general programs of study that aim to enhance students employability, those in professions courses are focused on the integration of theory and practice and the development of skills, awareness and capabilities that will enable a successful transition from university to professional practice.

One of the challenges of professions-based programs is to help bridge the theory–practice divide. I recall once giving students in a professional program an assignment in a course on contradictions and dualities in practice to identify and explore a duality they had experienced. It was a surprise to find that many elected to write about the duality of their learning in university and the experience of practice. Students described how they found little alignment and many contradictions between the theories and practices taught in the university and the work they did in their professional experience. These differences indicate to me two challenges for universities. Firstly, leaders of professions-based programs such as teacher education, need to be more deliberate in engaging, being in dialogue with and partnering their related industries (Cooper & Orrell, 2016) so that there are shared understandings about what is important in education and research regarding practice and professions. Secondly, within the program itself there should be a shared understanding about the intent of the program and the aspired qualities of its graduates. It is not unusual in such programs to find the practicum and the theoretical elements of the program being pitted against each other by both students and staff, some placing greater value on practice while others place greater emphasis on theoretical knowledge. This duality is unhelpful but is rarely given sufficient deliberate attention.

Proposition 8: Have High Expectations and Foster Student Aspirations

Having high expectations is another key factor in making learning possible. Teachers who have high expectations for student success encourage students to also have high expectations of their own and to develop aspirations for success. Such aspirations need not be limited to academic success, but include helping students to develop a positive self-identify, one in which they can develop a sense of their own capability to meet challenges. It would be difficult for teacher education students to perceive this, if their own mentors and educators fail to model such expectations of education. I recall undertaking a peer review for one of my colleagues whose subject was "learning theory". His students reported that he had high expectations of them and was very supportive. They held him in high regard and reported that by the end of their course that they themselves had become far more effective learners as a result of the teacher's expectations. In addition to being pleased with their own achievement they had also wanted to do it for him because he had placed such value on their success. They also claimed that they now knew what they must do as teachers themselves and felt better prepared for the responsibility.

A doctoral student of mine undertook an ethnographic study of educational success for students from very low and marginalised socioeconomic backgrounds. All of the students reported that they had enjoyed and achieved success at school, had formed aspirations for their lives, gained entry to university, completed a degree and gained employment. When asked what a critical factor in their success had been, to a person they all described that their motivation derived from their teachers having high expectations of them and that this was coupled with the teachers' refusal to accept student failure. They described teachers who said, "You will not fail, we will now work out what you need to succeed". Behind the scenes of this school was a commitment from the leadership and all staff to enabling success for all students. This was coupled with a deliberate provision of resources, infrastructure and teacher professional development to ensure the appropriate support was available.

Proposition 9: Wise Practice is Fostered through Self-Reflection, Critical Collegial Conversations and Commitment to Continuous Improvement

Universities and schools have multiple systems of formal, multi-level evaluation and there are others imposed by governments to ascertain the status and efficacy of education at national and international levels. These systems are supported by expensive infrastructure. My problem with many of these systems is that they are largely focused on assurance to *proving* rather than *improving* learning. Even where an intention has been to identify where there is a need for improvement and resource allocation, such strategies largely result in producing league tables of excellence and for blaming of teachers for the failure of education to reached desired national and international standards.

My first year as a teacher was not very successful. My school was in a mill settlement, not even a town, buried in the middle of a karri and jarrah forest. There were two classes. I had Grades One to Three and the principal had Grades Four to Seven. While I had a lovely time with the students especially with reading, maths, music and drama, I really wasn't a good planner or record keeper and that was what mattered to the inspectors who visited and assessed us. I am not sure who was closest to tears in my inspection: the inspector or me. I learnt that I still had a lot to learn.

On my last day of my first year as I moved off to teach in a coal town with equal poverty, I composed a long list of things I had yet to learn and that I had done wrong and needed to improve. I also included some possible strategies that I had considered would address my initial mistakes and that I would try in my new post where I could have a clean slate. I made two copies of this reflection: one for me and one I left behind in a drawer for the next first year teacher who was destined to be thrown in at the deep end as I had been. Since then I have learnt that there is considerable value in doing such simple reflection for achieving constructive change especially if it is undertaken collegially. Such a simple process aims to improve teaching and learning.

It is my belief that ongoing evaluation and change is where experienced and effective teachers need to have a voice. Wise teachers and educational leaders are only too aware of where policy and resource allocation confound good teaching practices both in teacher education accreditation, government policy and educational resource allocation. Teachers and academics need to collaborate in conversations that seek to identify the focus and approaches that would lead to educational enhancement and become a voice for reason. Too many who lead education systems ignore the rich resource of teachers' practice wisdom and maintain a focus on accountability and proving at the cost of improvement and change.

CONCLUSION

This chapter has argued that teachers' knowledge developed within practice is valuable and should be valued. It has not intended to imply that all teachers' practice-based knowledge should be indiscriminately valourised as wise practice, because it is largely intuitive, implicit, uncritiqued and reliant on generalised past experiences. Neither is it a fundamental case that all teachers' knowledge should be grounded in intentional testing and formal theory. There is a question that must be asked; namely, is "wisdom of practice" "wisdom" in the true sense, or merely practical strategic adaptations and knowledge derived from accommodating the demands of the situation? Wise practice is value laden and takes the form of universal principles, not particularities and details but makes a significant contribution to high quality education and should not be ignored. It is also important that practice wisdom is shared, critiqued and utilised judiciously to mitigate the risk of reifying and embedding erroneous assumptions that can become generalised as commonly accepted educational practices. The question for leadership in teacher education is how student teachers can access wise practice and learn to recognise their own emerging practice wisdom in order to share it and to verify its value and utility. Considerable deliberateness is needed in designing teacher education programs in such a way as to enhance the capacity of student teachers to value, utilise and question their pedagogical assumptions about their students, and imposed curriculum, and to ensure their teaching designs make learning possible.

ACKNOWLEDGEMENTS

Thanks to Judith Condon, Christina Moutos and Sarah Wight for their conversations about practice, and to Norman Habel for his conversations about wisdom and his comments on drafts of this chapter.

REFERENCES

Biggs, J. (1999). What the student does: Teaching for enhanced learning. *Higher Education Research & Development, 18*(1), 57-75.
Boice, R. (2000). *Advice for new faculty members.* Boston, MA: Allyn & Bacon.
Boud, D., & Falchikov, N. (2007). *Rethinking assessment in higher education: Learning for the longer term.* London/New York: Routledge.
Britzman, D. (2003). *Practice makes practice: A critical study of learning to teach.* Albany State, NY: University of New York Press.
Cooper, L., & Orrell, J. (2016). University and community engagement: Towards a partnership based on deliberate reciprocity. In F. Trede & C. McEwen (Eds.), *Educating the deliberate professional: Preparing practitioners for emergent futures* (pp. 107-123). Switzerland: Springer.
Csikszentmihalyi, M., & Rathunde, K. (1990). The psychology of wisdom: An evolutionary interpretation. In R. J. Sternberg (Ed.), *Wisdom: Its nature, origins and development* (pp. 25-51). Cambridge, MA: Cambridge University Press.
Dweck, C. (2007). *Mindset: The new psychology of success.* New York, NY: Ballantine Books.
Evans, L. (2002). What is teacher development? *Oxford Review of Education, 28*(1), 123-137.
Kugel, P. (1993). How professors develop as teachers. *Studies in Higher Education, 18*(3), 315-328.
Noddings, N. (2005). *The challenge to care in schools: An alternative approach to education* (2nd ed.). New York, NY: Teachers College Press.
Ramsden, P. (1992). *Learning to teach in higher education.* New York, NY: Routledge.
Shulman, L. (1987). Knowledge and teaching: Foundations of the New Reform. *Harvard Educational Review, 57*(1), 1-22.
Shulman, L. S. (2004). The wisdom of practice: Managing complexity in medicine and teaching. In S. M. Wilson (Ed.), *The wisdom of practice: Essays on teaching, learning, and learning to teach* (pp. 251-271). San Francisco, CA: Jossey-Bass.
Tronto, J. (2005). An ethic of care. In A. E. Cudd & R. O. Andreasen (Eds.), *Feminist theory: A philosophical anthology* (pp. 251-263). Oxford, England & Malden, MA: Blackwell Publishing.
Witte, M., Kerwin, A., Witte, C. L., & Scadron, A. (1989). A curriculum on medical ignorance. *Medical Education, 23*(1), 24-29.
Zembylas, M., Bozalek, V., & Shefer, T. (2014). Tronto's notion of privileged irresponsibility and the reconceptualisation of care: Implications for critical pedagogies of emotion in higher education. *Gender and Education, 26*(3), 200-214.

Janice Orrell PhD (ORCID: https://orcid.org/0000-0003-1034-0642)
College of Education, Psychology and Social Work, Flinders University, Australia

NOTES ON CONTRIBUTORS

Gulnar Ali PhD, FHEA, MSc, MA, RN
School of Human and Health Sciences
University of Huddersfield, United Kingdom
Lecturer in Health and Social Care
University of Sunderland, London, United Kingdom

Ruth Bacchus PhD
Lecturer, School of Humanities
Charles Sturt University, Australia

Patricia Benner PhD, RN, FAAN
Professor Emerita
Department of Social and Behavioral Sciences
University of California, San Francisco, United States of America

Laura Béres MSW, RSW, MA, PhD
Associate Professor
School of Social Work
King's University College
London, Ontario, Canada

Deborah Bowman PhD, FRSA, MBE
Professor of Bioethics, Clinical Ethics and Medical Law
Deputy Principal (Institutional Affairs)
St George's, University of London, United Kingdom

David Carr
Emeritus Professor
Moray House School of Education
University of Edinburgh, United Kingdom

Nita L. Cherry PhD, MAM, ASH (Assoc.)
Adjunct Professor
Faculty of Business and Law
Swinburne University of Technology, Australia

Stephen Curran
Professor of Psychiatry for Older People/Consultant Psychiatrist
School of Human and Health Sciences
University of Huddersfield and South West Yorkshire Partnership NHS Foundation
Trust, Fieldhead, Wakefield, United Kingdom

NOTES ON CONTRIBUTORS

Phillip Dybicz PhD, LCSW
Assistant Professor
Dewar College of Education and Human Services
Department of Social Work
Valdosta State University, United States of America

Rachael Field PhD, SFHEA, Member ALTF
Professor of Law
Co-Director, Bond Dispute Resolution Centre
Bond University Faculty of Law, Australia

Jan Fook PhD, FAcSS
Professor and Chair
Department of Social Work
University of Vermont, United States of America
and
Professor of Professional Practice Research (Visiting)
Department of Social Work
University of London, United Kingdom

Joy Higgs AM, PhD, PFHEA, Member ALTF
Emeritus Professor, Charles Sturt University, Australia
Director, Education, Practice and Employability Network, Australia

Barbara Hill PhD, SFHEA
Senior Lecturer and Indigenous Curriculum & Pedagogy Coordinator
Lead, Gulaay Indigenous Australian Curriculum and Resources team
Learning Academy, Division of Learning and Teaching
Charles Sturt University, Australia

Elizabeth Anne Kinsella PhD
Professor
Faculty of Health Sciences
Western University, Canada

Niamh Kinsella MSc Occupational Therapy, BSocSci
Lecturer in Occupational Therapy
School of Health Sciences
Affiliate of Centre for Person-centred Practice Research
Queen Margaret University, Edinburgh, Scotland

Sheridan Linnell, PhD, AThR
Associate Professor in Art Therapy
School of Social Sciences and Psychology
Western Sydney University, Australia

NOTES ON CONTRIBUTORS

Bernard McKenna PhD
Associate Professor
UQ Business School
University of Queensland, Australia

Janice Orrell PhD, Member ALTF
Emeritus Professor of Higher Education and Assessment
College of Education, Psychology and Social Work
Flinders University, Australia

Sandy O'Sullivan (Wiradjuri) PhD, Member ALTF
Deputy Head of School
School of Communication and Creative Industries
University of the Sunshine Coast, Australia

Joy Paton, PhD, AThR
Lecturer in Art Therapy
School of Social Sciences and Psychology
Western Sydney University, Australia

Allan Pitman PhD
Professor Emeritus
Faculty of Education
Western University, Canada

Aunty Beryl Yungha-Dhu Philip-Carmichael
PhD Honoris Causa (University of Sydney)
Ngiyeempaa Elder
Menindee, Australia

Bradley Roberts MBA
PhD Candidate
Faculty of Business and Law
Swinburne University of Technology, Australia

Melanie Rogers PhD
University Teaching Fellow/Advanced Nurse Practitioner
School of Human and Health Sciences
University of Huddersfield, United Kingdom

Rodd Rothwell PhD
Senior Lecturer
Faculty of Health Sciences
University of Sydney, Australia

NOTES ON CONTRIBUTORS

Karolina Rozmarynowska PhD
Assistant Professor
Institute of Philosophy
Faculty of Christian Philosophy
Cardinal Stefan Wyszynski University, Warsaw, Poland

Diane Tasker PhD
Member, Education, Practice and Employability Network, Australia
Wentworth Falls, Australia

Lester J. Thompson PhD
Social Work Educator
School of Health
University of New England, Australia

Angie Titchen DPhil (Oxon), MSc, MCSP
Independent Practice Development & Research Consultant
Visiting Professor, University of Ulster, Belfast, Northern Ireland (2007–2018)

John Wattis FRCPsych
Professor of Psychiatry for Older People
School of Human and Health Sciences
University of Huddersfield, United Kingdom

Printed in the United States
By Bookmasters